N. McCALLUM.

THE
SWAPS
HANDBOOK

The Swaps Handbook

SWAPS AND RELATED RISK MANAGEMENT INSTRUMENTS

Kenneth R. Kapner

John F. Marshall

NEW YORK INSTITUTE OF FINANCE

NEW YORK   LONDON   TORONTO   SYDNEY   TOKYO   SINGAPORE

Kapner, Kenneth R.
    The swaps handbook : swaps and related risk management
instruments
    / Kenneth R. Kapner, John F. Marshall.
        p. cm.
    Includes bibliographical references and index.
    ISBN 0-13-879297-6
    1. Swaps (Finance)   I. Marshall, John F. (John Francis), 1952–
. II. Title.
HG3881.K284   1990
332.4′5—dc20   90-37442
                                                                   CIP

10 9 8 7 6 5 4 3 2 1

New York Institute of Finance
(NYIF Corp.)
2 Broadway
New York, New York 10004-2207

Contents

PART ONE

THE FINANCIAL ENVIRONMENT

PART TWO

THE INSTRUMENTS AND THEIR USES

PART THREE

INSTITUTIONAL CONSIDERATIONS

About the Authors

Kenneth R. Kapner is Vice President of Domestic Treasury for the Hongkong and Shanghai Banking Corporation Limited. He holds the M.B.A. degree. Mr. Kapner has extensive trading experience in both the foreign exchange and money markets and is a frequent user of the swap product for the hedging of his bank's positions. He has written extensively on swap finance.

John F. Marshall is Associate Professor of Finance in the Graduate School of Business at St. John's University, New York. He holds the M.B.A., M.A., and Ph.D. degrees. He teaches courses in corporate finance and investment finance. Dr. Marshall is a risk management and portfolio strategies specialist and serves as a consultant to several leading Wall Street firms. He has written extensively on futures, options, and swaps as risk management tools.

Foreword

Since the inception of currency swaps in the late 1970s and interest rate swaps in 1981, the market for swaps has exploded to the point that the U.S. dollar interest rate swap curve is considered by some to be second only to the U.S. Treasury term structure in significance. When we began the 1980s, capital market issues were rarely swapped while now it seems noteworthy if an issue is not swapped! The volume of new swaps increased from a few hundred million dollars in 1981 to over $700 billion in 1989. Related products, such as caps and floors, have developed rapidly as variations on the basic swap structure. Indeed, the market, now known variously as the derivative products or swaps market, has come to symbolize innovation in the financial markets in the 1980s.

The internationalization of the currencies of the swaps markets has been a key determinant in its exponential growth. While the dollar has maintained its dominant position for interest rate swaps, it increasingly shares the spotlight with, amongst many, Deutschemarks, yen, sterling, and Canadian, Australian, and New Zealand dollars.

One of the most significant and often overlooked forces behind the market's growth has been the advent of the personal computer. In the days of calculators and accountant's spreadsheets it was a monumental task to price and reprice a complex transaction, especially one involving more than two parties and a volatile rate environment. Indeed, early practitioners would often say "Three way deals don't close." Personal computers, such as the Apple II and the IBM and its compatibles, provided a dramatic impetus to the market by making the necessary computations far less formidable and providing the speed to perform the calculations and effect transactions while prices are still current.

The financial press has covered the development of swaps closely since its inception and authors with practical, legal, accountancy, and theoretical backgrounds have sought to explain its complexities. In their first book, *Understanding Swap Finance*, Ken Kapner and Jack Marshall provided a very thorough primer for the beginning student of swaps. They provided a conceptual and a practical framework for grasping this seemingly complex field. The authors made it clear that swaps need not be thought of as intricate or difficult if one understands the basic concepts that are the essential building blocks and remembers that all elaborate structures can ultimately be reduced to basic components.

In this, their second book on swaps, *The Swaps Handbook*, the authors have expanded the scope of their coverage to include such related instruments as futures, forwards, forward rate agreements, forward exchange agreements, and single period and multiperiod options. They have provided a more thorough examination of the cash markets for debt and a more detailed discussion of the determination of interest rates and exchange rates. The inclusion of new material on commodity swaps is also most welcome. They have also expanded their treatment of the theory and practice of risk management. The appendixes the authors have chosen to include have added greatly to the value of the book by providing both thought provoking theory and very practical information for the practitioner.

I am sure that the professional reader will appreciate the effort that Ken and Jack have put into this book and the clarity of the presentation that they have achieved. Nevertheless, the reader must understand that to fully appreciate the instruments and their uses some effort on his or her part is required. A trick to utilize in learning about swaps as you work your way through this book is to keep a pencil and a pad available so that you may draw the boxes, arrows, and cash flows that are essential to this trade. Work through the numbers with the authors and confirm each step in their calculations.

Robert J. Schwartz, Jr.
Senior Vice President
Capital Markets Group
The Mitsubishi Bank, Ltd.

Preface

In all the history of financial markets, no markets have ever grown or evolved as rapidly as have the swap markets. This is a testament to the efficacy and flexibility of the instruments, the resourcefulness and the professionalism of the new breed of financial engineer, and the increased appreciation by financial managers of the importance of risk management in a volatile interest-rate and exchange-rate environment. The swap markets have proven very adaptable. The original swap products, now known as "plain vanilla" swaps, have given way to dozens of variants designed to serve very special purposes. Swaps are now used by industrial corporations, financial corporations, thrifts, banks, insurance companies, world organizations, and sovereign governments. They are used to reduce the cost of capital, manage risks, exploit economies of scale, arbitrage the world's capital markets, enter new markets, and create synthetic instruments. New users, new uses, and new swap variants emerge almost daily. Clearly, it is difficult to overstate the importance of the swap markets to modern finance.

More than any other modern markets, the swap markets are dependent upon the existence and liquidity of other markets. These other markets include the market for corporate debt, the market for U.S. Treasury debt, the market for mortgage debt, the Eurodollar and Eurobond markets, the futures and options markets, the spot markets for currencies and commodities, and the forward markets for currencies and commodities. It is not surprising then that the explosive growth in swap volume has been accompanied by enormous growth in trading volume in these other markets. Today, if you want to understand these other markets, you cannot ignore the impact of the swap markets—both as substitutes for other instruments and as complements to them.

Because of the market interdependencies that have been fostered by the advent of swaps, we felt that it would be inappropriate to try to tackle swaps in isolation. For this reason, this book examines swaps *and* related tools of financial risk management. The related tools include futures, forwards, forward rate agreements, put and call options, interest-rate caps, interest-rate floors, and a number of interesting variants on these basic themes. We have also taken the time to review interest-rate and exchange-rate basics along with the structure and the instruments of the cash markets for debt securities—including the markets for zero coupon bonds and repurchase agreements. Finally, we have taken the time to review important elements of the theory of risk management. We firmly believe that the full flavor of swaps cannot be appreciated or exploited without a foundation in these other areas.

We have been careful to structure the text in such a way that the reader experienced in these other areas can skip sections of chapters or even whole chapters without a loss of continuity. We have also included a number of topics of more narrow interest to specific readership groups. These materials are incorporated in the form of appendices to the chapters and can also be skipped without a loss of continuity.

Much of the swap-specific material incorporated in this book also appears in an earlier book we wrote for South-Western Publishing Company. That book, *Understanding Swap Finance,* is directed, more narrowly, to an academic audience. The user interested in swaps from a purely academic perspective might wish to consider that publication. In any event, we are indebted to South-Western for allowing us to employ much of that material in this publication.

While swap structures are complex, they are founded on relatively simple concepts. For this reason, swaps are more easily understood if they are reduced to their elemental components. This is the approach we have chosen to take. How these individual components are combined determines the end product. By building up from the bottom, we believe that the swap product can be made understandable—even to a novice. The reader of this book is expected to have a reasonable grounding in financial theory. In particular, the reader should be familiar with present value arithmetic and standard statistical concepts associated with measuring risk and return in an uncertain world. Nevertheless, we have taken the step of reviewing these concepts, where appropriate, for the reader who may be a bit rusty.

We do not want to leave the mistaken impression that swaps are easy. They are not. This is not a book to be read lightly. If the book is to serve the purpose for which it is intended, the reader must work his or her way through it. Take paper and pen and run through each example we use. Try out each computation and be sure you understand it before proceeding.

The swap business is very quantitative and number crunching tools are essential to do many of the calculations necessary to price swaps and to decide if they are the best of available financial alternatives. In writing the text, we made extensive use of spreadsheets, graphics packages, and an applications package published by MicroApplications, Inc. The latter, a veritable tool kit of analytical techniques called *A-Pack,* greatly facilitated many of our calculations. We found A-Pack to be an efficient, inexpensive, and very easy to use tool. We are indebted to MicroApplications for providing it. Readers interested in this package should see Endnote 1 to Chapter 2.

In keeping with the practical orientation of this book, yet cognizant of the intellectual and quantitative sophistication of most of our readers, we have chosen to include, at the end of each chapter, a section entitled "References and Suggested Reading." This material is provided for two groups. The first is the practitioner who requires greater detail than we have provided on some particular point. The second is the academic reader interested in additional literature for research purposes.

One of the major problems we have had in writing the book is keeping it current. The markets have evolved so quickly that developments taking place in 1987, which seemed to clearly point to the future of the markets, were old and discarded by the time we neared completion. We have benefited more than we can possibly say from industry practitioners who have commented on various drafts of the manuscript.

These include Ravi Mehra and Steve Katz of the HongkongBank and Craig Messenger of Shearson Lehman, Inc. Our special thanks go to Bob Schwartz of The Mitsubishi Bank. Bob's readings of the several drafts of the South-Western manuscript and his detailed comments and suggestions have proven invaluable. We are also indebted to the International Swap Dealers Association which accommodated all of our requests for information and to its officers and directors, some of whom read and commented upon portions of the manuscript. It goes without saying that we are also deeply indebted to those who contributed articles and other material to the appendices to this book. In particular we would like to thank Vipul K. Bansal, Robert R. Bench, Sung R. Lee, Anthony F. Herbst, and Harold D. Schuler.

We would also like to thank several persons who have asked to remain anonymous. Their comments were no less valuable. Reviews and comments from members of the academic community have also been extremely helpful. In particular, we would like to thank Dr. Kevin Wynne of Pace University. Any errors which may remain are, of course, entirely our own. We would also like to thank The First Boston Corporation, The Chase Manhattan Bank, and Shearson Lehman for permitting us to reproduce some of their illustrations.

JACK MARSHALL

Graduate School of Business
St. John's University, New York

KEN KAPNER

The Hongkong and Shanghai Banking Corporation Limited

Comments should be addressed to the authors:

John F. Marshall, Ph.D.
Graduate School of Business
St. John's University, New York
Queens, NY 11439
(516) 689-2768

PART
ONE

THE FINANCIAL ENVIRONMENT

1

Introduction to the Swap Product

1.1 OVERVIEW

The primary focus of this book is on a class of derivative products known as **swaps**. These instruments are used by corporations, financial institutions, and other end users to reduce financing costs and to hedge various types of financial risk. Swaps, however, do not exist in a vacuum. They compete with various forms of debt for a share of the corporate finance market as well as competing with other derivative instruments for a share of the risk management market. While appropriately viewed as substitutes for other instruments, swaps are also complements to these other instruments. For example, a swap can be viewed as a substitute for futures contracts for an end user in need of a hedge; while at the same time, for the swap dealer in need of a hedge for his swap book, futures may be the tool. Swaps are also complemented by other derivative instruments—particularly **interest-rate** and **exchange-rate options**—with which they are often combined to create unique cash flow patterns. For these reasons, we cannot fully appreciate the swap product or its uses without also examining these other instruments.

In this chapter, we introduce the interest-rate and currency swap products in what are often called their "plain vanilla" forms. That is, we will look at the simplest types of swaps—unencumbered by any of

3

the many special provisions that are often worked into the "terms and conditions" of these products.

We begin with the definition of a swap and then briefly examine the history of the swap markets, the fundamental economic principles on which swap activity rests, the basic structure of currency and interest-rate swaps, and the institutional parties involved in swaps together with these parties' reasons for engaging in swap activity. We close the chapter with a description of the remainder of the book. We save this description for the end of the chapter because we believe that the plan of the book will make more sense to the reader after we have introduced the swap product.

1.2   THE SWAP PRODUCT DEFINED

A swap is a contractual agreement evidenced by a single document in which two parties, called **counterparties**, agree to make periodic payments to each other. Contained in the swap agreement is a specification as to:

1.   the currencies to be exchanged (which may or may not be the same);
2.   the rate of interest applicable to each (which may be fixed or floating);
3.   the timetable by which the payments are to be made; and
4.   any other provisions bearing on the relationship between the parties.

Financial swaps are of two major types: **interest-rate swaps** and **currency swaps**; although there are many variants of each. Currency swaps were introduced first but interest-rate swaps account for the bulk of today's swap activity.

The most common type of interest-rate swap is a **fixed-for-floating rate swap**. In this type of swap, the first counterparty agrees to make fixed-rate interest payments to the second counterparty in exchange for floating-rate interest payments to the first counterparty by the second counterparty. The fixed rate of interest is called the **swap coupon**. The interest payments are calculated on the basis of a hypothetical amount of principal called **notional principal**. The notional principal is not exchanged. Only the interest payments are exchanged. If the counterparties' payments to each other coincide, then only the **interest differential** between the two counterparties' respective commitments needs to be exchanged. This "no frills" swap is the basic or "plain vanilla" interest-rate swap. Variants of this basic structure include zero coupon-for-fixed and floating-for-floating interest-rate swaps.

In the basic currency swap, the two counterparties agree to an immediate exchange (technically a sale) of one currency for another at some exchange rate; this exchange rate is usually the current **spot rate**.[1] These currencies are later swapped back (repurchased) at the same exchange rate. In the interim, the counterparties exchange interest payments. In the most common currency swap, one counterparty pays a fixed rate of interest and the other pays a floating rate of interest. This basic currency swap is called an **exchange of borrowings**. As with interest-rate swaps, many variations on the basic currency swap are possible. For example, the currencies may be:

1. exchanged in installments together with interest in such a fashion that no final re-exchange of principal is required;
2. the agreement may require that the re-exchange take place in installments rather than as a single transaction; or
3. the agreement might involve floating-for-floating or fixed-for-fixed rates.

Swap contracts are tailor-made to meet the needs of the individual counterparties. As such, they are created with the aid of swap specialists who serve as either, or both, brokers and market makers. As tailor-made contracts, swaps trade in an **over-the-counter** (OTC) type environment—as opposed to the organized exchanges on which highly standardized contracts (like futures and listed options) trade.

1.3   ORIGINS OF THE SWAP MARKETS

An **exchange rate** (foreign-exchange rate) is the number of units of one currency that can be purchased for one unit of another currency. An exchange rate may be fixed or floating. A fixed exchange rate is maintained by active intervention on the part of the governments whose currencies are involved. A floating rate, on the other hand, is determined by the forces of the market—although government interventions may still occur.

Toward the close of World War II, representatives of 47 western nations met at the resort town of Bretton Woods, New Hampshire to develop a post-war monetary system. The key feature of this system was a fixed-rate convertibility between the dollar and gold as well as fixed-rate convertibility of other currencies and the dollar. In essence, this established a fixed exchange-rate system based on the dollar and gold. This multinational accord, known as the **Bretton Woods Agreement**, imposed both an internal and an external monetary discipline on each participant. But the agreement broke down in the early 1970s following excessive monetary expansion on the part of the United States and most exchange rates involving the dollar have been allowed to float ever since.

Exchange rates became extremely volatile following the collapse of the Bretton Woods Agreement.[2] This exchange-rate volatility created an ideal environment for a swap-like instrument that could be used by multinational corporations to hedge long-term foreign-exchange commitments. Nevertheless, the first swaps were created for an altogether different purpose and only later were the cost-reducing and risk-management uses of these instruments recognized.

Swaps were a natural extension of **parallel loans** and **back-to-back loans** that originated in the United Kingdom as a means of circumventing foreign-exchange controls designed to prevent an outflow of British capital.[3] Throughout the 1970s, the British government imposed taxes on foreign-exchange transactions involving its own currency. The government's intent was to make the outflow of capital more expensive in the belief that this would encourage domestic investment by making foreign investment less attractive. The parallel loan became a widely accepted vehicle by which these taxes could be avoided. The back-to-back loan was a simple modification of the parallel loan and the currency swap was a logical extension of the back-to-back loan. Parallel and back-to-back loans involve two separate loan agreements, each of which exists independently of the other. Swaps, on the other hand, are created via a single agreement. As we shall show later, this difference is crucial.

We will illustrate parallel and back-to-back loans by way of a simple example. We begin with the parallel loan, which involves four parties. Suppose that there is a parent company, domiciled in England, that has a subsidiary in the United States. Call this firm the "British parent." Suppose further that there is a second parent company, this one domiciled in the United States with its own subsidiary in England. Call this firm the "American parent." Now assume that the U.S. subsidiary of the British parent is in need of U.S. dollar (USD) financing for a period of T years. In the absence of foreign-exchange controls, the British parent would simply borrow pounds sterling (BP) in its domestic market for a term of T years and exchange the pounds obtained for dollars at the current spot exchange rate. The British parent would then transfer the dollars to its subsidiary in the United States. For numerical illustration, assume that the British parent can borrow pounds in England at a rate of 9 percent.

Suppose now that the government of England imposes a stiff tax on currency transactions. If the British parent converts pounds to dollars, the government will tax the transaction. This tax is prohibitive and it encourages the British parent to search for an alternative way of obtaining financing for its U.S. subsidiary. One obvious solution is for the subsidiary to borrow in the U.S. capital markets on its own. Unfortunately, the subsidiary is not well known in the United States and, hence, the markets impose a substantial risk premium on its debt. In the extreme, the subsidiary may find the U.S. capital markets completely closed. We will assume that the capital markets are open but that the cost of funds is quite high. For purposes of numerical illustration, we will suppose that the American subsidiary of the British parent can borrow dollars in the United States at a rate of 12 percent.

As it happens, the American parent company finds itself with the mirror image problem of the British parent company. That is, its own subsidiary in England requires British pound financing. The American parent has the same options available to it as does the British parent. It can borrow in the U.S. capital markets and exchange the funds so obtained for pounds and then transfer the pounds to its British subsidiary. Assume that the American parent can borrow in the United States at a rate of 10 percent. But again, controls on currency flows render this option unattractive. Alternatively, the British subsidiary of the American parent can borrow on its own in the British capital markets. Suppose that the British subsidiary of the American parent can borrow pounds directly (in England) at a rate of 11 percent.

Assuming that each subsidiary borrows on its own, the cost of funds to the American subsidiary of the British parent is 12 percent (USD) and the cost of funds to the British subsidiary of the American parent is 11 percent (BP). If the two parent companies were to recognize that they have parallel financing requirements, they can simultaneously solve each other's problem. In the process, they can reduce each other's borrowing costs and they can avoid foreign-exchange taxes. The solution is for the British parent to borrow pounds in England and then lend the proceeds to the American parent's British subsidiary at the British parent's own cost (9 percent). At the same time, the American parent would borrow dollars in the United States and then lend the proceeds to the British parent's American subsidiary at the American parent's own cost (10 percent). The end result is that the British parent's American subsidiary obtains dollar financing at 10 percent (a 2 percentage point savings) and the American parent's British subsidiary obtains pound financing at 9 percent (again a 2 percent savings).

To fully understand the benefits of this arrangement, the cash flows between the parties need to be considered. We have divided the term of the loans into three distinct periods in order to facilitate this discussion. The first period represents the point of the initial transaction ($t = 0$), at which time the initial lending takes place. The second represents the period between time 0 and time T during which the two subsidiaries pay interest to each other's parent firm. The final period represents that point in time ($t = T$) when the principal sums are repaid and the loan obligations are retired. The cash flows for these three periods are depicted in Exhibits 1.1, 1.2, and 1.3, respectively.

Notice that each parent company has obtained the funds required by its subsidiary. This was accomplished without cost to either parent since the parent companies are, individually, borrowing and lending the same sums at the same rate. The parent firms are borrowing from third-party lenders (investors). Since no currencies are exchanged, no currency-transaction taxes are imposed on the parallel loans.

The back-to-back loan is very similar to the parallel loan. The main difference is that there are only two parties involved since the lendings take place between the parent companies directly. In this arrangement, the British parent agrees to lend pounds to the American parent, and the American parent agrees to lend dollars to the British parent. As before, we assume that the British parent lends to the American parent at the British parent's own cost and that the American parent lends to the British parent at the American parent's own cost. During the term of the loans, each company makes interest payments to the other. At maturity of the loans, each company repays the principal it borrowed. The cash flows for the three periods are depicted in Exhibits 1.4, 1.5, and 1.6.

There are two problems with back-to-back and parallel loans that limit their usefulness as financing tools. First, a party with a use for this type of financing must locate another party that has mirror image

EXHIBIT 1.1.   Parallel Loans
Initial Exchange of Principals

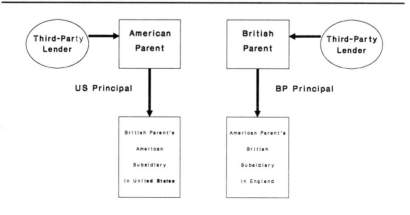

EXHIBIT 1.2.   Parallel Loans
                Debt Service Between Exchanges of Principals

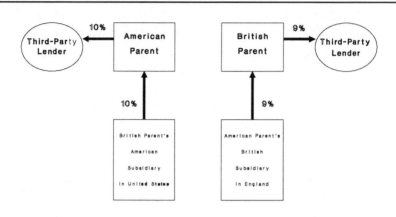

financing requirements—**matched needs**. These requirements include
the loan principal, the type of interest to be applied (fixed or floating),
the frequency of the coupon payments, and the term of the loan. The
search costs associated with finding this type of party can be
considerable—assuming it is even possible. Second, both the parallel
and back-to-back loans are actually two loans involving two separate
loan agreements. In the case of the back-to-back loan, the British
parent's debtor/creditor relationship with the American parent is inde-

EXHIBIT 1.3.   Parallel Loans
                Re-Exchange of Principals

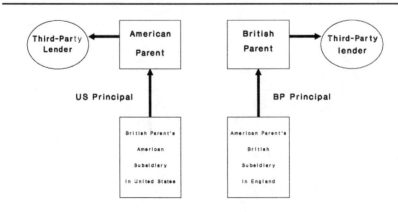

**EXHIBIT 1.4. Back-to-Back Loans
         Exchange of Principals**

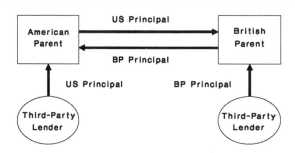

pendent of the American parent's debtor/creditor relationship with the British parent. Thus, if the British parent defaults on its obligations to the American parent, the American parent is not relieved of its obligations to the British parent. This can be very costly for the American parent. To avoid this problem, a separate agreement that defines the **rights of set-off** must be drafted. If this agreement is not registered, the outcome described above can still occur. On the other hand, registration itself can cause problems.[4]

Swaps provide the solution to the rights of set-off problem. The cash flows of the early swaps were identical to those associated with back-to-back loans. However, unlike the two loan agreements that characterize the back-to-back and parallel loans, the swap involves a single agreement. The agreement details all cash flows and provides for the release of the first counterparty from its obligations to the

**EXHIBIT 1.5. Back-to-Back Loans
         Debt Service Between Exchanges of Principals**

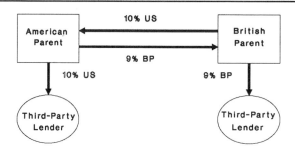

**EXHIBIT 1.6.   Back-to-Back Loans
Re-Exchange of Principals**

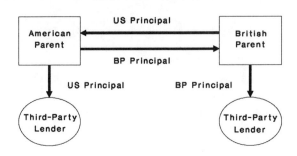

second if the second counterparty should default on its obligations to the first. This does not, however, prevent either counterparty from seeking damages from the other in the event of one counterparty's default. Thus, with a swap, the American parent's obligations to the British parent terminate if the British parent defaults on its obligations to the American parent. Yet, the American parent can still seek compensation from the British parent for damages to the American parent resulting from the British parent's default.

The other problem associated with back-to-back and parallel loans—finding a party with matched financing requirements—was solved through the intervention of swap brokers and market makers who saw the potential of this new financing technique. These players are discussed later in this chapter.

Although swaps originated from an effort to circumvent foreign-exchange controls, it was not long before the cost-reducing benefits of swap finance were recognized. The landmark currency swap, which brought the developing currency swap market from labor pains to actual birth, involved the World Bank and IBM as counterparties.[5] The swap was put together by Salomon Brothers. It allowed the World Bank to obtain Swiss francs and deutschemarks to finance its operations in Switzerland and West Germany without having to tap the Swiss and West German capital markets directly. The stature of the parties involved gave long-term credibility to currency swaps. The market grew rapidly thereafter.

It was a short step from currency swaps to interest-rate swaps. After all, if swaps could be used to convert one type of currency to another at the applicable interest rate on each currency, then why couldn't a similar type of contract be used to convert one type of borrowing (fixed rate) to another (floating rate)? The first interest-rate swap was put together in London in 1981.[6] The interest-rate swap product was introduced in the United States shortly thereafter when, in 1982, the Student Loan Marketing Association (Sallie Mae) executed a fixed-for-floating interest-rate swap.[7]

1.4 GROWTH OF SWAP ACTIVITY

The economic benefits from swaps can be enormous. Efforts to reap these benefits have led to the intense use of the swap instrument. In the years following the introduction of interest-rate swaps, swap activity exploded. The value of outstanding dollar swaps (currency and interest-rate swaps combined) grew from $5 billion, in 1982, to $45 billion, in 1984, to $430 billion, in 1986. The pace has continued to accelerate, and by the close of 1987, the dollar swap outstandings totaled $703.1 billion.[8] Of these outstandings, $540.5 billion represented interest-rate swaps and $162.6 billion represented currency swaps.[9] When nondollar swaps are added to the total, the year-end 1987 value of outstanding swaps worldwide exceeded the equivalent of $1.1 trillion.

The pace continued to accelerate through 1988 and the first half of 1989 (the latest period for which figures were available). For example, on December 31, 1988, the notional principal of interest-rate swaps outstanding amounted to $1 trillion and the currency swap outstandings amounted to $317 billion (US dollar equivalent) for a total of over $1.3 trillion dollars. In the final six months of 1988, the volume of new interest-rate swaps and currency swaps written increased by 54 percent and 47 percent, respectively, over the corresponding 1987 period. During the first six months of 1989, swap activity continued to grow at a 50 percent annual rate and total swap outstandings (interest-rate and currency swaps combined) stood at over $1.5 trillion on June

TABLE 1.1
International Swap Dealers Association Confidential Market Survey
Year-end Interest Rate Swaps Volume Comparison

Currency	1987 Number of Swaps	1987 Principal (millions)	1987 USD Equivalent	1988 Number of Swaps	1988 Principal (millions)	1988 USD Equivalent	Percent Change from Previous Year
USD	24,343	541,517	$541,517	29,349	728,166	$ 728,166	34.47%
AUD	2,060	14,793	$ 10,688	3,917	37,171	$ 29,341	151.27%
BEL	13	6,200	$ 185	60	20,554	$ 554	231.52%
CAD	659	8,473	$ 6,494	1,003	19,305	$ 15,771	127.84%
DEM	2,042	50,439	$ 31,640	4,935	99,356	$ 56,466	96.98%
WLG	52	1,950	$ 1,086	201	4,134	$ 2,086	112.00%
ECU	166	2,488	$ 3,221	426	7,800	$ 9,197	213.50%
FFR	1,015	60,448	$ 11,195	1,996	112,596	$ 18,871	86.27%
HKD	150	10,384	$ 1,336	330	18,320	$ 2,348	76.43%
NZD	31	442	$ 292	52	3,133	$ 2,042	608.82%
GBP	1,776	15,945	$ 29,706	3,376	29,357	$ 52,265	84.11%
CHF	345	6,482	$ 5,031	1,057	21,365	$ 14,610	229.61%
JPY	1,475	4,995,414	$ 40,498	2,860	10,052,213	$ 78,488	101.23%
Total	34,127		$682,888	49,560		$1,010,203	

Note: USD equivalent is expressed using the average FX rate for the applicable period.

Source: International Swap Dealers Association.

TABLE 1.2
International Swap Dealers Association Confidential Market Survey
Year-end Currency Swaps Volume Comparison

Currency	1987			1988			Percent Change from Previous Year
	Number of Swaps	Principal (millions)	USD Equivalent	Number of Swaps	Principal (millions)	USD Equivalent	
USD	6,031	162,606	$162,606	9,074	269,477	$269,477	65.72%
AUD	763	24,822	$ 20,438	1,581	42,539	$ 32,637	71.38%
BEL	65	60,917	$ 1,330	107	83,732	$ 1,857	37.45%
CAD	481	18,236	$ 13,881	938	36,828	$ 29,259	101.95%
DEM	729	44,204	$ 21,377	1,020	64,179	$ 33,979	45.19%
HLG	114	9,176	$ 3,987	161	12,198	$ 6,164	32.93%
ECU	726	19,341	$ 18,718	793	23,736	$ 24,497	22.72%
FFR	135	33,420	$ 4,827	184	33,154	$ 5,178	-0.80%
HKD	13	1,319	$ 197	22	3,031	$ 390	129.80%
NZD	388	14,289	$ 8,074	314	12,592	$ 7,473	-11.88%
GBP	352	7,106	$ 10,506	548	11,192	$ 17,704	57.50%
CHF	1,258	62,937	$ 39,928	2,003	122,658	$ 73,983	94.89%
JPY	2,169	10,823,518	$ 59,746	3,799	18,729,768	$131,033	73.05%
Total	13,224		$365,614	20,542		$633,642	
Total/2 to adjust for reporting of both sides	6,612		$182,807	10,271		$316,821	

Note: USD equivalent is expressd using the average FX rate for the applicable period.

Source: International Swap Dealers Association.

30, 1989. A more detailed picture can be obtained by examining Tables 1.1 and 1.2 which compare the 1987 and 1988 interest-rate and currency swap outstandings, respectively.

Similar growth was experienced by nearly all swap-related derivative instruments. For example, in 1988, the notional principal for new caps, floors, collars, and swaptions (all of which are discussed in detail in later chapters of this book) amounted to over $300 billion. This figure is not included in the swap outstandings for 1988 noted above. The growth in volume of these instruments was truly dramatic in the first half of 1989. For example, the volume of new swaptions (in terms of notional principal) grew by 163 percent over the corresponding period in 1988. The growth rate in volume for caps, floors, and collars was also quite impressive at over 70 percent. As of this writing, final figures for 1989 were not yet available, but all indications are that swap volume has continued to expand.

Given the enormous growth and usage of swaps and swap-related derivative products, it is not surprising that the phrase "swap driven" is frequently heard in discussions of capital markets, forward markets, and sometimes, futures markets. This is an explicit recognition of the profound effect the swap products have had on these markets. Indeed, the advent of swaps, as much as anything else, transformed the world's segmented capital markets into a single, truly integrated, international capital market.

1.5   ECONOMIC FOUNDATIONS OF THE SWAP PRODUCT

The viability of swap finance rests on several important economic principles. The most important of these are the principle of comparative advantage and the principle of offsetting risks. The **principle of comparative advantage** was long ago identified as the theoretical underpinning of international trade.[10] This principle is most easily illustrated in the context of a world having only two economic goods.

Consider two countries that are called X and Y. Each has 100 inhabitants and each produces only two goods: wine and cheese. Let's examine each country's annual production possibilities. Suppose that, given their productive endowments, the inhabitants of Country X can produce 400 bottles of wine *or* 200 pounds of cheese *or* any combination of the two goods that reflects the 2:1 trade-off of wine for cheese. At the same time, given their productive endowments, the inhabitants of Country Y can produce 1,200 bottles of wine *or* 300 pounds of cheese *or* any combination of the two goods that reflects the 4:1 trade-off of wine for cheese. Finally, suppose that the inhabitants of each country find that their utility is maximized when they consume wine and cheese in equal proportions.[11]

In the absence of trade, the collective utility of the inhabitants of Country X is maximized when the inhabitants of X produce and consume 133 bottles of wine and 133 pounds of cheese. Similarly, the collective utility of the inhabitants of Country Y is maximized when the inhabitants of Country Y produce and consume 240 bottles of wine and 240 pounds of cheese. It is clear that the inhabitants of Country Y enjoy a higher standard of living than do the inhabitants of Country X since both countries have the same number of inhabitants. We also observe that Country Y has an absolute advantage in the production of both wine and cheese. That is, if both X and Y produce just wine, Y can produce more wine per inhabitant. If both X and Y produce just cheese, Y can also produce more cheese per inhabitant.

Although Y enjoys an **absolute advantage** in both wine and cheese production, X nevertheless has a **comparative advantage** in the production of cheese. Y, on the other hand, has a comparative advantage in the production of wine. The comparative advantage that X holds in cheese production stems from X's 2:1 trade-off of wine for cheese. By giving up two bottles of wine, X can obtain an additional pound of cheese. If Y gives up two bottles of wine, it will only obtain an additional one-half pound of cheese. It is in this comparative sense that X holds an advantage in cheese production.

Whenever there are comparative advantages, there is a *possibility* that both countries can benefit from trade. For example, suppose each country concentrates more of its productive resources on producing that good in which it holds a comparative advantage and that all trade between X and Y takes the form of simple barter. For simplicity, we will assume the barter exchange rate is three for one. That is, three bottles of wine can be exchanged for one pound of cheese. It is easily shown that the optimal strategy to maximize the collective utility of the two countries' inhabitants is for X to produce 0 bottles of wine and 200 pounds of cheese, while Y produces 400 bottles of wine and 200 pounds of cheese. X would then trade 50 pounds of its cheese for 150 bottles of Y's wine. After this transaction, the inhabitants of Country X have 150 bottles of wine and 150 pounds of cheese while the inhabitants of Country Y have 250 bottles of wine and 250 pounds of cheese.

Notice that both countries' inhabitants enjoy improved living standards as a consequence of trade. In this specific case, the inhabitants of Country X gained proportionately more than did the inhabitants of Country Y. But *both* did gain. The extent of each country's gains from trade will depend on the barter exchange rate and the degree of comparative advantage that each enjoys.

It is clear that when comparative advantages exist, there can be benefits to all parties from trade. Whether actual benefits can be realized will depend on the exchange rate and the **transaction costs**. These are of paramount importance—both for simple barter and for the viability of the swap market. For purposes of the example, we implicitly assumed that wine and cheese could be costlessly traded. That is, there were no commissions to pay agents for arranging the barter trade and there were no transportation costs associated with moving wine and cheese between X and Y. To the extent that transaction costs exist, the gains from trade will be diminished.

We can easily show that swap finance rests on this same comparative advantage principle. Consider again the currency swap from our earlier example. Suppose that the British firm decides to borrow dollars in the United States to finance its operations in the United States. As a foreign entity in the United States, the British firm's credit is not as good as it might otherwise be and it is forced to pay 12 percent for dollars. In its own country, it can borrow pounds for 9 percent. At the same time, the American firm decides to borrow pounds in England to finance its operations in England. Again, as a foreign entity in England, the American firm's credit is not as good as it might otherwise be and it is forced to pay 11 percent for pounds. In its own country, it can borrow dollars for 10 percent. We may summarize as follows:

	Company	
Company	British Firm	American Firm
England	9.0%	11.0%
United States	12.0%	10.0%

It is clear that the British firm has a comparative borrowing advantage in England and that the American firm has a comparative borrowing advantage in the United States. The swap looks to exploit these comparative advantages. In the swap, the British firm borrows in its domestic market at 9 percent and lends the funds obtained to the American firm at the same 9 percent rate. At the same time and, as part of the same agreement, the American firm borrows in its domestic market at 10 percent and lends the funds obtained to the British firm at the same 10 percent rate. Thus, the British firm obtained dollars at 10 percent, for a net savings of 2 percent, and the American firm obtained pounds at 9 percent, for a net savings of 2 percent. Both counterparties to the swap have enjoyed a gain by exploiting their respective comparative advantages. Of course, the British firm did not have to lend to the American firm at the British firm's cost. Nor did the American firm have to lend to the British firm at the American firm's cost. The gains from the swap could just as easily have been split unevenly. In either case, if there are gains to be realized, the swap is viable.

It is not difficult to appreciate the comparative advantage that makes currency swaps viable. Indeed, it seems quite natural to expect a firm to have a comparative borrowing advantage in its domestic market relative to a nondomestic firm. The source of the comparative advantage in interest-rate swaps, in which both firms may be domiciled in the same country, is considerably more difficult to explain. Financial logic seems to suggest that such comparative advantages should not exist in efficient capital markets. This, however, is not necessarily the case. Included, as an appendix to this chapter, is a short paper by Sung Lee and Vipul Bansal of St. John's University that argues that, even in efficient capital markets, one domestic borrower may enjoy a comparative advantage in the fixed-rate market while another enjoys a comparative advantage in the floating-rate market. Their approach is interesting in that it is based on the intuitive logic of option pricing. They persuasively argue that all that is necessary for such advantages to exist is for there to be a quality differential in the borrowers' credit.

In banking circles, interest rates are most often quoted in terms of basis points. A **basis point** is 1/100 of 1 percent (0.01 percent). Thus, 2 percent is 200 basis points. We will often use this convention in our discussion of interest rates, interest-rate spreads, and interest-rate differentials.

The second principle on which swap finance rests is the **principle of offsetting risks**. Swaps are often used to hedge interest-rate risk and exchange-rate risk. **Interest-rate risk** is the risk that interest rates will deviate from their expected values and **exchange-rate risk** is the risk that exchange rates will deviate from their expected values. A **hedge** is a position that is taken for the purpose of reducing the risk associated with another position. This risk reduction is accomplished by taking a second position that has a risk that is opposite that of the original position. The result is that the two risks are offset. In this way, hedging involves the principle of offsetting risks.

One of the problems with the swaps we cited earlier was the difficulty of finding a potential counterparty with matching needs. This problem is resolved by intermediaries working for investment banks, commercial banks, and merchant banks. These professionals locate and match counterparties—a form of brokerage—or, in many cases, actually take one side of the transaction themselves. This is called **positioning the swap** or **booking the swap** and is a function performed by swap dealers (market makers). These swap facilitators (brokers and dealers) as they will be called for the moment, participate in the swap process in exchange for compensation for the services they provide. In the case of the swap broker, this compensation takes the form of a commission. In the case of a swap dealer, it takes the form of a bid-ask spread and/or an origination fee (called a **front-end fee**). The use of front-end fees has nearly disappeared in recent years except when the swap facilitator is called on to provide some special financial engineering. If the facilitator's fees are too large, they can wipe out the gains associated with each counterparty's comparative advantage.

1.6 BASIC STRUCTURE OF A CURRENCY SWAP

The cash flows associated with the basic currency swap (called an exchange of borrowings) are identical to those associated with a back-to-back loan. The principal difference, as already discussed, is that a currency swap includes termination provisions that relieve a counterparty of its obligations should the other counterparty default. The inclusion of termination provisions makes it unnecessary to detail the rights of set-off in a separate agreement as is typically done with a back-to-back loan.

The currency swap involves three distinct sets of cash flows:

1. the initial exchange of principals (usually obtained by borrowing from third-party lenders—hence the term ''exchange of borrowings'');

2. the interest payments of each counterparty to the other between the exchanges of principals; and

3. the final exchange (re-exchange) of principals at the *same* exchange rate used for the initial exchange of principals.

These cash flows are depicted in Exhibits 1.7, 1.8, and 1.9 for a swap involving a British firm and an American firm. The interest rate on U.S. dollars is assumed to be 10 percent and the interest rate on British

**EXHIBIT 1.7. Currency Swap
Initial Exchange of Prinicples**

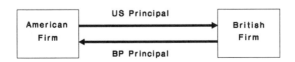

EXHIBIT 1.8.   Currency Swap
                 Interest Flows Between Exchanges of Principals

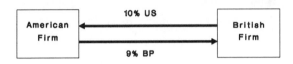

EXHIBIT 1.9.   Currency Swap
                 Re-Exchange of Principals

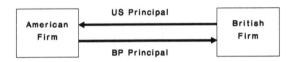

pounds is assumed to be 9 percent. Thus, this particular exchange of borrowings is a fixed-for-fixed rate currency swap. Today, the most common exchange of borrowings is fixed-for-floating. The floating rate is usually the London interbank offered rate, but it need not be. The London interbank offered rate is defined in the next section.

1.7   BASIC STRUCTURE OF AN INTEREST-RATE SWAP

There are important differences between currency swaps and interest-rate swaps. We shall begin by addressing these differences. In the exchange of borrowings currency swap, there are explicit exchanges of principals at the start of the swap and again at its termination. Both of these exchanges are made at the same exchange rate, which is usually the spot rate prevailing at the time the swap agreement is negotiated. In the interim, the parties exchange interest. These interest payments are made by the payer in the currency of the payee. Thus, there are ongoing full-interest exchanges.

In the plain vanilla interest-rate swap, both currencies are the same. That is, the counterparties are ''exchanging'' principals in the same currency. Since the principal exchanges are identical as well as in the same currency, the principal exchanges offset one another and are unnecessary. For this reason, the principal is referred to as "notional." This offsetting of principal exchanges occurs both at the start and at the end of the term of the swap contract. In the interim, the two parties exchange interest. However, since the interest payments are made in the same currency, they too are partially offset. It is, therefore, only the interest differential that needs to be exchanged in most cases.[12]

In the most common type of interest-rate swap, one counterparty is looking to exchange fixed-rate debt for floating-rate debt while the other counterparty is looking to exchange floating-rate debt for fixed-rate debt. As an example of a potential counterparty, consider a U.S. savings and loan association (S&L). The S&L has fixed-rate assets (conventional fixed-rate residential mortgages) but floating-rate liabilities (time deposits). This mismatch of fixed-rate assets and floating-rate liabilities exposes the S&L to considerable interest-rate risk. There are two ways the S&L can eliminate this risk:

1.   convert the fixed-rate assets to floating-rate assets; or

2.   convert the floating-rate liabilities to fixed-rate liabilities.

Both conversions are possible with a properly structured swap.

Any floating-rate obligation must be tied to some objectively determinable rate that is not easily manipulated by an interested party. This rate could be a short-term lending rate such as the 26-week Treasury bill (T-bill) rate or the prime rate offered by U.S. banks; or the rate could be a longer-term rate such as the 10-year Treasury note (T-note) rate or some average mortgage rate. As a practical matter, however, the rate of choice is usually the **London Interbank Offered Rate** (LIBOR). LIBOR is a widely recognized rate established daily by a sampling of lending rates offered by leading London banks. Unless specified otherwise, this rate is used for U.S. dollar lending. LIBOR originated with the London Eurodollar market. The LIBOR rate most often employed for swap purposes is six-month LIBOR. That is, it is the annual rate applicable on a six-month borrowing of dollars in London. Other common LIBOR terms are one month, three months, and one year. These rates change daily with fluctuations in the supply of and demand for U.S. dollars. As one would expect, LIBOR is highly correlated with the T-bill rate. All subsequent references to LIBOR should be understood as references to six-month LIBOR, unless specifically indicated otherwise.

The second thing to know about interest-rate swaps involving the U.S. dollar is that the fixed-rate side is usually pegged to T-note rates. That is, the fixed rate is typically set at some premium, stated in basis points, to the T-note rate for the note that has the same average term-to-maturity as the swap.

Treasury securities are **nonamortizing debt** instruments. That is, the principal is repaid in full at the time of the instrument's maturity. This type of principal repayment is sometimes called a **bullet transaction**. For this reason, swap pricing usually assumes bullet transactions on the swapped debt. In cases involving **amortizing debt**, the debt's maturity is not directly comparable to the Treasury instrument's maturity. In these cases it is customary to use average life in lieu of maturity. We discuss this issue, including the calculation of average life, in Chapter 8.

Let's consider an example of the plain vanilla fixed-for-floating interest-rate swap. Suppose Company A and Company B, both of whom are now domiciled in the United States, have matchable borrowing needs. Company A needs to raise $1 million of five-year money and would like a floating rate. Company A can borrow at a fixed annual rate of 12 percent or at a floating rate of LIBOR plus 2.5 percent. At the same time, Company B needs to raise $1 million of five-year money but wants a fixed rate. Company B can borrow at a fixed rate of 14 percent or a floating rate of LIBOR plus 3.5 percent. Notice that Company A has an absolute advantage in both fixed- and floating-rate borrowings but Company B nevertheless has a comparative advantage in floating-rate borrowings. To see this, simply substitute any percentage you like for LIBOR and divide the floating rate by the fixed rate. For example, if LIBOR is 8 percent then the ratio of Company B's floating to fixed rate is 11.5:14 or 0.821 and the ratio of Company A's floating to fixed rate is 10.5:12 or 0.875. Thus, Company B can trade off a "unit" of fixed rate (1 percentage point) for 0.821

units (percentage points) of floating rate, while Company A can trade off a "unit" of fixed rate for 0.875 units of floating rate. Since the goal is to minimize borrowing costs, Company B has a comparative advantage in floating rate. If some value other than 8 percent is substituted for LIBOR, the ratios will be different, but Company B will still have a lower ratio of floating to fixed rates than Company A.

If, Company A and Company B can reduce their floating- and fixed-rate borrowing costs, respectively, by entering into a swap, then swap finance is more attractive than straight borrowings. And this is exactly what they can do. If Company A borrows floating-rate money directly, it will pay LIBOR plus 2.5 percent. If Company B borrows fixed-rate money directly, it will pay 14 percent. Now consider the costs to each company if each borrows in the market in which it has a comparative advantage and then enters an interest-rate swap. For the moment, we will ignore any costs associated with arranging the swap.

Suppose Company A borrows fixed-rate money from a third party agreeing to pay 12 percent. This is the market in which Company A has a comparative advantage. At the same time, Company B borrows floating-rate money from another third party agreeing to pay LIBOR plus 3.5 percent. This is the market in which Company B has a comparative advantage. Next, suppose the two companies agree to a swap in which Company B would pay Company A a fixed rate of 13.5 percent on $1 million. This is 1.5 percent more than Company A must pay its third party. At the same time, Company A will pay Company B a floating rate of LIBOR plus 3.5 percent. Since there are no ex- changes of notional principal, the only cash flows between the counter- parties we need to consider are the interest transfers. These are de- picted in Exhibit 1.10. In this exhibit, the flows to the third parties are included as well as the flows between the counterparties to the swap.

Consider first the true cost of Company A's $1 million of five-year money and the form of its *net* interest obligation. Since Company A is receiving 1.5 percent more from Company B than it must pay its third party, it can apply this excess toward the rate it pays Company B; its true interest cost is then LIBOR + 2.0 percent (3.5% − 1.5%). Further, since Company A's fixed-rate commitment to its third party is offset by its fixed-rate receipts from Company B, Company A's only

**EXHIBIT 1.10.   Interest-Rate Swap
Interest Flows Between Counterparties**

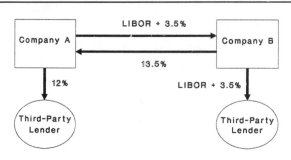

remaining obligation is the floating-rate it pays Company B. Thus, Company A achieved what it wanted, that is, floating-rate five-year money. Moreover, it has achieved this borrowing at an effective rate of LIBOR plus 2 percent (after adjusting for its fixed-rate excess of 1.5 percent). This rate is 50 basis points less than Company A would have paid had it borrowed floating-rate money directly. Now consider Company B's situation. Company B wanted to raise $1 million of fixed-rate five-year money. Although Company B pays a floating rate to its third party, this floating-rate payment is completely offset by the floating-rate payment it receives from Company A. Company B's only real cost is the 13.5 percent fixed rate it pays Company A. Thus, Company B has achieved its objective of borrowing fixed-rate five-year money. Furthermore, Company B is paying 50 basis points less than it would have paid had it borrowed fixed-rate money directly. The costs and net benefit from these transactions are summarized in Table 1.3.

Both Company A and Company B have reduced their borrowing costs through the interest-rate swap and each has achieved the type of borrowing it required. In this particular case, both companies reduced their borrowing costs by 50 basis points. We should point out that it is coincidental that the two companies enjoyed identical gains from the swap. They could just as easily have split the gains unevenly.

Suppose now that while Company A and Company B have matching needs, each is unaware of the other. If they are unable to identify each other, the potential gains from an interest-rate swap will be

TABLE 1.3
Comparison of Borrowing Costs With and Without a Swap

Without a Swap		
Company	Fixed Rate	Floating Rate
A	12%	LIBOR + 2.5%
B	14%	LIBOR + 3.5%

With a Swap		
Company A		
Pays fixed to third party		+ 12%
Pays floating to B		+ LIBOR + 3.5%
Receives fixed from B		− 13.5%
Net cost to A		LIBOR + 2%
Net savings to A = 50 basis points		
Company B		
Pays floating to third party		+ LIBOR + 3.5%
Pays fixed to A		+ 13.5%
Receives floating from A		− (LIBOR + 3.5%)
Net cost to B		13.5%
Net savings to B = 50 basis points		

foregone. Now suppose a facilitator could identify the two parties as having matching needs. Might Company A and Company B be willing to pay something for this service? Suppose the facilitator demanded 75 basis points from each. Would the swap still be attractive? Clearly not. But suppose the facilitator only required 25 basis points from each. In this case, the swap would still be attractive. Thus, the role of the swap facilitator can be justified when the gains from the swap are greater than the transaction costs imposed by the swap facilitator.[13]

1.8 SWAP FACILITATORS

In the absence of swap facilitators, there can be very significant search costs associated with finding potential counterparties who have matching needs. This introduces the role and the importance of swap facilitators. We will briefly discuss two types of swap facilitators—brokers and dealers. The financial institutions that serve these roles include investment banks, commercial banks, merchant banks, and independent broker/dealers. We will refer to these institutions collectively as "swap banks" or simply "banks."

1.8.1   Brokers

Financial institutions first became involved in swaps as swap brokers. The function of the **swap broker** is to find counterparties with matched needs. The swap broker performs the search to locate parties with matching needs and then negotiates with each on behalf of the other. The service is performed in exchange for a **commission**. During the search process and during the early stages of negotiation, the swap broker ensures the anonymity of the potential counterparties. Should the negotiations break off, neither party is at risk of having its financial condition divulged by the other. When serving as a swap broker, a bank assumes no risk, since it is not taking a position in the swap. Its role is limited to that of agent.

When the swap technique was first developed, the potential gains from swaps were often considerable. Gross benefits sometimes amounted to several hundred basis points. In such an environment, the brokers who arranged swap transactions could command significant fees. But, as the swap market attracted an ever growing number of participants, much of the potential cost-saving gains from swap finance were arbitraged away. This did not diminish the risk-management uses of swaps, but it did create a need for a more efficient and streamlined delivery system. Financial institutions soon created such a delivery system and, in the process, they discovered their own potential as market makers by assuming the role of a counterparty.

1.8.2   Dealers

The trick to streamlining the swap process and standardizing the swap product is for a bank to transform itself from a broker into a dealer or market maker. The **swap dealer** stands ready to match any client's currency or interest-rate requirements by offering itself as the counterparty to the swap. In order to limit its risk, the dealer must be able to lay-off the swap in another swap, called a **matched swap**, or in some standardized form of debt or its equivalent. We focus, for the moment, on the latter.

The broadest debt market in the world is the market for U.S. Treasury securities. The market for Treasury debt is made by U.S. Government securities dealers. These dealers make a market in short-term T-bills, intermediate-term T-notes, and long-term T-bonds. Because of the breadth and the immense volume of trading activity, this market is very liquid; and the **bid-ask spread** is typically very narrow. (The bid-ask spread is the difference between the asked price and the bid price.) Further, at any given time, there is a near virtual continuum of Treasury maturities ranging from a few days to 30 years. It is not surprising that the Treasury market was the market of choice for laying-off the dealer's swap risk. Also, it explains why swap dealers price their product as a spread over Treasuries having maturities matching the average life of the swap.

Consider a simple example involving a swap bank and an interest-rate swap. Each morning, the bank's swap staff prepares an **indicative swap pricing schedule**. This schedule specifies the prices at which the bank will enter into swaps for that day. Examine the pricing schedule in Table 1.4 which provides prices for five-year fixed-rate money.

These rates are interpreted as follows: The bank will pay the counterparty client **LIBOR flat** (meaning without a premium or discount) in exchange for the counterparty client paying the bank the five-year T-note rate plus 80 basis points. If the counterparty client wants to receive the fixed rate rather than pay the fixed rate, the bank will pay

TABLE 1.4
Indicative Swap Pricing Schedule
(01 June 19XX)

Maturity	Bank Receives	Bank Pays
5 years	TN rate + 80 bps sa	TN rate + 60 bps sa

Note: The notation "bps" denotes basis points and "sa" indicates that the rate is a semiannual rate. All quotes are against six-month LIBOR flat and assume bullet transactions. For amortizing loans, substitute average life for maturity.

its counterparty client the five-year T-note rate plus 60 basis points in exchange for the client paying the bank LIBOR flat. The bank makes its profit from the bid-asked spread that is easily seen to be 20 basis points. In addition, the bank might charge the client a front-end fee.

Assume the current five-year T-note rate is 9.15 percent. The bank will receive 9.95 percent or pay 9.75 percent against LIBOR. Suppose now that the bank's client can issue (sell) fixed-rate five-year debt at 11.5 percent and can issue floating-rate five-year debt at LIBOR plus 1.5 percent. The client would like to raise $1 million of five-year fixed-rate money. If the client borrows in the fixed-rate market, it will pay 11.5 percent. The bank suggests that the client issue $1 million of floating-rate money at LIBOR plus 1.5 percent and then swap this floating-rate debt for fixed-rate debt with the bank serving as the counterparty. In this swap, the bank will pay its counterparty client LIBOR, and the counterparty client will pay the bank 9.75 percent. There is, as pointed out earlier, no need for the client and the bank to exchange principals, since the principal sums are identical. The cash flows then look as depicted in Exhibit 1.11.

Observe that the counterparty client is paying the third-party lender LIBOR plus 1.5 percent, but the bank is paying the counterparty client LIBOR flat. At the same time, the counterparty client is paying the bank 9.75 percent. Thus, the counterparty client's actual cost for its $1 million of five-year money is 11.45 percent (9.95% + LIBOR + 1.5% − LIBOR).[14] Had the client borrowed fixed-rate five-year money directly, it would have paid 11.5 percent. Thus, the swap strategy has saved the client 5 basis points.

EXHIBIT 1.11.   Interest-Rate Swap and Capital Marketing Borrowing Cash Flows

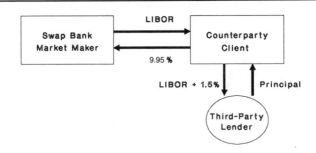

The swap bank, by entering into the swap, has assumed the risk that the interest rate it pays the client will change. This interest-rate risk exists because the bank is paying a floating rate. The ideal solution for the bank is to enter into another swap with another counterparty client who seeks to exchange fixed-rate debt for floating-rate debt. If such a party is found, the bank can be viewed as standing between the two counterparty clients in the traditional sense of a **financial intermediary**.

Suppose that it takes some time for the swap bank to locate a second counterparty client. How can the bank lay-off the risk in the interim? The answer is to short $1 million of five-year T-notes and use the proceeds from this sale to purchase $1 million of 26-week T-bills. If it was necessary to do so, the bank would roll these bills over every six months for five years. The T-bill rate is viewed as floating because it will be different with each **rollover**. This is the same sense in which the LIBOR rate is floating. The bank is then paying a fixed rate (T-note) and receiving a floating rate (T-bill). The bank's interest-rate risk from the swap with its counterparty client is thus offset. Importantly, the offset is not perfect because the floating-rate side of the swap is LIBOR based, while the Treasury hedge is T-bill based. While these two rates track each other very closely, they are not perfectly correlated, and thus there is some residual risk associated with the hedge. This risk is called **basis risk**.

There are other risks for banks making markets in swaps: counterparty credit risk, maturity risk, and several forms of mismatch risk. If the floating-rate portions are indexed to different rates, then there is also basis risk. When the swap involves different currencies, there may be sovereign risk and delivery risk. We will discuss in detail these risks and the management of swap risks in Chapter 9.

1.9 MISCELLANEOUS POINTS REGARDING SWAPS

In this section, we briefly consider two important areas involving swaps. The first is the off-balance sheet nature of swaps and the second is the efforts that have been made to standardize swap agreements.

Swaps are **off-balance sheet** transactions. That is, they do not show up on the assets side or on the liabilities side of a balance sheet. This accounting treatment of swaps has been attractive to both corporate users of swaps and to swap banks. In particular, banks found swap activity to be an easy way to boost bank return on equity—an important measure of profitability. The rapid growth of swap activity eventually became a source of concern to bank regulators who viewed swap activity as a threat to bank safety. In the mid-1980s, this concern led bank regulators to propose regulations that would stiffen capital requirements for such banks.[15] Banks responded by arguing that such measures would only increase the cost of swap finance to the end user and drive swap finance overseas.[16]

To address these and related concerns, the Federal Reserve, working with bank regulatory and supervisory bodies from Belgium, Canada, France, Germany, Italy, Japan, Luxemberg, the Netherlands, Sweden, Switzerland, and the United Kingdom, developed a preliminary set of proposals that became known as the **Basle Accord**. The Basle Accord was the culmination of a serious international effort to standardize the measurement of bank capital and to develop capital standards for banks. After a period of public comment and deliberation, the Federal Reserve issued final guidelines for U.S. banks on January 19, 1989. (The Federal Reserve's final guidelines provided a risk-based procedure for determining a bank's capital requirements. The guidelines took explicit consideration of swap and related activity. See Chapter 9.)

The second major consideration we briefly address is **swap documentation**. When the swap product was first introduced, each bank that entered the swap markets as a broker and/or dealer developed its own swap documentation. This documentation includes specification of terms, language, pricing conventions, and so on. Different banks used very different terminology and conventions. This lack of standardization limited the ability of banks to assign swaps and slowed the development of a **secondary market** in swap contracts. In June 1985, the New York-based **International Swap Dealers' Association** (ISDA) established a code listing standard terms for interest-rate swaps. Shortly thereafter, the **British Bankers' Association** offered its own set of documentation guidelines (British Bankers' Association Interest Rate Swaps or BBAIRS). These codes were later revised and, ultimately, led to the introduction of standard form agreements. The ISDA and BBAIRS alternative codes are referred to, colloquially, by persons in the swap trade as "is da" and "b bears." Swap documentation and ISDA's efforts toward standardization are discussed in detail in Chapter 10.

The standardization of documentation has increased the speed of transactions and has given an impetus to the development of a secondary market in swaps. The secondary market continues to evolve but is, as yet, not highly developed. For swaps to be easily tradeable, they would have to be written with **rights of assignment**. Rights of assignment pose a number of difficulties that are discussed in Chapter 9. In a related effort, some consideration has been given to the creation of a **clearinghouse** for swaps.[17] Such a clearinghouse could, theoretically, function in much the same fashion as the clearing associations used to clear and enforce futures and option contracts. These efforts appear to have been abandoned, and, in any case, the creation of a clearinghouse for swaps would make swaps too much like futures. This could pose regulatory problems for the industry. The absence of a well-developed secondary market for swaps is not, however, a serious problem for swap counterparties. A counterparty to a swap who finds that the swap no longer serves its purposes can negotiate a cancellation of the agreement directly with the other counterparty. We examine the mechanics for determining cancellation payments later.

1.10   PLAN OF THE BOOK

As we argued in both the preface to the book and the overview of this chapter, swaps do not exist in a vacuum. They both compete with and complement other instruments used in corporate finance. They also compete with other derivative instruments for a share of the risk management market. To fully understand the uses of swaps and the management of a swap portfolio, we must therefore also understand the financial environment in which swaps exist and the instruments with which they compete.

We have divided the book into three parts. The first, to which this chapter belongs and includes Chapters 2, 3, and 4, deals with the financial environment. Chapter 2 reviews interest-rate and exchange-rate basics. This review includes both a look at some theory and some institutional realities. Chapter 3 examines the cash markets for debt securities including U.S. Treasury debt, corporate debt, and mortgage debt. Finally, Chapter 4 considers the source of financial risks and the theory underlying the management of these risks.

The second part consists of Chapters 5, 6, 7, and 8. It examines derivative instruments that share the risk management market, and it examines the uses and the pricing of swaps. Specifically, Chapter 5 examines futures and forward contracts. Chapter 6 examines options—including the full range of over-the-counter interest-rate options. Chapter 7 considers the uses and structures of swaps from the end user's perspective. Chapter 8 focuses on the pricing of swaps from the dealer's perspective.

The final part, Chapters 9 and 10, involves institutional considerations. Chapter 9 considers the portfolio management problems of a swap market maker, and Chapter 10 examines the problems of swap documentation.

Throughout the book, we have highlighted important terms when they first appear or when they are first defined. These terms can be found in the glossary at the end of the book. We have also included appendices for some of the chapters. These appendices do not need to be read by all readers. They tend to be of narrow interest and will appeal to some readers but not to others. One side point on notation is in order. Different players in the markets employ different notation to represent the same things. For example, the U.S. dollar is denoted variously as $, US, US$, and USD. We have tried to be consistent in our use of currency notation but we have nevertheless deliberately varied our notation on occasion to better familiarize the reader with the different notational equivalents.

Lastly, we have avoided long literature recitals in the body of the text and we have tried to keep our use of footnotes to a minimum. Nevertheless, we recognize the considerable sophistication of the readers of this book. To better serve them, we have included reference lists of primary-source literature and suggested readings at the end of each chapter.

1.11 SUMMARY

Swap finance evolved from parallel and back-to-back loans. These latter financing devices originated as a mechanism to circumvent foreign-exchange controls. The first swaps were currency swaps, but interest-rate swaps, first introduced in 1981, account for the bulk of swap activity today. Swaps can be used to reduce financing costs and to manage interest-rate and exchange-rate risks.

Swap finance is facilitated by the intermediating roles played by swap brokers and dealers. Brokers arrange swaps between parties with matching needs. Dealers become counterparties to swaps and hedge their positions until such time as matched swaps can be arranged. Large swap dealers often carry swap portfolios that are measured in the tens of billions of dollars.

The off-balance sheet nature of swaps has led to some concern on the part of bank regulators as to the vulnerability of these financial institutions. Traditional bank accounting and regulation does not provide for explicit recognition of off-balance sheet items and the risks associated with them. This deficiency has been addressed by the Federal Reserve's new guidelines for risk-based capital requirements.

In 1985, the first steps were taken by the International Swap Dealers' Association and the British Bankers' Association toward a standardization of swap provisions and language. This has greatly facilitated the writing of swap contracts and has enhanced the prospects for the emergence of an efficient secondary market in swaps.

REFERENCES AND SUGGESTED READING

Baker, M. "Swaps—Driven Offerings Up," *Pensions & Investment Age*, 14:4, 53–54 (Feb 1986).

Beckstrom, R. "The Development of the Swap Market," in *Swap Finance*, vol. 1, Boris Antl, ed., London: Euromoney Publications (1986).

Celarier, M. "Swaps' Judgement Day," *United States Banker*, 98:7, 16–20 (Jul 1987).

Cooper, R. and A. Shegog "An Old-Fashioned Tug-of-War," *Euromoney*, Swaps Supplement, 22–27 (Jul 1987).

Crabbe, M. "Clearing House for Swaps," *Euromoney*, 345–351 (Sep 1986).

Falloon, W. "The ABC's of Swaps," *Intermarket Magazine*, vol. 5:5, 25–33 (May 1988).

Felgran, S. D. "Interest Rate Swaps: Uses, Risk, and Price," *New England Economic Review* (Federal Reserve Bank of Boston), 22–32 (Nov/Dec 1987).

Genova, D. and D. Thompson "A Guide to Standard Swap Documentation," *Commercial Lending Review*, 3:2, 44–49 (Spring 1988).

Kennrick, R. "Bank Regulators Suggest Control of Swap Volumes," *Asian Finance* (Hong Kong), 13:9, 16–18 (Sep 1987).

Klein L. B. "Interest Rate and Currency Swaps: Are They Securities?," *International Financial Law Review* (UK), 5:10, 35–39 (Oct 1986).

Nelson J. F. "Too Good to Last?," *United States Banker*, 97:6, 46–40 (Jun 1986).

Park, Y. S. "Currency Swaps as a Long-Term International Financing Technique," *Journal of International Business Studies*, 15:3, 47–54 (Winter 1984).

Powers, J. G. "The Vortex of Finance," *Intermarket Magazine*, vol. 3:2, 27–38 (Feb 1986).

Price, J. A. M. "The Technical Evolution of the Currency Swap Product," in *Swap Finance*, vol. 1, Boris Antl, ed., London:Euromoney Publications (1986).

Riley, W. B. and G. S. Smith "Interest Rate Swaps: Disclosure and Recognition," *CPA Journal*, 57:1, 64–70 (Jan 1987).

Samuelson P. A. and W. D. Nordhause *Economics*, 12d., New York: McGraw-Hill (1985).

Stoakes, C. "The London Inter-Bank Swaps Code," *International Financial Law Review* (UK), 4:10, 6 (Oct 1985a).

Stoakes, C. "Standards Make Swaps Faster," *Euromoney*, 19–21 (Nov 1985b).

Turnbull, S. M. "Swaps: A Zero-Sum Game," *Financial Management*, 16:1 15–21 (Spring 1987),

Wallich, C. I. "The World Bank's Currency Swaps," *Finance and Development*, 7:3, 197–207 (Fall 1984).

Wilford, D. S. "Strategic Risk Exposure Management, Working paper #3, in *Working Papers in Risk Management*, Chase Manhattan Bank (February 1987).

Whittaker, J. G. "Interest Rate Swaps: Risk and Regulation," *Economic Review* (Federal Reserve Bank of Kansas City), 72:3, 3–13, (Mar 1987).

ENDNOTES

[1] The *spot exchange rate* or *spot rate* is the current rate of exchange for currencies to be paid and received for *immediate delivery*. As a practical matter, this is usually taken to mean two business days. This is in contrast to *forward exchange rates*, which are current exchange rates for currencies to be paid and received for *deferred delivery*.

[2] For an examination of exchange rate volatility behavior before and after the collapse of the Bretton Woods Agreement, see Wilford (1987).

[3] For a discussion of the evolution of swaps from back-to-back and parallel loans, see Powers (1986).

[4] For a discussion of the problems that can result from the registration of the rights of set-off, see Price (1986).

[5] For an analytical examination of the World Bank's 1981 swap activity, see Park (1984). See also Wallich (1984).

[6] See Beckstrom (1986) for details of this swap.

[7] Ibid.

[8] Exact figures for the volume of swap activity do not exist. The numbers reported here for 1982, 1984, and 1986 are our own composites from estimates by Falloon (1988), Celarier (1987), Baker (1986), Powers (1986), and other sources. The figures for 1987, 1988, and 1989 are more accurate. They represent an aggregation of the values provided by reporting members of the International Swap Dealers Association (ISDA), a trade association founded in 1985. The ISDA now tracks the volume of swap activity world wide. Nevertheless, the ISDA's figures are still estimates as not all swap dealers report their transactions to the ISDA.

[9] One has to be careful in tabulating currency swaps because there are always two currencies involved. To avoid double counting, we should divide the currency swap outstandings in half. This has not been done here since only dollar swap outstandings are reported.

[10] The principal of comparative advantage, as the driving force behind international trade, was first formulated by David Ricardo in the early nineteenth century. For a more detailed discussion of the principle, see Samuelson and Nordhaus (1985, Chapter 38).

[11] The term "utility" is used in the economic sense. That is, utility is the benefit or satisfaction that an individual receives or expects to receive from some available alternative. The alternative is most often taken to mean consumption of some good or some basket of goods.

[12]The interest differential is exchanged when the swap payment dates are identical. In some cases the swap payment dates are mismatched. In these cases, there is a full-interest exchange on the payment dates. We address these cases more fully in Chapter 9.

[13]In the language of economics, the swap is profitable for the counterparties if the marginal benefits from the swap exceed the marginal costs of the swap. It is important to note that not all swaps are entered for the purposes of reducing financing costs. Many swaps are created entirely for risk management purposes. In such a case, a swap may be attractive even if it is not profitable. We discuss this possibility in more detail in Chapter 7.

[14]This is actually a simplification, fixed rates are based on a 365-day year using a yield measure called the bond equivalent yield while floating rates are measured on a 360-day year using a yield measure called the money market equivalent yield. Thus, the premium over LIBOR employed in this example is not directly addable to the fixed rate without first making an adjustment. We consider this adjustment in Chapter 8.

[15]See, for example, Celarier (1987), Cooper and Shegog (1987), Whittaker (1987), Riley and Smith (1987), Klein (1986), and Felgran (1987).

[16]See, for example, Nelson (1986) and Kennrick (1987).

[17]For a more thorough discussion of the standardization of swap documentation, see Stoakes (1985a, 1985b), and Genova and Thompson (1988). For discussion of the role of a swaps clearinghouse, see Crabbe (1986).

The Source of the Comparative Advantage in Interest-Rate Swaps

*Sung R. Lee and Vipul K. Bansal**

An interest-rate swap is an agreement in which two parties, called counterparties, agree to exchange interest payments without exchanging underlying debt. In most such swaps, one counterparty pays a floating rate of interest while the other pays a fixed rate of interest. This is called a fixed-for-floating interest-rate swap and it is the type we focus on here.

The counterparties to a fixed-for-floating interest-rate swap benefit by a reduction in their respective interest costs and/or a reduction in their interest-rate risks. It is generally accepted that these benefits are possible because some firms hold a comparative advantage in the fixed-rate market while other firms hold a comparative advantage in the floating-rate market.

The existence of comparative advantages in the capital markets seems, on the surface, to violate a fundamental tenet of financial theory (i.e., that capital markets are efficient). Bicksler and Chen (1986)[1], for example, argue that the existence of swap activity proves the existence of imperfections in the capital markets. Turnbull (1987)[2], on the other hand, argues that the comparative advantages may stem from externalities.

Financial theory holds that if a riskless arbitrage opportunity exists, firms will enter the market to exploit it. The rush to exploit price discrepancies will, eventually, cause the price discrepancies to disappear and the volume of activity to stabilize or decline. When swaps were first introduced, there was an immediate interest in the opportunities they presented. The volume of activity grew rapidly and the

---

*The authors are Assistant Professors, Graduate School of Business, St. John's University, New York, NY.

size of the gains did diminish. But the explosive growth of the swap markets has continued unabated—suggesting that the comparative advantages in the fixed-rate and floating-rate markets for debt are not solely the result of market imperfections. In fact, it is hard to believe that a market with a transaction volume of over $1 trillion is anything but efficient. This seems to suggest, at least to us, that the debt markets are both efficient and yet characterized by comparative advantage. The fundamental question then is "why should these comparative advantages exist in an efficient market?"

In this paper, we attempt to explain the source of the comparative advantages exploited by interest-rate swaps. We will argue that comparative advantage is not necessarily due to market imperfections or to externalities. Instead, comparative advantages exist because investors determine prices for securities in such a fashion that the risk premium differential for fixed-rate debt relative to floating-rate debt is greater for high-risk firms than it is for low-risk firms. Further, this relationship is true irrespective of the efficiency of the markets for debt. We will make our arguments at an intuitive level. A formal proof, however, is available for interested readers.[3]

Consider first the source of interest-rate risk. Suppose a mortgage lender, which we will call a bank, funds its mortgage lending through short-term borrowings from its depositors. The cost of these borrowings rises when interest rates rise and falls when interest rates fall. If the bank grants the mortgage borrower a conventional fixed-rate mortgage, then the bank runs the risk that its interest costs may rise above its interest revenues. But, if the bank grants the mortgage borrower an adjustable rate mortgage, then any increase in funding costs should be matched by increases in revenue. Thus, from the bank's point of view, floating-rate assets are preferable to fixed-rate assets. Now consider the situation from the borrower's point of view. The borrower prefers a fixed-rate mortgage because such a mortgage frees the borrower from the uncertainty associated with the future course of interest rates. The borrower knows precisely what he must pay each month. No nasty surprises await him.

Now let's consider a commercial firm in need of two-period financing. The firm has a choice of raising funds by selling fixed-rate debt or floating-rate debt. Two-period floating-rate debt, assuming this alternative is selected, can take any of several forms, but we will assume it takes the form of one-period debt rolled over for a second period.[4] If the firm sells fixed-rate debt, then its cost for each period is known. If the firm sells floating-rate debt, then only its cost in the first period is known. The risk-averse firm (borrower) prefers two-period fixed-rate debt. The potential lenders to this firm, on the other hand, are concerned about the possibility of a default. The longer the term of the lending, the greater the likelihood of such a default. All other things being equal then, the lenders to this firm prefer to buy the firm's one-period debt. If the lender lends for one period and then determines after one period that the firm's financial condition is no longer acceptable, it can simply elect not to re-lend for a second period or, equivalently, it can demand a significantly greater rate of interest to compensate for the greater risk. Thus, the lender who lends for one period possesses a valuable option. By initially lending for two periods, the lender forecloses on this option. The presence of default risk then suggests that a lender will demand a rate differential at least equivalent in value to the option surrendered when accepting two-period fixed-rate debt. The value of the option will, of course, be determined by the market and it will take the form of a rate on the two-period fixed-rate debt which is higher than the geometric average of the current one-period rate and the one-period rate expected to prevail one-period out.[5] The difference between the two-period fixed-rate and the one-period rate is the amount of the current rate-differential paid for fixed-rate debt relative to floating-rate debt.

Now, suppose we have two firms, called A and B, with different inherent risks. We'll suppose that debt ratings are accurate reflections of these risks and that Firm A is investment grade while Firm B is speculative grade. Should we expect the market to impose the same fixed-to-floating rate differential on both firms? Absolutely not. The longer the lender commits funds, the greater the likelihood that a default will occur. If the lender lends to Firm A, the lender will certainly feel secure for one period but will also feel fairly secure for two periods and so will only demand a small differential to lend two-period fixed-rate. Firm B, however, is a different story. The lender might feel reasonably secure to lend to Firm B for one period but very insecure to lend for two periods. Thus, the lender demands a greater differential for fixed-rate lending to Firm B than it does to Firm A. This is just another way of saying that the option the lender surrenders to lend to Firm B is more valuable than the option the lender surrenders to lend to Firm A.

In both the one-period case and the two-period case, Firm A's superior credit rating will guarantee it a borrowing advantage in absolute terms. But, Firm B will nevertheless possess a comparative advantage in one-period floating-rate debt. A typical scenario is:

	One-Period Rate	Two-Period Rate
Firm A	9%	10%
Firm B	10%	12%

The discussion above suggests that the poorer a firm's credit rating and the longer the term of the fixed-rate borrowing, the greater will be the rate differential between its fixed-rate and floating-rate borrowing opportunities. This does not imply a market inefficiency, but rather a reflection of the market's assessment of risks and the value of the options the lenders surrender. Nevertheless, it does give rise to exploitable comparative advantages. Therefore, it can be concluded that, even in efficient markets, higher risk firms enjoy comparative advantages in floating-rate markets (when floating rates are achieved by one-period lending with rollover) and that low risk firms enjoy a comparative advantage in the multi-period fixed-rate market. Further, while arbitrage will diminish the rate differentials, the rate differentials will not be fully removed by arbitrage unless all firms are equally risky.

ENDNOTES

[1]Bicksler J. and Chen, A. H. "An Economic Analysis of Interest Rate Swaps," *Journal of Finance*, 41:3 (July 1986).

[2]Turnbull, S.M. "Swaps: A Zero-Sum Game," *Financial Management*, 16:1 15–21 (Spring 1987).

[3]For a formal, but very mathematical, proof of the conclusions reached in this paper, please write: Sung R. Lee, Department of Economics and Finance, St. John's University, Queens, New York 11439.

[4]This type of floating-rate debt is discussed in Chapter 3 of this book. It has also been discussed, in the context of using swaps as a hinge between the money markets and the capital markets, by J. Walmsley, "Interest Rate Swaps: The Hinge Between Money and Capital Markets," *The Banker* (April 1985).

[5]The argument is analogous to the liquidity premium which is demanded by lenders in order to bear interest-rate risk. Importantly, the rate differential represented by the value of the option does not replace the liquidity premium. Rather, it exists in addition to the liquidity premium. The value of the option may be viewed as a default premium. We will not use this term, however, as the term default premium is traditionally employed to mean the rate differential between low-quality debt and high-quality debt of the same maturity.

Interest Rates and Exchange Rates: The Basics

2.1 OVERVIEW

Currency and interest-rate swaps are often used to transform the character of debt obligations. Sometimes this means transforming a fixed-rate obligation to a floating-rate obligation in the same currency. At other times, it means transforming an obligation in one currency to an obligation in another currency. Anyone with a serious interest in swaps must, therefore, have an understanding of the factors that determine interest rates and exchange rates and must have an appreciation for the risk exposures associated with fluctuations in these rates.

This chapter starts with a discussion of interest rates and the cash flows associated with debt instruments. The various forms of risk associated with debt instruments and some of the tools used to manage these risks will also be introduced in this chapter. (A more detailed discussion of the institutional characteristics of the various debt markets is presented in Chapter 3.)

Following the discussion of interest rates, the related topics of exchange rates and exchange-rate risks will be examined. Much of this examination concerns the determinants of spot and forward exchange rates. Our primary objective is to help the reader understand how exchange rates are related to interest rates (and vice versa), the risks that variations in these rates pose for borrowers and others involved in the international markets, and how interest-rate and exchange-rate discrepancies may be exploited for profit. All of these topics will prove important in our later discussion of the uses of swaps. It is important to note that we use the terms **debt markets** and **credit markets** synonymously to refer to the markets for debt securities.

2.2 DEBT INSTRUMENTS: THE BASICS

A debt instrument is a **promissory note** that evidences a debtor/creditor relationship. In such a relationship, one party borrows funds from another party. The borrowing party promises to repay the borrowed funds together with interest. The borrowing party is the **debtor** and the lending party is the **creditor**. The promissory note is satisfied when the borrowing party's obligations have all been met.

A debt instrument may be marketable or nonmarketable. Marketable debt instruments are considered **securities**. When the debt instrument takes the form of a security, the borrower is called the **issuer**. The issuer sells its securities to the lender who is called an **investor** or **holder**. All securities sold as part of the same issuance are called, collectively, an **issue**.

Some marketable debt securities, such as corporate bonds, require a neutral third party to oversee the issue. In these cases, the promissory note takes the form of an indenture. An **indenture**, which is called a **trust deed** in the United Kingdom, is an agreement that details all applicable terms and that appoints a **trustee** to serve as the neutral third party between the issuer and the holders of the securities. The provisions of the indenture designed to protect the holders of the securities are called **protective covenants**.

The length of time until the debt instrument matures is called its **term-to-maturity** or, more simply, its **term**. Debt instruments having maturities of less than one year (when issued) are often lumped together under the heading of **money market instruments**. Those with maturities of a year or more are generally considered **capital market**

instruments. The line of demarcation between money market and capital market instruments has become progressively more fuzzy and many professionals in the industry prefer looser language, such as "short-term," "intermediate-term," and "long-term" debt.

Most debt instruments call for a fixed rate of interest that is paid periodically: semiannually or annually, for example. The fixed rate of interest, which is always stated on an annual basis, is called the instrument's **coupon**. Some debt instruments, however, require a periodic resetting of the interest rate to reflect changes in market conditions. Such instruments constitute floating-rate or adjustable-rate debt.

Some debt instruments provide for periodic payments that include both interest and principal. Others only require periodic payment of interest. Still others require no payments of either interest or principal until such time as the instrument matures. In this book, the payments associated with a debt instrument are called the instrument's **cash flows** and the collection of cash flows is referred to as the **cash flow stream**.

When an instrument requires that each payment include some principal as well as interest in such a fashion that the principal is gradually repaid over the life of the instrument, the instrument is said to be **amortizing**. Residential mortgage debt is an example of amortizing debt. When the instrument provides for the full repayment of principal in a lump sum at maturity, with interim payments limited to interest, the instrument is said to be **nonamortizing**. Conventional bonds are examples of nonamortizing debt. When no payments are required until the instrument matures, the instrument is called a **zero coupon bond** or, more simply, a **zero**.

2.2.1 The Coupon

In the case of fixed-rate debt, the debt instrument's coupon is fixed at the time of issuance. The size of the coupon is determined by a number of factors. These include:

1. the general market conditions for debt of the maturity involved;

2. the creditworthiness of the issuer;

3. the tax status of the issue;

4. the value of any collateral offered to support the issue; and

5. any special features that might be included in the issue's indenture.

Since debt securities issued by the United States Treasury (called **Treasury securities** or simply **Treasuries**) include a near continuum of maturities out to 30 years, are of the highest quality, and are extremely liquid, the rates afforded by Treasuries are the logical starting point for setting coupon rates on other instruments. Beginning then with the prevailing Treasury rate for a given maturity, a premium will be added in order to reflect the relative riskiness of a particular new issue. This rate will then be adjusted up or down depending on the tax status of the issue. All other things being equal, the more heavily taxed the income provided by an instrument is, the higher the coupon the instrument must carry to attract investors. Thus, fully taxable corporate issues will carry higher coupons than tax-exempt municipals of similar maturities and risks. The provision of collateral reduces the financial injury to holders of an instrument in the event of the issuer's default. The greater the value of collateral and the more liquid the collateral, the more secure the holders of the instrument are and the smaller the coupon necessary to sell the issue. Some of the special features that affect the size of the coupon include callability, conversion, and sinking funds. A **call provision** grants the issuer the right to call back the issue on or after the **call date**. In the event that the call provision is exercised. the holder will receive the call price. The **call price** is equal to the instrument's par value plus a call premium specified in the indenture. An instrument is convertible if it can be converted into some other asset of the issuer at the discretion of the holder. In the case of corporate issuers, this asset is usually common stock. Call provisions are unattractive to potential investors and thus increase the coupon necessary to sell an issue. Conversion features are attractive to potential investors and thus reduce the coupon necessary to sell an issue. Both call and conversion features are forms of options. We discuss these features in an option's context in Chapter 6.

A **sinking fund** is a mechanism that provides for the gradual retirement of a debt issue. Sinking funds take one of two general forms. In the first, which is the most common in use today, the issuer must periodically repurchase a specified portion of the outstanding issue. These repurchases may be accomplished either by partial calls or by outright market purchases—depending on the terms of the indenture. In the second, the issuer makes periodic payments to a dedicated account, supervised by a trustee. The proceeds of this account are used to retire the issue at maturity. Bonds with sinking fund provisions are known, colloquially, as **sinkers**. In general, sinking funds reduce the level of uncertainty for the holders of the issue and thereby reduce the size of the coupon required to sell the issue.

2.2.2 Valuation of Debt Instruments

The valuation of debt instruments is an exercise in the mathematics of present value. That is, the cash flows that the instrument will provide to the investor must be discounted to their **present values**. The cash flows are discounted at what is commonly known as the instrument's **yield**. The sum of these present values is then the current market price of the instrument. The yield may be viewed as an opportunity cost. That is, the yield is the coupon rate that an equivalent instrument would have to pay in today's market to sell at par and, therefore, it is a reflection of the current level of interest rates. The yield is usually defined as the discount rate that equates the present value of all future cash flows with the current market price of the instrument. Symbolically, the yield is the value y that satisfies Equation 2.1.

$$\sum_{t=1}^{m \cdot T} \frac{CF(t)}{(1 + y/m)^t} = \text{Current market price} \qquad (2.1)$$

The left-hand side of Equation 2.1 discounts the successive cash flows, denoted $CF(t)$, at the rate of y and then sums these discounted values. The value m denotes the frequency of the payments. If the payments are made annually, then m is 1; if the payments are made semiannually, then m is 2; and so on. The frequency of the payments is important: When the payments are made semiannually, the yield is understood to be quoted on the assumption that it is compounded twice a year (semiannually). This is called a **semiannual rate** but it is still stated on an annual basis. As a general rule, there is only one value of y that will solve Equation 2.1. Let's consider a simple example.

A Treasury bond that matures in exactly three years has a $1,000 par value and pays a semiannual coupon 6.75 percent. The bond is currently selling for $967.50. Let's determine the bond's yield. Since the bond is selling below its par value (called a **discount bond**), the bond's yield must be greater than its coupon rate. Thus the bond's yield is greater than 6.75 percent. The bond will provide a cash flow of $33.75 every six months for three years (½ × $1,000 × 6.75%) and a final cash flow of $1,000 when the bond matures in three years. Suppose we arbitrarily try a discount rate of 7.30 percent. The cash flows, the discounted value of the cash flows, and the total value of the bond when discounted at 7.30 percent appear in Table 2.1.

Using a discount rate of 7.30 percent, the bond would have a market value of $985.41. This value is above the current market price of the bond and thus the discount rate we used, 7.30 percent, is too low. By successive approximations, we could eventually find the correct rate at which to discount the cash flows. As demonstrated in Table 2.2, this rate is 7.989 percent. Thus, the discount rate that equates the present value of the bond's future cash flows with its current market price is 7.989 percent. This discount rate is the bond's yield to maturity. While the calculations are tedious, they are also

TABLE 2.1
Discounting Cash Flows: First Iteration

Time	t value	Cash Flow	(at 7.300%) Discounted Value
0.5 years	1	$33.75	$32.56
1.0 years	2	$33.75	$31.41
1.5 years	3	$33.75	$30.31
2.0 years	4	$33.75	$29.24
2.5 years	5	$33.75	$28.21
3.0 years	6	$1,033.75	$833.68
		Total	$985.41

TABLE 2.2
Discounting of Cash Flows: Final Iteration

Time	t value	Cash Flow	(at 7.989%) Discounted Value
0.5 years	1	$33.75	$32.45
1.0 years	2	$33.75	$31.21
1.5 years	3	$33.75	$30.01
2.0 years	4	$33.75	$28.85
2.5 years	5	$33.75	$27.75
3.0 years	6	$1,033.75	$817.25
		Total	$967.52

repetitious and readily lend themselves to computer solutions. Everyone working in the bond trade has such analytical capability.[1]

While Equation 2.1 can be used to determine the value of any cash flow stream, there are short-cut methods that can be used when the cash flow stream takes the form of an annuity. An **annuity** is a series of cash flows of identical size that are spread out at equal intervals in time. The periodic coupon payments on a bond are an example of an annuity. The entire cash flow stream of a bond, however, is not an annuity because the final payment, representing the return of principal, differs from the coupon payments. Nevertheless, the mathematics of annuities is still valuable, as the bond can be viewed as consisting of two cash flow streams: The first represents coupon payments (an annuity) and the last represents a single cash flow valued using a simple present value formula. The cash flow stream in an annuity form is depicted in Table 2.3. The annuity formula is given by Equation 2.2 and the simple present value (PV) formula is given by Equation 2.3.

$$PVA = PMT \cdot \left[\frac{1 - (1 + y/m)^{-T \cdot m}}{y/m} \right] \qquad (2.2)$$

$$PV = PR \cdot (1 + y/m)^{-T \cdot m} \qquad (2.3)$$

In Equation 2.2, PMT denotes the annuity payment, which is the coupon portion of the cash flow stream. In Equation 2.3, PR denotes the principal repaid at time T.

TABLE 2.3
Cash Flows Associated with a Bond

Time	t value	Cash Flow	Type
0.5 years	1	$33.75	Coupon
1.0 years	2	$33.75	Coupon
1.5 years	3	$33.75	Coupon
2.0 years	4	$33.75	Coupon
2.5 years	5	$33.75	Coupon
3.0 years	6	$33.75	Coupon
3.0 years	6	$1,000.00	Principal

The present value of the coupon payments in Table 2.3 can now be obtained by Equation 2.2 and the present value of the principal payment in Table 2.3 can be obtained by Equation 2.3. Using a yield of 7.989 percent, the former is found to be $176.954 and the latter is found to be $790.565. Together, these values total $967.52. This is precisely the same result we got with Equation 2.1. The present value of an annuity formula is used to price swaps in Chapter 8.

The example above makes it clear that as interest rates rise (causing yields to rise) debt instrument prices will fall. Thus we see that yields and prices are inversely related. This inverse relationship between yields and prices is a fundamental principle of finance and it is the source of one of the most important sources of risk for those involved in the debt markets.

Two small points are in order. First, the bond above has a par value of $1,000. Another debt instrument might have a par value of $5,000 or $500. To eliminate the potential confusion associated with comparing debt instruments that have different par values, it is customary to quote the prices of debt instruments as a percentage of their par values. Thus, the bond above would be quoted at 96.75. The decimal portion of this value (.75) might be quoted as a fraction based on thirty-seconds or eighths.

For example, Treasury bonds are usually quoted in thirty-seconds of a percentage point. Thus 96.75 would be reported as 96^{24}/$_{32}$, (i.e., 96 and 24 thirty-seconds). Bond prices are usually quoted on an **and interest** basis.[2] That is, the price *does not* include the interest that has accrued on the bond. The accrued interest is calculated separately and the purchaser pays the seller the accrued interest in addition to the agreed purchase price. The accrued interest is calculated using standard interest-accrual formulas and is then added on to the purchase price.

There are several interest-accrual formulas and which applies depends upon the type of bond. For example, Treasury bonds accrue interest on an "actual over 365 day" basis while corporate bonds accrue interest on a "360 over 360 day" basis. Thus, Treasury bonds accrue one day's interest each day with interest calculated as if a year consists of 365 days. Corporate bonds (or "corporates") accrue and pay interest on the assumption that the year consists of 360 days and each month consists of 30 days. Thus, February pays two days extra interest while the 31st day of a month having 31 days is a "bad day" in the sense that no interest accrues on that day.

The second point we need to make involves basis points. Yield changes and interest-rate spreads are usually quoted in basis points. A basis point (bp) is one one-hundreth of one percent (0.01%). One-hundred basis points is, therefore, one percentage point.

The mathematics of yield measurement are the same whether measuring the yield of a nonamortizing debt instrument (such as a bond) or an amortizing instrument (such as a mortgage). The concept of "yield" is one of the most important concepts in fixed-income security analysis. It is important to understand, however, that different instruments have different yields. As indicated earlier, the yield, like the coupon at the time of initial issue, is explained by the market conditions associated with the maturity of the instrument, by the creditworthiness of the issuer, by the quantity and the quality of any collateral provided, and by various other features specific to the bond. Of the many factors that influence an instrument's yield, the two most important are the instrument's maturity and the riskiness of the issue. The next two sections examine these issues.

2.2.3   The Yield Curve

We focus on the role of maturity by holding default risk constant. This is most easily done by limiting ourselves to conventional coupon-bearing Treasury securities. We use Treasury securities because this is the only class of securities widely regarded as completely free of default risk. Each bond of a given maturity is priced by the market and this price can be transformed, by the arithmetic we have already described, into a yield. We can then plot these yields against maturity. The relationship between yield and maturity is called the **term structure of interest rates**. When graphed, the term structure is called a **yield curve**. A typical yield curve is depicted in Exhibit 2.1.

   Notice that the yield curve depicted in Exhibit 2.1 is upward sloping. This is considered normal and is called an **ascending** or **upward sloping** yield curve. There are several competing, although

EXHIBIT 2.1.   Upward Sloping Yield Curve
(Conventional U.S. Treasury Securities)

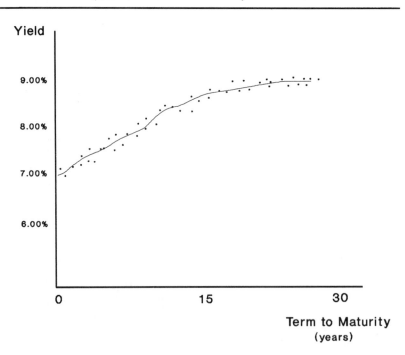

not mutually exclusive, explanations for the shape of the yield curve. First, long-term yields (yields on long-term instruments) should reflect market expectations of successive future short-term rates since an alternative to holding a long-term instrument is to hold a series of successive short-term instruments. If this is the only determinant of long-term rates, then long-term rates should be the geometric average of expected future short-term rates. This explanation for the shape of the yield curve is called the **pure expectations theory**.

The second explanation for the shape of the yield curve is called the **liquidity premium theory**. The liquidity premium theory holds that since, as we will demonstrate shortly, long-maturity instruments are more price sensitive than are short-maturity instruments, holders of long-term instruments are exposed to more price risk from a general change in the level of interest rates than are holders of short-maturity instruments.

The final theory, called the **segmented markets theory** or **segmentation theory**, argues that there are reasons to believe that demand and supply conditions for different maturities are different and that these maturity-specific demand/supply conditions are the determinants of yields. This theory views the debt markets as a continuum of individual, separate maturity markets. The problem with this theory, at least in its pure form, is that it fails to allow for arbitrage between maturities. Nevertheless, there are undoubtedly maturity-specific demand and supply considerations and they must certainly have some affect on yields. Most players in the credit markets have concluded that all three explanations for term structure play a role but that the relative importance of each varies with market conditions.

The yield curve is not static. It is continuously changing in response to evolving credit market conditions. Occasionally, the curve will shift up or down. Such shifts, however, are usually not parallel. Rather, the short-maturity end of the curve (short end) might shift by more than the long end. During periods of Federal Reserve tightening, for example, the entire curve will typically move higher but the short end will move by a greater amount— this results in a flattening, or even an inversion, of the yield curve. Such an inversion is depicted in Exhibit 2.2.

EXHIBIT 2.2. Normal versus Inverted Yield Curve
(Conventional U.S. Treasury Securities)

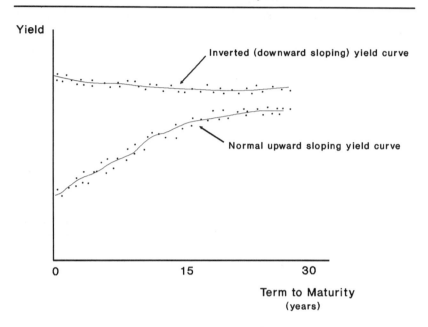

2.2.4   Investment Risks in the Debt Markets

There are a number of risks associated with holding a debt instrument. These include interest-rate risk, default risk, reinvestment risk, call risk, prepayment risk, and purchasing power risk. We will briefly consider each of these in a few moments. First, however, some general obervations about risk must be made.

Any financial risk consists of two basic components called systematic risk and unsystematic risk. The **systematic component** of risk represents the degree to which manifestations of the risk are associated with more general market behaviors. The **unsystematic component** of risk represents the degree to which manifestations of the risk are independent of more general market behaviors. These different risk components are most easily illustrated in the context of common stock.

To some degree, variations in the rate of return on common stock are associated with variations in the rate of return on the entire stock market. This covariability exists because changes in variables that affect one stock's price will often also affect the prices of many other stocks and, therefore, will have an effect on the overall market. For example, an increase in interest rates will increase the cost of doing business and tend to negatively impact most stocks. Thus, if interest rates rise and the stock market declines, the degree to which a specific stock declines with the rest of the market is a manifestation of that stock's systematic risk.

Now consider some event that is specific to a particular company. For example, suppose the company is a toy manufacturer and one of its most popular toys is found to be unsafe and sales must be discontinued. Upon release of this news, the stock's price declines. The market, however, is not significantly affected by the event because the event is company specific. Such manifestations of risk are unsystematic in nature.

The various types of risk associated with holding debt instruments also have systematic and unsystematic components. The systematic component of a risk to which the holder of a debt instrument is exposed is the degree to which that instrument's value fluctuates with the values of other debt instruments. The unsystematic component is the degree to which the value changes in the debt instrument are independent of the value changes in other debt instruments.

The importance of the distinction between systematic and unsystematic components of risk has to do with the management of risk. Unsystematic risk disappears with diversification. That is, the greater the degree of diversification in a portfolio, the less unsystematic risk one will find. Systematic risk, however, does not disappear with diversification and must, therefore, be managed by other means.

A more specific examination of the forms of risk associated with holding debt instruments follows.[3]

2.2.4.1 INTEREST-RATE RISK

Interest-rate risk is examined first because this form of risk usually dominates the other risks associated with holding debt instruments. **Interest-rate risk** is the risk that evolving market conditions will bring about a change in interest rates. Since yields on existing instruments must respond to reflect prevailing interest rates, a change in the level of interest rates will mean a change in market values for existing debt instruments. Manifestations of interest-rate risk are felt broadly since a change in market conditions that leads to an upward or downward shift in the yield curve will influence most debt securities similarly and simultaneously.

Interest-rate risk is of great significance to both issuers and holders of debt instruments. For issuers, changes in interest rates affect the cost of funds and may affect the return on rate-sensitive assets. The latter is particularly important if the return on the assets is used to meet the interest expense on the issuer's liabilities.

As mentioned earlier, long-term instruments are more price sensitive to changes in interest rates than short-term instruments. This point is very important and worth some elaboration. Suppose we have five instruments that have maturities of six months, one year, two years, five years, and 20 years, respectively. Each instrument is initially priced at par, (that is, the yields and the coupons match) and each instrument pays a semiannual coupon. Consider the effect on the prices of these instruments from a 20 basis point parallel shift upward in the yield curve. This parallel shift in the yield curve is depicted in Exhibit 2.3 and the resultant values and value changes are reported in Table 2.4.

The values of the bonds, both before and after the 20 basis point change in yield, are calculated using Equation 2.1. Now consider the column labeled "Price Change." Notice that the instrument with six months to maturity declined in value by $0.097 for each $100 of face value as a result of the 20 basis point increase in yields. Notice also that the bond with 20 years to maturity declined in value by $1.767 for each $100 of face value as a result of the same 20 basis point increase in yields. The 20-year bond declined in value by *more than 18 times as much* as the bond with six months to maturity. Thus, we see that the longer the maturity, all other things being equal, the more price sensitive a debt instrument is to a change in its yield.

The price changes discussed above measured the change in bond values for a 20 basis point change in yields. Bond traders and others involved in interest rate risk management need to know very precisely how changes in yield will affect prices. There are a number of related

EXHIBIT 2.3.   Parallel Shift in the Yield Curve

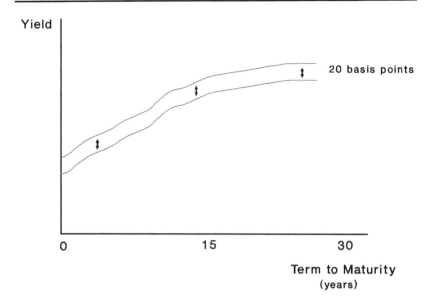

measures that are used for this purpose. Two of the most important are "duration" and the "dollar value of a basis point."

2.2.4.1.a *Duration*   We have demonstrated that the longer a debt instrument's maturity, all other things being equal, the more sensitive is its price to changes in its yield. Maturity, however, is not the only factor that influences a debt instrument's price sensitivity to

TABLE 2.4
Debt Instrument Maturity and Price Sensitivity

Maturity (Years)	Coupon	Initial Yield (%)	Initial Price	New Yield (%)	New Price	Price Change
0.5	7.000	7.000	$100.000	7.200	$99.903	−0.097
1.0	7.750	7.750	$100.000	7.950	$99.811	−0.189
2.0	8.250	8.250	$100.000	8.450	$99.639	−0.361
5.0	8.750	8.750	$100.000	8.950	$99.208	−0.792
20.0	9.375	9.375	$100.000	9.575	$98.233	−1.767

Note: The prices and price changes are reported per $100 of face (par) value.

yield changes. Four other factors also play a role. The other factors are:

1. the size of the instrument's coupon;
2. the frequency of the coupon payments;
3. the speed with which the loan principal amortizes; and
4. the instrument's present yield.

In 1938, Frederick Macaulay developed a measure of price sensitivity to yield changes that incorporates all the factors that influence price sensitivity.[4] This measure is known as **duration**. Assuming equal basis point changes in yield (i.e., a parallel shift in the yield curve), two debt instruments that have identical durations will have identical interest-rate sensitivities. Further, the ratio of two debt instruments' durations is an accurate measure of their relative price sensitivities to equivalent yield changes when such price sensitivity is stated on a percentage basis. Duration, which is measured in years and denoted here by D, is a weighted average-time-to-maturity of an instrument. The weights are the ratios of the present values of the future cash flows (including both interest and principal) to the current market price of the instrument. The current price of the instrument is, of course, the sum of the present value of all future cash flows associated with the instrument. That is,

$$D = \sum_{t}^{m \cdot T} w_t \cdot (t/m) \qquad \textbf{(2.4)}$$

where
$$w_t = \frac{CF(t/m) \cdot (1 + y/m)^{-t}}{\sum_{t} CF(t/m) \cdot (1 + y/m)^{-t}}$$

$$t = 1, 2, 3, \ldots m \cdot T$$

$CF(t/m)$: Cash flow at time t/m (time measured in years).

y: Present yield on instrument.

m: The number of payment periods per year.

Let's consider the duration calculation for a simple bond. Consider the two-year bond in Table 2.4. It has a coupon of 8.250 percent and an initial yield of 8.250 percent—so it is priced at par. The duration calculation for this bond, which reveals a duration of approximately 1.88 years, is shown in Table 2.5. The durations for all the bonds in Table 2.4 are listed in Table 2.6.[5]

Notice that Table 2.6 also includes a **modified duration**. Shortly after Macaulay introduced the concept of duration, another researcher showed that the slope of the present value curve (the value of a bond versus its yield) is a natural indicator of an instrument's price sensitivity.[6] This slope, as it turns out, is equal to Macaulay's duration divided by one plus the instrument's periodic yield $(1 + y/m)$. This slope became known as the modified duration. The calculation of modified duration, denoted here by D_m, is related to duration by Equation 2.5. It is important to note that all subsequent references to duration are references to modified duration.

$$D_m = \frac{D}{(1 + y/m)} \qquad (2.5)$$

(Duration has a great many theoretical as well as practical applications. The interested reader can get some idea of the many applications by consulting the "References and Suggested Reading" section which appears at the end of this chapter.)

TABLE 2.5
Duration Calculation

t value	Cash Flow	Discounted Value of Cash Flow	Weight $w(t)$	Time (t/m)	Product $w(t) \cdot (t/m)$
1	$4.125	3.961	0.0396	0.5	0.0198
2	$4.125	3.805	0.0381	1.0	0.0381
3	$4.125	3.654	0.0365	1.5	0.0548
4	$104.125	88.580	0.8858	2.0	1.7716
	Totals	100.000	1.00000	Duration =	1.8843

TABLE 2.6
Comparative Durations

Maturity (Years)	Coupon	Initial Yield (%)	Initial Price	Duration (Years)	Modified Duration
0.5	7.000	7.000	100.000	0.50	0.48
1.0	7.750	7.750	100.000	0.98	0.94
2.0	8.250	8.250	100.000	1.88	1.81
5.0	8.750	8.750	100.000	4.15	3.98
20.0	9.375	9.375	100.000	9.38	8.96

Consider one such application; compare the duration of the 20-year bond to the duration of the five-year bond. Notice that the 20-year bond has a duration that is approximately 2.25 times that of the five-year bond. This means that the yield change necessary to cause a 1 percent decline in the market value of the five-year bond will cause a 2.25 percent decline in the market value of the 20-year bond. Duration ratios, like the one we just used to compare the above two bonds, provide a measure of relative price sensitivities in terms of percentage changes in value. To convert these values to dollar terms, we must multiply the duration ratio by the ratio of the bonds' prices:

$$\frac{D_{20\text{-yr}}}{D_{5\text{-yr}}} \times \frac{P_{20\text{-yr}}}{P_{5\text{-yr}}}$$

Since both of these bonds were priced at par, the price ratio is 1.0. This will, of course, usually not be the case. Since it happens to be the case here, however, we can say that the yield change just sufficient to cause a $1 change in the value of the five-year bond would cause a $2.25 change in the value of the 20-year bond.

   2.2.4.1.b *Dollar Value of a Basis Point.*   Another widely used measure of price sensitivity is the **dollar value of a basis point** or **DVBP** (sometimes called the price value of a basis point or PVBP). An instrument's DVBP is the amount of value change per $100 of face value that will occur if yields change by one basis point. The DVBP values for the five bonds in Table 2.4 appear in Table 2.7.

The DVBPs in Table 2.7 were obtained by dividing the price change resulting from a 20 basis point change in yield by 20 to obtain the price change from a 1 basis point change in yield (this method of calculation results in a slight rounding error.) Consider for a moment the DVBP of the five-year and the 20-year bonds. The five-year bond has a DVBP of 0.0396 while the 20-year bond has a DVBP of 0.0884. The ratio of the DVBPs provides a relative measure of the dollar value changes that are associated with equivalent changes in yield. Thus, the 20-year bond is 2.23 times as price sensitive to yield changes as is the five-year bond. This is almost the same result we got from the duration calculation (after multiplying by the price ratio). We see then that DVBPs and durations provide similar information and have many of the same applications. For the remainder of this discussion, we consider DVBP only.

Those involved in the management of interest-rate risk, including those who use swaps, often have positions in instruments of different maturities. A position in an actual instrument is called a **cash position**. Some of these cash positions may be long positions while others are short positions. Clearly, a short position in one debt instrument is a partial hedge for a long position in another debt instrument. Unfortunately, knowledge of the instruments' DVBPs is not sufficient, in and of itself, to effectively manage interest-rate risk. The reason is simple. The DVBP measures the dollar value change that results from

TABLE 2.7
Comparative DVBPs

Maturity	Yield	Price	Approximate DVBP
0.5	7.000	100.000	0.0048
1.0	7.750	100.000	0.0094
2.0	8.250	100.000	0.0181
5.0	8.750	100.000	0.0396
20.0	9.375	100.000	0.0884

a single basis point change in yield. But, not all yield curve shifts are parallel and, hence, not all yields change by the same number of basis points.

To deal with this problem, risk managers typically convert all interest-rate exposures to some **baseline** or **benchmark** equivalent. This is usually an instrument on which a futures contract is written. For example, the **baseline instrument** might be the 20-year Treasury bond or the 10-year Treasury note. Next, the historic yield changes for the cash instrument in which the firm has a position is regressed against the corresponding historic yield changes for the baseline instrument to get what is called a **yield beta**. The yield beta measures the number of basis points the yield of the cash instrument is likely to change for each 1 basis point change in the yield of the baseline instrument. For example, suppose that a bond trader has a long position in $2,000,000 (face value) 15-year bonds of Issuer X. The bonds have a DVBP of 0.0792. The baseline 20-year Treasury bond has a DVBP of 0.0884. Finally, the yield beta (β_x) of the 15-year bonds of Issuer X is 0.84. Then the DVBP hedging model can be used to determine the face value of the baseline instrument which is equivalent to this long position. The DVBP model is given by Equation 2.6, in which FV denotes face value. Face value is also called par value.

$$FV_b = FV_x \times \frac{DVBP_x}{DVBP_b} \times \beta_x \qquad (2.6)$$

$$FV_b = 2,000,000 \times \frac{0.0792}{0.0884} \times 0.84$$

$$= 1,505,158$$

From this calculation, we see that the long position in $2,000,000 of Issuer X's bonds is equivalent to a long position in $1,505,158 of baseline T-bonds.

Suppose that the firm also has a short position in $1,800,000 (face value) of nine-year notes of Issuer Y. Using the DVBP model, these notes are found to be equivalent to a short position in $1,066,500 of baseline Treasury bonds. By converting all positions to the same baseline equivalent, the risk managers can accurately assess the degree to which the firm's various exposures are offsetting. For example, the risk managers sum the baseline equivalent of the long position in Issue X with the baseline equivalent of the partially offsetting short position in Issue Y to obtain a net exposure equivalent to a long position in $438,658 of the baseline security. Since a futures contract on the baseline security exists, the risk manager can hedge by taking a short position in the futures. In this case, each 20-year Treasury bond futures covers $100,000 of face value bonds. Thus, to fully hedge, the risk manager needs a short position in approximately 4.4 futures. (Futures and futures hedging are discussed more fully in Chapter 5.)

2.2.4.2 DEFAULT RISK

Default risk on debt is the risk that the borrower will fail to make timely payments of interest and/or principal on its debt. Most issuers of debt securities have their debt rated by debt rating agencies. As a general rule, underwriters will not handle unrated issues. The two principal rating agencies are Moody's and Standard and Poor's. The rating systems of these two rating agencies are similar but not identical. The best grade is the top **investment grade** (Aaa or AAA, respectively) and the poorest grade is for those bonds that are already in default. The higher the rating, the lower the yield an instrument will provide. A decade ago, very few issuers could sell debt that had a less-than investment grade rating. But this has changed dramatically during the last decade as **speculative grade** (also called **high-yield** or **junk**) issues have become a major source of finance for those involved in takeovers and leveraged buyouts. The dramatic change in the volume of this type of debt is illustrated in Exhibit 2.4.

Default risk is not a hedgeable risk, but investors can manage it in several ways. One way is to enhance the creditworthiness of the borrower by insisting on collateral. Another way is to limit the size of the position in any one issuer's debt.

Default risk is largely unsystematic in nature and hence, it can be greatly reduced by diversification. In a well-diversified, high-yield

EXHIBIT 2.4.   The High-Yield Market

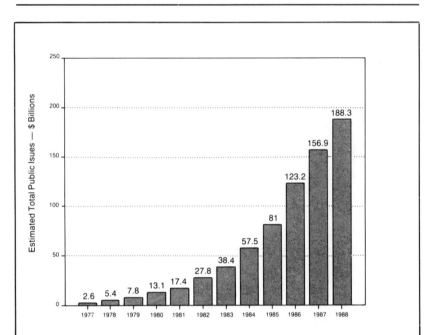

FIRST BOSTON HIGH YIELD RESEARCH

Source: First Boston High Yield Research, *First Boston Corporation High Yield Handbook* (1989)

portfolio, the risk premium on high-yield debt has tended to exceed the default rate on the debt. The difference is an excess premium. The excess premium on high-yield corporate debt for the last several years is depicted in Exhibit 2.5.

2.2.4.3   REINVESTMENT RISK, CALL RISK, AND PREPAYMENT RISK

Reinvestment risk, call risk, and prepayment risk are closely related forms of risk. When an investor purchases a debt instrument that has a known yield, the investor takes the risk that the instrument's value will fluctuate in response to changes in its yield. This is the interest-rate risk we discussed earlier. But, if the investor purchases an instrument with a maturity that is identical to his or her investment horizon (that

EXHIBIT 2.5. Excess Premiums vs. Default Losses 1977–1988

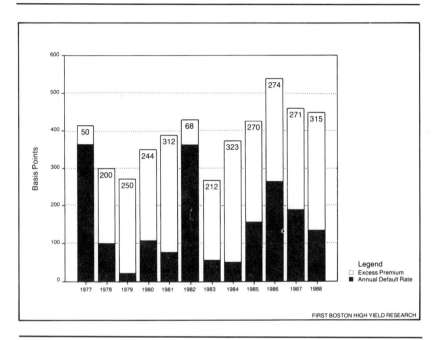

Source: First Boston High Yield Research, *First Boston Corporation High Yield Handbook* (1989)

is, the investor purchased the instrument in order to have some known terminal wealth), then these fluctuations in value are really quite irrelevant. Regardless of interim changes in value, the instrument will ultimately be redeemed for its full face value (par) and, thus, for this investor, interim fluctuations are not very important. But if the investment provides periodic income, such as coupon payments, then there is still a risk that the terminal wealth will deviate from initial expectations. The concept of yield implicitly assumes that income generated by an investment can be reinvested to earn the same rate. But if yields are fluctuating, then the investor may very likely find that the reinvestment rate differs from the yield that prevailed at the time the instrument was purchased. These reinvestment rates might be higher or lower than the purchase-time yield and so the terminal wealth may deviate from the expectation held at the time of the instrument's purchase. The deviations from expected terminal wealth that result from fluctuations in the reinvestment rate are manifestations of **reinvestment risk**.

Call risk and **prepayment risk** are the risks that the issuer will choose to repay the loan principal before maturity. In the case of callable bonds, the issuer can choose, at its discretion, to call the bond on or after the call date. If a bond is called, the holder gets the call price as specified in the bond's indenture. In the case of mortgages debt, the mortgagor usually has the right to prepay the mortgage balance at any time. The mortgage balance is the portion of the principal that has not amortized plus any accrued interest. In both the case of the call and the prepayment, the holder of the debt instrument receives proceeds sooner than expected and, presumably, sooner than desired. This premature receipt of funds forces the investor to look for an avenue to reinvest.

A debt instrument is most likely to be called or prepayed when interest rates have declined. Lower interest rates provide an incentive for the issuer to issue new debt at the prevailing lower rates and to use the proceeds to pay off the existing debt. This tendency for calls and prepayments to occur when rates decline implies that the investor will find that the available investment alternatives after a call or a prepayment are usually poorer than the original investment in the debt instrument. It is for these reasons that call risk and prepayment risk are closely related to reinvestment risk.

One way to avoid reinvestment risk is to invest exclusively in securities that are not callable or prepayable and that do not provide periodic coupons. Noncallable zero-coupon bonds are such an instrument. A zero coupon bond (zero) is sold at a deep discount from face value and gradually rises in value as it approaches maturity. At maturity the instrument is redeemed for its full face value. Zero coupon bonds are more price sensitive to changes in yields than are equivalent maturity coupon bearing bonds. However, the investor who matches the maturity of the zeros to his or her investment horizon, assuming his or her investment horizon is known with certainty, is unconcerned about interim fluctuations in value and is, therefore, freed from concern over interest-rate risk and reinvestment risk. If the zeros are derived from U.S. Treasury securities the investor is also freed from concern over default risk.

2.2.4.4 PURCHASING POWER RISK

The last form of risk we consider is purchasing power risk. This is the risk that the terminal wealth from an investment will have less purchasing power than the investor expected at the time of the instrument's purchase. This form of risk is associated with any investment that is not indexed to the rate of inflation. While some debt instruments have coupons that are indexed to various measures of inflation, such as the consumer price index, debt with indexed coupons are not common in the United States, although they are more common in Europe. Floating-rate debt, however, is, in a sense, inflation indexed. As we will argue later in this chapter, interest rates tend to reflect inflationary expectations. Thus, a change in inflationary expectations should be accompanied by a change in interest rates. Floating-rate debt should then adjust to offer a greater nominal rate of interest when inflationary expectations are high and a lower nominal rate of interest when inflationary expectations are low. (We discuss floating-rate debt in greater detail in the Chapter 3.)

2.3 EXCHANGE RATES: THE BASICS

An exchange rate (or foreign-exchange rate) is the number of units of one currency that can be purchased (exchanged) for one unit of another currency. An exchange rate is therefore the price of one currency stated in terms of another currency. This price is determined by a number of related factors, including:

1. the general price level for goods in the two countries;
2. the expected rates of inflation in the two countries;
3. the rates of interest in the two countries; and
4. the degree to which the governments of the two countries restrict trade and/or manipulate exchange rates involving their currencies for economic or political gain.

There are actually two different kinds of exchange rates: spot and forward. **Spot exchange rates** are the rates of exchange for immediate payment and delivery of a currency.[7] A typical exchange rate quote for deutschemarks (DM) in terms of dollars (US) would be 1.4555 DM/US. This means that one U.S. dollar will purchase 1.4555 deutschemarks for immediate delivery. **Forward exchange** rates are current rates of exchange for deferred delivery of a currency. Deferred delivery means that the price of the currency is agreed to now but the delivery and payment for the currency will not occur until some specified later date. Forward exchange rates are stated in exactly the same way as spot rates but the length of the delivery deferral must be added. For example, the 30-day forward rate for deutschemark in terms of dollars might be 1.4552 DM/US 30-days.

The difference between the forward rate and the spot rate is called a **forward premium** if the forward rate is above the spot rate, and a **forward discount** if the forward rate is below the spot rate. In the example above, the 30-day forward deutschemark for dollar rate is at a discount to the spot rate (1.4552 DM/US as opposed to 1.4555 DM/US). In the case of this particular exchange rate, a forward discount has been the historic norm. This is generally attributed to the lower rate of inflation in West Germany. We will ignore this historic relationship in some of the examples that follow in order to illustrate certain pertinent points.

The markets for both spot and forward foreign exchange are called **currency markets** or **foreign exchange markets** and are known in the trade as **FOREX** or **FX markets**. These markets are made, for the most part, by banks with the banks acting as both dealers and brokers in currencies.

The foreign exchange markets are very liquid for the major hard currencies. While trading is decentralized, with each broker/dealer maintaining its own trading room and associated facilities, brokers and dealers are nevertheless tied together electronically and the markets are very competitive and very efficient.

Banks, corporations, institutional investors, and private individuals often have commitments in currencies that differ from their domestic currency. These commitments may require exchanges of currencies at a single later date or at a series of later dates. For example, a British bank might make a 60-day dollar loan to an American borrower. The British bank made the loan by taking British pound (BP) deposits and converting them, at the spot rate, to dollars. The American borrower will repay the dollars, together with interest, in 60 days. Thus, the British bank knows the number of dollars to be received 60 days forward. Or a German automaker might agree to sell cars to an American distributor for a specified number of dollars. The agreement might require the autos to be delivered and payment to be made in 90 days. Thus, the German firm knows the number of dollars to be received 90 days forward. In both of these situations, the receiver of dollars does not really want dollars. The British bank wants pounds and the German automaker wants deutschemarks. Both the bank and the automaker have "long" forward positions in dollars.

Both the bank and the automaker just described can deal with their forward dollar positions in a variety of ways. The simplest way is to wait until they receive the dollars and then convert the dollars to their domestic currency at the prevailing spot rate. The trouble with this strategy is that the spot rates that will prevail 60 or 90 days forward are not known at the time of the initial transactions; that is, at the time the British bank makes its loan to the American firm and at the time the German automaker agrees to sell cars to the U.S. distributor. It is quite possible, indeed it is highly probable, that the spot exchange rates will have changed from their initial levels by the time of the final currency translation. If the dollar weakens between the time of the initial agreements and the time of the final exchanges, the British bank and the German automaker could find themselves with serious losses on what seemed like profitable transactions.

Fluctuations in exchange rates are the source of exchange-rate risk. This is the kind of risk to which both the British bank and the German automaker were exposed. When such a risk exists, it is often prudent to hedge the risk. A hedge is a position taken in some instrument for the purpose of offsetting the risk associated with some other position. Swaps are often used for this purpose. They compete, in this regard, with other hedging instruments including forward contracts and futures contracts.

It is important at this point to distinguish between **foreign curren-cy transactions** and **foreign currency translations**. For accounting purposes, it is often necessary or desirable to restate profits and losses (as well as balance sheet values) in another currency. Such restate-ments are referred to as foreign exchange translations. Actual ex-changes of currencies, on the other hand, represent foreign exchange transactions.

2.3.1 The Determinants of Exchange Rates

In free markets, changes in exchange rates are determined, more than anything else, by changes in interest rates and in inflationary expecta-tions. The role of interest rates is explained by the concept of **interest-rate parity** and the role of inflation is explained by the concept of **purchasing-power parity**. These two explanations are, in turn, related to one another by the **Fisher Equation**. Since this is not meant to be a formal treatise on exchange rate theory, we will keep the discussion short and relatively nonquantitative. The reader interested in a more formal treatment of these topics should see the suggested reading at the end of this chapter.[8]

2.3.1.1 INTEREST-RATE PARITY

Suppose that the nominal rate of interest for some given maturity in Country X is higher than the nominal rate of interest in Country Y for instruments that have comparable risk. Suppose further that the spot and forward exchange rates of Currency X for Currency Y are identi-cal. Then investors with surplus funds in Country Y have an incentive to convert their Currency Y to Currency X at the current spot exchange rate. The Currency X obtained from this translation can then be invested in Country X at Country X's higher rates. The debt instrument purchased, however, will mature at a known future date and the Country Y investors, therefore, have unwanted long forward positions in Currency X. To eliminate the risk associated with these long forward positions in Currency X, the Country Y investors can contract forward to convert their future Currency X back to Currency Y. The Country Y investor who engages in this related series of transactions will earn a higher return than the Country Y investor who invests domestically at lower rates. Yet, because the investor has hedged his exchange-rate risk, the higher return is achieved without bearing greater risk.

Suppose that an American investor observes that six-month (182 day) U.S. Treasury securities are currently yielding 8.20 percent while six-month (182 day) West German government securities are yielding 9.30 percent. The spot exchange rate of deutschemark for dollars is 1.9550 and the 182-day forward exchange rate is also 1.9550. The investor has $100,000 that he plans to invest in 182-day U.S. Treasury securities. After observing the higher yield on West German securities, however, he decides to convert his dollars to deutschemark and then invest these deutschemark in West German securities. At the current spot exchange rate, US $100,000 will purchase DM 195,500. If the deutschemarks are invested at 9.30 percent for 182 days (half of a year), the American investor will have DM 204,691.75 in 182 days. The interest portion is calculated as DM 195,500 $\times$ 9.3% $\times$ 182/360. Thus, if the investor engages in this strategy, he will have a long position in 204,691.75 182-day forward deutschemarks the moment he purchases the German securities.

To hedge this, he would sell DM 204,691.75 182 days forward for dollars at the current 182-day forward rate. This will yield US 104,701.67. If the American investor invested his US $100,000 in U.S. securities, on the other hand, he would only have had $104,145.56. For this American investor, the German investment, with the appropriate hedge, is clearly superior to the straight U.S. investment.

The strategy we have just described is actually a sophisticated and widely practiced form of arbitrage called **covered interest arbitrage**. In this strategy, the investor borrows funds in one country, converts the funds to the currency of another country at the spot exchange rate, lends the currency obtained at the prevailing interest rates in that country, and simultaneously contracts in the forward foreign exchange market to convert the future proceeds from this lending back to his own currency. The proceeds at delivery can then be used to repay the original lending source. For example, suppose that the American investor, whom we will now call an arbitrager, had borrowed the $100,000 he used for the transaction in the United States at a cost of

8.20 percent. Then assume the German investment, coupled with the currency translations, will provide a terminal value of $104,701.67. After repaying the sum he borrowed and the interest (a total of $104,145.56), the arbitrager will have a riskless profit of $556.11. What's more, this profit was earned without any actual investment of the arbitrager's own funds.

Continuing with the example, consider what happens if this covered interest arbitrage activity becomes widespread. The sales of dollars (for deutschemarks) in the spot market will depress the value of the dollar relative to the deutschemark. Thus the spot exchange rate of DM for USD will decline. At the same time, the forward sales of deutschemark for dollars will cause the forward exchange rate of DM for USD to rise. The spot and forward rates will eventually reach an equilibrium in which no further riskless arbitrage profits are possible. Assuming no change in the 182-day interest rates on the U.S. and German securities, we might find that the equilibrium is reached when the spot DM/USD rate is 1.9495 and the 182-day forward rate is 1.9599. (We leave it to the reader to prove that no riskless arbitrage profits are possible at these exchange rates.)

The spot and forward rates arrived at in the preceding example do not represent a unique solution to the exchange rate equilibrium. Other combinations of spot and forward exchange rates will also yield a result in which arbitrage profits are not possible. Nevertheless, it is clear that competition among investors to earn the highest returns possible on their money and competition among arbitragers to exploit interest rate and exchange rate discrepancies are responsible for maintaining logical relationships between spot and forward exchange rates.

The interest-rate parity theorem is summarized by Equation 2.7. In Equation 2.7, $E_{y,x}$ denotes the spot exchange rate; $E_{y,x}(D)$ denotes the D-day forward exchange rate; and $r_y(D)$ and $r_x(D)$ denote the interest rates on comparable risk instruments having maturities of D days.

$$\frac{E_{y,x}(D)}{E_{y,x}} = \frac{1 + r_y(D)}{1 + r_x(D)} \qquad (2.7)$$

2.3.2   Purchasing Power Parity

The interest-rate parity theorem explains the relationship between spot and forward exchange rates in terms of interest-rate differentials between countries. Once the spot rate is known, for example, the forward rates are all determined by relative interest rates. The theory does not, however, explain why the spot rate is what it is. And without some means of determining the spot rate, the forward rates cannot be determined.

The current spot rate is explained by the concept of purchasing-power parity, which, in turn, is derived from a theorem called the **law of one price.** The law of one price argues, quite simply, that the price of a good in one country cannot exceed the price of the good in another country by more than the cost of transporting the good between the two countries. If it should, merchants, acting in the role of arbitragers, would buy the good in the cheaper market, transport it to the higher-priced market and then resell it. Included in the transportation cost is a "normal profit" for the merchant and the cost of converting the good from the standard of the originating country to the standard of the destination country (if the two standards differ). The theory obviously assumes that there are no artificial barriers to trade. The law of one price is stated algebraically in Equation 2.8.

$$P_y = P_x \cdot E_{y,x} + R_y \qquad \text{where} \qquad -T_y \leq R_y \leq T_y \qquad (2.8)$$

Equation 2.8 says that the price of the good in Country Y, stated in terms of Currency Y, must be equal to the price of the good in Country X stated in terms of Currency X times the spot exchange rate of Currency Y for Currency X, denoted here as $E_{y,x}$, plus a stochastic component, R_y, which is bounded by the cost of transportation, stated in terms of Currency Y, T_y. Anytime the prices of the goods between the two markets deviate from the law of one price, arbitragers will become active. The arbitragers' purchases will bid the price up in the lower-priced market and the arbitragers' sales will drive the price down in the higher-priced market.

Now, suppose we average this law of one price relationship over all the goods that trade in the two countries. If we do so, the stochastic component, which averages zero, will disappear. If we use a common base period, the "averaged" values may be interpreted as price indexes. In this form, the relationship is known as purchasing-power parity and is given by Equation 2.9.

$$\tilde{P}_y = \tilde{P}_x \cdot E_{y,x} \qquad (2.9)$$

In Equation 2.9, $\tilde{P}_y$ and $\tilde{P}_x$ denote the price indexes in Country Y and Country X, respectively. We can manipulate the price indexes to obtain an expression for the spot exchange rate. This is given by Equation 2.10.

$$E_{y,x} = \frac{\tilde{P}_y}{\tilde{P}_x} \qquad (2.10)$$

From Equation 2.10, we see that the spot exchange rate between the currencies of two countries should be a reflection of the relative price levels in the two countries.

Purchasing-power parity helps explain why the spot exchange rate is what it is and interest-rate parity helps explain why the forward rates are what they are given the spot rate. If price levels determine spot rates, however, shouldn't we expect expectations of future changes in the price level (inflation) to influence forward rates? The answer is, of course, a decided yes. But the influence is felt through interest rates. To see this, we need to consider one last relationship—the Fisher Equation.

2.3.3 The Fisher Equation

The Fisher Equation, named for Irving Fisher (an important economist of the late nineteenth and early twentieth centuries), argues that nominal interest rates are related to real interest rates by Equation 2.11.

$$r_{y,n}(D) = r_{y,r}(D) + i_{y,e}(D) \qquad (2.11)$$

Equation 2.10 states that the nominal rate of interest in Country Y for a maturity of D days, denoted here by $r_{y,n}(D)$, equals the required real rate in Country Y for that number of days, denoted here by $r_{y,r}(D)$, plus the expected change in the price level in Country Y over that number of days, denoted here by $i_{y,e}(D)$. (The latter is, of course, just the expected rate of inflation in Country Y.) The theory is predicated on the assumption that lenders and borrowers formulate their lending and borrowing plans on the basis of real rates of interest. In its modern form, the theory is also usually taken to assume that investors form rational expectations of future rates of inflation.

Together, interest-rate parity, purchasing-power parity, and the Fisher Equation form a complete and workable explanation for the structure of spot and forward exchange rates. Although we will not do so here, it can also be shown, by combining Equations 2.7 and 2.11, that the real rate of interest should be equalized across all countries (assuming no artificial constraints on the flow of capital or the flow of goods). We leave this to the reader. We note however, that the equations suggest, and practice proves, that an increase in inflationary expectations will lead to a weakening of a currency's value vis-à-vis other currencies and that an increase in real rates of interest for a currency will lead to a strengthening of that currency's value vis-à-vis other currencies.

2.3.4 Other Factors Influencing Exchange Rates

Our discussion of the determination of spot and forward exchange rates has focused primarily on the roles played by interest rates and inflation rates. Other factors also play a role—partly because they influence interest rates and inflation rates and partly because they have a direct influence on the demand for or the supply of a currency. Currency traders watch these other factors very carefully. They know when each economic statistic is due to be released and they try to predict the values that are to be reported. Examples of these important factors include such things as the growth rate of **gross national product** (GNP), the size of trade deficits, capital flows between countries, central bank interventions, monetary policy decisions, fiscal policy decisions, unemployment rates, and so on.

2.4 SUMMARY

A debt instrument represents a debtor/creditor relationship. The most basic features of these instruments include the instrument's coupon, its term-to-maturity, its yield, and the process by which the debt will be amortized. Debt instruments often include special provisions that are written into the contract's indenture. Some of these special provisions are callability, convertibility, and sinking funds.

A debt instrument's value is determined with the aid of present value arithmetic. Ignoring the specialty provisions that influence value, the value of a debt instrument is simply the sum of the present value of all futures cash flows that the instrument is expected to provide. The instrument's yield plays a critical role in this discounting process because it serves as the discount rate.

A yield curve is a graphic depiction of the relationship between a debt instrument's yield and its term to maturity when all other yield-influencing factors are held constant. Other factors that influence yield include various types of risk, particularly default risk, tax status, and the provision of collateral. We observed that the price sensitivity of a debt instrument to changes in its yield is largely a function of the instrument's maturity. But, we also argued that price sensititiy is influenced by the instrument's coupon, the present yield of the instrument, and the frequency of the coupon payments. The influence of all four sensitivity-influencing factors are captured by a single measure known as duration. An equivalent, but more intuitive, way to measure price sensitivity is via a measure called the dollar value of a basis point. From this latter measure, we can construct a very effective hedge by translating all interest-rate risk exposures to a common denominator in the form of a baseline instrument.

In addition to the risk stemming from an instrument's price sensitivity to yield changes, called interest-rate risk, a debt instrument can expose its owner to a variety of other risks as well. These include default risk, reinvestment risk, call risk, prepayment risk, and purchasing power risk.

Exchange rates represent the price of one currency in terms of another currency. Spot rates represent the price of a currency for immediate delivery and forward rates represent the price of a currency for later delivery. Currencies trade in foreign exchange markets, which are known in the trade as FOREX or FX markets. For the most part, these markets are made in an over-the-counter-like setting by major banks.

In completely free markets, spot rates are explained, at least in theory, by a relationship known as purchasing-power parity. Forward rate premiums (or discounts) are explained by a relationship known as interest-rate parity. Finally, the relationship between interest rates and expected rates of inflation is explained by the Fisher Equation.

Just as fluctuations in interest rates expose borrowers and lenders to interest-rate risk, so do fluctuations in exchange rates expose those with currency positions to exchange-rate risk. These risks need to be hedged and very sophisticated strategies exist for the hedging of these risks—some of which involve swaps.

REFERENCES AND SUGGESTED READING

A-Pack: An Analytical Package for Business, MicroApplications, Inc. (telephone: 1-516-821-9355).

Arak, M., L. S. Goodman, and J. Snailer "Duration Equivalent Bond Swaps: A New Tool," *Journal of Portfolio Management*, 26–32 (Summer 1986).

Bierwag, G. O., G. G. Kaufman, and C. Khang "Duration and Bond Portfolio Analysis: An Overview," *Journal of Financial and Quantitative Analysis*, 671– 679 (Nov 1978).

Bierwag, G. O., G. G. Kaufman, and A. Toevs "Duration: Its Development and Use in Bond Portfolio Management," *Financial Analysts Journal*, (Jul/Aug 1983).

Bierwag, G.O., G.G. Kaufman, and A. Toevs (eds.) *Innovations in Bond Portfolio Management: Duration Analysis and Immunization*, Greenwich CT: JAI Press (1983)

Booth, G.G., J. E. Duggan, and P.E. Koveos "Deviations from Purchasing Power Parity, Relative Inflation, and Exchange Rates: Recent Experience," *The Financial Review*, 20(2), 195–218 (May 1985).

Gay, G. D. and R. W. Kolb "Removing Bias in Duration Based Hedging Models: A Note," *Journal of Futures Markets*, 4:2, 225–228 (Summer 1984).

Grove, M. A. "On Duration and the Optimal Maturity Structure of the Balance Sheet," *The Bell Journal of Economics* (Autumn 1974).

Gushee, C. H. "How to Hedge a Bond Investment," *Financial Analysts Journal*, 41– 51 (Mar/Apr 1981).

Hicks, J.R. *Value and Capital*, Oxford: Claredon Press, (1939).

Khang, C. "Bond Immunization when Short-term Rates Fluctuate More than Long-term Rates," *Journal of Financial and Quantitative Analysis* (Dec 1979).

Leibowitz, M. L. "The Dedicated Bond Portfolio in Pension Funds—Part II: Immunization, Horizon Matching and Contingent Procedures," *Financial Analysts Journal*, 47–57 (Mar/Apr 1986).

Macaulay, F. R. *Some Theoretical Problems Suggested by the Movement of Interest Rates, Bond Yields, and Stock Prices in the United States since 1856*, New York: Columbia University Press for the National Bureau of Economic Research (1938).

Maloney, K. J. and J. B. Yawitz "Interest Rate Risk, Immunization, and Duration," *Journal of Portfolio Management*, 41–48 (Spring 1986).

Marshall, J.F. *Futures and Option Contracting: Theory and Practice*, Cincinnati: South-Western (1989).

Weston J. F. and T. E. Copeland *Managerial Finance*, 8th ed., New York: Dryden Press (1986).

ENDNOTES

[1] Many inexpensive "financial calculators" have built in algorithms for finding a bond's yield. Additionally, many popular software packages have routines capable of solving for bond yields. One software package which we like is *A-Pack: An Analytical Package for Business* from MicroApplications. A-Pack offers a veritable tool kit of analytical techniques useful for anyone involved in financial analysis. We used many of these techniques to perform our calculations as we wrote this book. For information about *A-Pack*, contact MicroApplications (telephone: 1-516-821-9355).

[2] Bonds that are in default and "income bonds," whose coupon payments vary with the financial fortunes of the issuer, are exceptions. They are quoted on a **flat** basis. When a bond is quoted flat, the purchase price is understood to include accrued interest.

[3] The reader who would like to delve more deeply into systematic and unsystematic risks and the measurement of these risks should see Marshall [1989], Chapter 6.

[4] See Macaulay [1938].

[5] These durations were calculated using *A-Pack*.

[6] See Hicks [1939].

[7] As a practical matter, immediate delivery is understood to mean two business days.

[8] In particular, see Marshall [1989], Chapter 11.

3

The Cash Markets
for Debt

3.1 OVERVIEW

This chapter examines the cash markets for public and private debt. We briefly examine four specific debt markets:

1. the market for U.S. government debt;
2. the market for corporate debt;
3. the market for mortgage debt; and
4. the Eurodollar/Eurobond market.

This look at the debt markets will greatly facilitate our later discussion of swap structures and their uses. We assume in this chapter that the reader is familiar with the interest-rate and exchange-rate basics discussed in Chapter 2.

In any discussion of securities, we need to distinguish between the primary and secondary markets. The **primary market** is the market through which the initial distribution and sale of securities takes place. The proceeds of these sales, less distribution costs, are funneled through to the issuer. The **secondary market** is the market in which existing investors (owners of the securities) transfer their claims on an issuer to other investors. These transactions result in a change of ownership of the securities but do not generate any additional proceeds for the issuer.

The market for U.S. government debt includes the debt of various U.S. government agencies. Our primary interest, however, is in the direct debt of the U.S. Treasury. The Treasury issues debt instruments in order to finance current budget deficits and to carry the national debt. The market is very liquid and the instruments are relatively homogeneous.

The market for corporate debt includes an array of debt instruments. Some have long maturities while others have very short maturities. Some issues are of high quality while others are very poor. For these reasons, the market for corporate debt is less homogeneous than the market for Treasury debt. It is also considerably less liquid, although the degree of liquidity varies considerably by issuer and by issue.

The mortgage market is a classic example of financial engineering at work. For many decades, mortgages were routinely held until maturity by the institutions that originated them. During the last two decades however, it has become common practice to pool mortgages and issue security interests in the pools. This process of securitization has since been applied to other types of debt.

The Eurobond/Eurodollar market originated in London in the early 1960s as a way to put U.S. dollars held outside the United States back to work. After a slow start, the Eurobond/Eurodollar market grew rapidly and, today, it is a centerpiece of the world financial system.

The reader who is thoroughly familiar with these markets might want to skip this chapter.

3.2 THE CASH MARKET FOR U.S. TREASURY DEBT

The U.S. Treasury routinely issues Treasury bills (T-bills), Treasury notes (T-notes), and Treasury bonds (T-bonds) in its effort to finance the ongoing needs of the U.S. government. These instruments are sold at periodic auctions held by the Federal Reserve Bank of New York. The funds are used to refund existing debt (**refunding**) and to raise new money. The principal bidders at Treasury auctions are **primary government securities dealers**. They enter competitive bids for the securities and then resell the securities to the ultimate investors. Together, the Federal Reserve and the primary government securities dealers make the primary market for Treasury securities. Government securities dealers, including the primary government securities dealers, also make an active secondary market in Treasuries. They buy and sell in an effort to profit from the difference between their bid and ask prices.[1] Most government securities dealers are commercial banks or investment banks and most engage in a variety of other activities including swaps. As we shall see later, the Treasury market activity of these banks greatly facilitates their swap activity.

The government securities market is the least regulated of all securities markets. For this reason, this market has been the market of choice for those interested in experimentation and innovation. For example, the government securities market gave rise to the first widely accepted zero coupon products and also gave birth to the repo/reverse market.

3.2.1   The Instruments

Treasury bills are issued in maturities of three months (13 weeks or 91 days), six months (26 weeks or 182 days), and one year (52 weeks or 364 days). In addition, the Treasury occasionally issues very short-term "cash management bills" to cover funding gaps. Unlike conventional notes and bonds, T-bills do not pay periodic interest coupons. Instead, they are sold at a discount from face value and redeemed at face value. The interest is then the amount of the discount. For this reason, these instruments are correctly viewed as short-maturity zeros.

Since 1977, T-bills have been issued exclusively in **book-entry** form. This means that there are no physical certificates evidencing ownership. Instead, ownership is evidenced by entries in a computer data file. The computer data file constitutes the "book." At present, T-bills represent about 40 percent of all outstanding Treasury debt. Interest on T-bills is exempt from state and local taxes, but the interest is subject to federal income taxation.

T-bill yields are not quoted on the same basis as bond yields.

Instead, yields on bills are quoted on a **bank discount basis** (also known as a **discount basis** and, sometimes, as a **bank basis**). The **bank discount yield** (BDY) understates the true yield relative to the conventional yield measure for bonds. To see this, we will consider a quick example: Suppose that a newly issued 26-week (182 day) T-bill having a face value of $100,000 is sold to "yield" 9 percent; that is, the bank discount yield (BDY) is 9 percent. The amount of discount is calculated using the actual number of days (actual) in the life of the bill but assuming the year has only 360 days. The precise formula for determining the amount of discount is given by Equation 3.1 in which *DD* denotes the dollar amount of discount, and *FV* denotes the face value of the bill.

$$DD \ = \ FV \ \times \ BDY \ \times \ \frac{\text{Actual}}{360} \tag{3.1}$$

In this example, the calculation is:

$$DD \ = \ 100,000 \ \times \ 9\% \ \frac{182}{360}$$

$$= \ 4,550$$

The investor purchasing this $100,000 six-month T-bill would actually pay $95,450. This purchase price (or present value) is obtained by deducting the amount of discount from the face value of the bill. This relationship is given in Equation 3.2.

$$\text{Present value} \ = \ FV \ - \ DD \tag{3.2}$$

As already noted, a T-bill is simply a short-term zero coupon bond. In this example, the T-bill may be viewed as a zero coupon bond purchased for $95,450 and redeemed 182 days later for $100,000.

The bank discount yield understates the true yield for two reasons. First, the bank discount yield calculates the amount of discount on the basis of the bill's face value even though the investor actually pays a price that is less than face value. Second, interest is paid on all days (182 in this example) even though the daily interest rate assumes that the year only has 360 days.

Note and bond prices are quoted on the basis of what is called the **bond equivalent** or **coupon equivalent yield**. This is the yield to maturity that equates the present value of the instrument's cash flow to its current price when the yield is stated on the assumption of semiannual compounding. The discount yield may be converted to a bond equivalent yield (BEY) when the bill has a maturity of six months or less by Equation 3.3. Notice that the bond equivalent yield employs actual days over 365 while the discount yield uses actual over 360.

$$BEY = \frac{365 \times BDY}{360 - (BDY \times \text{Actual})} \qquad \textbf{(3.3)}$$

Using Equation 3.3, the BEY on the bill in our earlier example is found to be 9.56 percent. The difference between the discount and bond equivalent yield measures is clearly quite substantial. Such a difference in yield measures is not inconsequential—as we will later see when we price what are called off-market swaps.

Another way to get this same result, while treating the bill as a zero coupon bond, is to employ a simple present value/future value relationship. The necessary relationship is given as Equation 3.4

$$FV = PV \cdot (1 + k) \qquad \textbf{(3.4)}$$

where FV is \$100,000, PV is \$95,450 and k is the periodic discount rate. Solving for k yields 4.76689 percent. But this discount rate represents a period of only 182 days. To re-express the rate on the basis of 365 days, we must multiply by 365 over 182. This adjustment produces a bond equivalent yield of 9.56 percent.

By convention, bond equivalent yields assume semiannual compounding. As a result, they are not equivalent to effective annual rates of return. An effective annual rate of return is often called a **simple rate of interest** and it is the clearest, most direct way to compare alternative investment opportunities. An effective annual rate of return (r) can be obtained from a bond equivalent yield using Equation 3.5.

$$ROR = \left(1 + \frac{BEY}{2}\right)^2 - 1 \qquad (3.5)$$

In this specific case, the effective annual rate of return is found to be 9.79 percent. The calculation is depicted below.

$$r = \left(1 + \frac{0.0956}{2}\right)^2 - 1$$

$$= 9.79 \text{ percent}$$

Thus, a 182-day T-bill with a quoted yield of 9 percent using the customary bank discount basis, provides an investor with an effective annual rate of return of 9.79 percent.

The conversion of discount yields to bond equivalent yields for bills that have a maturity of greater than six months (182 days) is considerably more complex than Equation 3.3.[2] Those involved in the trading of these instruments, however, need not concern themselves with the actual calculations—as traders invariably have computer-based analytics that provide the converted values at their disposal. For those interested, Appendix 1 to this chapter provides one method of making the BDY-to-BEY conversion for T-bills of any maturity.

While the conversion of discount yields to bond equivalent yields makes T-bills and coupon bearing securities more directly comparable, a different conversion is necessary to make T-bills comparable to interest-bearing money market instruments, such as certificates of deposit, which use a yield measure called **money market yield**. Yield quotes in terms of money market yield are said to be on a "money market basis" or, simply, a "yield basis." In this case, our goal is to make the yield on a *discount instrument*, stated actual over 360, equivalent to the yield on an interest-bearing instrument, which is also stated actual over 360. The problem is that an instrument quoted on a discount basis pays interest on the full-face value even though *the purchaser only pays the discount price* to get the instrument. An instrument quoted on a money market basis also pays interest on the full face value but, in these cases, the *purchaser really does pay the* *full face value* to get the instrument. The money market yield (MMY) is obtained from the bank discount yield using Equation 3.6.

$$MMY = \frac{360 \times BDY}{360 - (BDY \times \text{actual})} \tag{3.6}$$

The 9 percent bank discount yield we used in our previous example is equivalent to a money market yield of 9.43 percent. The calculation is as follows:

$$MMY = \frac{360 \times 0.09}{360 - (0.09 \times 182)}$$

$$= 9.43 \text{ percent}$$

The different yield conventions used for quoting yields on different instruments is very important in the pricing of swaps. For example, in a typical fixed-for-floating interest-rate swap, the floating-rate is usually tied to LIBOR. LIBOR is quoted actual over 360 and it is the rate on interest-bearing Eurodollar deposits. Thus, LIBOR is quoted as a money market yield. Because LIBOR is the rate paid on Eurodollar deposits, the money market yield convention is often called the **Eurodollar convention**. The fixed-rate side is usually quoted on a bond equivalent basis and, hence, actual over 365. The different conventions used for quoting fixed and floating rates becomes particularly important when pricing off-market swaps. The different conventions for quoting yields on money market instruments becomes very important when pricing basis swaps. (Basis swaps are floating-for-floating-rate swaps in which the two rates are tied to different money market instruments. We will consider this issue again more carefully in Chapter 8.)

Treasury notes and Treasury bonds both carry semiannual coupons and are often referred to, collectively, as "coupons" to distinguish them from the Treasuries' discount instruments. Treasury notes are sold with original maturities from two to 10 years. More specifically, they are sold in original maturities of two, three, four, five, seven and

10 years. There is a regular issue cycle for each of these maturities. For example, two-year notes are issued monthly and four-year notes are issued quarterly. Treasury bonds have original issue maturities of 30 years. The issue of 20-year bonds was discontinued in 1986. Treasury bonds are issued quarterly as part of the Treasury's quarterly refunding cycle.

Because notes are issued frequently and in different maturities, there are multiple issues of similar maturity at any given time. For example, a five-year original maturity note has a four-year maturity after one year. Of course, a new four-year note also has a four-year maturity. The most recently issued of any given maturity is considered the current issue. The current issues are the most liquid and trading in them is active. Trading in all maturities greater than 10 years is active. Many investors and traders prefer to be in actively traded issues in order to be assured of the liquidity necessary to exit positions quickly and cost effectively. The actively traded issues (most current issues of any given maturity) are called the **on the runs**. The demand for the on the runs is greater than the demand for **off the run** securities and traders pay a premium to be in the on the runs. Investors who buy coupon Treasuries with the intention of holding them to maturity will consequently do better by buying off the run securities. Coupons with less than a year to maturity tend to be very illiquid. Those with an interest in trading short-maturities are much more inclined to trade bills.

Treasury notes and bond yields are quoted as bond equivalents. While secondary market trading takes place in terms of price (as a percentage of par value), the auctions are held in terms of yield. The Treasury announces a new auction at least one week in advance and then solicits competitive bids. Bidders submit secret bids to two decimal places (e.g., 8.63 percent) and the quantities desired. The Treasury then awards the issue to the lowest yield bidder first and progresses upward until the full issue is sold. The highest accepted bid (which translates to the lowest accepted price) is called the **stop out bid**, or, when translated to a price, the **stop out price**. The Treasury then sets the issue's coupon to the nearest one-eighth of a percentage point so that the average price paid is as close to par as possible without exceeding par. Each successful bidder is then charged a price that corresponds to its bid and the bond's coupon. Some bidders will pay a premium, others a discount, and some will pay par. The difference between the average bid and the stop out bid is called the **tail**.

Noncompetitive bids for small denomination bidders are accepted at Treasury auctions. All noncompetitive bidders pay the average competitive bid price.

The secondary market in Treasuries is quite active except as noted above. Bills trade in terms of yield but notes and bonds trade in terms of price. On the run bid-ask spreads tend to be very narrow; one thirty-second is typical and one sixty-fourth is not unusual. Off the run spreads are considerably greater, often running to an eighth (⅛) or more.

As mentioned earlier, the Treasury market is not highly regulated. This has allowed a great deal of experimentation that has fostered a number of innovations—many of which are very important to the swap trade. Two of these are zero coupon products and repurchase agreements.

Zero coupon bonds were briefly discussed in Chapter 2. To summarize, a zero coupon bond, or "zero", is a debt instrument that is sold at a deep discount from face (par) value. These instruments do not pay periodic coupons. Instead, interest accrues via a gradual rise in the value of the instrument as it approaches maturity. At maturity, zeros are redeemed for full face value.

Although the advent of Treasury-based zero coupon bonds gave a major boost to the general market for zero coupon bonds, corporate experimentation and municipal experimentation in zeros had occurred earlier. The volume of this early corporate and municipal activity was minimal and we do not consider it further. The first zero coupon products involving Treasury securities were actually derivative products and not Treasury securities at all. These were introduced in 1982 by Merrill Lynch, which called its product "Treasury Investment Growth Receipts," or TIGRs. Merrill Lynch purchased conventional coupon-bearing Treasury securities and removed the coupons— thereby separating the coupons and the final redemption payment into separate cash flows. These individual cash flows, each corresponding to a different maturity, were then used to create irrevocable trusts with a custodial bank. The custodial bank then issued shares in the trusts. These shares were the TIGRs that Merrill Lynch then marketed to its clients.

Although the TIGRs were not themselves issues of the Treasury, they were fully collateralized by Treasury obligations and nearly equivalent to Treasuries in terms of default risk.[3] As we saw in Chapter 2, zeros are also free of reinvestment risk, call risk, and interest-rate risk when the investor matches the maturity of the zero to his or her investment horizon. In addition to this, early investors in zeros benefited from favorable tax treatment of the accruing interest on these instruments.

The zero coupon product introduced by Merrill Lynch soon had competition as other investment banks created their own zero coupon Treasury derivatives. These products, which traded under various acronyms called **trademarks**, included such names as CATS, LIONs, COUGARs, DOGs, and EAGLEs, to mention just a few. The secondary market for each of these proprietary products was rather illiquid since the only dealer for each product was the investment bank that created it. In an effort to address this problem, a group of government securities dealers, led by The First Boston Corporation, created a generic Treasury-based zero coupon product. These products are known as **Treasury Receipts**.

The risk management uses and the tax benefits of zeros combined to make these derivative products very attractive to investors and they quickly became popular. Although the tax benefits were eliminated by changes in the tax law that became effective in 1982, the instruments remained popular and by 1985 the par value of outstanding zeros exceeded $100 billion. For the investment banks, the incentive for creating zero coupon products was two-fold. First, the investment bank purchased a bond, stripped it to create a series of zeros, and then sold these zeros to the public. The investor benefits afforded by zeros were reflected in their price so that the series of zeros that could be created from a conventional bond had a collective value that exceeded that of the bond. Thus, buying and stripping Treasuries was a classic exercise in **conversion arbitrage**. In conversion arbitrage, an instrument (or group of instruments) with a given set of investment characteristics is converted into an instrument (or group of instruments) that has a different set of investment characteristics.

The U.S. Treasury was a major beneficiary of the popularity of Treasury-based zero coupon products. The demand for the zeros created a demand for the bonds that are the raw material for making zeros. The demand for strippable bonds by investment banks and other government securities dealers drove up the price and drove down the yields on these issues. The Treasury then benefited from the lower yields. Nevertheless, until June of 1982, the Treasury objected to the stripping of bonds and actively tried to dissuade investment banks from engaging in the practice. The Treasury's objections were based on the tax avoidance opportunities that were possible with zeros. With the change in the tax law noted earlier, the Treasury dropped its objections and, in 1984, the Treasury created its own program for stripping bonds. The program, called **Separate Trading of Registered Interest and Principal of Securities (STRIPS)**, allowed the stripping of specially designated note and bond issues. The program proved popular and was later extended to allow the stripping of all noncallable coupon issues with original maturities of 10 years or more. These zero coupon bonds are direct obligations of the U.S. Treasury and, hence, completely default free. All such securities are held in book-entry form.

Zero coupon Treasuries have become very important to the swap markets. The yield on these instruments is the purest measure of the demand/supply conditions for debt of a given maturity. The yield curve for zeros, called the **zero coupon yield curve**, is often plotted and compared to the conventional yield curve. An example of such a comparison appears in Exhibit 3.1.

The market for Treasuries also gave rise to the repo/reverse market. A repo or, more precisely, a **repurchase agreement** (also known as an **RP**), is the sale of a security with an accompanying promise to buy back the security at a specific later date and at a specific price. Thus, a securities dealer holding temporarily unneeded securities can sell them to an investor, which might be another securities dealer, under a repurchase agreement. The selling dealer might, for example, sell $20 million dollars (face value) six-month bills to an investor for

EXHIBIT 3.1.   Conventional versus Zero Coupon Yield Curve
(January 1990)

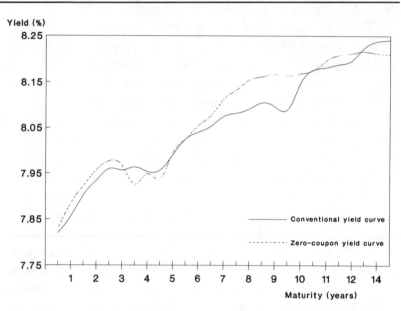

$19,199,200 with a promise to repurchase the bills three days later at a price of $19,212,400. The difference between the selling price and the repurchase price, $13,200 in this case, represents interest paid by the selling dealer to the investor for a three-day loan. From the investor's perspective, the loan is very safe since it is fully collateralized by Treasury securities. The motivation of the selling dealer is the short-term loan it receives at a very low interest rate.

The repo market is attractive to investors for several reasons. First, this market provides a ready means for investing surplus funds for very short periods of time. Indeed, a large volume of repos are done on an overnight basis—these are called **overnight repos**. Rates on overnight repos are usually lower than the Fed funds rate. While this is very low, it is still better than no return for the investor who lacks access to the Fed funds market. Second, by rolling over overnight repos, the investor can effectively manage surplus funds when the available quantity of surplus funds is uncertain from day to day.

Repos can also be done for longer terms. A repo of 30 days or more is called a **term repo**. Interest rates on term repos generally rise with the length of the term. Although the overnight repo market is very liquid, the term repo market is considerably less liquid.

Just as securities dealers can enter the repo market as sellers of securities, they can also enter the market as purchasers of securities. That is, the securities dealer can purchase securities with an accompanying promise to sell them back at a specific later date and at a specific price. This kind of transaction is called a **reverse** or **reverse repurchase agreement**. The usual motivation for a securities dealer doing a reverse is to obtain securities to cover **short sales**. That is, when a securities dealer sells securities it does not own, it must borrow the securities in order to make the required delivery. The reverse market is a very effective way to acquire the securities for such short sales.

Repos and reverses are identical transactions. Whether a transaction is called a repo or a reverse depends on which side initiated the transaction. But, in fact, one party's repo is always another party's reverse.

Repos (and reverses) are regarded, for obvious reasons, as short-term financing tools and they are often used by securities dealers as vehicles to help carry very large inventories of securities at very low cost. They are also very important instruments for managing securities inventories, particularly when securities are needed for short sales—a situation that often arises when swap dealers are hedging swaps. We will consider this use of repos in Chapter 8.

3.3 THE CASH MARKET FOR CORPORATE DEBT

Like the U.S. Treasury, financial and nonfinancial corporations (including banks) in the United States issue large quantities of debt. These issues include both long and short maturities and both fixed- and floating-rate instruments. The type of instrument issued will depend on the nature of the issuer (bank or nonbank), the length of time the funds are needed, the type of collateral available, the type of interest rate desired (fixed or floating), and the all-in cost of the different financing alternatives available. In this section, we examine fixed-rate and floating-rate securities, beginning with the former. We postpone discussion of all-in cost considerations until Chapter 8.

3.3.1 Fixed-Rate Instruments

The intermediate- to long-term fixed-rate instruments include notes and bonds. The short-term fixed-rate instruments include commercial paper and certificates of deposit.

Notes and bonds are intermediate- to long-term promissory notes of issuing corporations. Notes have original maturities of 10 years or less and bonds have original maturities of more than 10 years (20 or 30 years is typical). Short-maturity issues are often not callable but long-maturity issues usually are. For the remainder of this section, we will use the term ''bond'' to include both bonds and notes.

Issuers are most likely to call a callable issue after interest rates have declined. In these cases, the funds necessary to retire the issue can be obtained by issuing new debt at the prevailing lower interest rates. You will recall from Chapter 2 that callable bonds expose their holders to call risk. To protect investors from a call accomplished with proceeds obtained from a new issue of debt securities bond indentures often contain **refunding restrictions** which specifically bar the issuer from calling the bond with funds from this source. It is important for investors in corporate bonds to distinguish between protections from call and protections from refunding. The former is an absolute protection from a call while the latter is only protection from calls accomplished via funding from new debt issues.

Bonds are classified with respect to a number of characteristics. These include the issuer, the purpose of the issue, the type of security pledged on the issue, the method of interest payment, and the method of repayment. Bond rating agencies distinguish between types of issuers, which are lumped into several major categories. For example, Moody's lists four categories: public utilities, transportations, industrials, and banks and financial corporations. Each of these categories can be more finely divided. For example, public utilities can be divided into gas distribution companies, electric power companies, telephone companies, and so on. Even finer subdivisions are possible. Electric utilities, for example, can be divided into nuclear based and nonnuclear based.

The title of a bond often gives a clue to the issuer's purpose in issuing the bond, but title alone is not a reliable indicator. Some bonds are issued to raise funds that will be used to retire an existing debt issue (**refunding**) or to change the mix of debt to equity in the firm's capital structure (**debt-for-equity swaps**). Other issues are used to finance specific acquisitions or other forms of corporate investments. Sometimes, the purpose is to raise funds for discretionary corporate purposes—having an available war chest for corporate takeovers, for example.

Bonds are also classified by the type of security pledged by the issuer. Security can take the form of a pledge of real property, a pledge of personal property, or a guarantee by another entity. Bonds secured by real property are called **mortgage bonds**. In a mortgage bond, the issuer grants the bondholders a first mortgage on some or all of its property. Such bonds are often issued as part of a **series**, with the holders of each series having an equal claim to the mortgaged property in the event of default. Some bond indentures allow for new series to be issued and added to the first mortgage, others do not. Not all series need have the same maturity and, often, multiple series, each with its own maturity, are issued simultaneously. Bonds secured by personal property, securities and inventory for example, are called **collateral trust bonds**. The personal property constitutes the **collateral**.

Some bonds are guaranteed by another entity. For example, an issuer with a weak credit rating might persuade another firm with a strong credit rating to guarantee its debt. The issue then gets the rating of the guaranteeing entity which reduces the coupon necessary to sell the issue at par. This kind of guarantee is quite common in parent/subsidiary relationships. Such bonds are called **guaranteed bonds**. When no security or guarantee is available, the issue is called a **debenture**. In the event of default, the debenture holders become general creditors of the issuer. At times, corporate issuers will sell **subordinated debentures**. In the event of default, claims by holders of these instruments are satisfied only after the claims of general creditors have been satisfied. To reduce the coupon necessary to sell debentures and subordinated debentures, issuers will often make such instruments convertible to other assets—usually some number of shares of the issuer's common stock. These are called **convertible debentures**.

Bonds may be **bearer bonds** or **registered bonds**. The ownership of bearer bonds is evidenced by the physical securities. The owner of the bond collects interest by clipping the appropriate coupon and sending it to the designated paying agent. For this reason, bearer bonds are sometimes called **coupon bonds**. Neither the issuer nor the issuer's agent keeps a record of the ownership of bearer bonds. Registered bonds may be **fully registered** or **registered as to principal only**. The issuer, or issuer's agent, keeps continuous track of the ownership of fully registered bonds and sends the coupon payments and principal repayment without any action on the part of the bondholder. When registered as to principal only, the holder must still send the appropriate coupon in order to collect interest.

While most bonds require the periodic payment of fixed amounts of interest (the coupon) and any failure to pay the coupon in full and on time constitutes a default, there is an exception. The exception is income bonds. **Income bonds** provide for a fixed coupon, but the issuer, under terms specified in the indenture, can elect not to pay a coupon upon the occurrence of certain events without triggering default. In this sense, these bonds are very much like preferred stock. Missed coupon payments may be cumulative or noncumulative. An income bond is **cumulative** if missed coupons must be paid at a later date; if not, the bond is **noncumulative**.

Bondholders typically expect their principal to be repaid at the time of the bond's maturity. Most longer-term corporate bonds, however, are callable: That is, the issuer has reserved the right to demand that the bond be returned in exchange for the call price stipulated in the bond's indenture. The call price is usually the bond's par value plus a call premium. At one time, the call premium was routinely set at one year's interest, but today, the call premium is usually set on a sliding scale and grows smaller as the bond approaches maturity. Interest stops accruing on bonds that have been called, so holders of called bonds have a financial incentive to turn them in immediately.

Call features are often associated with sinking fund provisions. When sinking funds were first introduced, they most often provided that the issuer periodically place funds in escrow in order to assure that it will have sufficient funds on hand to retire the issue at maturity. Today, sinking fund provisions typically require the orderly retirement of the issue over its life. This usually means retiring a specified minimum portion of the issue each year. This can be accomplished in either of two ways: the issuer can provide sufficient funds to the trustee and the trustee will randomly select bonds to call, or the issuer can purchase the bonds in the open market and tender these bonds to the trustee. The latter course is preferable from the issuer's perspective when the bonds are trading below the call price.

There is a difference between a serial bond and a bond that is retired by periodic calls. When a bond is callable, no holder knows if his or her bond will be called and, if so, when that call will occur. In the case of a **serial bond**, the bond is divided into a number of series each with a specific maturity date and a specific coupon. Thus, the purchaser of a serial bond can specify which series he or she wants and thereby know, quite precisely, when that bond will be redeemed (assuming that it is not also callable).

The primary market for public offerings of corporate debt is made by investment banks in the role of **underwriter**. The underwriter buys the issue from the issuing firm at a discount from the **offering price**. The underwriter then sells the issue to investors, at the offering price, either directly or through a syndicate established for this purpose. From the issuer's perspective, the difference between the issue's par value and the proceeds actually received represents a **flotation cost**.[4] This is not, however, the only cost associated with a debt issue. The issuing firm is also required to bear some miscellaneous expenses and these miscellaneous expenses must be included when considering the total cost of floating a new debt issue.

The secondary market for corporate bonds consists of two parts—an exchange market and an over-the-counter (OTC) market—both of which are centered in New York City. The New York Stock Exchange lists a great many specific bond issues and trading in these issues does take place on a floor of the New York Stock Exchange designated for this purpose. The bulk of bond trading however is made in an OTC dealer market by several dozen investment banks. Some regional firms also make a market in bonds but not on the same scale as the New York investment banks. The dealers provide quotes, which include both bid and offer (asked) prices. They stand ready to buy or sell at any time and they make their income from the bid-ask spread. Dealers usually keep their inventories hedged against interest-rate risk.

While individual investors do purchase corporate bonds, the bulk of investment activity is on the part of institutional investors. These institutional investors include insurance companies, mutual funds, pension funds, and so on. Such investors often have very specific maturity needs and bonds fit these needs quite well. The market made by bond dealers is largely a **wholesale market** (large denomination trades with narrow bid-ask spreads) which appeals to the institutional investor. The exchange-based trading is largely a **retail market** (small denomination trades with wider bid-ask spreads for small investors).

The liquidity of bond issues is measured by the volume of trading in the issue and by the size of the bid-ask spread. As a general rule, the greater the volume of trading, the narrower will be the spread.

Banks issue intermediate- and long-term debt in order to leverage up their returns. Bank regulators count such issues as part of a bank's capital for purposes of meeting capital requirements. Regulators, however, prefer equity capital to debt capital as a cushion against bank losses.

Our discussion of the intermediate- and long-term debt issues of domestic corporations applies equally well to banks. When we get to the short-term markets, however, there is a significant difference. Corporations issue short-term liabilities called **commercial paper** while banks (and other depository institutions) issue short-term liabilities called **certificates of deposit**. While both of these instruments are lumped together under the general heading of money market instruments, we will look at them separately.

Commercial paper is an unsecured promissory note with a maturity of 270 days or less.[5] For a long time, commercial paper, like T-bills, was sold at a discount from face value. Increasingly, however, commercial paper is marketed with add-on interest. In either case, the yield is quoted on a bank discount basis.

Commercial paper is issued both by industrial corporations and by financial corporations. Industrial paper is issued through a handful of commercial paper dealers who sell the paper to institutional investors. Financial corporations place most of their paper directly, but some finance company paper is placed through dealers. The largest firm engaged in the direct placement of its own commercial paper is General Motors Acceptance Corporation or GMAC and, consequently, GMAC's paper rates are important industry benchmarks.

Commercial paper is an effective financing tool for firms with investment grade ratings when funds are only needed for a short period of time. Interestingly, however, commercial paper is also used as the foundation of an intermediate- to long-term financing strategy. In such a strategy, a firm issues commercial paper with the intent of refunding the paper by periodically rolling the paper over. For example, a firm might need funds for four years. Rather than issue a four-year note, the firm might choose to issue six-month paper and then roll this paper over seven times, with six-month maturities each time, until the funding need terminates.

There are several good reasons why a firm might choose to finance with successive short-term rollovers rather than a single intermediate-term note issue. First, when the yield curve is upward sloping, the normal situation, the short end of the yield curve offers the lowest rates. Thus, short-term financing is cheaper than intermediate-term financing. If the yield curve does not change, each successive paper issue will cost the firm less than the coupon on an intermediate-term note. Second, the flotation costs for paper are a small fraction of the flotation costs for note and bond issues. For example, a four-year note issue might involve a discount to the underwriter of 4.5 percent of the offering price. On commercial paper, this might be as little as one-eighth of one percent per year. Over a four-year period, this translates to only one-half of one percent. Third, the amount of finance needed might change periodically. With an intermediate-term note issue, the issuer might find itself overfinanced if some or all of the assets the financing supports are prematurely liquidated. In the case of commercial paper, the firm can easily reduce the amount of funding on subsequent rollovers. A final reason for employing a series of paper rollovers instead of a single fixed-rate note issue involves the nature of the assets supported by the financing. If the assets' return is responsive to changes in interest rates, so that return rises when rates rise and return falls when rates fall, then a series of paper rollovers might be a better match than intermediate- or long-term financing by way of a note or bond. Each time the paper is rolled over, the issuer agrees to pay the then prevailing rate on paper of the given maturity. While the rate is fixed for the life of the paper, it is better viewed as floating over the life of the entire financing. That is, in our example, the series of rollovers can be viewed as a four-year financing in which the rate is reset every six months. If the assets are interest-rate responsive and the supporting liabilities are also interest-rate responsive, then the issuer has a natural interest-rate hedge.

The user of the commercial paper rollover strategy is of course, subject to the risk that rates might rise before the next rollover. If the assets are not interest-rate responsive, then the user of the paper rollover strategy is exposed to considerable interest-rate risk. For example, suppose that a firm sells six-month paper at 7.5 percent and uses the proceeds to purchase three-year automobile receivables yielding 9.9 percent after costs. If the yield curve does not change at all, then each new rollover resets the firm's cost of funds at 7.5 percent. But suppose that the yield curve shifts sharply upward in response to a tightening in monetary policy and the next paper issue is sold at 10.4 percent. The return on the receivable assets is now below the firm's cost of funds.

The yield on paper is always higher than the yield on T-bills of similar maturity. The spread reflects the small, but ever present, risk of default that can occur on paper and a modest difference in the tax treatment of the interest earned on these money market instruments (T-bill interest is exempt from state income tax while paper interest is not). While the yields on T-bills and commercial paper may be different, they do track each other rather closely—but not perfectly. Historically, however, paper rates have been somewhat more volatile than T-bill rates. This difference in volatility and the fact that paper and T-bill rates do not track each other perfectly, leads to a special form of risk for those who engage in basis swaps. We address this point in Chapter 9.

Unlike T-bills, there is no active secondary market in commercial paper and purchasers generally hold it to maturity. Nevertheless, both dealers and direct placers generally guarantee liquidity by standing ready to buy back their paper at any time.

The bank counterpart of commercial paper is negotiable certificates of deposit otherwise known as CDs. A CD is a receipt from a bank for funds deposited at the bank for a specific period of time and at a specific rate of interest. CDs have maturities of at least seven days and can run to several years. Original issue maturities of less than thirty days are, however, not very common. Similarly, original issue maturities of more than one year are also uncommon.

CDs are issued by all major money center banks and many regional banks as well. Yields are somewhat higher than T-bills of similar maturity. There is a viable secondary market for the CDs of well-established issuers but, for most issues, the bid-ask spreads are considerably greater than those in the more homogeneous T-bill market.

Banks can achieve long-term financing via CDs using the same type of rollover strategy we described for issuers of commercial paper. The strategy is often used, by both banks and thrifts, to finance long-term fixed-rate assets such as conventional mortgages. This gives rise to interest-rate risk and makes these institutions logical candidates for swaps as risk-management tools.

Before leaving this section, it is worth considering the degree to which the various money market rates track one another. We have already indicated that the tracking or, in statistical terms, the "correlation," is not perfect. This less-than-perfect correlation exposes some money market participants to basis risk and explains why these same parties often engage in basis swaps. As already indicated, we address these issues in detail in Chapters 8 and 9. Nevertheless, an illustration at this point will help to crystallize the issue. Exhibit 3.2 depicts 36 weekly observations for the T-bill rate, the commercial paper rate, and the CD rate (all three-month maturities) for a selected period in the mid 1980s. The vertical axis has been expanded to make it easier to distinguish between the three interest-rate paths.

EXHIBIT 3.2. Comparative Money Market Rates

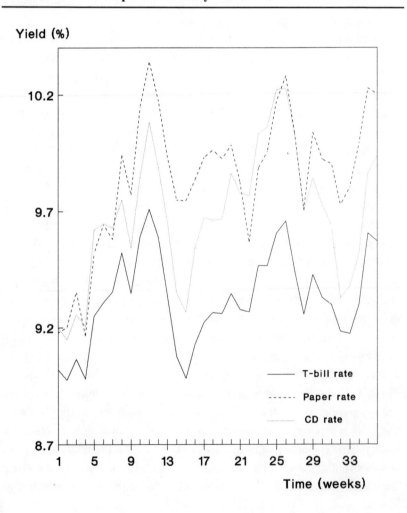

Notice in Exhibit 3.2 that the three curves do track each other closely, but the spread between them is not fixed. The fluctuation in the spread is the source of the basis risk.

3.3.2 Floating-Rate Instruments

We have already demonstrated how short-term fixed-rate instruments, such as commercial paper and certificates of deposit, can be rolled over to provide intermediate- to long-term financing that has a floating-rate character. Although each short-term instrument pays a fixed rate, the rate is revised with each rollover and, in this sense, the overall financing strategy has a floating rate. An alternative way to achieve a floating rate on an intermediate- to long-term financing is to issue a single, intermediate- to long-term, instrument with a floating-rate coupon. **Floating-rate debt**, also sometimes called **variable-rate debt** or **adjustable rate-debt**, is an obligation in which the interest rate is periodically reset in response to changing market conditions. These corporate instruments are called, collectively, **floating-rate notes**, and are known by the buzzwords **FRNs** and **floaters**. Banks also issue floating rate securities called **floating-rate CDs**. We will explain these instruments together.

Floating-rate notes are bond-type debt instruments that have floating-rate coupons rather than the fixed-rate coupons that characterize more conventional long-term debt instruments. The term ''floating-rate note'' is often used generically to mean any type of debt security in which the coupon is adjusted periodically to reflect changes in the rate to which the coupon is pegged. These periodic adjustments may be made very frequently, say monthly, or only occasionally, say once every several years or so. For example, a floating-rate note (FRN) with a four-year maturity might have its coupon reset every six months. A one-year floating-rate CD might have its interest rate reset once a month.

As used more narrowly, the term floating-rate note is taken to mean an intermediate- to long-term debt security whose interest rate is pegged to a short-term rate or rate index and adjusted frequently (more than once a year). For example, the rate to which these instruments' coupons are pegged might be the prime rate, the 26-week T-bill rate, or a six-month commercial paper index.

FRNs originated in Europe. They first appeared in the United States in 1973. The U.S. market for FRNs grew rapidly thereafter and, for a time, demand for these new instruments far exceeded the quantities offered.[6]

By offering a floating-rate note, a corporate issuer can achieve nearly the same outcome as if it had employed the commercial paper rollover strategy. For example, a corporation with a top investment grade rating can sell a four-year note with a floating rate tied to the rate on top tier six-month commercial paper. Every six months the coupon is reset for the following period. The coupon rate is reset, on predetermined reset dates, to the rate prevailing on those dates for top tier six-month paper.

What factors should a firm consider when choosing between a floating-rate note and a paper rollover strategy? There are a several important considerations. First, the firm should compare the rate at which it can issue paper to the rate at which it can issue a floating-rate note. While the rates will generally be close, they will not necessarily be identical. Purchasers of the notes are committing their funds for an extended period of time and may demand a premium to compensate for a possible deterioration of the issuer's creditworthiness over the life of the instrument. Second, the issuer should compare the flotation costs associated with the financing alternatives. Finally, commercial paper is a short-term liability and, therefore, not counted as part of the issuer's capital. A note with a maturity greater than one year, on the other hand, is counted as part of the issuer's capital. The firm's long-term-debt-to-total-capitalization ratio and other measures of financial leverage are, therefore, affected by the choice of financing alternatives.

Another way to achieve floating-rate financing is for the firm (or bank) to issue an intermediate-term fixed-rate note and then employ a fixed-for-floating interest-rate swap strategy to convert this fixed-rate obligation to a floating-rate obligation. This latter possibility will be considered in much more detail in later chapters. Again, the same factors mentioned above must be considered when the issuer chooses among the available alternatives. It would, of course, help greatly if we could reduce the choice to a single quantifiable value. All-in cost is the value most often used for this purpose.

All-in cost is the total cost of a financial transaction, including the interest expense, front-end and/or underwriting fees, periodic servicing fees, etc. This cost is typically stated as a per annum rate and can be thought of as the mirror image of an internal rate of return. Consider an example: A domestic corporation provides variable rate financing to purchasers of its products. In order for the corporation to provide financing to one of its larger customers, it needs to raise $20 million of new capital. To hedge interest-rate risk, the corporation would prefer floating-rate financing to fixed-rate financing. The corporation considers the all-in cost of two financing alternatives.

The first alternative is to sell $20 million of floating-rate notes. The corporation estimates that the notes can be sold at par if it offers a coupon equal to the 26-week T-bill rate plus 1.5 percent. Suppose that the all-in cost, including the cost of underwriting the issue, is determined to be the T-bill rate plus 1.85 percent.

The second alternative is to sell $20 million of fixed-rate notes and then to swap this fixed-rate debt into floating-rate debt. Suppose that the fixed-rate debt can be sold at par with a coupon of 9.25 percent, and that this can be swapped for six-month LIBOR plus 0.25 percent. Finally, suppose that six-month LIBOR is almost perfectly correlated with the 26-week T-bill rate and that six-month LIBOR averages 0.5 percent over the 26-week T-bill rate. Given this, this form of floating-rate financing will cost the firm the 26-week T-bill rate plus 0.75 percent. Finally, after including the underwriting costs of the fixed-rate note issue and the front-end fees for the interest-rate swap, suppose that the all-in cost from this latter financing alternative is determined to be the 26-week T-bill rate plus 1.15 percent. After comparing the all-in costs of the two alternatives, the corporation in this example chooses the fixed rate note issue coupled with an interest-rate swap.

We have deliberately avoided a careful examination of the cash flows and the all-in cost in this brief presentation of this cost-comparing approach. We will, however, take a very careful look at these cash flows and the calculation of all-in cost in Chapter 7.

All floating rate debt must specify an objectively measurable market-determined rate (often called a benchmark or reference rate) to which the instrument's rate can be pegged. Further, this rate must not be easily manipulated by interested parties. Common benchmarks include the CD rates (one month, two months, and so forth), prime rate, T-bill rates (one month, two months, and so forth), Fed funds rate, commercial paper rates, and LIBOR.

3.4 THE CASH MARKET FOR MORTGAGE DEBT AND MORTGAGE-BACKED SECURITIES

A **mortgage** is a loan secured by real property such as a building or land. In the residential mortgage market, the subject of this section, the borrower approaches a mortgage lender for a loan. If approved, the lender provides sufficient funds for the purposes of the borrower (usually funds to purchase the property) and the borrower signs a document agreeing to repay the loan, together with interest, according to some payment schedule. Since most mortgage lending involves amortization of the loan principal, the payment schedule is sometimes called an **amortization schedule**. The document constitutes the mortgage. The borrower is called the **mortgagor** and the lender is called the **mortgagee**. The mortgage must be serviced; that is, mortgage payments must be collected and recorded, real estate taxes must be collected and passed along to the appropriate taxing jurisdictions, and foreclosure proceedings must be instituted in the event of a default.

In the **conventional mortgage**, which is becoming increasingly rare, the mortgage rate is fixed for the life of the mortgage and the mortgage payments are all of equal size. For the latter reason, these mortgages are often called **level-payment mortgages**. Payments on residential mortgages are usually made monthly, but other payment frequencies are possible. Mortgages amortize over their lives so that each payment includes both interest and principal. Since each payment includes some repayment of principal, the mortgage balance (the remaining principal) gets progressively smaller with each payment. This makes conventional mortgages self-amortizing forms of debt.

Conventional mortgages typically have a term of 30 years but shorter terms are not uncommon. Since each payment includes some principal, each subsequent payment must include less interest since the mortgage balance declines with each payment. If each payment is the same size but the interest component is declining, the principal component must get larger with each payment. Portions of a typical mortgage amortization schedule appear in Exhibit 3.3.

As can be seen in Exhibit 3.3, the early mortgage payments are mostly interest while the latter mortgage payments are mostly principal. Mortgagors are usually permitted to make payments on their mortgages in excess of that which is required. Such excess payments are called **prepayments** and are credited directly against the mortgage balance.

In recent years, mortgage lenders have been discouraging borrowers from taking out conventional fixed-rate mortgages in favor of **adjustable rate mortgages** (ARMs). There are a great number of variants of ARMs, but they share one common characteristic—the mortgage rate may change in response to changing market conditions. To persuade borrowers to take these mortgages, the originating institu-

EXHIBIT 3.3   Conventional Mortgage Amortization Schedule

Payment Number	Total Payment	Principal Component	Interest Component	Principal Balance
1	1,755.15	88.48	1,666.67	199,911.52
2	1,755.15	89.22	1,665.93	199,822.30
3	1,755.15	89.96	1,665.19	199,732.33
.	.	.	.	.
180	1,755.15	390.84	1,364.31	163,326.60
.	.	.	.	.
251	1,755.15	704.51	1,050.64	125,371.88
.	.	.	.	.
358	1,755.15	1,712.10	43.05	3,453.35
359	1,755.15	1,726.37	28.78	1,726.98
360	1,741.37	1,726.98	14.39	0.00
.				

Notes: Principal $200,000
Mortgage rate   10.00%
Term   30 years, monthly payments

Source: A-Pack: An Analytical Package for Business

tion often provides an artificially low mortgage rate for the first year or so. This initial low rate is sometimes called a **teaser rate**. Following the period in which the rate is artificially held below market, the rate adjusts to a market level. Thereafter the rate periodically adjusts to keep pace with market conditions. Such mortgages often have **caps** on each rate revision as well as life-time caps. These caps are intended to protect the mortgagor from excessive changes in mortgage rates.

A variety of other mortgages have been introduced in recent years including **graduated payment mortgages** (GPMs), **graduated equity mortgages** (GEMs), **pledged-account mortgages** (PAMs), **shared-appreciation mortgages** (SAMs), and **reverse-annuity mortgages** (RAMs). These latter mortgages represent relatively small segments of the overall mortgage market and we do not dwell on them further.

Mortgage lending was, at one time, a very routine affair. Using customer deposits as their primary source of funds, banks and thrifts originated mortgages that they placed in their portfolios. These mortgages were serviced by the originating institution and held by that same institution until maturity. Of course, with its funds tied up in existing mortgages, the institution was unable to originate additional mortgages until either:

1. it had collected sufficient repayments from existing mortgagors; or
2. attracted additional deposits.

In an effort to add liquidity to the secondary mortgage market, Congress sponsored the creation of several organizations, the last such creation was the **Government National Mortgage Association** (GNMA), more popularly known by its nickname **Ginnie Mae**, which was created in 1968. Since 1970, GNMA has provided a vehicle for the pooling and guaranteeing of mortgages. The GNMA guarantee covers the full and timely payment of both interest and principal. Once pooled and guaranteed, undivided interests in the pools, called **pass-through certificates** or **participation certificates**, are sold to investors.

Variations of the basic mortgage pass-through securities are also marketed by the other federally sponsored organizations including the **Federal Home Loan Mortgage Corporation** (FHLMC), nicknamed **Freddie Mac**, and the **Federal National Mortgage Association** (FNMA), nicknamed **Fannie Mae**, and by a number of private parties—usually large commercial banks. The nature of the guarantee provided by these organizations varies. FHLMC, for example, guarantees the timely payment of interest and the ultimate, but not necessarily timely, payment of principal. Private issuers of pass-throughs may or may not purchase payment guarantees (insurance). The rest of our mortgage-oriented discussion will concentrate on GNMA pass-throughs.

The pooling process separates the mortgage from the mortgage servicing function. The mortgage originator may keep the servicing rights or may sell them to another institution. The servicing rights have value because of a fee collected by the servicing agent. For example, in the GNMA pool, the servicing fee is set at 44 basis points (calculated on the principal balance) that is deducted from the mortgage interest. Six additional basis points are paid as a fee (premium) to the GNMA for its guarantee. Together, these deductions total 50 basis points (one-half of one percent). Thus, a 10.75 percent mortgage coupon will return, if sold at par, 10.25 percent to investors in the pass-throughs. This rate is called the **pass-through rate**. The originating institution also derives profit from the **points** it charges the borrower to originate the mortgage. A point is defined as one percent of the mortgage principal. The funds made available by the sale of the mortgages can be used to originate additional mortgages—which, in turn, produces additional revenue from points collected on the new originations and from new servicing fees.

The pooling of mortgages, whether government sourced or privately sourced, has dramatically transformed the mortgage market. It is now routine for banks and thrifts to originate mortgages, pool them, and sell off the pools (either keeping the servicing rights for themselves or selling the servicing rights to another institution). While the pools themselves are large ($1 million dollars is the minimum size and most are considerably larger), the pass-throughs can be purchased in denominations as small as $25,000. Thus, they appeal to many private investors. The structure of the pass-through market is depicted in Exhibit 3.4.

Because mortgage pass-throughs represent undivided claims on the mortgage pool—meaning that each pass-through owner holds a pro rata claim to all interest and principal repayments—the investor in pass-throughs is subject to both reinvestment risk and substantial prepayment risk. Further, if the investor sells the pass-throughs prior to their maturities, he or she is also exposed to considerable interest-rate risk. The source of the interest-rate risk is the same as for any other debt instrument and, therefore, we do not discuss it further. The reinvestment risk and the prepayment risk, however, require a little more explanation. Recall that mortgages are amortizing forms of debt. That is, the investor receives periodic payments that include principal as well as interest. Since the periodic payments on amortizing debt are larger than the periodic payments on nonamortizing forms of debt, the reinvestment risk is greater on pass-throughs than on coupon-bearing Treasury and corporate bonds. The prepayment risk stems from the fact that the mortgagors have the right, which they frequently exercise, to prepay all or part of the mortgage balance. That is, they may pay back the principal before they are required to do so. These prepayments are passed along to the holders of the pass-throughs who must

EXHIBIT 3.4   Interest Flows in GNMA Pass-throughs
(Conventional mortgages)

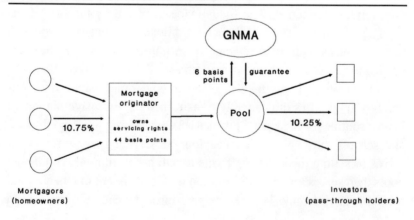

then reinvest. Prepayments occur for a variety of reasons including the sale of the home, a sudden availability of funds for the homeowner, the death of the homeowner, or a refinancing of the mortgage in response to lower interest rates. The last of these reasons accounts for the greatest number of prepayments on mortgages that are written during periods of high interest rates. A great deal of research has gone into modeling prepayment behavior.[7]

From the beginning, the prepayment risk problem has been a bane to investors. In June of 1983, in an effort to address this problem, investment banks, led by the First Boston Corporation and Salomon Brothers, introduced **collateralized mortgage obligations** (CMOs). CMOs were a dynamic innovation and quickly captured a major portion of the mortgage market. From a financial engineering perspective, the process by which CMOs are created is similar to that by which the early zero coupon bonds were created from conventional coupon bonds. The investment bank purchases mortgage pass-throughs (or whole mortgages) and then issues special bonds that are collateralized by the mortgages (hence the name). The bonds are divided into a series of distinct groups called **tranches**. In the basic or plain vanilla CMO, each tranche is entitled to receive a pro rata share of interest, just as with a pass-through, but only one tranche at a time receives principal. For example, at the beginning, only the first tranche receives principal. This tranche, called the **fastest-pay tranche**, receives all principal collected by the servicers, whether paid on time or prepaid, until all of the tranche's principal has been amortized. The tranche is then retired and the second tranche becomes the fastest-pay tranche. The structure of the CMO, using pass-throughs or whole mortgages as the collateral source, is depicted in Exhibit 3.5 with the second tranche as the fastest-pay tranche (the first tranche has already been retired).

Many variants of the basic CMO have evolved since this product was first introduced. Some have structures considerably more complex than that depicted in Exhibit 3.5. For example, there are CMOs in which more than one tranche receives principal at a time, there are zero coupon CMOs, and there are CMOs that are based on adjustable-rate mortgages.

While the CMO does not eliminate prepayment risk, it greatly

EXHIBIT 3.5   Cash Flows on a CMO

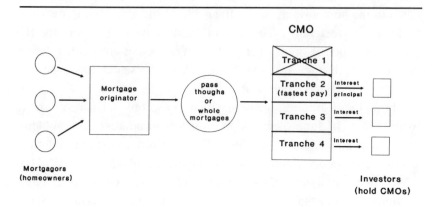

reduces it. The structure of the tranches guarantees that the first tranche will have a very short life, that the second tranche will have a somewhat longer life, that the third tranche will have a still longer life, and so on. Thus, a long-term instrument, the mortgage or pass-through, is used to create a series of distinct instruments, the tranches, that have short, intermediate, and long lives. The investor can pick the tranche that most closely mirrors his or her needs. Because investors can purchase need-specific securities and, hence, have less risk than that associated with whole mortgages or pass-throughs, they are willing to pay a little more for these instruments. The collective value of the CMO tranches can then be more than the value of the mortgages (or pass-throughs) used to create them. This value difference is the source of a large portion of the investment bank's profit. The investment bank also makes the secondary market in CMOs, acting as a dealer, and derives profit from the bid-ask spread.

While a large percentage of newly originated mortgages are sold off soon after origination, most lending institutions still keep mortgages in their investment portfolios. These mortgages are supported by customer deposits, including the CDs discussed earlier. For these lending institutions, interest rate mismatches between mortgage assets and CD liabilities are a very real concern. These interest-rate mismatches can, fortunately, often be rectified by appropriately structured swaps. It is not surprising then that thrifts are the largest single class of users of swap products. We consider a thrift's use of an interest-rate swap to hedge a mortgage portfolio in an appendix to Chapter 7.

3.5 THE CASH MARKETS FOR INTERNATIONAL DEBT

When talking about international debt markets, we must distinguish between domestic issues and foreign issues. **Domestic issues** are debt issues of governments, corporations, and other entities, sold within the country of the issuer and in the currency of the issuer. Dollar-denominated U.S. Treasury bonds and U.S. corporate bonds sold in U.S. markets are examples of U.S. domestic issues. German government and German corporate bonds denominated in deutschemarks and sold in Germany are domestic deutschemark issues. **Foreign issues** are debt issues sold in one country and currency by an issuer of another country. Deutschemark denominated bonds sold by a U.S. corporation in Germany or dollar denominated bonds sold by a German corporation in the U.S. are examples of foreign issues. For purposes of a consistent framework for discussion, we will assume throughout the remainder of this section that the domestic market is the United States.

We often distinguish between issues denominated in dollars, called **U.S.-pay**, from issues denominated in other currencies, called **foreign-pay**. The prices of U.S.-pay issues respond to changes in U.S. interest rates and the prices of foreign-pay issues respond to changes in foreign interest rates. We will begin this section with a discussion of U.S.-pay foreign bonds.

In the early 1960s, a small market in U.S.-pay and foreign-pay bonds began to develop in London. This market became known as the **Eurobond market**. Eventually, trading in Eurobonds spread to other European centers and, still later, spread to countries outside of Europe. Despite the extension of the market to non-European countries, the market for these bonds continued to be called the Eurobond market. The Eurobond market grew rapidly during the 1970s and exploded in the 1980s. This explosive growth is largely explained by the ready availability of swaps beginning in the early 1980s.

Since its inception, the Eurobond market has been dominated by U.S.-pay issues. This has changed somewhat in the last few years but dollar-pay bonds still account for more than 50 percent of the total new-issue volume. German-pay bonds are the next most important and now account for upwards of 15 percent of new-issue volume.

U.S.-pay Eurobonds are often called **Eurodollar bonds**. They share three characteristics:

1. they are denominated in U.S. dollars;
2. they are underwritten by an international syndicate; and
3. they are sold at issue to investors outside the United States.

Because the bonds are sold outside the United States, they are exempt from registration with the Securities and Exchange Commission (SEC). There are no comparable registration requirements for debt issues sold in the Eurobond market. The absence of registration requirements and the costly due diligence investigation that precedes registration, suggests that there can be a cost advantage to offerings made outside the U.S. Once a Eurodollar issue has become "seasoned," however, U.S. investors can purchase the issue in the secondary market. A bond is **seasoned** once it has traded for a sufficiently long period of time (at least 90 days) following completion of distribution.

While most domestic U.S.-pay bonds carry a semiannual coupon, Eurodollar bonds, and most foreign-pay bonds, carry an annual coupon. Thus, a conversion is necessary to make the yield quotes on Eurobonds comparable to the yield quotes on domestic bonds. The mathematics for this conversion is discussed in Chapter 8 in the context of semiannual versus annual swap coupons.

Issuers of Eurodollar bonds include U.S. issuers who prefer to raise dollars outside the United States, non-U.S. issuers who have a need for dollars, and U.S. and non-U.S. issuers who raise dollars in the Eurodollar bond market and then swap these dollar liabilities into liabilities denominated in other currencies.

In recent years, an increasing number of foreign entities in need of dollar financing have chosen to sell their bonds in the U.S. capital markets rather than the Eurobond market. These U.S.-pay bonds are called **Yankee bonds**. There are counterparts to Yankee bonds issued in many major capital markets. For example, non-Japanese entities sometimes issue yen denominated bonds in the Japanese capital markets. These issues are nicknamed **Samurai bonds**.

The market of choice for issuing debt will depend principally on the comparative costs of alternative issuing arenas. Some issuers may hold a comparative advantage in one market while others may hold a comparative advantage in another market.

Foreign-pay Eurobonds, like U.S.-pay Eurobonds, are underwritten by an international syndicate that sells them in a number of international markets. The issuing entity may or may not be domiciled in the country and currency of issue. For example, a German firm may issue deutschemark bonds but a British firm may also issue deutschemark bonds.

While U.S.-pay issues have long dominated the Eurobond market, deutschemark issues, as already noted, are also a major component of this market. Floating rate notes are very popular in the Eurobond markets, irrespective of the currency of denomination, but, they are particularly popular among investors in deutschemark issues.

At the short-end of the maturity spectrum, there is a very big market for short-term Eurodollar deposits. A Eurodollar deposit is a time deposit, denominated in dollars, that is held in a bank outside the United States. London is the principal center of the Eurodollar market. Banks acquire these deposits by issuing Eurodollar CDs. These Eurodollar CDs are purchased by other banks and by corporations—often U.S. corporations.

Eurodollar deposits are actively borrowed and lent among major banks both in Europe and elsewhere. London banks quote an important interest rate for interbank lending of these deposits. This rate, known as the London Interbank Offered Rate, or LIBOR, is always a dollar-based rate quote unless specifically indicated otherwise.[8] LIBOR is routinely quoted for one-month through 12-months, but three-months, six-months, and 12-months are generally the most active.

When investing in foreign-pay debt issues, investors are exposed to two additional forms of risk. These are **sovereign risk** and **exchange-rate risk**. Sovereign risk is the risk that an issuer may be barred by its government from making timely payments of interest and principal. Such an event might occur as a consequence of the overthrow of a government or as a result of a national financial crisis. The second kind of risk, exchange-rate risk, is the risk that the exchange rate between the investor's domestic currency and the currency in which the instrument is denominated may change unfavorably. For example, a U.S. investor investing in deutschemark bonds will benefit from a strengthening of the deutschemark but will be hurt by a weakening of the deutschemark vis-à-vis the dollar.

Swaps are often used to manage exchange-rate risk. They can also be used to exploit discrepancies between exchange rates and interest rates in two countries. These subjects will be examined further in later chapters.

3.6   SUMMARY

Swaps are often used to convert one form of debt to another form of debt. Sometimes this means converting a fixed rate to a floating rate (or vice versa) in the same currency and sometimes it means converting a liability denominated in one currency to a liability denominated in a different currency. In order to fully understand the uses of swaps, it is necessary to have a fairly complete overview of the various markets for debt.

The largest debt market in the world is the market for U.S. Treasury debt. The major instruments trading in these markets are bills, notes, and bonds. T-bills have short maturities, are sold at a discount from face value, and trade in terms of yield with yield quoted on a bank discount basis. T-notes and T-bonds are coupon bearing securities that trade in terms of price. Yields on these instruments are quoted on a bond basis. Treasury debt is very homogeneous with a near continuum of maturities ranging from a few days all the way out to thirty years. The market for Treasury securities, which is made by government securities dealers, is largely unregulated. This has been important in the development of both zero coupon bonds and repurchase agreements.

The U.S. corporate (financial and nonfinancial combined) debt market is very heterogeneous. Nonbank institutions issue short-term debt in the form of commercial paper while banks issue short-term debt in the form of certificates of deposit. These same corporations issue a variety of intermediate- to long-term forms of debt that include both fixed-rate and floating rate notes and fixed-rate bonds. These instruments sometimes have substantial collateral backing and at other times lack collateral altogether. The primary market for corporate notes and bonds is made by investment banks acting as underwriters and the secondary market is made by bond dealers, although some exchange trading does occur.

The mortgage market was a rather humdrum affair until the introduction of mortgage pass-throughs. Most newly originated mortgages created today are pooled with other mortgages for eventual sale as pass-throughs or for conversion into CMOs. The pooling process separates the mortgage debt from the mortgage servicing rights. A mortgage originator will often find it advantageous to sell off the mortgages but to keep the servicing rights to the mortgages. The last decade has witnessed a major shift from conventional level-pay mortgages to various forms of adjustable rate mortgages.

The Eurobond market has grown to become a mainstay of the world financial system. Bonds denominated in any currency can be sold in the Eurobond market. U.S.-pay bonds have long dominated this market and continue to do so, but German-pay and other foreign-pay bonds have become an increasingly important segment of this market. There are advantages to selling U.S.-pay bonds outside the United States. One of the most important of these is the avoidance of a time consuming and expensive registration with the Securities and Exchange Commission (SEC). The Eurobond market's growth was stimulated by the advent of swaps. It is now quite common to raise capital by selling bonds in one currency and then immediately swapping the proceeds from the sale into another currency. Thus, the Eurobond markets provide an efficient mechanism to tap the capital markets of the world in order to raise funds at the least possible cost.

This would not be possible without the availability of swaps or swap-like instruments.

REFERENCES AND SUGGESTED READINGS

Carron, A. *Prepayment Models for Fixed and Adjustable Rate Mortgages*, New York: First Boston, Fixed Income Research (Aug 1988).

Fabozzi, F.J and I.M. Pollock (eds.), *The Handbook of Fixed Income Securities*, 2nd ed., Homewood, IL: Dow Jones-Irwin, (1987).

Fage, P. *Yield Calculations, Credit Swiss First Boston Research* (Oct 1986).

First Boston Corporation, *High Yield Handbook (1989)*, High Yield Research Group, The First Boston Corporation (Jan 1989).

Gelardin, J. "A Complex Market for Floating Rate Notes," *Euromoney*, 17–19 (Jan 1986).

Madura, J. and C. Williams "Hedging Mortgages with Interest Rate Swaps vs Caps: How to Choose," *Real Estate Finance Journal*, 3:1, 90–96 (Summer 1987).

Smith, D.J. "The Pricing of Bull and Bear Floating Rate Notes: An Application of Financial Engineering, *Financial Management*, vol. 17(4) (Winter, 1988).

Stigum, M. *The Money Market*, revised ed., Howewood, IL: Dow Jones-Irwin (1983).

Wilson, R.S. "Domestic Floating-Rate and Adjustable-Rate Debt Securities," in *Handbook of Fixed Income Securities*, F.J. Fabozzi and I.M. Pollack, eds., 2nd ed., (Homewood, IL: Dow Jones-Irwin, 1987).

ENDNOTES

[1]In all dealer activity, the bid price is the price the dealer will pay to buy a security. The ask or asked price, also known as an offer, is the price at which the dealer is willing to sell the security. The difference between the higher asked price and the lower bid price is called the bid-ask spread. Note, when securities are traded on the basis of yield (as is the case with T-bills), the bid will be higher than the asked. This is a reflection of the inverse relationship between prices and yields.

[2]The reader interested in the conversion of discount yields to bond equivalent yields should see Fage (1986), Chapter 1. One way to convert T-bill yields of any term to bond equivalent yields is to first convert the T-bill yield to a simple rate of interest and then convert this simple rate of interest to a semiannual bond equivalent yield. The procedure is described in Appendix 1 to this chapter.

[3]There is some modest risk that the custodial bank might fail and that holders of the derivative zero coupon products might suffer payment delays or other losses.

[4]The offering price will usually be at or close to par. The securities, however, may be sold for less than the offering price but never for more than the offering price. From the underwriter's perspective, the difference between the offering price and the proceeds paid to the issuer is called the **underwriter's discount**.

[5]Commercial paper with a maturity greater than 270 days is rare because any publicly offered issue with a maturity greater than 270 days must be registered with the SEC. This registration, and the accompanying due diligence investigation conducted by the underwriting team, is time consuming and expensive.

[6]The first documented public offering of FRNs in the United States is attributed to Mortgage Investors of Washington, which offered on 1 November 1973, $15 million of floating rate (eight percent to 12 percent) senior subordinated notes due 1 November 1980. For a more detailed discussion of the history of floating-rate debt, see Wilson (1987). For a discussion of the role of FRNs in financial engineering, see Smith (1988).

[7]Carron (1988) provides a very good starting point for anyone interested in mortgage prepayment models.

[8]For example, there is a deutschemark LIBOR, usually denoted DM LIBOR, that represents the interest rate in London for loans involving deutschemark deposits held with London banks.

CHAPTER 3

Conversion of Bank Discount Yields to Bond Equivalent Yields

A very straightforward and intiutive way to convert bank discount yields (BDY) to bond equivalent yields (BEY) is to first convert the BDY to a simple rate of interest (also known as an effective annual rate of return). This simple rate of interest can then be converted to its BEY equivalent. The complete process takes five steps.

Step 1. Calculate the dollar amount of the discount using Equation 3.1.

$$DD = FV \times BDY \times \frac{\text{Actual}}{360} \qquad (3.1)$$

Step 2. Calculate the present value of the T-bill using Equation 3.2.

$$PV = FV - DD \qquad (3.2)$$

Step 3. Calculate the periodic discount rate k using Equation 3.4 or its equivalent below.

$$k = \frac{FV}{PV} - 1 \qquad (3.4)$$

Step 4. Convert the periodic discount rate k to a simple rate or interest, denoted here by r, using Equation 3.A.1.

$$r = (1 + k)^a - 1 \qquad \text{where} \qquad a = \frac{365}{\text{Actual}} \qquad (3.A.1)$$

Step 5. Convert the simple rate of interest to a bond equivalent yield using Equation 3.A.2.

$$BEY = 2 \cdot [(1 + r)^{\frac{1}{2}} - 1] \qquad \text{(3.A.2)}$$

The calculation is complete at this step and you now have the bond equivalent yield stated in its conventional form as a semiannual rate.

4

Understanding and Managing Financial Risk

4.1 OVERVIEW

Most firms are affected to some degree by changes in one or more financial prices. These include interest rates, exchange rates, commodity prices, and stock prices. A firm that employs floating-rate financing or that holds floating-rate assets, for example, will be affected by a change in interest rates. A domestic firm that sells its products in foreign markets will be directly affected by fluctuations in the exchange rate between its currency and that of its foreign market. A firm in the manufacturing sector will be affected by changes in the market prices of its raw materials and/or the prices of its finished goods. A mutual stock fund will be affected by changes in equity values. Fluctuations in financial prices are then a source of significant risks. These risks are called, collectively, **price risks**.

A firm does not have to be directly involved in a market in which prices are changing to be affected by the changing prices. For example, a retailer may not employ debt financing at all and may hold no rate-sensitive assets. Yet, it may have considerable interest-rate risk. If the retailer's sales are sensitive to interest rates, then the firm will suffer a loss of sales should interest rates rise. Such a situation is typical of the housing, automobile, and durable goods industries in which buyers often finance their purchases.

As a second example, consider a manufacturer that purchases all of its inputs domestically and sells its output domestically. At first glance, such a firm would not seem to be affected by fluctuations in exchange rates. But, if the firm has foreign competitors that sell their products in the firm's domestic market, then fluctuations in exchange rates will affect the prices of the competitors' products and, through this effect, impact the firm's sales.

Similarly, an increase in the price of one commodity can affect the prices of other commodities by shifting demand toward or away from those other commodities as consumers try to substitute one commodity for another. Consider, for example, the situation of a livestock producer that feeds its livestock corn. Suppose that a fungus seriously damaged wheat crops and so caused wheat prices to rise. The livestock producer is not directly affected by the rise in wheat prices. But, as some of the wheat consumers respond to the increase in wheat prices by substituting corn for wheat, the demand for corn increases and corn prices rise. This example serves to highlight the fact that exposure to price risks may be direct or indirect and indirect exposures are just as real, but usually harder to measure, than direct ones.

Most successful firms are adept at dealing with their **core business** risks. These core business risks involve such things as the choice of technology in production, the method of delivering goods and services to clients, ongoing research and development efforts, and so on. But price risks are a type of **environmental risk**. That is, they are caused by events that occur outside the firm. Manifestations of this risk can wreak havoc on even the best managed and most efficient of producers. For this reason, it is not sufficient to only manage core business risks; price risks must be managed as well.

In this chapter, we consider the measurement of price risk, the measurement of exposure to price risk, and certain concepts and techniques associated with managing price risk.

4.2   VOLATILITY: THE SOURCE OF PRICE RISK

Price risk is defined as the potential for a future price to deviate from its expected value. A deviation from an expected price is not necessarily for the worse. Indeed, if expectations are unbiased, beneficial deviations are just as likely as detrimental ones. Nevertheless, we define any deviation from the expected value as a manifestation of price risk. When we want to limit our definition of risk to injurious outcomes, we will refer to risk as **downside risk**. For now, we will concentrate on price risk.

The definition of price risk suggests a way to measure it. Since price risk takes the form of deviations from expected values, the more volatile the prices, the more price risk the exposed parties will bear. This volatility can be quantified with the aid of well-defined statistical measures. The most often used of these measures are the **variance** and the **standard deviation**. The standard deviation is the square root of the variance and so, if you know one of these values, you also know the other. It has become common practice to equate the terms "volatility" and "standard deviation." Many financial institutions, for example, use the term **volatility unit**, to mean one standard deviation.

The definition of price risk also suggests a way to deal with it. Since price risk represents the potential for actual prices to deviate from expectations, one can try to improve the accuracy of the expectations. For example, suppose that we have a series of "market forecasts," in the form of forward prices, and a corresponding series of realized prices. Sample values are given in Table 4.1. The forward prices may be viewed as the value "expected" by the market (expected value).

TABLE 4.1
Market Forecasts versus Realized Prices

Time	Market Forecast One Period Out	Actual Price One Period Later	Deviation
1	145	152	−7
2	163	158	5
3	156	175	−19
4	164	180	−16
5	188	151	37
		Total	0

Observe first that the deviations sum to zero, which suggests that, on average, the market's forecast is unbiased. But notice also that the market forecast has missed the mark each time, as represented by the individual deviations. There is clearly some price risk in relying on the market for one's forecasts. One solution, it would seem, is to make better forecasts than the market.

Beginning in the early 1970s, market prices became progressively more volatile. Corporations, banks, and other institutions responded by hiring more economists to forecast prices. This intense utilization of the economics profession led to a spate of advances in forecasting theory and forecasting models. The volatility growth tapered off in the mid 1980s but, for most prices, volatility never returned to its pre-1970s level. During much of this period, there were no forward markets in many assets for comparative market forecasts. As time went on, however, more forward (and futures) markets were introduced. And, as market forecasts became increasingly available, a frustrating, and at first surprising, picture began to emerge. Market forecasts tended to outperform individual economists' forecasts. This is not to say that individual economists did not sometimes come closer to correctly forecasting the future price but, rather, that they could not do so consistently enough to produce a lower forecast volatility than that produced by the market.

Today we have a well-advanced theory to explain this phenomenon. The theory, called the **efficient markets hypothesis**, holds that the market may be viewed as a great gatherer and channeler of information. Each market participant gathers and processes information but none has a complete picture. That is, each participant possesses a subset of the total relevant knowledge and its importance. By buying and selling, the individual market participants register their private forecasts in the market and channel their private information into the market price. The market price reflects all available information rather than just one participant's private knowledge. The collective wisdom embodied in the market then produces a better forecast than that which can be produced by any individual economic prognosticator.

The upshot is that forecasting, regardless of the individual forecaster's talents, is not a solution in and of itself to the price-risk problem. If price risk cannot be eliminated by forecasting, then the only remaining solution is to manage the price risk. This is the strategy that has emerged as advances in theory, development of new instruments, and technological improvements have all conspired to make risk management practical and cost-effective. The development of risk management theory and techniques has, as one might expect, been accompanied by a dramatic cutback in the number of economists employed by industry.

Before leaving this section, consider the extent to which price volatilities have changed. Exhibit 4.1 provides a graphic illustration of the degree of price volatility over the period from 1960 to 1985 for interest rates (shown on Panel A, using five-year T-notes), exchange rates (shown on Panel B, using the DM/USD rate), and commodity prices (shown on Panel C, using a price index). A more recent history of volatility is provided for interest rates in Panel D which covers the period from 1977 to 1990. Notice the extraordinary difference between the 1977 to 1979 period and the 1987 to 1989 period.

EXHIBIT 4.1.   Panel A—U.S. Five-year Treasury Notes: Interest Rate Volatility
(Monthly changes in basis points)

Basis points

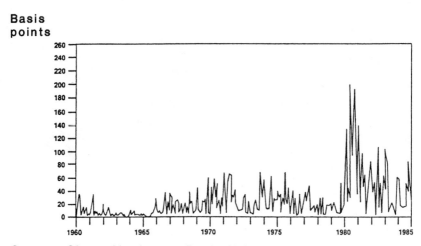

Source: Chase Manhattan Bank, N.A.

EXHIBIT 4.1. **Panel B—Spot Deutschemark/Dollar: Exchange Rate Volatility**
(Monthly percent change)

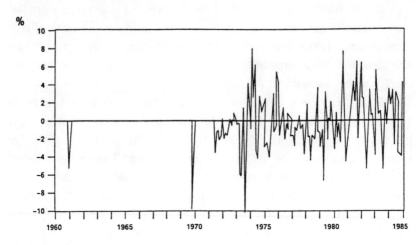

Source: Chase Manhattan Bank, N.A.

EXHIBIT 4.1. **Panel C—Relative Price of Commodities: Price Volatility**
Commodity price index/producer price index

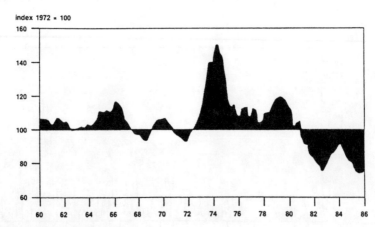

Source: Chase Manhattan Bank, N.A.

EXHIBIT 4.1.   Panel D—On-The-Run Treasury Yield Interest Rate Volatility
20-day historical volatility

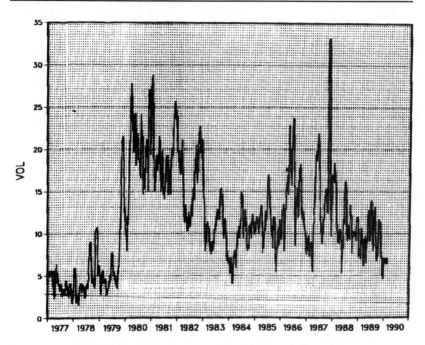

Source: Shearson Lehman Hutton

4.3   MEASURING EXPOSURE TO PRICE RISK

Knowledge of the existence of a price risk is not sufficient to manage it. The risk manager needs to know the degree of exposure to the price risk. Two different firms can have an exposure to the same price risk but the extent of the exposures can be quite different. Consider two firms: The first is a passenger airline and the second is a large lawncare company. Both firms employ oil derivatives in their business. The airline uses kerosene to fuel its planes and the lawncare firm uses gasoline to power its mowers. Both firms have an exposure to a change in oil prices because both kerosene and gasoline will fluctuate in price with the price of oil.

As it happens, expense for fuel represents 38 percent of the airline's operating costs and 4 percent of the lawncare firm's operating costs. Thus, a change in the price of oil will dramatically influence the financial performance of the airline but may have only a very modest effect on the lawncare firm's financial performance.

The first step after measuring the volatility of a price is then to measure the firm's exposure. This is done by constructing separate risk profiles for each price risk to which the firm is exposed. A **risk profile** is a specification of the relationship between a performance measure and price. Sometimes we find it convenient to use price changes from the current price level (which, in the case of forward and futures prices, can be interpreted as a forecast of the future spot price) instead of the price. Performance is usually plotted on the vertical axis and price, or price change, is plotted on the horizontal axis. These alternative forms of the risk profile are depicted in Exhibit 4.2, Panels A and B, respectively. Notice that when a risk profile employs price changes from expected values, as in Panel B, the risk profile will pass through the origin.

The performance measure most often used in developing risk profiles is a change in the present value of the firm's cash flows. The

EXHIBIT 4.2a.   Risk Profiles—Alternative Forms.—Panel A: Performance versus Price

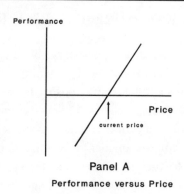

Panel A
Performance versus Price

EXHIBIT 4.2b.   Risk Profiles—Alternative Forms.—Panel B: Performance versus Price Change

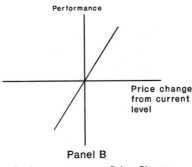

Panel B

Performance versus Price Change

"change in value" measure is particularly useful when the goal of exposure measurement is to neutralize the risk. Let's consider an example. A U.S. financial corporation has just acquired $12 million of five-year fixed-rate assets (loans) paying 10 percent semiannually. It has financed these assets with floating-rate liabilities. Specifically, the liabilities take the form of six-month commercial paper. This paper will be rolled over every six months for five years (this financing strategy was discussed in Chapter 3). The first paper issue required a paper rate of 7 percent and the firm expects that this is a good estimate of future paper rates.

The difference between the payments the firm will receive at 10 percent and the payments the firm will make at 7 percent represents a cash flow stream from the firm's business as a finance company. Under current expectations and a discount rate of 10 percent, the firm concludes that the cash flow stream has a present value of $1,389,913. The calculation, which uses Equation 2.1 from Chapter 2, is illustrated in Table 4.2.

Now consider how the value of the firm would change if commercial paper rates suddenly increase by 1 percent. The firm's *initial* net cash flow (period 1) would not change since the rate on the firm's assets is fixed at 10 percent and the cost of its commercial paper financing is fixed at 7 percent for the first six months. It is the

TABLE 4.2
Calculating the Present Value of an Expected Cash Flow Stream

Period	Known Cash In	Expected Cash Out	Net Cash Flow	Discounted Value (at 10 percent)
1	$600,000	$420,000	$180,000	$ 171,429
2	600,000	420,000	180,000	163,265
3	600,000	420,000	180,000	155,491
4	600,000	420,000	180,000	148,087
5	600,000	420,000	180,000	141,035
6	600,000	420,000	180,000	134,319
7	600,000	420,000	180,000	127,923
8	600,000	420,000	180,000	121,831
9	600,000	420,000	180,000	116,030
10	600,000	420,000	180,000	110,504
			Total Value	$1,389,913

refunding rate six months out that rises to 8 percent, with each subsequent refunding now expected to cost 8 percent. The expected cash flow for periods 2 through 10, therefore, declines to $120,000.

Discounting all the net cash flows at the same 10 percent used earlier, we find that the value of the firm's cash flow declines to $983,751. Thus, a 1 percent rise in commercial paper rates results in a $406,162 decrease in that portion of the firm's value associated with this particular financing. This seemingly modest one percentage point rise in interest rates can be seen to translate into a 29 percent decrease in the firm's value.

We can repeat this calculation for all new levels of interest rates and plot the value changes against the rate changes to get the firm's risk profile. The risk profile for this firm, with respect to changes in the commercial paper rate, is depicted in Exhibit 4.3. This profile is downward sloping because an increase in rates leads to a decrease in value and vice versa.

Risk profiles, like the one on the next page, can be drawn for any price exposure. This can be an exposure to interest rates, exchange rates, any of hundreds of commodity prices, and even stock prices. Risk profiles are useful for several reasons. First, the very act of

EXHIBIT 4.3.   Risk Profile—Paper Rate

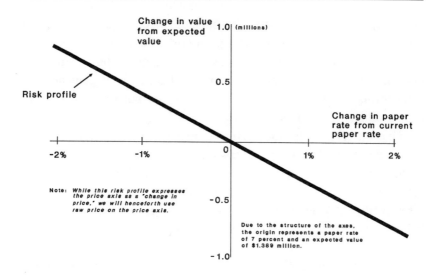

developing risk profiles forces those exposed to give serious thought to the existence of the exposures. Second, without a serious effort to measure the exposures, it is impossible to efficiently manage them. Finally, the nature of the exposures and the shape of the risk profiles might suggest appropriate risk management techniques.

4.4   MANAGING RISK

There are three different, but related, ways to manage financial risks. The first is to purchase **insurance**. Insurance, however, is only viable for the management of certain types of financial risks. Such risks are said to be insurable. The second approach is **asset/liability management**. This approach involves the careful balancing of assets and liabilities so as to eliminate net value changes. Asset/liability management is most often used in the management of interest-rate risk and exchange-rate risk. The final approach, which can be used either by itself or in conjunction with one or both of the other two, is **hedging**.

Hedging involves the taking of offsetting risk positions. It is very similar to asset/liability management but while asset/liability management, by definition, involves on-balance sheet positions, hedging usually involves off-balance sheet positions. This distinction between asset/liability management and hedging is important but often overlooked. In fact, many people consider asset/liability management strategies forms of hedging and vice versa. For our purposes, it is worth maintaining the distinction.

Our interest in the tools of risk management is primarily with swaps, but we will also look at forwards, futures, and options. All four of these instruments are off-balance sheet contracts and, hence, hedging tools. But, because hedging tools are often used to take up where asset/liability management leaves off, or as an alternative to asset/liability management, it is important to look at this activity as well. Insurance is of less importance to us but we will say a few words about it in order to be clearer as to which risks are insurable and which are not. We will look at insurance, then asset/liability management and, finally, hedging.

4.4.1   Insurance

An **insurable risk** is a risk to which many firms (or individuals) are exposed, for which manifestations of the risk are not highly correlated among those exposed, and for which the probability of a manifestation of the risk is known with a high degree of certainty. Insurable risks include such risks as death, loss from fire, loss from theft, liability, and medical expense. Consider the case of fire. Damage from fire results in financial loss and the risk of fire is, therefore, a financial risk.

The financial risk to which the firm is exposed from fire is a function of the probability of the firm experiencing a fire and the value of the assets at risk. The risk of losses from fire is an insurable risk because many firms experience a similar exposure and these individual exposures have a near zero correlation. That is, the probability of a fire at Firm A is the same whether or not Firm B experiences a fire.[1] Additionally, while we cannot say that Firm A will or will not experience a fire, we do know with great certainty the statistical likelihood (probability) that Firm A will experience a fire. The latter is established through careful actuarial studies.

For simplicity, suppose that there are 1,000 identical firms each with a net worth (equity) of $2 million. Each is subject to the same 2 percent probability of a fire. Should a fire occur at any of the firms, the loss will average $5 million (in terms of replacement cost of assets and lost business). For any of the firms then, a fire would be devastating— wiping out all equity and leaving unpaid debts. Thus, not only are the owners of a firm exposed to a financial risk from fire but so are the firm's creditors.

The amount of the exposure, per year, can be obtained by multiplying the probability of a fire (2 percent) by the loss resulting from fire ($5 million). The exposure is then $100,000. Now, suppose that an insurance company offers to cover any fire losses at any of the firms for an annual premium of $120,000. The excess covers administrative costs and profit for the insurer. If a fire occurs, the insurer pays out $5 million. If not, the insurer benefits by the amount of the premium.

For the insured firms, the payment of the insurance premium, even if in excess of the amount of the exposure, may be money well spent. First, the risk-averse nature of both the firms' owners and managers suggest that they will be willing to pay, up to a point, for the removal of the risk. In the language of economics, we say that they enjoy a "utility" (or satisfaction) gain from risk reduction. Second, the firms' creditors will view the firms as more creditworthy if they minimize their risks. As more creditworthy, the creditors may be willing to extend credit to the firms at lower cost. This reduced financing cost offsets, to some degree, the cost of the insurance.

While the insurer has assumed the risk of all of the individual firms it is, in fact, not at significant risk because the individual risks of fire were not highly correlated. In the language of finance, the risks are unsystematic in nature. If we assume zero correlation, a reasonable approximation in this case, the insurer's *per firm risk* is quite small. This is a rather simple application of portfolio theory. Since the risks are independent of one another, the premiums received from all the firms tend to offset the payments to the firms that do experience a fire.

The more policies the insurer writes, the greater the degree to which the premiums and policy payouts are offsetting. From the insurer's perspective, its average per-firm risk decreases with each new firm added to its policy base. The average per-firm risk to the insurer is given by Equation 4.1.

$$PFR = \frac{IFE}{\sqrt{N}} \tag{4.1}$$

where PFR = denotes average per-firm risk to insurer,

        IFE = denotes the individual firm's exposure, and

        N = denotes the number of identical firm's insured.

Another way to look at this is to consider the insurer's risk per dollar of premiums received. The relationship between the number of firms insured and the insurer's per-dollar risk exposure is depicted in Exhibit 4.4.

EXHIBIT 4.4.   **Insurer's Average Risk Exposure**
                      (Per firm insured)

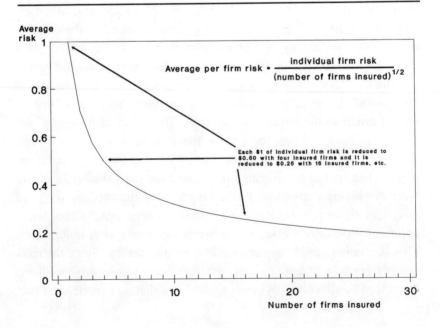

Insurance works because the insurer's risk, when spread across a large policy base, is a small fraction of the insured's risk. The keys to the principal of insurance then is the independence of the individual exposures and the spreading of the risk across a large policy base. The latter is called, in the language of statistics, the "law of large numbers." In a sense, insurers are practicing arbitrage. Instead of arbitraging across space or time, however, they are arbitraging across risk.

There are two problems with removing risks by insuring them. First, the introduction of an intermediary, the insurer, suggests that the cost of insurance will exceed its expected monetary value. The insurer, after all, must cover its own administrative costs and its owners expect to earn a reasonable profit. Second, not all risks are insurable and price risks are generally not insurable. The reason is simple; the financial performances of firms with an exposure to the same price risk are not independent of one another. In fact, they lie at the opposite end of the statistical spectrum—they are nearly perfectly positively correlated. That is, if *one* firm experiences financial injury from a manifestation of the risk, *all* similarly exposed firms will experience financial injury from a manifestation of the risk. This would be like insuring firms against fire while knowing that if one policyholder experiences a devastating fire, all policyholders will experience a devastating fire. In such a situation, insurance has no meaning.

Should the insurer be required to pay off on all policies simultaneously, it could not possibly do so and so the insurance is useless. And this is precisely the case in price risk. If the yield curve shifts upward for example, all firms experience a similar increase in the cost of funds. If the dollar weakens, all firms with an exposure to the dollar are impacted. If the price of corn falls, all corn farmers will suffer.

4.4.2   Asset/Liability Management

Asset/liability management is an effort to minimize exposure to price risk by holding the appropriate combination of assets and liabilities so as to meet the firm's objectives (such as achieving a stated earnings target) and simultaneously minimize the firm's risk. The key to this form of risk management is holding the *right* combination of on-balance sheet assets and on-balance sheet liabilities.

Asset/liability management is most highly developed for managing interest-rate risk. Indeed, few discussions of this approach to risk management are conducted in any other context. But asset/liability management can be used and is often used in the management of exchange-rate risk, commodity-price risk, and stock-price risk. Indeed, in the case of mutual stock funds, the fund itself is at no risk from stock price fluctuations because, by construct, asset/liability management works perfectly to balance the claims of the funds' shareholders against the value of the funds' assets.[2] Despite its applicability to other forms of price risk, we will limit our look at asset/liability management to the management of interest-rate risk and exchange-rate risk.

The first users of asset/liability management techniques were pension funds. Banks, insurance companies, savings and loans, and finance companies soon followed suit. The following example discusses how a pension fund uses asset/liability management.

Pension funds are exposed to considerable interest-rate risk and it was this risk that the funds needed to manage. A pension fund sells policies to clients. These policies can take a variety of forms. One of the most popular in use today are **guaranteed income contracts** or GICs. GICs guarantee a fixed stream of future income to their owners, (i.e., the policyholders) and constitute liabilities of the pension fund. The proceeds obtained from the sale of these policies are invested, by the fund, in financial assets which provide a return for the fund. Fluctuations in market interest rates, however, can and will cause the return on the firm's assets to deviate from the return promised to the fund's policyholders. For example, if rates decline the fund might find itself investing future cash flows in assets that are yielding an insufficient return to meet the fund's obligations—as represented by the claims of the policyholders. An equivalent, but alternative, way to look at this problem is to consider the market value of the firm's assets and the market value of the firm's liabilities. While theses values should initially be the same, they may not be equally sensitive to changes in interest rates. Thus, a fluctuation in rates may impact the value of the fund's assets more than the value of the fund's liabilities, or vice versa. The risk is then that the fund's liabilities might be underfunded at the time the fund is due to pay off.

Ideally, asset/liability management should strive to match the timing and the amount of cash inflows from assets with the timing and the amount of the cash outflows on liabilities. An asset portfolio constructed to precisely match cash flows is called a **dedicated portfolio**.[3] Unfortunately, it can be extremely difficult, if not impossible, to precisely match cash flows. Furthermore, even when it can be done, it may be too expensive or may require the fund to pass up more attractive investment opportunities. The solution is to forget about matching cash flows and to concentrate instead on the value of the fund's assets and the value of the fund's liabilities and to make the value difference completely interest-rate insensitive.

The selection of assets so as to minimize the rate sensitivity of the difference between asset and liability values is called, in the context of asset/liability management, **portfolio immunization**. The concept of immunization and the strategy for implementing it were first developed by F.M. Redington in a paper published in 1952.[4]

Since the goal of immunization is to make the asset/liability mix insensitive to interest-rate fluctuations, the logical starting point for an immunization strategy is the duration tool that we discussed in Chapter 2. Duration is a relative measure of a debt instrument's interest-rate sensitivity. In its original form, duration is calculated as a weighted average of the time to the instrument's maturity. The weights are the present values of the individual cash flows divided by the present value of the entire stream of cash flows. The weights (denoted here by $w(t)$) are then multiplied by the time at which the cash flow will occur (t/m), where t denotes the period of the cash flow and m denotes the number of cash flows per year). The products are then added to get duration. The duration calculation from Chapter 2 is repeated here as Equation 4.2. The calculation produces a duration value measured in years.

$$D = \sum_{t=1}^{m \cdot T} w(t) \cdot (t/m) \qquad \textbf{(4.2)}$$

The duration value is often modified by dividing by one plus the instrument's yield (y) divided by the number of cash flows per year (m). This modified duration (denoted below by D_m) is given by Equation 4.3. It was also discussed in Chapter 2.

$$D_m = \frac{D}{(1 + y/m)} \tag{4.3}$$

The concept of duration is closely related to the concept of a risk profile. To see this, consider the relationship between the present value of a debt instrument and the instrument's yield. This is depicted in Exhibit 4.5.

It can be shown, though we will not do so here, that the negative of the slope of the "value curve" in Exhibit 4.5 is the instrument's modified duration.[5] If we subtract the starting present value from the new present value to get a "change in present value," we will not affect the slope of the value curve because we have merely shifted the vertical axis. However, once we have shifted the axis, we have, by our earlier definition, a risk profile. Thus, we see that, at least in the context of interest rates, modified duration is the slope of the risk profile.

Let us now compare the risk profiles associated with holding three different debt instruments. The first is a long-maturity instrument, the

EXHIBIT 4.5.   Relationship Between a Risk Profile and Duration

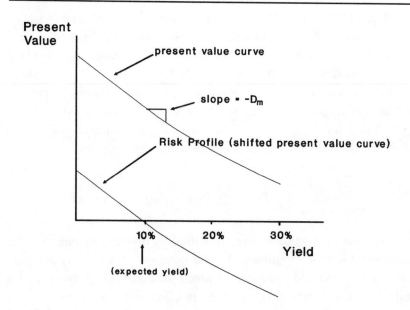

second is an intermediate-maturity instrument, and the third is an overnight-money instrument. The latter instrument refers to money that is lent overnight at the overnight money rate and then re-lent at the next day's overnight money rate. Think of this as an instrument with a floating rate of interest that is reset daily (as close to continuously as is currently practical). The risk profiles associated with these three instruments are depicted in Exhibit 4.6.

Notice that the long-maturity instrument has the steepest risk profile. The risk profile of the cash instrument is absolutely flat. This is consistent with the long duration of the long-maturity instrument and a zero duration for the overnight-money instrument. This suggests that the concept of duration is useful in the same way as is a risk profile—it can be used to assess the extent of an interest-rate exposure.

An interesting property of duration is that the duration of a portfolio of assets is a weighted average of the durations of the individual assets included in the portfolio when the instruments' weights are taken to be the market values of the instruments divided by the entire market value of the portfolio. This type of weighting is called **value weighting**.

This duration property of asset (and liability) portfolios is the key to immunization strategies. In the immunization strategy developed by Redington, the fund manager determines the duration of the firm's liabilities and then selects two assets with different durations. Finally,

EXHIBIT 4.6.   Interest-Rate Risk, Maturity, and Duration

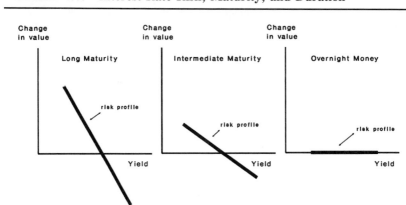

the manager determines the weights on the two assets in the asset portfolio so that the portfolio has a duration that matches precisely the duration of the liabilities. Those who employ immunization strategies generally use the original (Macaulay) duration, but the modified duration can also be used. We employ the latter.

Let's consider a simple example. Suppose that the pension fund sells a new policy that commits the fund to pay $100 each year for the next 15 years. The cash flows of the liability stream, together with their discounted values (using a 10 percent discount rate) and their contributions to duration (products), look as depicted in Table 4.3. We see that the liability stream has a present value of $760.61 and a modified duration of 5.708.

The problem for the fund is how to invest the $760.61 proceeds from the sale of the policy to earn a return of at least 10 percent while assuring itself that the assets in which the fund invests will have a value at least equal that of its liabilities at each and every point in time in the future. Suppose now that the fund has two instruments in which it can invest. The first is a 30-year Treasury bond paying a coupon of 12 percent and selling at par. The second is six-month T-bills yielding 8 percent (bond equivalent). The bond has a modified duration of 8.080 years and the bill has a modified duration of 0.481.[6]

TABLE 4.3
The Calculation of Modified Duration

Time	Cash Flow	Discounted Value of Cash Flow	Weight	Product
1	100	90.909	0.120	0.120
2	100	82.645	0.109	0.217
3	100	75.131	0.099	0.296
.	.	.	.	.
.	.	.	.	.
.	.	.	.	.
15	100	23.939	0.031	0.472
	Total	760.608	1.000	6.279

Modified Duration $= 6.279 \div 1.1 = 5.708$

Fluctuations in yields will, of course, cause both the fund's assets and liabilities to fluctuate in value. For the immunization strategy to be completely effective, the fluctuations in the value of the asset portfolio must precisely match the fluctuations in the value of the liability portfolio. This means weighting the bond and the bill in such a fashion as to produce a portfolio duration precisely equal to the duration of the liabilities. The weights must, of course, sum to 1.0. The model is given by Equations 4.4 and 4.5 where w_1 and w_2 are the weights on the bond (instrument 1) and the bills (instrument 2), respectively. D_1 and D_2 are the corresponding durations and D_L denotes the overall duration of the liabilities.

$$w_1 \cdot D_1 + w_2 \cdot D_2 = D_L \tag{4.4}$$

$$w_1 + w_2 = 1 \tag{4.5}$$

Substituting the known duration values into Equation 4.4 and then solving renders the appropriate weights. The solution is illustrated below.

The Determination of Immunization Portfolio Weights

$$w_1 \cdot 8.080 + w_2 \cdot 0.481 = 5.708$$

and $\qquad w_1 + w_2 = 1 \qquad$ implying that $\qquad w_2 = 1 - w_1$

substituting for w_2:

$$w_1 \cdot 8.080 + (1 - w_1) \cdot 0.481 = 5.708$$

finally, solving for w_1:

$$w_1 = 68.79 \text{ percent}$$

The solution for w_1 implies that the solution for w_2 is 31.21 percent. Thus, we conclude that the pension fund should invest 68.79 percent of the proceeds it received from the sale of its policies in the 30-year bond and 31.21 percent in the six-month bill. This translates into a current investment of $523.23 in bonds and $237.38 in bills.

Now consider what happens if the yield curve moves upward by 10 basis points. This movement represents a parallel shift in the yield curve. The liabilities are now discounted by 10.1 percent instead of 10, the bond is discounted by 12.1 percent instead of 12, and the bill is discounted at 8.1 percent instead of 8. The old values and the new values are depicted in Table 4.4.

Notice that the change in the value of the fund's assets (- $4.32), obtained by combining the value change in the bond and the value change in the bill, is precisely equal to the value change in the fund's liabilities. Thus, the immunization strategy has successfully protected the fund from a 10 basis point change in asset and liability yields. In addition, this portfolio is "profitable" in the sense that the return on the assets exceeds the 10 percent cost of the liabilities. Had this not been the case, the fund would not have offered the policy for sale. The return on the fund's portfolio is computed as the weighted average of the return on the individual assets. In this case, the calculation is: (68.79% × .12) + (31.21% × .08) = 10.75 percent.

There are three problems with the immunization approach described above. First, the duration values are only reliable for short periods of time. That is, as time passes, the durations of the individual assets and the duration of the liabilities change, and these changes are not equal for all the instruments involved. Thus, a weighting scheme that works perfectly today will probably not work perfectly tomorrow. This is not to say that it will not work well tomorrow, only that it will not work as well as it does today; and, with each passing day, the weighting scheme becomes less reliable.

The second problem is that durations also change with changes in yields and these duration changes are not necessarily the same for all

TABLE 4.4
Performance of the Immunized Portfolio

	Pension Liabilities	Assets		
		30-Year Bond	6-Month Bill	
Old value	760.61	523.23	237.38	
New value	756.29	519.03	237.26	
Change in value	-4.32	-4.20 +	-0.12 =	-4.32

the instruments. Thus, for small changes in yield, the duration matching strategy will work very well. But for large changes in yield, the duration matching strategy will work less well. Both of these problems, however, are easily solved. The solution is to recompute the durations frequently, recalculate the weights, and adjust the portfolio accordingly.[7]

The third problem with the simple duration matching strategy described here concerns the assumption that all movements of the yield curve take the form of parallel shifts. As we argued in Chapter 2, this is simply not the case. Shorter term rates are more sensitive than are longer term rates; the rates on different types of instruments have different sensitivities, even if they have the same maturities; and the same types of instruments with the same maturities may have different sensitivities due to different degrees of default risk.

A very workable solution however is to adjust the size of the asset positions on the basis of the historical relationship between the yield changes on the liabilities and the yield changes on the assets. That is, if we assume that there is a proportionality to the yield change on the liabilities and the yield change on the assets, then we can measure this proportion using historical data. The statistical procedure used for this purpose is linear regression. In this procedure we regress the past changes in the yield of the liabilities against the historical changes in the yield of the 30-year bond. The resultant coefficient is the required proportion. In Chapter 2, we called this coefficient the yield beta. The regression is given by Equation 4.6 in which Δy_L denotes the yield change on the liabilities, Δy_b denotes the yield change on the bond, and β denotes the yield beta that represents the proportionality factor.

$$\Delta y_L = \beta \cdot \Delta y_b \qquad (4.6)$$

We then measure a yield beta for the liabilities and the six-month bill using the same procedure. Once we know the yield betas, we can adjust the duration model so as to account for nonparallel shifts in the yield curve.

There are more sophisticated immunization models, but none has been shown to be consistently superior to Redington's original model (with the adjustments we have noted) and so we do not go into these any further.[8] We should note that the risk profile for the pension fund, (i.e., changes in its value with respect to changes in interest rates) will be perfectly flat if the portfolio weighting is done correctly.

Now consider the asset/liability management approach as it can be applied to the management of exchange-rate risk. We use a U.S. bank with global operations as the basis of our example. The bank makes loans to corporations worldwide. These loans are usually made in the currency of the borrower. Thus, a loan made to a British firm is usually made in sterling (BP). A loan made to an Italian firm is usually made in lira (IL), and so on. These loans are recorded on the bank's books as assets. But some of the assets are denominated in sterling, some in lira, and some in other currencies.

Now, suppose that the bank raises the funds that it lends to these firms by borrowing dollars in the United States. These dollars are then converted, at the prevailing spot exchange rate, to the currency of the lender. The borrowings are recorded as dollar liabilities of the bank.

The bank described in this example has a serious currency mismatch in its asset/liability structure. The bank's balance sheet for example, for one day's activity at the end of the day of that activity, might look something like that depicted in Table 4.5.

TABLE 4.5
Global Bank's Balance Sheet
(one day activity)
(all values in millions)

Assets		Liabilities	
Loans (sterling)	2.50	Demand deposits (dollars)	3.51
Loans (lira)	1,480.00	CDs (dollars)	11.48
Loans (dollars)	12.40	Other time deposits (dollars)	2.70
		Total liabilities	17.69

Exchange Rates: USD/BP = 1.6550
USD/IL = 0.0007785
USD/USD = 1.0000

At the current exchange rates, the bank's assets have a current dollar-value equivalent of 17.69 million. This is to be expected since the value of the assets and the value of the liabilities should be equal at the moment they are created—that is what Table 4.5 depicts. But, suppose that the dollar strengthens over the next few weeks. For example, suppose that the USD/BP rate declines to 1.6385 and the USD/IL rate declines to 0.0007625. In such a case, the value of the bank's assets, when translated to their dollar-value equivalent, is significantly below the value of its liabilities: 17.62 million versus 17.69 million. The difference, 0.07 million will show up as a translation loss and will be reflected in the bank's equity account (not shown here).

The asset/liability management of this bank's exchange-rate exposure is conceptually quite simple. The bank should borrow lira to fund lira loans and the bank should borrow sterling to fund sterling loans. Dollar borrowings should be reserved for funding dollar loans. By matching the currency denomination of liabilities to the currency denomination of the assets, the bank eliminates a large portion of its exchange-rate exposure. A simplified breakdown of the bank's balance sheet by currency appears as Table 4.6.

The asset/liability **currency-matching** strategy does not completely eliminate the bank's exchange-rate exposure. The bank still bears the risk associated with the ultimate repatriation of its profits from its global activities. But, this exposure is very small compared to the nonmatched strategy depicted in Table 4.5.

For institutions with exchange-rate exposures, which includes global banks like the one above and multinational corporations, there are usually interest-rate exposures as well. These can also be managed with immunization techniques. For example, the global bank could use the currency-matching strategy to solve its exchange-rate exposure and, within each currency, use an immunization strategy to manage its interest-rate exposure—just as the pension fund did.

As a closing point to this section on asset/liability management, we should mention that immunization strategies and currency-matching strategies are not necessarily the best way to manage interest-rate risk and exchange-rate risk. Such strategies often require the sacrifice of

TABLE 4.6
Global Bank's Balance Sheet (by currency)
(one day activity)
(all values in millions)

Assets		Liabilities	
		Sterling	
Loans	2.50	Demand deposits	1.30
		Time deposits	1.20
Total BP assets	2.50	Total BP liabilities	2.50
		Lira	
Loans	1,480.00	Demand deposits	330.00
		Time deposits	1,150.00
Total IL assets	1,480.00	Total IL liabilities	1,480.00
		Dollar	
Loans	12.40	Demand deposits	3.56
		Time deposits	8.84
Total USD assets	12.40	Total USD liabilities	12.40

better, more profitable, opportunities. For this reason, hedging strategies can sometimes prove superior. Such strategies are discussed in the next section.

4.4.3 Hedging

Although closely related to asset/liability management and often used in conjunction with asset/liability management, hedging is a distinct activity. A hedge is a position that is taken as a temporary substitute for a later position in another asset (liability) or to protect the value of an existing position in an asset (liability) until the position can be liquidated. Most hedging is done in off-balance sheet instruments. The instruments most often used for hedging are forwards, futures, options, and, of course, swaps. It is important to note, however, that a hedge can take the form of an on-balance sheet position. This is often the case, for example, when swap dealers hedge their swaps in Treasury bonds and bills. The key, in this case, is the temporary nature of the cash market hedge.

We will discuss forwards, futures and options in the next two chapters. The remainder of the book is devoted to swaps. For now, we need to focus on the underlying theory of hedging rather than the instruments used to hedge.

Consider once again the standard risk profile. For illustration, we will consider a West German firm's exposure to exchange-rate risk. This firm's long position in dollars stems from a $500,000 T-bill it owns that matures in 30 days. The risk profile appears as Exhibit 4.7. Note that value change, which for consistency we will henceforth call "profit," is on the vertical axis and price, in this case the DM/USD 30-day forward exchange rate, is on the horizontal axis.

The upward sloping nature of this risk profile suggests that the German firm's exposure stems from a long forward position in dollars. That is, an increase in the DM/USD 30-day forward rate represents a

EXHIBIT 4.7.   Risk Profile—Exchange Rate

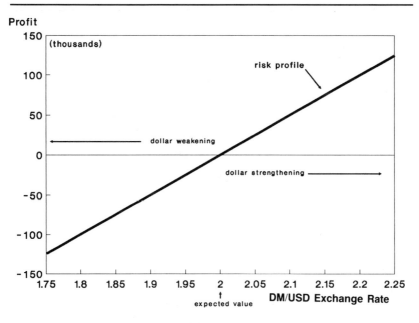

strengthening of the dollar vis-á-vis the deutschemark. The German firm benefits from any such strengthening. On the other hand, the German firm will suffer financially from any weakening of the dollar.

The slope of the risk profile suggests something about the extent of the German firm's exposure but it does not tell the whole story. The other consideration is the degree of volatility of the DM/USD exchange rate. This volatility is measured, as we argued earlier in this chapter, by the standard deviation of the exchange rate (price). Suppose that one standard deviation, for a 30-day period, is 0.0625 DM/USD and that the exchange rate is approximately normally distributed. Given this knowledge, we can translate the exchange-rate risk into a dollar exposure risk. This is depicted in the three panels of Exhibit 4.8.

This three-panel approach is easy to understand. Panel A is the same risk profile depicted in Exhibit 4.7. Panel B depicts a normal distribution for the 30-day forward exchange rate. By using the properties of the normal distribution, we can make confidence interval

EXHIBIT 4.8. Panel A

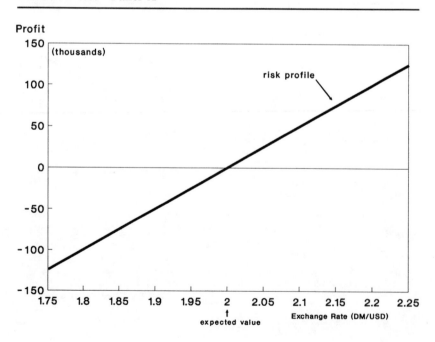

EXHIBIT 4.8. Panel B

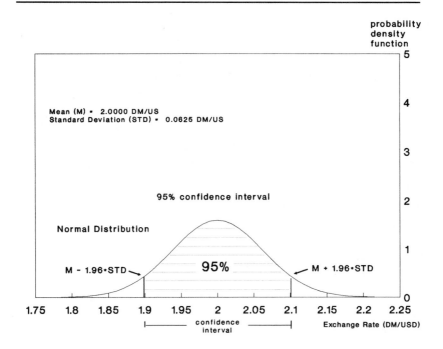

EXHIBIT 4.8. Panel C

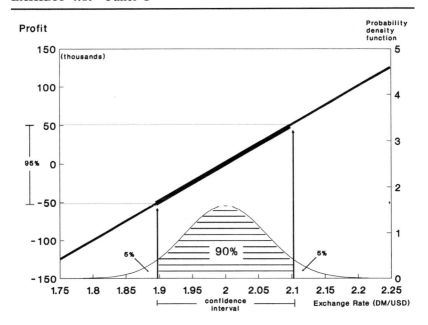

151

statements, conduct hypothesis tests, and determine the probabilities of the exchange rate falling outside of any specific range.

A **confidence interval** is a range of values symmetrically distributed around the expected value that captures a specified probability for the actual outcome. The probability is called the **confidence level** and the range of values is called the confidence interval. For example, a 90 percent confidence interval is given by the range that begins with the "expected value plus 1.64 standard deviations" and ends with the "expected value less 1.64 standard deviations." A 95 percent confidence interval is given by the expected value plus 1.96 standard deviations to the expected value less 1.96 standard deviations. In statistical work, the expected value is often called the **mean**. We will suppose that the mean exchange rate, as represented by the current 30-day forward rate, is 2.0000 DM/USD.

To return to Panel B, since the mean is 2.0000 and a standard deviation is 0.0625, the 90 percent confidence interval is (1.8975, 2.1025). This is calculated as the mean (2.0000) less 1.64×0.0625 to the mean (2.0000) plus 1.64×0.0625. Panel B depicts this confidence interval. Now, if we superimpose the confidence interval in Panel B on the risk profile in Panel A, we can determine the 90 percent confidence interval for the firm's profit. This is depicted in Panel C. We conclude that, for this firm, the 90 percent confidence interval for value change is the range DM $-51,250$ to DM $51,250$.

The nice feature of this approach to assessing risk exposure is that the standard deviation of the price change, for whatever price being considered, is the same for any and all firms. The risk profile, on the other hand, is unique to each firm. By combining the two, we convert a standard measure of risk to a firm-specific measure of risk.

There are other, more quantitative, ways to look at this same relationship.[9] For example, we can calculate the value impact on the firm from a one unit change in price. In the preceding example, this would be DM 500,000 per 1 DM/USD. This value can then be multiplied by the standard deviation of DM/USD exchange rate.

$$\text{Profit Risk} = \frac{\text{Value per}}{\text{Price Unit}} \times \begin{array}{c} \text{Standard Deviation} \\ \text{of the Price} \\ \text{(price risk)} \end{array} \qquad \textbf{(4.7)}$$

For our German firm, this is:

$$= DM\ 500,000 \div 0.0625\ DM/USD$$

$$= DM\ 31,250$$

The value DM 31,250 is then the profit risk, stated in terms of a standard risk measure (one "standard deviation" or one "unit of volatility"), that is specific for this firm. This firm-specific profit risk can be converted to a confidence interval by using the same properties of the normal distribution. For example, the 90 percent confidence interval is the mean, now equal to zero, plus and minus 1.64 times 31,250 (a standard deviation). This interval covers all values from DM −51,250 to DM +51,250. It can be seen that this is the range of values on the vertical axis covered by the bolder portion of the risk-profile depicted in Panel C of Exhibit 4.8 and it is also equal to the range of profit values we generated using the first approach.

As already defined, a hedge is a position taken as a temporary substitute for another position or, a position taken to protect the value of another position until the first position can be terminated. While the position to be hedged gives rise to a "risk profile," the hedge itself gives rise to a **payoff profile**. Payoff profiles and risk profiles are actually the same thing. The latter term is used to emphasize the risk associated with holding a cash market position and the former is used to emphasize the "profit/loss" potential associated with holding the hedge instrument. The hedge eliminates risk if the risk profile and payoff profile are mirror images of one another.

Consider Exhibit 4.9. This exhibit depicts the payoff profile for a short position in 500,000 30-day forward dollars. The German firm in the preceding illustration arranged this forward contract through a German bank. That is, the firm agreed to the sale of $500,000 for delivery in 30 days. The agreed price on this exchange is 2.0000 DM/USD. If the dollar's value rises, the German firm stands to lose on its forward contract with the German bank. If the dollar's value falls, the German firm stands to benefit on its forward contract with the German bank.

Observe that in a payoff profile, "profit" is usually placed on the

EXHIBIT 4.9. **Payoff Profile**
(Forward sale of USD for DM)

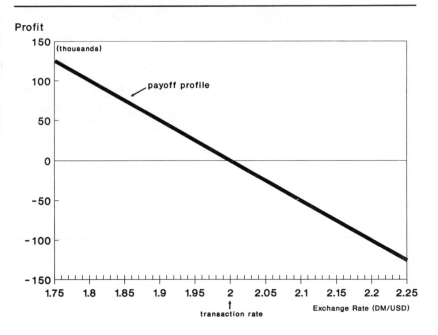

vertical axis. Nothing is lost, however, if "profit" is interpreted as a value change. This representation makes the risk profile and the payoff profile directly comparable. As we mentioned before, however, we will henceforth refer to "value changes" as profit. Profit, in this sense, is any value deviation from the expected value.

Notice that the German firm's payoff profile on the forward position with the bank and the risk profile on its forward position from its T-bill are mirror images of each other. These are depicted on the same graph in Exhibit 4.10, Panel A. Since a payoff profile is itself a risk profile, the forward position with the bank represents a second risk exposure, but one that is opposite that of the original exposure. This offsetting of risks is the key to successful hedging. A hedge creates a second risk equal to, but opposite, that of the original exposure. The two exposures are then offsetting and the end result is no net risk. This is depicted by the flat exposure line, representing net risk in Panel B of Exhibit 4.10.

EXHIBIT 4.10. Risk Profile and Payoff Profile—Panel A

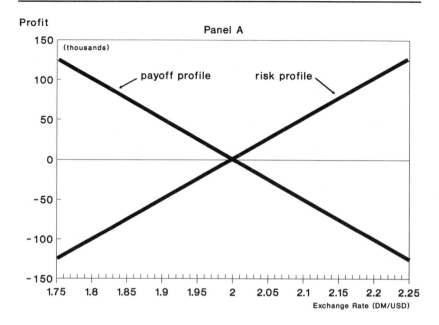

EXHIBIT 4.10. Residual Risk Profile—Panel B

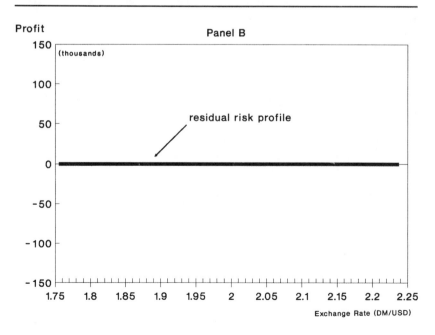

The approach taken above considers any deviation from the expected outcome to be a manifestation of price risk. When management wishes to hedge this risk in this way, forward contracts, futures contracts, and swaps can be used to formulate the hedge. But, often, management only wants to formulate a hedge to cancel the downside risk. That is, management wants to construct a hedge that protects the firm from unfavorable price changes but that still permits the firm to benefit from favorable price changes. Such hedges can be engineered with the use of options and options coupled with other hedging instruments. These considerations and instruments are examined more carefully in the next two chapters.

There are three hedging considerations that need to be addressed before closing this chapter. The first involves the size of a hedge, the second involves the effectiveness of a hedge, and the third involves the cost of a hedge. The size of a hedge is measured relative to the size of the cash position to be hedged. This relative measure is called the hedge ratio. The effectiveness of a hedge is measured by the degree to which the hedge reduces the price risk to which the firm is exposed. The forward hedge we used to manage the German firm's exposure to exchange-rate risk seems to have been perfectly effective, and indeed it was. But not all hedges are that perfect. Sometimes a hedge eliminates some of the risk but not all of the risk. The cost of a hedge is the degree to which the hedge reduces the firm's expected profit.

4.4.3.1 SIZE OF THE HEDGE

The number of units of the hedging instrument necessary to fully hedge one unit of the cash position is called the **hedge ratio**. For example, if on average it takes two units of five-year T-note futures to offset the risk exposure from one unit of corporate debt, then the hedge ratio is 2:1. (We discussed the most often used procedure for determining hedge ratios for debt positions in Chapter 2.) For currency positions, the hedge ratio is always 1:1 when hedging in a futures or forwards on the same currency. For commodity-price risk and stock-price risk, the hedge ratios are more complex. The reader interested in pursuing this subject further should refer to the appropriate reference material at the end of this chapter.[10] For the remainder of our discussion, we assume that the correct hedge ratio is always used.

4.4.3.2 EFFECTIVENESS OF A HEDGE

The degree of correlation between two prices represents the closeness with which their movements track one another. The correlation is measured with the aid of a statistic called the **correlation coefficient**. Correlation coefficients always lie in the range of negative one, called **perfect negative correlation**, to positive one, called **perfect positive correlation**. We will denote the correlation coefficient by ϵ. Assuming that the appropriate hedge ratio is employed, the risk that remains after a hedge is placed is called **basis risk**. The relationship between basis risk (when measured as a variance) and price risk (when measured as a variance) is given by Equation 4.8.

$$\text{Basis risk} = (1 - \epsilon^2) \cdot \text{Price Risk} \qquad \textbf{(4.8)}$$

Notice that Equation 4.8 employs the square of the correlation coefficient rather than the correlation coefficient. This squared value is called the **coefficient of determination.** It is an exact measure of the percentage of the original risk that is removed by the hedge. For example, suppose ϵ^2 is 0.87, then, the hedge will reduce the price risk by 87 percent. Of course, 13 percent of the original risk will remain. This remaining part is the basis risk.

Hedgers are often interested in the source of basis risk. By better understanding its source, one gains insights into how to construct better hedges. Basis risk exists because the cash price and the price of the hedging instrument are not perfectly correlated. This is so because the demand and supply conditions in the cash market may evolve somewhat differently than the demand and supply conditions in the market for the hedging instrument. The prices cannot ordinarily stray too far from one another without giving rise to arbitrage opportunities. But the prices can stray to some degree without giving rise to profitable arbitrage opportunities and so some basis risk will exist. Consider, for example, a corporate investor's efforts to hedge his or her planned three-month commercial paper issue in a three-month T-bill futures contract. The bills and the paper have the same maturity and their rates tend to track each other fairly closely—although paper rates are always at a premium to bill rates. The tracking isn't perfect as illustrated in Exhibit 4.11 and so the firm that hedges its planned paper issues in bill futures will bear some basis risk.

EXHIBIT 4.11. Commercial Paper Rate versus T-bill Rate

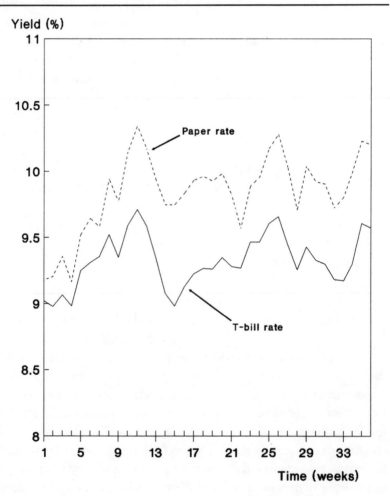

4.4.3.3 COST OF A HEDGE

The final consideration to be addressed before closing this chapter is the cost of a hedge. There is a great deal of literature on the subject of the cost of hedging. The general consensus is that hedging is relatively cheap but not free. There are two good reasons not to expect hedging to be costless.

First, the risk that hedgers seek to shed when they take on a hedge must be borne by the counterparty to the hedge contract. If the counterparty is another hedger with a mirror image exposure, then both hedgers enjoy some benefit and we would not expect either to have to compensate the other. But, more often, the counterparty to the contract is a speculator. The speculator is taking a position in order to earn a speculative profit. If speculation is privately costly to the speculator (resources expended) and if speculators are risk averse, then we would expect speculators to require compensation for their risk-bearing services. To the extent that speculators are compensated for risk bearing, hedgers must bear the cost.

The second reason for expecting hedging not to be costless is the presence of transaction costs. Every trade involves some transaction costs in the form of a commission, a bid-ask spread, or both.

Although hedging is not costless, not all hedges will be equally costly. It may be, due to inefficiencies in the market, that one type of hedge is less costly than another. Furthermore, the relative costs may change from one day to the next so that the cheaper hedge today might not be the cheaper hedge tomorrow. The prudent hedger compares the cost of alternative hedging strategies before committing to one.

The upshot of these closing remarks is that the hedger must consider both the effectiveness of the hedge and the cost of the hedge. Together, these factors determine the **efficiency of the hedge**. **Efficient hedges** are those that provide maximum risk reduction per unit of cost. From among the set of available efficient hedges, the hedger must select the optimal one. The **optimal hedge** is that which maximizes the hedger's utility—as this term is used in economics. Consider the five hedges depicted in Exhibit 4.12.

Notice that Hedge C is **inefficient** compared to Hedge A because

EXHIBIT 4.12.   Efficient versus Inefficient Hedges

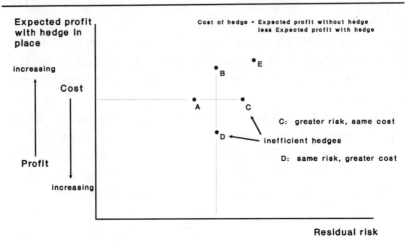

Hedge C is less effective than Hedge A at the same cost. Notice also that Hedge D is inefficient compared to Hedge B because Hedge D is more costly than Hedge B while only equally effective. The efficient hedges then are Hedges A, B, and E.

The hedger who derives positive utility from reducing risk and negative utility from paying the cost must choose a hedge so as to balance these competing considerations. The hedge that maximizes the user's utility is then the optimal hedge. Importantly, the optimal hedge for one hedger may not be optimal for another hedger. This is a reflection of the individual's own, very personal, utility function. The selection of a hedge must consider these differences.

There has been some confusion in recent literature concerning the meaning of the terms "effectiveness," "efficiency," and "optimality," as these terms have been applied to hedging theory. The distinctions become exceedingly important when composite hedging is considered. A **composite hedge** is a hedge that involves more than one hedging instrument. The advantage of composite hedging is that such a hedge can reduce the basis risk otherwise associated with simple hedges. (An article by Tony Herbst and Jack Marshall dealing with these issues, and the mathematics of composite hedging in the context of futures, appears at the end of this chapter. The interested reader may wish to consider it. Those unfamiliar with futures contracts may find it helpful to read Chapter 5 before reading the appendix to Chapter 4.)

4.5 SUMMARY

Price risk is the potential for a future price to deviate from its expected value. Price risk itself is measured with the aid of a statistic called variance or, its square root, which is called standard deviation. It is quite common to refer to a standard deviation as a volatility unit.

Price risks exist independently of individual firm's exposures. But, individual firms are exposed to price risks. The extent of an exposure, however, will vary considerably from one firm to another. Such exposures must be identified and measured.

There are a number of useful and well-established tools for measuring the extent of a firm's exposure to a price risk. One way is to use a risk profile. A risk profile is a graphic depiction of the relationship between the change in a firm's value (which we will henceforth call profit), and the changing price that gives rise to this profit. With the aid of a distributional assumption, such as the assumption that a price is normally distributed, we can convert the price risk to a profit risk. That is, we can determine a particular confidence interval so that we know the range of values that profit may assume with any desired degree of confidence.

Financial risks, of which price risk is just one form, can be managed in several ways. Some financial risks can be managed by the purchase of insurance. Risks that can be managed in this way are said to be insurable. Most price risks, however, are not insurable. For these risks, the sophisticated manager will employ either or both asset/liability management techniques or hedging strategies. These strategies are very closely related but the former usually involves on-balance sheet positions and the latter usually involves off-balance sheet positions.

Asset/liability management techniques are most highly developed for the management of interest-rate risk. Two such techniques are cash flow matching strategies and immunization strategies. Asset/liability management is also used to manage exchange-rate exposures. In this case, we attempt to match our assets in each currency with liabilities in the same currencies.

Although very useful, asset/liability management is not a complete answer to the exposure problem. In many cases, an asset/liability approach to risk management will result in the loss of more attractive investment or financing alternatives. In addition, asset/liability management strategies often take some time to implement. In either case, the manager should consider hedging strategies. A hedge is a position taken as a temporary substitute for a position in a cash asset (liability) or to offset the risk associated with holding a cash asset (liability) until the position is liquidated. The instruments most widely used for hedging are futures contracts, forward contracts, options contracts, and swaps. Collectively, these instruments are often called derivative instruments.

REFERENCES AND SUGGESTED READINGS

Brown, K.C. and D.J. Smith, "Recent Innovations in Interest Rate Risk Management and the Reintermediation of Commercial Bank Lending," *Financial Management*, 17(4) (Winter 1988).

Hodges, S.D. and S.M. Schaefer, "A Model For Bond Portfolio Improvement," *Journal of Financial and Quantitative Analysis*, 12(2), pp. 243–260 (1977).

Liebowitz, M.L. "How Financial Theory Evolves into the Real World-Or Not: The Case of Duration and Immunization," *Financial Review*, 18(4), pp. 271–280 (1983).

———— "Total Portfolio Duration: A New Perspective on Asset Allocation," *Financial Analysts Journal*, 42(5), pp. 18–29 (1986a).

———— "The Dedicated Bond Portfolio In Pension Funds—Part I: Motivations and Basics," *Financial Analysts Journal*, 42(1), pp. 68–75 (1986b).

———— "The Dedicated Bond Portfolio In Pension Funds—Part II: Immunization, Horizon Matching, and Contingent Procedures," *Financial Analysts Journal*, ·42(2), pp. 47–57 (1986c).

Marshall, J.F. *Futures and Option Contracting: Theory and Practice*, Cincinnati, OH: South-Western (1989).

Redington, F.M. "Review of the Principle of Life Office Valuations," *Journal of the Institute of Actuaries*, 18, pp. 286–340 (1952).

Schaefer, S. M. "Immunization and Duration: A Review of Theory, Peformance and Applications," in *The Revolution in Corporate Finance*, J.M. Stern and D.H. Chew (eds.), Oxford, UK: Blackwell (1986).

Wade, R. E. "Managing a Negative Gap in a Rising Interest Rate Environment," *Financial Managers' Statement*, 9(4), 33–37 (Jul 1987).

ENDNOTES

[1] In the language of statistics, we would say that the marginal and conditional probabilities are the same.

[2] Technically, the shareholders of a mutual fund have an equity interest in the fund and, therefore, their claims are not liabilities. But, the concept is the same. The value of the assets is fixed in relation to the value of the claims on those assets. In this case, the value is fixed by defining, on a daily basis, a **net asset value** (NAV) for the fund's shares. The NAV is equal to the per share value of the fund's holdings less the per share value of the fund's liabilities.

[3] For a more detailed discussion of dedicated portfolios, see Hodges and Schaefer (1977) and Liebowitz (1986a, 1986b, 1986c)

[4] See Redington (1952).

[5] See Schaefer (1986).

[6] These duration values were determined using the financial analytics package A-Pack. A more detailed discussion of A-Pack can be found in the footnotes to Chapter 2.

[7] Any adjustment in the size of positions will have an effect on profitability. For example, the adjustment might result in an increase in 30-year bond holdings and a decrease in six-month bill holdings, or the adjustment might require a less-than-full investment of the proceeds from the sale of policies—allowing the fund to direct the remaining proceeds elsewhere.

[8] For further discussion of the empirical performance of the Redington model versus other, more sophisticated models, see Schaefer (1986).

[9] For a thorough discussion of the theory of hedging together with the mathematical detail, see Marshall (1989), Chapter 7 with applications in later chapters.

[10] Ibid., Chapters 7 and 10 through 13.

Effectiveness, Efficiency, and Optimality in Futures Hedging: An Application of Portfolio Theory

*Anthony F. Herbst and John F. Marshall**

Recent papers have attempted to offer measures of futures hedge effectiveness which improve on the coefficient of determination offered by Johnson[1] and popularized by Ederington.[2] In some cases, these papers have confused effectiveness with efficiency and, in others, they have confused effectiveness with optimality.[3] Thus, there appears to be a serious definitional problem when it comes to defining hedge effectiveness. This appendix, does two things:

1. it demonstrates the importance of distinguishing among effectiveness, efficiency, and optimality when discussing a futures hedge; and

2. it offers a very practical extension of portfolio theory to futures hedging which we call composite hedging.

A composite hedge is distinguished from the simple hedge of traditional hedging theory in that the former allows for multiple hedge instruments while the latter is limited to a single hedge instrument. In this sense, the composite hedge generalizes the simple hedge.

We begin with a review of basic hedging theory and then develop the composite hedge. In the process, the importance of distinguishing among the aforementioned concepts is shown. We then summarize and conclude.

---

*Anthony Herbst is Professor of Finance in the College of Business Administration of the University of Texas at El Paso. Professor Herbst holds the C.R. and D.S. Carter Chair. John Marshall is Associate Professor of Economics and Finance in the College of Business Administration of St. John's University, New York.

BASIC HEDGING THEORY

The purpose of a hedge is defined to be risk reduction. That is, a hedge is put on in order to reduce the risk associated with a cash position or an anticipated cash position. Any other motivation is either speculation or arbitrage. For purposes of this paper, it is assumed that the hedger is a producer with no quantity risk who holds a long cash position. The concept of a producer is very general and includes any firm which adds value through production, conversion, storage, or transport. Production of quantity q is undertaken at time t with a cash market sale planned for time T. The cost of production, denoted $C(q)$, is known at time t. The spot price at time T, which is not known at time t, is denoted P_T.

The risk inherent in a cash position can be stated either as a per-unit price risk or in terms of dollar profit on the overall position. When defined as a per-unit price risk, the appropriate measure of risk is the variance of the time T spot price as perceived at time t. When defined on overall profit, the appropriate measure of risk is the variance of profit on the cash position.

The producer's profit on unhedged production, denoted π, is related to the time T spot price by Equation 4.A.1.

$$\pi = P_T \cdot q - C(q) \qquad \textbf{(4.A.1)}$$

Since P_T is not known at time t, profit is uncertain. This uncertainty is the source of the producer's risk. This risk can be measured as the variance of profit which, it is easily shown, is a function of the variance of the spot price.[4] Let σ_P^2 denote the variance of the spot price and let σ_π^2 denote the variance of profit. Then, the variance of profit is related to the variance of price by Equation 4.A.2 and the expected profit is related to the expected price by Equation 4.A.3.

$$\sigma_\pi^2 = \sigma_P^2 \cdot q^2 \qquad \textbf{(4.A.2)}$$

$$E[\pi] = E[P_T] \cdot q - C(q) \qquad \textbf{(4.A.3)}$$

For any planned output q, profit can be plotted in standard risk/ return space, where return is defined as expected profit and risk is defined as the standard deviation of profit. This is depicted in Exhibit 4.A.1.

Now, let there be a futures-type hedging instrument which matures at time T. The time t price of this futures contract is denoted $F_{t,T}$. That is, $F_{t,T}$ is the price of the time T delivery futures at time t. For simplicity, we assume that the appropriate hedge ratio is $1:1$ and that a futures contract covers one unit of the cash asset.[5] Let the producer now hedge a portion of its output in futures. That is, the producer will sell futures at time t at price $F_{t,T}$ and offset these futures at time T at price $F_{T,T}$ (the classic short hedge). In particular, let the producer hedge x units of output by selling x futures short. The size of the hedge is bounded such that $q \geq x \geq 0$. The producer's profit on the hedged production, denoted π_H, is given by Equation 4.A.4.

$$\pi_H = P_T \cdot q + F_{t,T} \cdot x - F_{T,T} \cdot x - C(q) \qquad \textbf{(4.A.4)}$$

While $F_{t,T}$ is known at time T, $F_{T,T}$ is not. Equation 4.A.4 can be rewritten, after a little manipulation, as Equation 4.A.5.

EXHIBIT 4.A.1.   Producer Profit and Risk
                     (Unhedged position)

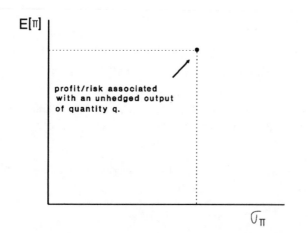

$$\pi_H = P_T \cdot (q - x) + (B_T + F_{t,T}) \cdot x - C(q) \quad \textbf{(4.A.5)}$$

where B_T is the time T basis. Basis is the difference between the spot and futures prices; that is, $B_T = P_T - F_{T,T}$. We now reconsider the expected profit and the risk associated with production but, this time, with the hedge in place. These values are given by Equations 4.A.6 and 4.A.7, respectively.

$$E[\pi_H] = E[P_T] \cdot (q - x) + (E[B_T] + F_{t,T}) \cdot x - C(q) \quad \textbf{(4.A.6)}$$

$$\sigma_{\pi H}^2 = \sigma_P^2 \cdot (q - x)^2 + \sigma_B^2 \cdot x^2 + \\ 2 \cdot (q - x) \cdot x \cdot \sigma_{P,B} \quad \textbf{(4.A.7)}$$

where σ_B^2 denotes the variance of the basis, and $\sigma_{P,B}$ denotes the covariance of the basis and the spot price. The basis at time T and the spot price at time T should be independent (as perceived at time t) and so the covariance between B_T and P_T is identically zero.[6] This reduces the complexity of Equation 4.A.7 which becomes:

$$\sigma_{\pi H}^2 = \sigma_P^2 \cdot (q - x)^2 + \sigma_B^2 \cdot x^2. \quad \textbf{(4.A.8)}$$

Consider now the risk/return space for the producer's profit. For purposes of illustration, we assume $E[B_T] + F_{t,T} < E[P_T]$.[7] When the producer chooses not to hedge at all, then $E[\pi_H] = E[\pi]$ and $\sigma_{\pi H}^2 = \sigma_\pi^2$ as in point A of Exhibit 4.A.2. If the producer chooses to hedge all production such that $x = q$, then the hedge outcome is given by point B. The difference in expected profit between points A and B represents the producer's cost of hedging. There is a cost to hedging because we assumed that $E[B_T] + F_{t,T} < E[P_T]$. This is a critical point, which will be returned to shortly.

It is important to note that the producer need not choose between the two extremes depicted in Exhibit 4.A.2. Indeed, x can take any value between zero and q. By varying the value x between these two extremes, we can map out the set of hedging possibilities available to the producer. These are depicted in Exhibit 4.A.3 together with the producer's indifference map which suggests that, at least for this producer, the optimal (utility maximizing) hedge is quantity x^*.

EXHIBIT 4.A.2. **Profit/Risk Trade-off as a Function of the Quantity Hedged**

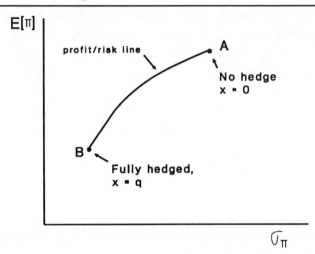

We now consider the cost of hedging. Remember the assumption $E[B_T] + F_{t,T} < E[P_T]$. Substituting for B_T the value $P_T - F_{T,T}$ (the definition of B_T), *we see that this assumption implies* $F_{t,T} - E[F_{T,T}] <$ 0. This is the source of the cost of hedging for a short hedger. It states that the cost of a hedge, as perceived at time t, is equal to the difference between the current futures price $F_{t,T}$ and the futures price

EXHIBIT 4.A.3. **The Optimal Profit/Risk Trade-off for a Risk Averse Utility Maximizer**

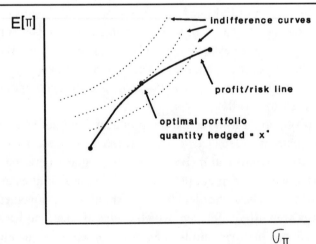

expected to prevail at the time the hedge is offset $E[F_{T,T}]$. This suggests that, contrary to many naive views on hedging, a producer cannot ignore his or her expectations as to the later futures price when formulating an optimal hedge (unless the producer holds the view that hedging is costless or very nearly so). Thus, the corollary: "Optimal futures hedging requires forecasting."

From this point on, discussion is restricted to those situations in which the producer practices routine and complete hedging. Such a situation will almost surely occur whenever $F_{t,T} - E[F_{T,T}]$ is greater than or equal to zero (implying a negative cost to hedge) and is still quite likely whenever $F_{t,T} - E[F_{T,T}]$ is negative but small. We shall assume that there is a cost to hedging for all available hedges.[8]

When hedging is complete, the variance of profit, given by Equation 4.A.8, reduces to Equation 4.A.9.

$$\sigma_{\pi H}^2 = \sigma_B^2 \cdot q^2 \tag{4.A.9}$$

Compare Equation 4.A.9, in which all output is hedged, with Equation 4.A.2, in which no output is hedged. Note that with complete hedging price risk is replaced by basis risk. This explains the view of those who have argued that "hedging is speculation in the basis."[9]

The obvious question can now be asked as to how one should measure the effectiveness of a futures hedge. Equations 4.A.9 and 4.A.2 are the keys. Johnson[10] showed that basis risk σ_B^2 is related to price risk σ_P^2 by Equation 4.A.10.

$$\sigma_B^2 = (1 - \epsilon^2) \cdot \sigma_P^2 \tag{4.A.10}$$

where ϵ is the coefficient of correlation between the spot price and the futures price. When squared, this value is often called the coefficient of determination and it is easily obtained as a by-product of a simple linear regression.[11] The coefficient of determination measures the fraction of the price risk (variance of the spot price) statistically "explained" by, and therefore eliminated by, the futures hedge. As expected, the value ϵ^2 must lie in the range of 0 to 1. When ϵ^2 is 1, the hedge is completely effective in the sense that no risk remains. When ϵ^2 is 0, the hedge is completely ineffective in the sense that risk has not been reduced at all. Clearly then, ϵ^2 is a logical measure of hedge effectiveness. This was Johnson's seminal contribution to hedging theory.

We can now define a hedge's effectiveness as the degree to which it reduces the risk associated with a cash position. *This definition deliberately ignores the cost of hedging.*

THE COMPOSITE HEDGE

We have seen that a futures hedge has the potential to increase a producer's utility by reducing the risk otherwise associated with a cash position. Since producers are risk averse (a critical working assumption in all financial theory), producers should enjoy a utility gain from hedging. However, hedges may be costly. To the degree that a hedge is costly, the hedge reduces producer profit with a concomitant reduction in producer utility.

The principal contribution of this paper is the consideration of hedging opportunities when more than one futures instrument is available for hedging a given cash position. A composite hedge is one which consists of multiple hedging instruments. The mathematics of composite hedging are a simple extension of portfolio theory but one which seems not to have been extensively considered thus far in the hedging literature.

To keep this presentation as simple and as intuitive as possible, we retain all of the assumptions made earlier and we add the following: The producer routinely hedges all output, the correct hedge ratio for each available hedge instrument (relative to the cash position) is $1:1$, and none of the instruments are perfect hedges in the sense that none are perfectly effective.[12] We denote the time t price of the ith futures by $F_{t,T}(i)$, for $i = 1, 2, 3, \ldots, n$; and we denote the ith basis by $B_T(i)$. We denote the correlation between the ith and the jth bases by $\epsilon(i,j)$, and we denote the correlation between the spot price and the ith futures by $\epsilon(i)$. The fraction of output hedged by instrument i is denoted $w(i)$ where $w(i) = x(i)/q$. And, where, as implied by the earlier assumption, $\Sigma\, w(i) = 1$.

The producer's profit when employing the composite hedge, denoted π_c, is then given by Equation 4.A.11.

$$\pi_c = q \cdot \sum_{i=1}^{n} w(i) \cdot [F_{t,T}(i) + B_T(i)] - C(q) \qquad \textbf{(4.A.11)}$$

The expected profit is given by Equation 4.A.12 and the variance of profit by Equation 4.A.13.

$$E[\pi_c] = q \cdot \sum w(i) \cdot \{F_{t,T}(i) + E[B_T(i)]\} - C(q) \qquad \textbf{(4.A.12)}$$

$$\sigma_\pi^2 = \sigma_P^2 \cdot q^2 \cdot [\sum w(i)^2 \cdot (1 - \epsilon(i)^2) + 2 \cdot \sum_{i>j} \sum w(i)$$

$$\cdot w(j) \cdot (1 - \epsilon(i)^2)^{1/2} \cdot (1 - \epsilon(j)^2)^{1/2} \cdot \epsilon(i,j)] \qquad \textbf{(4.A.13)}$$

While the right-hand side of Equation 4.A.13 seems rather formidable, it is actually a simple extension of modern portfolio theory. The term associated with the first summation (i.e., $\sum w(i) \cdot (1 - \epsilon(i)^2)$), constitutes unsystematic risk and the term associated with the double summation constitutes systematic risk. The source of the systematic and unsystematic components of total risk are the individual basis risks. That is, each basis risk consists of a systematic and an unsystematic component. As the composite hedge is expanded to bring in increasingly more hedging instruments, the unsystematic component of basis risk vanishes and the systematic component converges to the average covariance among the bases of the different hedging instruments.

Unlike other applications of portfolio theory, however, there are relatively few instruments to be combined in developing a composite hedge. For example, a corporate bond underwriter might hedge in a combination of Treasury note and Treasury bond futures; a commercial paper dealer might hedge in certificate of deposit, Treasury bill, and Eurodollar futures; an equities portfolio manager might hedge in Major Market Index, Standard & Poor's 500, New York Stock Exchange Composite, and Value Line futures; a farmer might have three wheat futures available; and so on. The point is that the typical composite hedge might contain from two to five different futures, rarely more. Given this limited availability of hedging instruments, we cannot treat unsystematic risk in a composite hedge the way we treat it in other applications of portfolio theory. Limited opportunity for diversification is such that this risk, although reduced, simply does not vanish in its entirety.

The composite hedge is best illustrated graphically. Suppose that there are three futures, 1, 2, and 3, which can be combined to formulate composite hedges. A complete hedge in a single instrument, that is, $w(i) = 1$, is depicted in Exhibit 4.A.4 for each of the three possible simple hedges. These are denoted H_1, H_2, and H_3, respectively.

Note that hedges H_1, H_2, and H_3 all have different risk/return characteristics. H_1 is the most effective in that it reduces risk the most. Unfortunately, it is also the most costly. H_2 is less effective but also less costly. H_3 is more costly than H_2 *and* less effective than H_2. H_3 is clearly an inefficient hedge. At first glance, H_1 and H_2 appear to be efficient hedges. Indeed, this has been the position of traditional hedging theory. However, the conclusion is premature.

Suppose that the three hedge instruments are combined using every conceivable combination of weights. The resultant set of feasible hedges is depicted in Exhibit 4.A.5. Note that simple hedge H_1 is now also inefficient in the sense that there are superior composite hedges.

EXHIBIT 4.A.4.   Three Simple Hedges

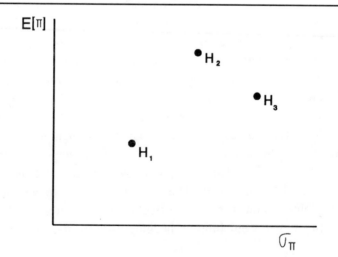

EXHIBIT 4.A.5.   The Feasible Set and the Efficient Set

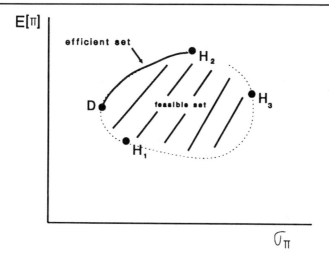

One can now see the importance of distinguishing between an effective hedge and an efficient hedge. *A hedge is effective if it reduces risk relative to no hedge. A hedge is efficient if there does not exist another hedge offering greater expected profit with the same or less risk.* Equivalently, a hedge is efficient if there does not exist another hedge offering less risk with the same or greater expected profit. The

EXHIBIT 4.A.6.   The Optimal Composite Hedge

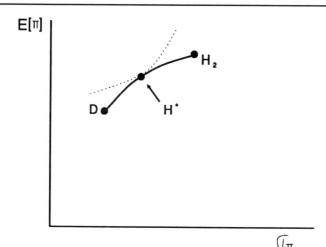

collection of efficient hedges, line DH_2 in Exhibit 4.A.5, is the efficiency frontier.

As a final step, we superimpose the producer's indifference map to find the optimal composite hedge just as we find an optimal portfolio. This is done in Exhibit 4.A.6. In this case, hedge H^* is found to be optimal. Thus, the optimal hedge is that composite hedge which maximizes the producer's utility.

As defined here, the terms effectiveness, efficiency, and optimality are completely consistent with traditional portfolio theory. This has not always been true of other uses of these same terms.

SUMMARY AND CONCLUSION

Many researchers in recent years have tried to improve on Johnson's measure of hedge effectiveness but, in so doing, they have confused critical definitions. This appendix has sought to show the need to distinguish between effectiveness, efficiency, and optimality when discussing hedges. The importance of these distinctions becomes apparent only when it is realized that hedge performance can be enhanced by taking a composite hedging approach. While research has largely ignored the potential benefits from composite hedging, portfolio theory suggests that the benefits can be considerable. Additionally, this appendix has introduced the mathematics of composite hedging. As one would expect, the simple hedges of traditional hedging theory are special cases of composite hedges. As the mathematics demonstrates, simple hedges may be inferior to composite hedges and producers should consider the potential of composite hedging for improving hedge performance.

ENDNOTES

[1] See L.L. Johnson, "The Theory of Hedging and Speculation in Commodity Futures," *Review of Economic Studies.* 27: 139–151 (1960).

[2] See L. Ederington, "The Hedging Performance of the New Futures Markets," *Journal of Finance*, 34: 157–170 (1979).

[3]Examples of papers which have used the terms "effectiveness" and "efficiency" synonymously include C. Howard and L. D'Antonio, "A Risk-Return Measure of Hedging Effectiveness," *Journal of Financial and Quantitative Analysis*, 19: 101–112 (1984), and J.S.K. Chang and L. Shanker, "A Risk-Return Measure of Hedging Effectiveness: A Comment," *Journal of Financial and Quantitative Analysis*, 22: 373–376, (1987). A very recent example that has used the terms "effectiveness" and "optimality" synonymously is J.S.K. Chang and H. Fang, "The Hedging Effectiveness of Stock Index Futures: An Intertemporal Risk-Return Approach," Financial Management Association Meetings, Boston, (October 1989).

[4]See J.F. Marshall, *Futures and Option Contracting: Theory and Practice*, Cincinnati: South-Western (1989).

[5]Nothing is lost by the assumption of a 1 : 1 hedge ratio. As shown in Marshall, Chapter 7, any hedge instrument can be redefined in such a fashion as to force a hedge ratio of 1 : 1. Specifically, if the appropriate hedge ratio is b and if the hedge instrument is redefined such that 1 unit of the "adjusted" instrument equals b units of the "unadjusted" instrument then the hedge ratio between the spot and the adjusted futures is 1 : 1. The "adjusted" futures price, F^*, is related to the unadjusted futures price by $F^* = b \cdot F$. All subsequent references to futures hedges assume the use of "adjusted" instruments.

[6]The argument for independence is simple. The expected value of the maturity basis, using the redefined hedge instrument described in footnote 5 ($B = P - F^*$), is the same irrespective of the level of the spot price at maturity. Thus, the spot price at maturity and the maturity basis are independent and the covariance between them is zero. This argument ignores the implications of convergence between spot and futures prices. In the presence of convergence, the covariance may not be zero. As a practical matter, however, it should still be small. The actual significance is an empirical issue which we do not address here.

[7]It need not be that $E[B_T] + F_{t,T} < E[P_T]$, but, as we will demonstrate shortly, in any other situation hedging would be complete and the example trivial.

[8]Many empirical studies have failed to find any systematic bias in $F_{t,T}$ which has led most investigators to conclude that $F_{t,T}$ is an unbiased estimator of P_T and, by implication, an unbiased estimator of $F_{T,T}$. If so, $F_{t,T} - E[F_{T,T}]$ should be zero. Others have found some systematic bias indicating a cost to hedging, but, in general, this bias has been small. For a review of these studies see Marshall, Chapter 9.

[9]The view that hedging is "speculation in the basis," was first expressed by H. Working, "Futures Trading and Hedging," *American Economic Review*, 43 (1953).

[10]Johnson, "The Theory of Hedging and Speculation in Commodity Futures."

[11]The regression requires that the spot price at time T be regressed against the T-delivery futures price at time T. That is, the regression has the form: $P_T = b \cdot F_{T,T} + a + e$. The R^2 value from this regression is the coefficient of determination. As a side point, the value b is the hedge ratio. Importantly, however, a simple linear regression is not always the best way to estimate a hedge ratio.

[12]The results obtained here are not obviated by the existence of perfectly effective hedges, but the illustration of the concepts involved would look somewhat different.

PART
TWO

THE INSTRUMENTS
AND THEIR USES

CHAPTER 5

Futures and Forwards

CHAPTER 6

Options: Calls, Puts, Caps, and Floors

CHAPTER 7

Corporate Objectives and the Structure of Swaps

CHAPTER 8

The Pricing of Swaps

5

Futures and Forwards

5.1 OVERVIEW

Futures and **forwards** are contracts made between two parties that call for some specific action, usually the delivery of some underlying asset, to take place at a later date. For this reason, they are often described as contracts for "deferred delivery." This definition distinguishes between contracts for deferred (or later) delivery and contracts for immediate delivery. The latter constitute spot contracts. The spot and forward markets together constitute the "cash markets."

Futures contracts differ from forward contracts in several important ways. First, futures contracts trade on futures exchanges while forward contracts trade in over-the-counter dealer-type markets.

Second, futures contracts are highly standardized—with all contract terms, except price, defined by the exchange on which they trade. Forward contracts are negotiated between the contracting parties with all contract terms subject to mutual agreement.

Third, a clearing association stands between the parties of a futures contract. As a result, counterparties' identities are irrelevant. In a forward contract, each party is directly responsible to the other and, consequently, the identities of the counterparties are critically important.

Fourth, futures markets (in the United States) are regulated by the **Commodity Futures Trading Commission** (CFTC). Regulations are very specific and detailed. Forward markets, in general, are not regulated.

Fifth, the financial integrity of the futures markets is protected by requiring each party to a contract to post a performance bond called **margin**. Through a daily marking-to-market process, with corresponding transfers of margin, each party to a contract is assured of the other party's performance. No such market-wide systematic margining requirement is employed in the forward markets. Consequently, market makers in the forward markets tend to limit their contracting to parties who are well-known to them. Finally, the institutional structure of futures contracts makes them very easy to terminate via a simple offsetting transaction. Forward contracts are much more difficult to terminate—in fact, termination is often not possible.

This chapter takes a closer look at the futures and forward markets. Its goal is to help the reader understand the instruments and their uses.

5.2 FUTURES

Futures are highly standardized contracts that call for either **deferred delivery** of some underlying asset or a final **cash settlement** based on some clearly defined rule. These contracts trade on organized **futures exchanges** with a **clearing association** that acts as a middleman between the contracting parties. The contract seller is called the **short** and the contract purchaser is called the **long**. Both parties post a performance bond, called margin, that is held by the clearing association. Margin transfers, called **variation margin**, are made daily in response to a **marking-to-market** process based on daily **settlement prices**.

Each futures contract has an associated month that represents the month of contract delivery or final settlement. Individual contracts are identified by their **delivery month**. Examples would include December corn and June T-bills. All contracts on the same underlying asset, that trade on the same exchange, and have the same delivery month are identical and constitute a **futures series**. Thus, all December corn contracts on the **Chicago Board of Trade** (CBOT) are part of the December series in corn. July corn contracts are part of the July series.

Margin requirements vary by the nature of the position held. If the position is a speculation without any type of risk-mitigating position, the margin might run as high as 5 to 7 percent of the contract's value. If the position is a speculation but the speculator is long one series and short another (called a **spread**), margin may be only 1 to 3 percent of contract value. If the position represents a hedge, margin will typically be in the 2 to 4 percent range.

The oldest futures exchange in the United States is the Chicago Board of Trade. For over a hundred years, the CBOT's market was limited to agricultural futures—mostly grains and the soybean complex. But, with the increased volatility in the financial markets, the CBOT and other futures exchanges began to make markets in financial futures. Today there are financial futures in debt instruments, called **interest-rate futures**; foreign-exchange rates, called **currency futures**; and equity derivatives, called **stock-index futures**.

Financial futures differ from commodity futures in several ways. Probably the most important is that many financial futures are not "deliverable" in the traditional sense. To make this clear, it is important to understand the delivery process associated with commodity futures. When a contract is deliverable, the actual delivery is restricted to a narrow delivery period. Within the bounds of the delivery period, the actual time of delivery is left to the discretion of the short. That is, the short notifies the clearing association that delivery will be made. The clearing association then assigns the delivery to a long. The long makes payment and the short turns over **warehouse receipts** that evidence ownership of the stored commodity.

Although the delivery process works, it is of limited use for two reasons. First, if the long or short is a hedger, the commodity hedged might not be exactly the same as that specified in the futures contract. Thus, if the hedger is short, the commodity might not be acceptable for delivery. If the hedger is long, the commodity to be delivered might not be exactly what the hedger needs. The second reason is that the delivery takes the form of the transfer of warehouse receipts from an approved warehouse. But only a limited number of warehouses are approved and they may not be conveniently situated.

For these reasons, very few futures contracts are actually delivered. Instead, hedgers take positions in futures as a temporary substitute for later cash market transactions. For example, a commodity producer who expects to "harvest" 5,000 units in July will short July futures covering 5,000 units of the commodity. Later, in July, when the producer harvests his production, the crop is sold in the local cash market and the futures contract is terminated by an offsetting transaction. This procedure allows the producer to hedge efficiently but not actually use the futures market for any transactions in the physical commodity. By holding the short position in futures while awaiting harvest, the producer "locks in" a harvest price. This converts the hedger's price risk to a much smaller basis risk. Basis risk is the risk that the cash price and the futures price at harvest (July) will differ by more or less than some expected amount.

The fact that very few futures contracts are actually delivered led many exchanges to consider eliminating the delivery feature altogether. To date, this has not happened in commodity futures. But, many of the financial futures were created as non-deliverable instruments. The stock-index futures and some of the interest-rate futures are examples. In lieu of delivery during a defined delivery period, these contracts are settled in cash on a specific **final settlement** date. Stock-index futures, for example, are settled in cash on the third Friday of the contract month. The final settlement amount is determined by the value of the underlying stock index at the time of the final settlement. Thus, final settlement is simply another marking-to-market where the final settlement price is the actual index value.

Some financial futures that do provide for delivery offer the short more than one instrument to deliver. Treasury bond futures are an example. These futures allow the short to select any of a number of different T-bond series for the actual delivery. Adjustment rules are required to "equalize" the values of the permissible delivery instruments. Nevertheless, at any given point in time, one approved delivery instrument may be cheaper to deliver than another. This has led to a great deal of study of the **cheapest-to-deliver** instruments. Studies have shown that T-bonds behave differently when they are the cheapest to deliver than when they are not.[1] Anyone involved in the government securities markets must consider these behaviors.

Traders continuously monitor the various deliverable T-bonds in order to determine which is the cheapest-to-deliver. As one bond moves into cheapest-to-deliver status and another bond moves out of cheapest-to-deliver status, profitable trading opportunities can arise. One bond, for example, may be the cheapest to deliver today while another may be the cheapest to deliver tomorrow. Strategies that exploit the cheapest-to-deliver status of a bond are forms of arbitrage—but they are not necessarily riskless. There are many option-like strategies, for example, that can be used to exploit relative value differentials created as individual bonds move into and out of the cheapest-to-deliver status. Table 5.1 depicts the cheapest-to-deliver T-bond on the CBOT's T-bond futures contract on 13 October 1988. Notice that, at the current futures price, the cheapest-to-deliver bond is the bond with a coupon of 7.25 percent and maturing in 2016. If, however, the yield on the T-bond futures were to decline by 33 bps, then the cheapest-to-deliver instrument would be the bond paying a 10.375 percent coupon and maturing in 2012.

In addition to their uses as hedging instruments, futures are also extremely efficient as speculative instruments. Margin requirements are a small percentage of contract value and this gives the speculator considerable **leverage**. A small percentage change in a futures price will result in a large percentage change in the value of the speculator's margin. Futures speculators look for this type of leverage. In addition to the leverage afforded by futures, speculators like these instruments because the transaction costs are very small relative to contract value and the markets are symmetric. The symmetry involves the ease with

TABLE 5.1
Treasury Bond Futures
(October 13, 1988)

	At Current Market	After 33 bp Decline
Futures price	89-04	92-14
Cheapest deliverable	TSY 7.25s '16	TSY 10.375s '12

Source: The First Boston Corporation

which either a short or a long position can be taken. Not all markets facilitate short positions as easily as do futures markets.

A final point involving margin is in order. Margin, as the term is used in futures, is a performance bond—not "equity" in the sense that margin is equity in stock and bond markets. Because its function is to guarantee performance, margin need not be tendered in the form of cash and only very small players would tender margin in the form of cash. Larger market players meet their margin requirements with T-bills or other forms of security. This feature is important because T-bills are interest-bearing assets. When the true purpose of margin is appreciated and margin is tendered in interest-bearing form, it is appropriate to view futures markets as markets in which a position can be taken without investment. Like swaps and other derivative instruments, futures positions are off-balance sheet. That is, they do not appear on either the asset side or the liabilities side of a balance sheet.

The role of the clearing association in futures contracting is very important. Futures trades involve two private parties usually acting through an agent on the floor of the exchange called a **floor broker**. Neither party, as a general rule, knows the identity of the opposing party to a trade. The very instant that the trade is made, however, the obligations of the two parties are replaced by matched obligations to the clearing association. That is, the long's obligation to the contract seller is replaced by an obligation to the clearing association and the clearing association assumes the short's obligation to the long. Similarly, the original short's obligation to his counterparty is replaced by an identical relationship with the clearing association. This intermediary role of the clearing association frees both of the contracting parties from any need to know the opposing trader's identity and from any worry about the financial integrity of the other party. The clearing association, on the other hand, is protected from price risk by the fact that it is always long and short an identical number of contracts; and it is protected from counterparty credit risk through the margining system.

There is much literature on the pricing performance of futures markets. Most academic literature has concluded that futures prices are **informationally efficient**. In the extreme, an efficient market is one in which prices *fully and instantaneously* reflect the value of all relevant information. In the case of futures prices, this would imply that futures prices are unbiased estimates of future spot prices and efficient indicators of true value given all known supply/demand influencing information. If correct, this theory would suggest that futures are a costless hedging instrument for those with a need to hedge price risk whether the price involved is a commodity price, an interest rate, an exchange rate, or a stock index.

There are problems with the argument that futures prices are fully and instantaneously efficient. Prices, be they futures prices or any others, are determined by the buying and selling activities of producers (hedgers), speculators, and arbitragers. The latter two groups are motivated by a desire to earn speculative profits. It is their competitive activity—gathering, processing, and reacting to information—that is the supposed source of market efficiency. But, if information is fully and instantaneously reflected in prices, then these groups could not earn profits except by random chance. It is inconsistent to believe that those responsible for market efficiency, after expending resources to gather and process costly information, would not be rewarded for their efforts. Speculators and arbitragers would, presumably, realize the absence of reward and withdraw from the market. But, if they withdrew from the market, how could the market continue to be efficient?

The only consistent argument, at least in the authors' opinion, is that markets are very efficient at pricing assets, including futures, but not perfectly so. There is just enough inefficiency that those who expend resources to gather and process information are rewarded for their efforts but not so much inefficiency that these rewards are either easy to earn or excessive. These arguments lead to what has been called an "equilibrium degree of inefficiency."[2]

While futures are used to hedge price risk, including commodity-price risk, equity-price risk, interest-rate risk and foreign-exchange risk, our concern in this book is primarily with the latter two forms of price risk. Let's consider a commercial interest that needs to hedge an interest-rate exposure. Suppose that it is currently May 15th and an industrial corporation's board is trying to decide whether or not to build a new production facility. The firm has a top investment grade rating and the firm's chief financial officer (CFO) would like to raise $50 million in new long-term debt capital. Specifically, the firm would sell 30-year mortgage bonds. In selling the idea to the firm's board, the CFO has argued that the current corporate yield curve for top invest-ment grade bonds suggests that the firm can sell its debt at par if it is willing to pay a coupon of 9.75 percent. Unfortunately, from the time the board approves the plan until the time the bonds can actually be sold will take some months. During this period, the firm's investment bank will undertake the required due diligence investigation, file the offering with the SEC, wait for approval from the SEC, and put together the underwriting syndicate. This will, in all likelihood, take anywhere from two to four months.

The CFO has had bad experiences as a result of "offering lags" after approval of new security issues by the firm's board. On one occasion, interest rates increased by 80 basis points between the time of the decision to go ahead with a financing and the actual public offering. The rise in rates increased the firm's cost of funds and demonstrated the extent of the interest-rate exposure associated with offering lags. The CFO assures the board that he or she can hedge the offering and greatly reduce the firm's interim exposure to shifts in the yield curve. On the strength of his or her word, the board approves the project and the financing plan.

The CFO notifies the firm's investment bank that the offering is a "go." The investment bankers say that the offering will be ready in three months (August). The CFO calculates the hedge requirements using a **dollar value basis point** (DVBP) model,[3] and chooses T-bond futures as the hedging instrument.

Suppose that thirty-year investment-grade corporate bond yields have a yield beta of 0.45 and, at an assumed yield of 9.75 percent and selling at par, have a DVBP of 0.096585. The T-bond futures, written on 20-year 8.00 percent T-bonds, in which the firm hedge will happen to be selling at par (100) and have a DVBP of 0.098891. To hedge the yield until the offering, the CFO calculates the hedge requirement using the DVBP model given by Equation 5.1.

$$FV_h = FV_c \times \frac{DVBP_c}{DVBP_h} \times \beta_y \qquad (5.1)$$

FV_h and FV_c denote the face value of the hedging instrument and the cash instrument (the firm's 30-year bond), respectively; $DVBP_h$ and $DVBP_c$ denote the dollar value of a basis point of the hedging instrument and the cash instrument, respectively; and β_y represents the yield beta.

Substituting for the values in Equation 5.1, the CFO finds the face value of the T-bonds required to hedge the offering to be $21.98 million.

$$FV_h = \$50 \text{ million} \times \frac{0.096585}{0.098891} \times 0.45$$

$$= \$21.98 \text{ million}$$

The CFO translates the face value of the hedge into the required number of futures using Equation 5.2. That is, the face value of the required hedge is divided by the face value of a single T-bond futures FV_f ($0.1 million).

$$N_f = \frac{FV_h}{FV_f} \tag{5.2}$$

$$= \frac{\$21.98 \text{ M}}{\$0.1 \text{ M}} = 219.8 \text{ futures}$$

Thus, the CFO sells 220 September T-bond futures.

To check that this was the correct course of action, consider what happens to the firm if corporate yields rise by 80 basis points by the time of the actual offering so that the firm commits itself to pay a semiannual coupon of 10.55 percent. The firm will then pay $200,000 more interest every six months than it would if rates stay at 9.75 percent. This $200,000 semiannual sum is found by multiplying $50 million by 80 basis points and then by multiplying the product by 0.5 since this is a semiannual amount. Using the new 10.55 percent coupon to discount this stream over a 30-year period produces a present value of $3.618 million. This means that the increase in yield, and, therefore, the increase in the coupon the firm must pay to sell its bonds at par, costs the firm the equivalent of $3.618 million. This sum is found using present value annuity arithmetic.[4]

Now consider the return on the firm's short position in 220 T-bond futures. If the corporate yield rose by 80 basis points, the T-bond yield should have risen by about 178 basis points. This is the information conveyed by the yield beta. What effect does this increase in T-bond yield have on the firm with a short position in T-bond futures equivalent to $22 million of T-bonds? The answer is obtained using the same bond valuation arithmetic discussed in Chapter 2 and repeated here as Equation 5.3. The present value of the bond, denoted PV_{bond}, is found as the sum of the present values of the individual cash flows, denoted $CF(t)$, using the bond's yield, denoted y, as the discount rate.

$$PV_{bond} = \sum_{t=1}^{2 \cdot N} CF(t) \times \left(1 + \frac{y}{2}\right)^{-t} \tag{5.3}$$

Equation 5.3 indicates that the T-bonds decline from par to about 84.495 percent of par. On $22 million of T-bond equivalents, this is equal to a market value change of about $3.411 million (the calculation appears below). Since bond values decline and the firm is short, this value accrues to the firm. Thus, while the actual issue of bonds by the firm costs the firm $3.618 million more than expected, the hedge offsets $3.411 million of the additional cost. The hedge, therefore, reduces the impact from yield changes considerably.

$$\text{Profit on hedge} = VPT \times NOP \times TPP \times NF$$

where VPT = Value per tick ($31.25).

NOP = Number of points by which price changed (100 − 84.495 = 15.505).

TPP = Ticks per point (32).

NF = Number of futures (220).

$$\text{Profit} = \$31.25 \times 15.505 \times 32 \times 220 \approx \$3,411,000.$$

A reasonable question to ask at this point is "why wasn't the hedge perfect?" That is, the loss of $3.618 million on the cash market commitment is only partially offset by the $3.411 million profit on the hedge. The answer is simple. The DVBP model provides a very accurate and effective hedge for relatively small changes in yields (1 basis point at a time). As the yields change, the DVBPs of the T-bond and the corporate bond both change but not necessarily by equal percentage amounts. Thus, as yields rise or fall from the level at which the DVBPs were calculated, the hedge becomes progressively less precise. This is not really a serious problem. In practice, a hedge can be periodically "adjusted" to reflect these DVBP changes. Only the hedger who fails to periodically recalculate and adjust is likely to experience the kind of "less than full offset" experienced by this hedger. A handy rule of thumb used by some risk managers is too recalculate the hedge after each 5 basis point change in yields. Periodic recalculation and adjustment of the size of the hedge introduces some additional cost in the form of commissions and back-office resources. From a purely practical perspective, any hedge strategy must consider these costs.

Ignoring the recalculation suggested above, let's now consider how the hedge performs in terms of the risk profiles and payoff profiles described in Chapter 4. Exhibit 5.1 depicts the firm's risk profile with respect to yield changes (over the period encompassed by the offering lag). Performance on the vertical axis is measured as the change in the present value of the future coupons the firm will have to pay starting with a coupon of 9.75 percent. As suggested in Chapter 4, we will call this performance value "profit."

The payoff profile from the hedge is depicted in Exhibit 5.2 assuming, as indicated, no adjustments to the hedge as yields change. Notice that we have defined the horizontal axis as the yield on the corporate bond rather than the yield on the T-bond. We made this adjustment, using the yield beta, in order to make the firm's risk profile and the payoff profile from the firm's futures hedge directly comparable.

Combining Exhibits 5.1 and 5.2, we obtain the residual risk profile from the hedge. This is depicted in Exhibit 5.3.

If the hedge were adjusted after each 5 basis point change in yields, the payoff profile would look like that depicted in Exhibit 5.4.

EXHIBIT 5.1. Risk Profile—Offering Lag

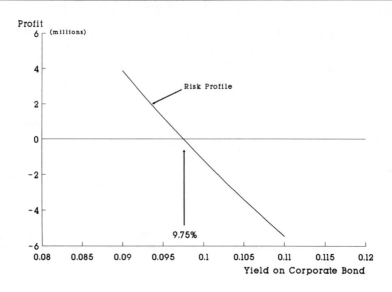

EXHIBIT 5.2. Payoff Profile—Hedge
(Short T-bond futures)

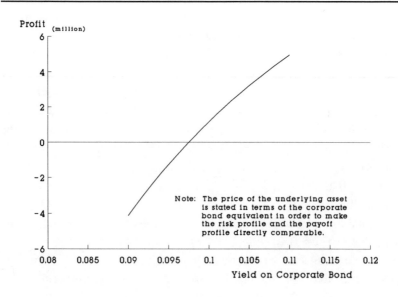

EXHIBIT 5.3.   Residual Risk Profile—Futures Hedge
(Risk profile + payoff profile)

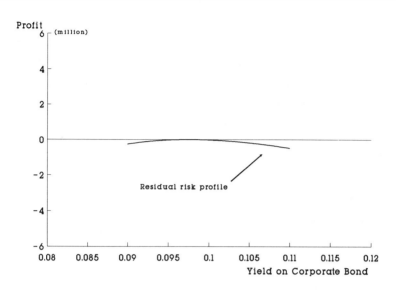

The unadjusted payoff profile is also depicted in Exhibit 5.4 to facilitate comparison.

Combining Exhibits 5.1 and 5.4, we get the residual risk profile for the hedger who recalculates and adjusts the hedge frequently. This is depicted in Exhibit 5.5. Notice that this "fine tuning" of the hedge has a favorable impact on residual risk and may be worth the extra effort.

The commercial firm in this example needed to hedge against the possibility of a rise in the level of interest rates. To do so, the hedger took a short position in interest-rate futures. This point will prove quite important later since the hedge position is reversed in certain types of forward contracts.

Exchange-rate risk is more easily managed than interest-rate risk. The reason is simple: The hedge ratio for a direct hedge is always, by definition, 1:1. The currency units of a given country are standardized. Thus, 1 currency unit of Country X to be received at some future point in time is identical to every other currency unit of Country

EXHIBIT 5.4. Payoff Profile of Adjusted Futures Hedge
(Relative to unadjusted hedge)

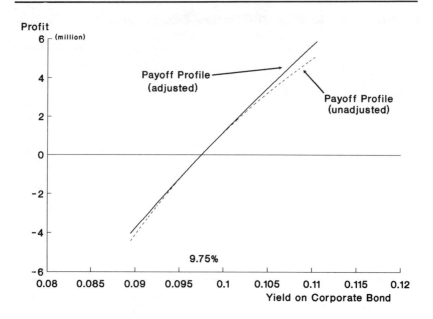

EXHIBIT 5.5. Residual Risk Profile—Future Hedge
(Adjusted versus unadjusted)

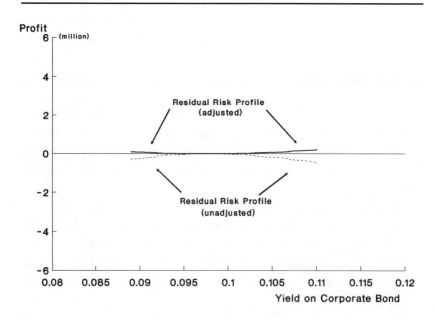

X to be received at that same point in time. The only time we might need to consider a hedge ratio other than 1:1 is if the hedge is a cross hedge. (A cross hedge is defined in the next section.) A cross hedge would only be considered if there were no futures written on the currency that was the subject of the hedge. In these cases, however, a direct forward contract would almost surely provide a better hedge than a cross hedge in futures. For this reason, we do not consider hedge ratios other than 1:1 for currency futures.

The leading futures exchange for currency contracts is the **International Monetary Market** or IMM. The IMM is an affiliate of the **Chicago Mercantile Exchange** or CME. The IMM's currency contracts are very important because they are widely used by swap dealers, foreign exchange dealers, and other market makers in nonexchange derivative instruments to hedge their positions and to engineer new products or product variants. The IMM also makes a market in Eurodollar futures that, as we will see later, play an important part in determining the pricing of a swap-related over-the-counter instrument called a **forward rate agreement**.

5.3 FORWARDS

If futures are so effective as hedging instruments, why would anyone want to hedge in forwards? The answer is a bit complex. Since forward contracts are not standardized, the end users can tailor-make the contracts to fit very specific needs. This makes forward contracts better suited for certain purposes. Another reason is that futures contracts do not exist on all commodities and all financials. Furthermore, even when they do exist, the futures standard and the actuals may differ in one or more significant ways.[5] In these cases, the best the futures hedger can do is engage in a cross hedge. A **cross hedge** involves a hedge in a futures written on a commodity or a financial instrument that differs in a meaningful way from the futures standard. Our hedging of corporate bonds in T-bond futures in the preceding section is an example of a cross hedge, and, as it happens, a fairly effective one.

There are times when a good cross hedge in futures is not possible.

In these situations, the hedger should consider forwards. But even when a futures hedge does exist, the hedger might want to consider forwards as the hedging instrument. This has traditionally been the case when the subject of the hedge is an exchange-rate exposure. The forward markets in currencies are the most highly developed of all the forward markets. These markets are made by large banks—particularly those with a global view. Most forward transactions in these markets are interbank, but banks can and do effect transactions on behalf of nonbank clients.

Consider the example of a U.S. importer that needs to hedge an exposure to fluctuations in the yen/dollar exchange rate. We will denote the Japanese yen by JPY. On July 12th, the importer entered a contract to buy merchandise from a Japanese manufacturer for the sum of JPY 256,450,000. At the time, the spot exchange rate of yen for dollars is 143.50 JPY/USD. The terms of trade, however, require the importer to make the payment on October 28th (which is 107 days later). The importer could purchase the yen immediately in the spot market and hold the yen until payment is required; but the importer does not want to tie up its capital in this way. At the same time, the importer cannot afford to run the risk of a significant change in the JPY/USD exchange rate, so the importer must consider his hedging alternatives.

There are futures contracts on the yen traded on the International Monetary Market (IMM) but only four delivery months are traded. These are March, June, September, and December. The U.S. importer could hedge in the September futures and, when these mature, go unhedged until October. Or, the importer could hedge in the December futures and lift the hedges in late October. Neither of these alternatives is optimal as each exposes the importer to some risk. In the first alternative, the importer is exposed to the risk of being unhedged for over a month. In the second alternative, the importer is exposed to some basis risk from the timing mismatch between the hedge and his actual needs.

A case like this is ready made for a forward contract. The importer can negotiate a 107-day forward yen-for-dollar purchase involving 256.45 million yen at the bank's 107-day forward yen/dollar rate (suppose that this is 142.15 JPY/USD). The importer is now hedged and the hedge horizon matches his requirements perfectly. Fluctuations in the yen/dollar exchange rate no longer need concern him.

There are other good reasons for hedging in forwards rather than futures. One is the different accounting treatment afforded to futures and forwards in some countries. (This will be addressed in the next section.) Another reason is the potential for a mismatch between the length of the hedger's hedging horizon and the maturity date of the futures. Futures typically have rather short lives. They only go out as far as two years and many do not go out that far. Even when futures are available for more distant delivery dates, these tend to be very illiquid and the consequent cost of transacting in them is high. Until recently, forward contracts have rarely run as long as a year. A hedger with longer term needs was simply out of luck. But, in recent years, long-dated forward contracts have evolved for interest rates and exchange rates. These long-dated forwards are made possible, as we will show later, by an ability to synthesize forwards from swaps and vice versa.

In the next two sections, we examine two specific types of forwards: forward rate agreements and forward exchange agreements. Both of these products have become popular among global banks that make markets in swaps.[6] While they are readily available in short-dated form, long-dated variants are becoming increasingly common. Long-dated forward contracts in commodities are also possible but these are usually negotiated directly between producers and end users. For example, major food processors often have multi-year contracts with farmers for the purchase of the latter's crops.

A final solution for the hedger with a very long horizon is the swap. Swaps, whether they be interest-rate swaps, currency swaps, or the new breed of commodity swaps, may be viewed and often are viewed for modeling purposes as a series of forward contracts. We will not dwell on swaps in this chapter, however, since swaps are thoroughly discussed later in this book.

5.4 FORWARD RATE AGREEMENTS

Forward rate agreements, or FRAs, are a type of forward contract originally introduced by banks in 1983. They originated in London, and British banks remain the principal market markers. New York banks, however, are rapidly catching up.

In a forward rate agreement, the two contracting parties, which we will call counterparties, agree on some interest rate to be paid on a "deposit" to be received (or made) at a later date. The size of the deposit, called the notional principal, together with the agreed upon contract rate of interest and the value of the **reference rate** of interest prevailing on the contract settlement date, serve to determine the amount to be paid or received in the form of a single cash settlement. The notional principal (deposit) itself, however, is not actually exchanged. The actual amount paid or received is determined in two steps. In the first step, take the difference between the reference rate on the **settlement date** and the agreed contract rate and then multiply this difference by the notional principal and the term of the deposit (because rates are always stated on an annual basis). The second step, discounts the sum obtained in the first step using the reference rate as the rate of discount. The resultant present value is the sum paid or received. We will explain the purpose of the discounting shortly. The reference rate is most often LIBOR, but it can just as easily be the prime rate, the T-bill rate, or any other well-defined rate that is not easily manipulated.

A party that is seeking protection from a possible increase in rates would buy FRAs. Such a party is sometimes called the "purchaser." A party that wants protection from a possible decline in rates would sell FRAs. Such a party is sometimes called the "seller." Note that these hedge positions are the exact opposite of the hedge positions that would be employed if hedging in futures. This difference in hedge positions is a source of some initial confusion for those experienced in futures who subsequently enter the FRA market.

The difference between the futures and FRA hedging positions is explained by a difference in the pricing conventions used in futures and FRAs. Interest-rate futures are quoted in terms of a "dollar price" that is stated as a percentage of par. FRAs, on the other hand, are quoted in terms of yield. Since prices and yields are inversely related, a long position in a futures contract behaves like a short position in an FRA and vice versa. This dichotomy in the futures/forwards conventions dates back to the origins of interest-rate futures. To make financial

futures more appealing to the traditional commodity futures trader, the
futures exchanges decided to trade futures on a "price" basis rather
than a "yield" basis. While trading bond and note futures on the basis
of price is consistent with the trading practices in the cash markets for
these intermediate- to long-term instruments, it is not consistent for
short-term instruments that trade on the basis of yield. That is, T-bill
futures, Eurodollar futures, and CD futures trade on the basis of price
while the cash versions of T-bills, Eurodollar deposits, and certificates
of deposit trade on the basis of yield. Since prices are inversely related
to yields, the hedging strategies that employ futures appear to be
reversed—relative to hedging strategies employing forwards—but, in
fact, they are not.

Because forwards are not as standardized as futures, a much wider
range of rates can be quoted by market makers. Conventions are, of
course, required to avoid confusion. The quote convention in the FRA
market is to identify the point in time when the "deposit" is to
commence and the point in time when the deposit is to terminate. For
example, the phrase "three-month against nine-month LIBOR" means
a six-month LIBOR deposit to commence in *three* months and to
terminate in *nine* months. In industry shorthand, this FRA term would
be denoted "3 × 9" and read "three by nine."

We can now explain the purpose of the discounting in the calculation of the FRA settlement sum. Unlike other contracts, including
swaps, that are cash settled at the "end" of a settlement period, FRAs
are cash settled at the beginning of their term. For example, if a dealer
and a client enter into a LIBOR-based three-month against nine-month
(3 × 9) FRA, the cash settlement would be effected three months out,
which corresponds to the beginning of the six-month term. In order to
make a cash settlement effective at the beginning of a period equivalent in value to a cash settlement effective at the end, the ending value
must be discounted.

The following example illustrates the above scenario. Suppose a
U.S. bank needs to lock in an interest rate for $5 million six-month
LIBOR-based funding that commences in three months. That is, in
three months the bank will lend $5 million to a client for a period of six
months. The client, however, needs a rate commitment from the bank
immediately. The bank, on the other hand, cannot commit itself to a

rate unless it can "lock in" the cost of its funds. The bank approaches a market maker in FRAs. At the time, six-month LIBOR (the spot rate) is quoted at 8.25 percent. The bank asks the FRA market maker for a quote on three-month against nine-month LIBOR. The market maker bank offers a rate of 8.32 percent. That is, the FRA market maker bank is offering a six-month LIBOR deposit at a rate of 8.32 percent to commence in three months. The U.S. bank accepts (entering as contract buyer). Based on this rate, the U.S. bank offers its client a rate of 8.82 percent on its borrowing from the bank. The bank arrived at this figure by using its own in-house lending rule for its best-rated customers of "LIBOR plus 50 bps." That is, the bank adds 50 basis points to its cost of funds (LIBOR) to allow for profit and to cover its credit risk.

What happens now? Suppose that interest rates rise substantially so that at the time the FRA is due to settle (three months), six-month LIBOR is at 8.95 percent. The bank then obtains $5 million of LIBOR deposits in the Eurodollar market at a rate of 8.95 percent and lends these funds to its corporate client for six months at its commitment rate of 8.82 percent. Clearly, the bank loses money on the actual lending. The amount of profit or loss on the actual lending to the customer is determined by Equation 5.4.[7]

$$\text{Profit/loss} = (\text{Rate received} - \text{Rate paid}) \times \text{Principal} \quad \textbf{(5.4)}$$
$$\times \text{Term}$$
$$= (8.82\% - 8.95\%) \times \$5 \text{ million} \times \frac{182}{360}$$
$$= -\$3.286.11$$

Nevertheless, the bank comes out ahead because it was hedged. The hedge brings a positive cash flow (profit) to the bank. The calculation is given in Equation 5.5.

$$\text{Hedge profit/loss} = D \times (RR - CR) \times NP \times \text{Term} \quad \textbf{(5.5)}$$
$$= 1 \times (8.95\% - 8.32\%) \times \$5 \text{ million}$$
$$\times \frac{182}{360}$$
$$= \$15,925$$

In Equation 5.5, *RR* denotes the reference rate, *CR* denotes the FRA contract rate, and *NP* denotes the notional principal. The value *D* is a dummy variable with the value $+1$ if the counterparty is the FRA purchaser and -1 if the counterparty is the FRA seller. The purpose of the dummy variable is simply to give the hedge outcome the right sign (i.e., " $+$ " if a profit and " $-$ " if a loss). The sum obtained by Equation 5.5 must still be discounted in order to arrive at the amount paid or received. This is done using Equation 5.6—remember that the reference rate serves as the discounting rate and must be adjusted to reflect the six-month nature of (182-day) the deposit term.

$$\text{Amount received/paid} = \frac{\overset{\text{Hedge Profit/loss}}{}}{1 + \dfrac{RR \times 182}{360}} \qquad (5.6)$$

$$= \frac{15{,}925}{(1 + 0.04525)}$$

$$= \$15{,}235.59$$

The bank's overall profit (or loss) is then obtained by summing the profit/loss on the lending and the profit/loss on the hedge. In this case, this is $12,639. Notice that the bank's overall profit or loss is found using the hedge profit/loss ($15,925) rather than the amount received/paid on the hedge ($15,236). This is important because the lending profit/loss and the hedging profit/loss are *realized* at the same point in time (in a present value sense) but the lending profit/loss and the amount received/paid on the hedge are *received* at different points in time (again in a present value sense).

The hedger bank in this example hedged by "buying" an FRA. As was noted earlier, had this same bank wanted to hedge in futures, it would have "sold" the appropriate number of futures contracts.

Notice in the example used to illustrate the FRA process that the bank that purchased the FRA did not actually take delivery of the "deposit." Instead the bank and the FRA market maker settled upfront in cash for a sum dictated by Equations 5.5 and 5.6. The bank then met its deposit needs by purchasing deposits in the Eurodollar cash market. This procedure is analogous to lifting a futures hedge through an offsetting transaction and then transacting in the cash market. It differs however from the traditional use of forward contracts as physical delivery instruments. This cash settlement feature then distinguishes FRAs (and, as we will see shortly, forward exchange agreements) from forward contracts more generally.

There is one other important reason why a user might prefer a forward contract to a futures for hedging purposes. This is the different accounting treatments of profits and losses on futures and forwards in some countries. In the United States, accounting conventions are defined by the **Generally Accepted Accounting Principles** or **GAAP**. Under GAAP rules, profits and losses on speculative positions in futures are treated as though they were realized during the accounting period in which they accrued. That is to say, a marking-to-market process is applied for accounting purposes. However, if the futures position is part of a clearly identified **micro-hedge**, that is, the futures position is matched against a specific asset or liability (cash position), then the profit or loss can be amortized over the same period as the profit or loss on the cash position. This option is generally not available for a **macro-hedge**. The latter would involve a hedge taken to offset any net risk associated with the hedger's overall asset/liability mix. (It should be stressed that the accounting treatment of profits and losses on futures hedges is still a gray area.) Forward rate agreements are generally not, at this point in time, required to be marked-to-market for accounting purposes.

In the case of a macro-hedge, in which futures are marked-to-market on a daily basis but forwards are not, there can be clear accounting advantages to hedging with forwards. For a futures hedger, the profits (or losses) on the futures are largely offset by losses (or profits) on the underlying cash position. However, because the losses (or profits) on the cash position are not realized until the cash position is closed, the losses (or profit) might easily occur during a different accounting period than that of the profits (or losses) on the hedge. These different accounting treatments of futures profits and cash market profits can result in accounting-profit volatility which, in turn, can make the hedge appear more risky than it really is. It can also have unwanted, although temporary, tax effects. Because FRA profits (or losses) need not be marked-to-market, these accounting distortions may not occur when hedging in FRAs.

To see this accounting problem a little more clearly, consider again the example of the bank using the FRA to hedge its lending commitment to its corporate client. We will treat this as a macro-hedge, even though in practice it may not be. Suppose the bank enters the FRA as contract purchaser on 15 October 1990 with settlement due on 15 January 1991. This is a 3 × 9 FRA, so the "deposit" commences on 15 January and matures on 15 July (but it is nevertheless cash settled on 15 January). Since there is no marking-to-market, all profit on the FRA is realized in 1991. This corresponds to the year in which the losses on the cash lending are realized. The end result is that the bank shows a net profit of $12,639 on its overall position for 1991 and $0 for 1990.

Suppose now that the bank hedges in futures (by selling Eurodollar futures) and achieves an identical overall performance. But, on 31 December 1990, the futures price is such that the bank has a mark-to-market profit for the year of $32,500. And in 1991 the bank has a futures profit of −$16,575. Over the two years, the bank earns the same $15,925 profit on its hedge but investors see greater volatility in the bank's financial statements. In addition, if the bank hedges in futures it will pay substantial income taxes in 1990. Although a large portion of these taxes can be recovered in 1991, the time value of the money paid in taxes in 1990 is still lost.

It is important to appreciate that the scenario of large taxes in 1990 with some tax recovery in 1991 is only one possible outcome of the mark-to-market process. It could just as easily have gone the other way and worked to the advantage of the bank. But in either case, the mark-to-market process increases accounting-profit volatility and this is unattractive.

It is worth noting that there has been increasing regulatory and accounting interest in recent years in extending the mark-to-market principle to all derivative instruments and, potentially, to cash instruments as well. It is not clear however, whether or not this interest will culminate in uniform accounting treatment of all financial positions.

The FRA market is largely an **interbank** dollar-denominated market. That is, the bulk of transactions are bank to bank and most transactions involve dollars. There is relatively little involvement on the part of investment banks, but investment bank involvement seems to be increasing. The size of transactions has increased considerably since the contracts were first introduced and transactions involving notional principal of $50 million or more are not uncommon. In the early days, market makers typically quoted rates for every three-month and every six-month period up to one year. But broken dates are now common and long-dated forwards are also common. The latter can extend out to several years. A partial listing of one broker's quotes from 1 December 1989 is depicted in Table 5.2. The contract rates (rate) represents the "last" rather than a bid or an asked.

TABLE 5.2
FRA Rates—Cash & IMM Dates*
(1 December 1989)
Part I: Non-IMM (Cash)

3 Months	Rate	6 Months	Rate	9 Months	Rate
1 × 4	8.28	1 × 7	8.10	1 × 10	8.05
2 × 5	8.09	2 × 8	7.98	2 × 11	7.99
3 × 6	7.90	3 × 9	7.86	3 × 12	7.92
4 × 7	7.77	4 × 10	7.79	6 × 15	7.95
5 × 8	7.74	5 × 11	7.79		
6 × 9	7.68	6 × 12	7.78		
7 × 10	7.68	7 × 13	7.82		
8 × 11	7.73	8 × 14	7.89		
9 × 12	7.74	9 × 15	7.94		

Part II: IMM

IMM Contract		FRA	Rate	FRA	Rate
DEC-89	91.64	0 × 3	8.360	6 × 9	7.640
MAR-90	92.23	0 × 6	8.147	6 × 12	7.765
JUN-90	92.36	0 × 9	8.083	6 × 15	7.955
SEP-90	92.26	0 × 12	8.116	6 × 18	8.121
DEC-90	91.98	3 × 6	7.770	9 × 12	7.740
MAR-91	91.87	3 × 9	7.780	9 × 15	7.958
JUN-91	91.74	3 × 12	7.868	9 × 18	8.125
SEP-91	91.65	3 × 15	8.026	9 × 21	8.286

* These rates are indicative only. Actual market quotes occur above or below these rates.

Part I of Table 5.2 depicts a "snapshot" of non-IMM FRA rates for one broker as they appeared at about 4 PM (EST) on 1 December 1989. The broker is providing rates for sequential three-month FRAs, six-month FRAs, and nine-month FRAs. The table is not complete because this broker also provided dates beyond those indicated and provides rates for 12-month FRAs as well. As noted earlier, these FRAs are identified by notation such as "$w \times y$" where w indicates the time of commencement (in months) and y indicates the time of termination (in months). Thus, the FRA identified as 1×4 commences exactly one month from the spot date and terminates exactly four months from the spot date (FRAs follow Eurodollar date conventions).

Part II of Table 5.2 depicts IMM FRAs. IMM FRAs are FRAs that are priced off the IMM's Eurodollar futures contracts and that use **IMM settlement dates**. For example, at the time this "snapshot" was taken, the December 1989 IMM contract was priced at 91.64, which implies that the market's expectation of the three-month Eurodollar rate (LIBOR) to commence on the settlement date of the IMM contract was 8.36 percent—calculated as $100 - 91.64$. Since the "snapshot" was taken in December, the three-month FRA that commenced in December 1989 and terminated in March 1990 is denoted 0×3. The IMM 0×3 FRA has a rate of 8.36 percent. Similarly, the March 1990 IMM contract is priced at 92.23 implying a rate of 7.77 percent. The corresponding FRA is the FRA that commences in three months and terminates in six months and that would be described as 3×6. The reader will observe that the IMM 3×6 FRA rate is indeed 7.77 percent.

Three-month IMM Eurodollar futures can be used to price longer maturity Eurodollar-based financial instruments. This is accomplished by calculating the implied longer maturity rate from a sequence of shorter maturity rates (the actual calculation is demonstrated shortly). The set of implied prices generated in this way is called the Eurodollar strip. The IMM FRAs were introduced to "piggy-back" off this strip. The FRAs that are priced off the Eurodollar strip use IMM settlement dates and are themselves called **strips**. It is now typical to use three-month Eurodollar futures to price six-month, nine-month, and 12-month FRAs. The three-month strip has already been demonstrated.

For this strip, the contract rate is simply the LIBOR rate implied by the appropriate Eurodollar contract.

The pricing of strips longer than three months is more difficult to explain. Remember that the rates implied by Eurodollar contracts are market expectations of three-month LIBOR but stated on an annual basis. For example, the implied rate for March 1990 was 7.77 percent. But, this rate only applies for three months (approximately one-quarter of a year). The actual return for the three-month period would be about one-fourth of 7.77 percent or 1.9425 percent. An investor in three-month Eurodollars would, therefore, earn 1.9425 percent for his or her three-month deposit. This deposit could then be rolled over for another three months at the new three-month LIBOR rate. This could be repeated over and over again. The result is that the rate is compounded four times a year. We know that an annual rate of 7.77 percent compounded four times a year is not the same as an effective annual rate of 7.77 percent and not the same as an annual rate of 7.77 percent compounded twice a year. To find an equivalent rate for a six-month FRA, a nine-month FRA, or a 12-month FRA, this compounding must be taken into consideration.

As in our first example, let's suppose we want to price a six-month FRA off the three-month IMM Eurodollar contracts. Suppose further that this FRA is to commence in six months and terminate in twelve months, so it is a "6 × 12." Since the current time was December 1989, six months out is June 1990. The two three-month periods involved are then the ones that began in June 1990 (and ended in September 1990) and September 1990 (which takes us to December 1990). Part II of Table 5.2 indicates that the JUN-90 IMM contract is at 92.36, implying a three-month LIBOR of 7.64 percent that is equivalent to a three-month return of about 1.91 percent. The SEP-90 IMM contract is at 92.26, which implies a three-month LIBOR of 7.74 percent that is equivalent to a three-month return of about 1.935 percent. The implied six-month LIBOR rate can be found using the approximation formula given by Equation 5.7. This formula only provides an approximation because it ignores the differing number of days in different three-month periods.

$$6 - \text{M LIBOR} \approx \{[(1 + \text{JUN}/4) \cdot (1 + \text{SEP}/4)] - 1\} \times 2 \quad \textbf{(5.7)}$$

In this particular case, the calculation is:

$$6 - \text{M LIBOR} \approx \{[(1.0191) \cdot (1.01935)] - 1\} \times 2 =$$
$$7.764 \text{ percent}$$

The value 7.764 percent is almost identical to the price of the 6×12 IMM FRA depicted in Part II of Table 5.2. As already noted, the difference—0.001—is explained by the uneven number of days in the different three-month periods (these can be anywhere from 90 to 92 days). The rate, 7.764 percent, is interpreted as the implied six-month LIBOR with semiannual compounding. The same calculation can be done to price a one-year strip. Let's suppose we want to calculate a 9 $\times$ 21, that is, a one-year strip that commences in September 1990 and terminates in September 1991. We would use the SEP-90, DEC-90, MAR-91, and JUN-91 IMM contracts for this purpose. The calculation is:

$$12 - \text{M LIBOR} = \{[(1 + \text{SEP}/4) \cdot (1 + \text{DEC}/4) \cdot (1 + \text{MAR}/4)$$
$$\cdot (1 + \text{JUN}/4)] - 1\} \times 1$$

In this case, the calculation yields one-year LIBOR of 8.283 percent. This is almost identical to the contract rate in Part II of Table 5.2 for the 9×21 FRA (again, the difference is due to the approximate nature of Equation 5.7). The one-year rate is interpreted as the contract rate on one-year LIBOR using annual compounding.

In 1985, the British Bankers' Association published standardized terms for FRAs. These terms are known as the **FRABBA terms** and they have become the standard, unless specifically stated otherwise, for all interbank FRAs among London banks. Similar standardization efforts have occurred in the United States. (We will discuss documentation standardization efforts in Chapter 10.)

Forward rate agreements have a number of uses. In addition to their use as a hedging vehicle, they can be used by banks to arbitrage among related instruments. For example, the bank can arbitrage FRAs against futures, or FRAs against swaps, or FRAs against cash deposits, to mention just a few of the possibilities.

Like swaps and futures, FRAs are off-balance sheet transactions.

That is, they do not appear on either the asset side or the liability side of the balance sheet. Before the adoption of the Federal Reserve's revised capital guidelines in January of 1989, these instruments, like swaps, presented banks with the opportunity to increase earnings without inflating the balance sheet. By avoiding an inflation of the balance sheet and thus avoiding negative consequences in terms of additional capital requirements, the bank could enhance its return on equity. These considerations, however, have changed somewhat with the adoption of the new guidelines. We will consider this issue more fully in Chapter 9.

Because FRAs are not marked-to-market with variation margin transfers, the parties to an FRA are exposed to more risk than are parties to futures contracts. This point was made earlier. As a result, the FRA market tends to be limited to institutions with strong credit. Some risk, nevertheless, remains. The risk is measured in exactly the same fashion as the risk on a swap. (We will consider the measurement and the management of these risks in Chapter 9.) For now, however, suffice it to say that the exposure at any point in time is equal to the replacement cost of the forward, should the counterparty default. That is, the exposure is the amount the market-maker bank would have to pay as a front-end fee to secure a replacement FRA with identical terms to the one in default.

All of the illustrations involving futures and forwards have been cast in the context of hedging. While risk management is the primary focus of this book and our examples are, therefore, quite appropriate, we would be remiss not to at least mention the speculative uses of these instruments. Both futures and forwards can be used to speculate on the direction of financial prices, including interest rates. A speculator, for example, who believes that rates will rise can speculate on this belief by either selling interest-rate futures or by buying forward rate agreements. Once the position has been taken, the speculator can offset the position by taking an equal-but-opposite position. The speculator would want to offset the position once his or her expectations were realized or if the expectations changed in such a way as to no longer warrant the position.

It is important to appreciate that futures and forward positions do not have to be held until they are actually delivered or cash settled.

Offsetting positions can be taken. This is particularly important to speculators who must be nimble in an ever changing interest-rate environment. The highly standardized nature of futures contracts makes futures easier to offset than tailor-made forward contracts, but both can be offset.

5.5 EURO-RATE DIFFERENTIAL FUTURES (DIFFs) AND FORWARD EXCHANGE AGREEMENTS (FXAs)

There are two remaining instruments we will take a brief look at (we will treat them together as they have similar uses). One is a type of futures contract and the other is a type of forward contract. The futures contracts, called **Euro-rate differential futures** contracts, trade on the Chicago Mercantile Exchange or CME (a U.S. futures exchange). These contracts can be used as hedging instruments when the risk exposures stem from changes in the **interest-rate differential** between a dollar-based interest rate and a nondollar-based interest rate. The forward contracts, called **forward exchange agreements**, are marketed by European banks, but are not, as yet, widely used in the United States. They can be used as hedging instruments when the risk exposures stem from changes in **exchange-rate differentials**. A discussion of Euro-rate differential futures follows first.

A Euro-rate differential futures contract or, as it is known in market jargon, a **DIFF**, is a futures contract tied to the differential between a three-month nondollar interest rate and three-month LIBOR. These contracts can be used to hedge rate differential exposures between currencies. DIFFs were introduced on 6 July 1989 and, as of this writing, three contracts were available: dollar/sterling DIFFs, dollar/mark DIFFs, and dollar/yen DIFFs.

A DIFF is ultimately cash settled for a sum based on the difference between USD three-month LIBOR and some other interest rate. For example, if USD three-month LIBOR is at 9.45 and DM three-month LIBOR is at 6.20 at the time the March dollar/mark DIFF is due to settle, then the DIFF would be priced at 96.75—which is calculated as 100 less the difference between USD LIBOR and DM LIBOR (i.e., $100 - (9.45 - 6.20)$). Note that all values are understood to be percentages. Suppose now that it is currently January and the March mark/dollar DIFF is currently priced at 96.90. This would suggest that the market currently expects the differential between USD LIBOR and DM LIBOR to be 3.10 percent at settlement in March. By contract design, each basis point 0.01% has a value of $25 (this is the same value as a basis point on a Eurodollar futures contract on the IMM). Thus, if you were to buy this DIFF at 96.90 (go long) and hold the DIFF to final settlement at 96.75, you would suffer a loss of 15 basis points, worth $25 each, for a total loss of $375. The calculation is $(96.75 - 96.90) \times 100 \times \$25$.

The DIFFs can be used to:

1. lock in or unlock interest-rate differentials when funding in one currency and investing in another;

2. hedge exposures associated with nondollar interest-rate sensitivities;

3. manage the residual risks associated with running a currency swap book; and

4. manage the risks associated with changing interest-rate differentials for a currency dealer.

Consider a simple example. Suppose that the treasurer of a U.S.-based corporation with a subsidiary in West Germany funds the subsidiary with short-term deutschemark borrowings. For simplicity, assume that the firm is able to borrow at DM three-month LIBOR. The treasurer occasionally rolls over the firm's debt if the funding need still exists. Now suppose that it is currently early August and the treasurer determines that he or she will need to rollover the firm's current 18 million deutschemark funding. Suppose further that the current dollar/deutschemark exchange rate is 0.7545. At this rate, the deutschemark funding has a dollar value of $13,581,000. The current debt matures in September. The treasurer could simply wait until September and take a chance with a spot DM LIBOR or he or she could hedge in dollar/mark DIFFs.

The IMM's September three-month Eurodollar contract is currently priced at 90.75 implying a market expectation of 9.25 percent for three-month LIBOR in September. At the same time, the September mark/dollar DIFF is priced at 97.25. At current prices, the treasurer could lock in a DM three-month LIBOR rate of 6.50 percent. This is calculated as $(100 - 90.75) - (100 - 97.25)$ or, more simply, as 97.25 less 90.75. To effect this hedge, the treasurer will sell an appropriate number of September Eurodollar futures and buy the same number of September dollar/mark DIFFs. The treasurer can then hold these contracts until the actual time of the rollover. At that time, the treasurer can borrow deutschemarks at the prevailing DM LIBOR rate. Assuming no serious manifestations of other risks, such as basis risk, the profit/loss on the DIFF and Eurodollar contracts will be just sufficient to offset any rise/fall in the DM three-month LIBOR rate.

As with any hedge, an important consideration is the calculation of the correct hedge ratio. This is rather straightforward with DIFFs. We begin by determining the dollar value of a basis point on the cash position. For example, the firm in the example above would calculate the DVBP of its funding requirement (the cash position) as follows:

$$DVBP = \$13.581 \text{ million} \times 0.01\% \times \frac{91}{360}$$

$$= \$343.30$$

Since, by contract construction, the dollar value of a DIFF basis point and a Eurodollar basis point are both $25, the number of futures contracts needed is $343.30 ÷ $25, or approximately 14.

DIFFs are still very new and the full range of uses is only beginning to be discovered. Trading volume in DIFFs has been light, but that is typical for some time after the introduction of a completely new type of futures contract. It will be a few years before we know whether or not DIFFs have found a permanent home in the modern financial marketplace. We now turn our attention to the over-the-counter counterpart to DIFFs.

Forward exchange agreements or **FXAs** were intended by their creators to be to the forward foreign-exchange market what FRAs had become to the forward Eurocurrency market. They allow parties to hedge movements in exchange-rate differentials without entering a conventional currency swap. From a conceptual perspective, an FXA combines two notional forward foreign-exchange contracts into a single instrument. At the termination of the agreement, a single payment is made by one counterparty to the other based on the direction and the extent of movement in the exchange-rate differential. These contracts can be used to hedge a form of exchange-rate risk, to use a bank's foreign-exchange limits more efficiently, to speculate on the direction of exchange-rate differentials, and to engage in various types of arbitrage, such as that between FXAs and currency futures, FXAs and currency swaps, and FXAs and actual currency positions. Because interest-rate differentials and exchange-rate differentials are closely related, as we demonstrated in Chapter 2, the difference between DIFFs and FXAs is not as great as the definitional distinctions suggest.

Forward exchange agreements have the same advantages and disadvantages relative to DIFF futures that FRAs have relative to interest-rate futures, so we will not waste time repeating the comparisons. Instead, we will concentrate on an example of the use of an FXA and the calculation of the cash settlement amount.

The cash settlement formula is given by Equation 5.8.[8] The actual settlement amount indicated by Equation 5.8 is determined on the **calculation date**, which occurs a few days prior to the settlement date.

$$\text{Settlement Amount} = D \times NP$$

$$\times \left[\frac{(SD - SC) + (FD - FC)}{(1 + ((R \times N) \div (100 \times Y)))} - (SD - SC) \right] \quad \textbf{(5.8)}$$

where
NP = Notional Principal.
SD = Near forward exchange rate at time of contracting.
SC = Spot exchange rate at settlement.
FD = Contract forward points.
FC = Settlement forward points.
R = LIBOR, expressed in percentage form but reported as a number rather than as a percentage, (i.e., 9.5 percent is entered as 9.5).
N = Actual number of days between the two exchanges (i.e., period covered by the agreement).

Y = Number of days in the year, which may be 360 or 365 depending on the custom in the contractual currency.

D = Represents a dummy variable having the values $+1$ (if the counterparty is the contract purchaser) or -1 (if the counterparty is the contract seller).

Before proceeding to the example, the terms above need to be clarified. The notional principal is the amount of principal on which the final cash settlement will be based. As with FRAs, the notional principal is not exchanged.

There are a number of exchange rates involved in the determination of the cash settlement amount and so it is important to be very clear as to which rate is which. Let's denote the time of initial contracting by the letter c, the time of the first (near) forward exchange by the letter t, and the time of the second (far) forward exchange by the letter T. Then we can denote any exchange rate we like by using the letter E to mean an "exchange rate" together with two subscripts: the first represents the current time and the second representing the time of the forward transaction. For example, the notation $E_{t,T}$ would denote the exchange rate at time t for a transaction that will take place at time T. Since time T follows time t, $E_{t,T}$ denotes a forward rate. When the two subscripts are the same, as in $E_{t,t}$, the exchange rate is a spot rate. At time c, we know $E_{c,c}$, $E_{c,t}$, and $E_{c,T}$ but we do not know $E_{t,t}$ and $E_{t,T}$. The latter two are, however, known at the time of contract settlement. The settlement date is the same date that the near forward comes due.

We can now define the terms in Equation 5.8 using the notation we defined above:

$$SD = E_{c,t} \qquad\qquad FD = E_{c,T} - E_{c,t}$$

$$SC = E_{t,t} \qquad\qquad FC = E_{t,T} - E_{t,t}$$

Now lets consider an example. It is currently 6 January 1991 and a U.S.-based customer has approached an FXA market-maker bank looking for a three-month against nine-month deutschemark-for-dollar FXA having notional principal of DM 5 million. Specifically, the customer wishes to buy three-month deutschemarks and sell nine-month deutschemarks. The market-maker bank's current set of "dollar for deutschemark" (USD/DM) exchange rates are given in Table 5.3.[9]

The bank and its customer enter the FXA with the bank as contract seller and the customer as contract buyer (the convention is that the purchaser of the near forward, who is also the seller of the far forward, is considered the contract purchaser). Three months later on the contract's calculation date, 6 April 1991, the bank calculates the amount of the cash settlement based on the prevailing forward rates and six-month USD LIBOR. This amount will be paid to the customer if positive and paid by the customer if negative. The market maker's rates on the calculation date appear in Table 5.4.

The components of Equation 5.8 can be generated using the definitions for SD, SC, FD, and FC that we introduced before. These are:

$$SD = 0.40404 \quad FD = 0.40016 - 0.40404 = -0.00388$$

$$SC = 0.37807 \quad FC = 0.37258 - 0.37807 = -0.00549$$

The dummy variable is $+1$ since the customer was the contract buyer, the notional principal is DM 5 million, LIBOR is 8.00 percent, the number of days involved is 183, and the number of days in the year is 360 in this case. Substituting these values into Equation 5.8 produces the cash settlement amount of \$2,732.18. Since this sum is positive, the bank pays the customer the settlement amount.

An FXA contract exactly reproduces the cash flows associated

TABLE 5.3
FXA Market Maker's Exchange Rates USD/DM*
(6 January 1991)

Date for Value	Type	Rate	Notation
8 January 1991	Spot	0.40917	$E_{c,c}$
8 April 1991	Forward (near)	0.40404	$E_{c,t}$
8 October 1991	Forward (far)	0.40016	$E_{c,T}$

**Note:* The standard two-day settlement is assumed.

TABLE 5.4
FXA Market Maker's Exchange Rates USD/DM
(6 April 1991)

Date for Value	Type	Rate	Notation
8 April 1991	Spot	0.37807	$E_{t,t}$
8 October 1991	Forward	0.37258	$E_{t,T}$

6-M USD LIBOR: 8.00 percent.

with conventional cash market transactions. This is the key to understanding how these instruments can be used to hedge and arbitrage other positions. Suppose that on 6 January 1991, the customer had simply bought a three-month forward contract and sold a nine-month forward contract as two separate cash market transactions. How would the cash flows have looked from the customer's perspective? The answer is illustrated in Table 5.5.

Now consider the cash flows associated with the FXA. In addition to the cash flow resulting from the FXA settlement, the customer would purchase deutschemarks on 6 April 1991 (for 8 April settlement) as a spot transaction and would sell deutschemarks forward on 6 April 1991 for settlement on 8 October 1991. The first of these two transactions would require the expenditure of $1,890,350 and the second would result in the receipt of $1,862,900. These sums are based on the exchange rates given in Table 5.4. The customer would also borrow (or lend) a sum in dollars equal to the difference between the dollar amount of the October transaction if made in April and the dollar amount of the October transaction if made in January, discounted for the appropriate number of days at six-month LIBOR. This

TABLE 5.5
Cash Flows Associated with Two Cash Market Transactions
Effected on 6 January 1991

Date	DM	USD	Relevant Exchange Rate
8 April 1991	5,000,000	(2,020,200)	0.40404 USD/DM
8 October 1991	(5,000,000)	2,000,800	0.40016 USD/DM

TABLE 5.6
Cash Flows Associated with FXA (as adjusted)

Date	DM	USD	Origin of Payment
8 April 1991	5,000,000	(1,890,350)	Spot transaction DM for USD
		(132,582.18)	Dollar amount of lending
		2,732.18	FXA settlement amount
	5,000,000	(2,020,200)	
8 October 1991	(5,000,000)	1,862,900	Forward transaction USD for DM
		137,900	Lent funds returned + interest
	(5,000,000)	2,000,800	

borrowing (or lending) is required to offset the movement in the spot rate between January and April. These cash flows are summarized in Table 5.6.

Now compare the net cash flows from the cash market transactions in Table 5.5 and the net cash flows from the FXA and associated transactions in Table 5.6. Clearly, the FXA has replicated the conventional cash transactions perfectly.

FXAs are more difficult to understand than FRAs because they involve more variables. The FRA involved only two interest rates: the contract rate and the value of the reference rate on the calculation date. The FXA, on the other hand, involved six rates: two spot exchange rates, three forward exchange rates, and one interest rate. In addition, unlike the FRA whose cash settlement amount is a function of a change in rates, an FXA's cash settlement amount is largely a function of a change in rate differentials. As noted earlier, FXAs are not widely used by U.S. banks.

5.6 FORWARD RATE AGREEMENTS, FOREIGN EXCHANGE AGREEMENTS, AND SWAPS

Swaps and forwards, particularly swaps and FRAs, are closely related. In fact, a swap can be viewed as a series of forward contracts. For example, the cash flow stream of a three-year semiannual fixed-for-floating interest-rate swap can be replicated by simultaneously entering six sequential forward rate agreements that each span six months.

This ability to replicate swaps from forwards means that there is the potential to create synthetic swaps from forwards. A **synthetic instrument** is an instrument that is created by combining other instruments so as to replicate the real instrument's cash flow stream. Synthetic instruments are created and used for a variety of purposes. The most obvious are to reduce the cost of hedging by creating synthetic hedging instruments when the synthetic instrument is more cost-effective than the real hedging instrument, and to arbitrage between the synthetic instrument and the real instrument.

Less immediately obvious, but just as real, is the opportunity to use swaps to synthesize forwards. For example, a swap dealer might enter a two-year interest-rate swap as fixed-rate payer and might simultaneously enter a one and one-half-year swap as fixed-rate receiver. These swaps are not perfectly matched and so the swap dealer has a residual position. But the residual position is equivalent to an 18-month against 24-month FRA. The swap dealer could then sell an appropriate FRA, acting as an FRA dealer, to earn the bid-ask spread and simultaneously cover his residual risk from the mismatched swaps.

The point is that FRAs, like futures contracts, may be viewed as substitutes for swaps but, in many instances, are just as appropriately viewed as complements to swaps. Clearly, there are economies of scale for swap dealers who also make markets in FRAs and related instruments.

We will not dwell on FRAs and FXAs in the remainder of this book. Instead, the similarity of swaps and forwards suggests that most of what we have to say about swap pricing, swap risks, and swap uses also applies to these special types of forwards.

5.7 SUMMARY

Futures and forward contracts are contracts that allow users to hedge price risks by locking in prices on instruments that are to be delivered (or cash settled) in a single transaction. The payoff profiles associated with these instruments suggest that their hedging uses are best suited to hedging against price risk—as opposed to downside risk only. That is to say, the user of these instruments will profit if prices move favorably but suffer losses if prices move unfavorably.

Futures contracts are highly standardized instruments. Forward contracts are much more tailor-made but many forward markets have evolved a degree of standardization that approaches that of futures contracts. Futures markets are made by futures exchanges and trading takes place through a dual auction system on the floor of the futures exchange. The markets tend to be liquid with narrow bid-ask spreads. Forward contracts are traded in dealer-type markets by market-maker banks. They tend to be less liquid than futures and characterized by larger bid-ask spreads. Because they are less standardized, however, a wider range of contract terms are possible.

The integrity of a futures market is maintained by requiring all parties to a contract to post a performance bond called margin. The margin is held by a clearing association that guarantees performance on all contracts. No system-wide margining is employed in the forward markets. As a result, participation in these markets tends to be limited to strong credits or to those who are in a position to offer collateral.

The markets for interest-rate and exchange-rate contracts has grown rapidly in recent years. Futures contracts are written on T-bills, Eurodollars, CDs, T-bonds, T-notes, mortgage instruments and other debt instruments. Some of these are cash settled contracts while others are deliverable. Currency futures exist for all major currencies. Foreign exchange markets are very highly developed and large banks make both spot and forward markets in currencies. Banks also make forward markets on interest rates in the form of forward rate agreements or FRAs. If adjusted for the difference in the timing of the cash settlement, FRAs may be viewed as single-period swaps.

The most recent innovations in the futures and the forward markets are the advent of Euro-rate differential futures, which allow for the hedging of interest-rate differentials between short-term interest rates in different currencies, and forward exchange agreements, which allow for the hedging of changes in exchange-rate differentials. These instruments are similar in concept and have similar uses.

Forwards, futures, and swaps are all substitutes for, and complements to, one another. There are clear economies of scale for firms that make markets in swaps to also make markets in forward contracts in currencies and forward rate agreements.

REFERENCES AND SUGGESTED READING

Arak, M. and L.S. Goodman "Treasury Bond Futures: Valuing the Delivery Options," *Journal of Futures Markets*, 7(3), pp. 269–286 (1987).

Bank for International Settlements, *Recent Innovations in International Banking* (1986).

British Bankers' Association, *Forward Rate Agreements: FRABBA Terms* (1985).

Chew, L. "FRAs: Managing the Gap," *Risk*, 2(8) (1989).

Dominguez, N. and J. Brauer, "Strategies: Taking Advantage of Delivery Options in Treasury Futures Contracts," First Boston, Derivative Products Group (Oct 18, 1988).

Grannan, L. "Futures: DIFFs Make All The Difference," *Risk*, 2(8) (1989).

Grossman, S.J. and J.E. Stiglitz "On the Impossibility of Informationally Efficient Prices," *American Economic Review* (June 1980).

Hume, J. G. "Remaining Calm in Troubled Markets: The Growth of Risk Hedging Vehicles," *Journal of Commercial Bank Lending*, 7:7 36–44 (Dec 1984).

Kawaller, Ira G. "Hedging with DIFFS," *Market Perspectives: Topics on Options and Futures*, (Chicago Mercantile Exchange) 7(3) (June/July 1989).

Kolb, R.W. *Understanding Futures Markets*, 2d ed., Glenview, IL: Scott, Foresman (1988).

Kuhn, B.A. "A Note: Do Futures Prices Always Reflect the Cheapest to Deliver Grade of a Commodity, *Journal of Futures Markets*, 8(1), pp. 99–102 (1988).

Livingston, M. "The Cheapest Deliverable Bond for the CBT Treasury Bond Futures Contract, *Journal of Futures Markets*, 4(2), pp. 161–172 (1984).

Marshall, J.F. *Futures and Option Contracting: Theory and Practice*, Cincinnati, OH: South-Western (1989).

Meisner, J.F. and J.W. Labuszewski "Treasury Bond Futures Delivery Bias," *Journal of Futures Markets*, 4(4), pp. 569–577 (1984).

Nadler, D. *Eurodollar Futures/Interest Rate Arbitrage*, Quantitative Strategies Group, Shearson, Lehman, Hutton (April 1989).

ENDNOTES

[1]For a discussion of the role played by cheapest-to-deliver bonds, see Livingston (1984), Meisner and Labuszewski (1984), and Kolb (1988). For an excellent discussion of the embedded options associated with cheapest-to-deliver bonds and strategies for exploiting the value of these embedded options, see Dominguez and Brauer (1988).

[2]This argument was first put forward by Grossman and Stiglitz (1980) who referred to the inefficiency as an "equilibrium degree of disequilibrium."

[3]The dollar value basis point model (DVBP) is the most widely used model for determining the size of a hedge by institutions which hedge fixed-income securities in futures. This model is discussed in this book in Chapter 2. The academic literature, on the other hand, prefers to use duration-based models. It has been shown that these two approaches to hedging fixed-income securities, if adjusted to reflect the yield beta, produce identical hedge ratios. See Marshall (1989), Chapter 12.

[4]The present value annuity formula is given as follows:

$$PVA = AMT \times \left[\frac{1 - (1 + r/m)^{-nm}}{r/m} \right]$$

where, in this case, AMT, the periodic annuity amount, is \$200,000; r, the annual discount rate (yield), is 10.55 percent; m, the number of payments per period (compoundings), is 2; and n, the number of years, is 30. This calculation was discussed in Chapter 2.

[5]The terms "actuals," "physicals," and "cash" are used interchangeably to refer to a physical commodity or financial instrument as distinguished from a derivative instrument (such as a futures, a forward, or an option) which is written on the "cash" instrument.

[6]Forward exchange agreements (FXAs) are not widely used in the United States but they are popular in London.

[7]To call the result of this calculation "profit" is actually a misnomer as costs in addition to interest expense must be considered to arrive at profit. The value obtained is more correctly called "net interest," but, we will continue to refer to it as profit to be consistent with the hedging theory offered elsewhere in this book.

[8]This version of the FXA settlement formula is taken from Midland Bank. We have added a dummy variable D to make it clearer as to who pays whom.

[9]These rates are for illustrative purposes only. They are not the actual rates that prevailed on 6 January 1991.

6

Options: Calls, Puts, Caps, and Floors

6.1 OVERVIEW

The instruments we will be discussing in this chapter differ from other financial instruments in that they are all, in some sense, options. An **option** is a contract between two parties in which one party has the *right but not the obligation* to do something—usually to buy or sell some underlying asset.

The concept of an option is quite general. The best known types are calls and puts. A call option grants its purchaser the right (but not the obligation) to buy some underlying asset while a put option grants its purchaser the right (but not the obligation) to sell some underlying asset. Only the purchaser of the call or put has "a right without an obligation." The contract seller has an absolute obligation.

Calls and puts are not the only types of options. For example, many bonds have option-like features. The two most frequently encountered of these features are the "conversion feature" associated with convertible bonds and the "call feature" associated with callable bonds. A convertible bond is a bond in which the bondholder has the right, but not the obligation, to convert the bond into some other asset of the issuer. A callable bond is a bond in which the issuer has the right, but not the obligation, to call the bond (for redemption) prior to maturity.

Since rights without obligation have value, the option purchaser

219

must expect to pay the option seller for the option or option-like feature. That is, one does not get value without giving value. In the case of calls and puts, the price paid for the option takes the form of a flat up-front sum called a **premium**. In the case of a convertible bond, the bond purchaser gets the option-like feature as a part of the bond and pays for the option indirectly in the form of a reduced coupon. That is, the bondholder pays par at issue but accepts a coupon below market for the life of the bond. Thus, payment for the option is made in installments over the life of the bond.

The call feature on a bond is a little trickier to understand. The bondholder owns the bond but the bond issuer owns the option. Thus, when an investor purchases the bond from the issuer, he or she simultaneously "sells" the issuer an option. For this option, the issuer pays the bond purchaser. In this case, the payment takes the form of an above market coupon—relative to a noncallable bond—for the life of the bond and, so again, payment for the option is made in installments over the life of the bond.

There are many other types of options and option-like features associated with financial instruments. In this chapter, we are going to focus first on understanding calls and puts and their uses. Then, we are going to examine some relatively new forms of options called caps, floors, and collars. These instruments are, in some ways, similar to traditional options. At the same time, they are also quite different. It is the differences as well as the similarities that give these instruments their special risk-management uses. Finally, we will look at a few special options including an "option on a cap"—which may be regarded as an option on an option—and an "option on a swap." We will concentrate on the logic underlying options, the logic in option pricing, the efficiency of options as hedging instruments, and the costs to hedgers of hedging with options.

Option pricing is one of the most mathematically complex of all applied areas of finance. The first complete option pricing model was developed by Fischer Black and Myron Scholes and published in 1973. Most subsequently published option pricing models can be shown to be variants of the original Black/Scholes model. In most cases, the derivation of option pricing models rests on the mathematics of stochastic calculus and a presentation of such models without a solid background in these sophisticated quantitative tools would be confusing at best.[1] This is not a serious problem, however, as the calculations necessary to ascertain the fair market values of options have been automated and software for such purposes is available for both mainframe and micro-computers.[2] For these reasons, we will not examine in detail any of the option pricing models currently in use.

6.2 CALLS AND PUTS: THE BASICS

A **call** option grants its purchaser, called the **option holder**, the right to purchase a specified number of units of some **underlying asset** from the option seller, called the **option writer** or sometimes the **option grantor**, for some predetermined period of time (**time to expiration**) at some specified price called the **strike price**. The strike price is also known as the **exercise price**. The option writer is said to be **short the option** and the option purchaser is said to be **long the option**. For the rights bestowed by the option, the option purchaser pays the option seller a one time up-front fee called the option premium.

A put option has an identical definition except that the option purchaser has the right to sell ("put") the underlying asset to the option writer. This sale, if the option purchaser elects to exercise the option, is made at the option's strike price.

Calls and puts can be one of two types: European or American. (The names explain the origins but are no longer geographically meaningful.) A **European option** is an option that can only be exercised during a very limited exercise period near the end of the option's life. An **American option** can be exercised at any time from the moment it is created until the time it expires. Once an option expires, it is worthless if it has not been exercised. This difference between European and American options is depicted in Exhibit 6.1

In order to fully identify an option, several things must be specified. These include the underlying asset, whether the option is a call or a put, the strike price of the option, the expiration date of the option, and, if the option trades on more than one exchange, the exchange on

EXHIBIT 6.1.   Exercise Periods: European versus American

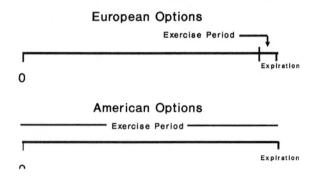

which the option trades. For example, a call option on IBM stock having a strike price of $100 and that expires in November would be identified as an "IBM November 100 call." In this case, the exchange is the **Chicago Board Options Exchange** or **CBOE**. Not all options trade on an options exchange, and, as we will see later, some of the most important options for risk management purposes are traded in over-the-counter dealer-type markets.

For any underlying asset on which options are written, there will be multiple options trading. For example, Table 6.1 lists some of the options on IBM stock as they appeared in *The Wall Street Journal* on Friday, 1 December 1989. These prices were the "last trade of the day" prices for these options on Thursday, 30 November 1989. We have deliberately limited the list to two strike prices below the closing price of IBM (90 and 95) and two strike prices above the closing price of IBM (100 and 105).

The structure of Table 6.1 is typical of the way options prices are reported whether in the financial press or on a computer screen. The calls are listed first and the puts are listed second. The expiration months are listed horizontally and the strike prices are listed vertically. The value 97-½, which appears directly under the name of the underlying asset (IBM), is the closing price of the underlying asset on the same day.

Option prices are always quoted and reported *per unit* of underlying asset regardless of the number of units of underlying asset covered

TABLE 6.1
Option Premiums
December 1, 1989

IBM	Strike	Calls			Puts		
		DEC	JAN	APR	DEC	JAN	APR
97-1/2	90	8-3/8	9-1/4	11-1/4	1/4	5/8	1-5/8
	95	3-5/8	5-1/2	7-7/8	5/8	1-11/16	3-1/4
	100	3/4	2-9/16	5-1/8	2-3/4	3-3/4	5-1/4
	105	3/16	1	3-1/8	7-1/8	7-5/8	8-3/8

by the option. For example, the price of the IBM December 90 call is $8-⅜ or $8.375. This represents the option price per unit of stock covered by the option. Since the option covers 100 shares of stock, the actual price of this option is $837.50. Different options cover different numbers of units of the underlying asset. For this reason, it is less confusing if each option is treated as if it covers just one unit of the underlying asset. This is also the reason why the **per unit pricing** convention has been adopted in actual trading. Nothing is lost by this treatment.

Almost all stock options and most other put and call options traded in the United States expire on the third Friday of the expiration month. That is, the December 1989 options expired on the third Friday of December 1989, which happened to be 15 December 1989. The actual date of expiration is very important as it can range anywhere from the 15th of the month to the 21st of the month. As we will see shortly, a large part of an option's value is derived from the time remaining to maturity. A few days can make a big difference in this value.

Listed options (i.e., options listed on an exchange) are cleared through a clearing house. All listed stock options and most other listed options in the United States are cleared through the **Option Clearing Corporation (OCC)** located in Chicago. An option clearing house serves the same function in options trading that a clearing association serves in futures trading. That is, the clearing house guarantees the performance on each option and, for this reason, the clearing house may be viewed as long to all shorts and short to all longs. As with futures, the clearing house holds margin to assure performance by the option writers. Option purchasers do not post margin as they have no obligations once they have paid the option premium.

Since OTC options are not traded on exchanges, they are not cleared through a clearing house. Instead, each party to the contract must know the other party and must have faith in the other party's ability to perform. Nevertheless, dealers in these markets may require margin or collateral from option writers to minimize the risk from a failure to perform.

Options have value for two entirely different reasons and the fair value of an option (i.e., the fair premium) is the sum of these two component parts. The two components of value are called **intrinsic value** and **time value**. Additional terminology will be explained in the following paragraphs—these terms will help the reader understand the above value components (it is assumed that the options discussed are of the American variety).

An option can be **in-the-money, at-the-money** or **out-of-the-money**. Which of these terms applies depends on the relationship between the current price of the underlying asset and the strike price of the option. For a call option, the option is in-the-money if the price of the underlying asset exceeds the strike price of the option. It is at-the-money if the price of the underlying asset exactly equals the strike price of the option. Finally, it is out-of-the-money if the price of the underlying asset is below the strike price of the option. The relationships between monieness and price are reversed for put options. These relationships are summarized in Table 6.2.

TABLE 6.2
Monieness and Options

Relationship	Calls	Puts
$A > S$	In-the-money	Out-of-the-money
$A = S$	At-the-money	At-the-money
$A < S$	Out-of-the-money	In-the-money

Notes: A denotes the current price of the underlying asset.
   S denotes the strike price of the option.

To make this notion of monieness clearer, let's apply the rules in Table 6.2 to the IBM options in Table 6.1. The IBM 90 calls and the IBM 95 calls are in-the-money because, at 97.50, the price of the underlying asset (i.e., IBM stock), is above the strike price of these options. The IBM 100 calls and the IBM 105 calls are out-of-the-money because the price of the underlying asset is below the strike prices of these options. For the IBM puts, the situation is reversed. The IBM 90 puts and the IBM 95 puts are out-of-the-money because the strike prices of these options are below the price of the underlying asset. The IBM 100 puts and the IBM 105 puts are in-the-money because the strike prices of these options are above the price of the underlying asset.

An option's intrinsic value is either the amount by which it is in-the-money or zero, whichever is greater. In terms of mathematical functions, this relationship can be written using a **MAX function**. A MAX function, for "maximum," is simply a function that selects the largest value from a set of values. The MAX function is given by Equation 6.1.

$$\text{Intrinsic Value} = \text{MAX} \{\text{in-the-money, zero}\} \qquad \textbf{(6.1)}$$

Since the conditions for a put to be in-the-money are exactly opposite those for a call to be in-the-money, the MAX functions are slightly different for calls and puts. These appear below.

	Intrinsic Value
Call	$\text{MAX}\{A - S, 0\}$
Put	$\text{MAX}\{S - A, 0\}$

For example, if the underlying asset has a price of 60 and the strike price is 55, then the call is in-the-money by 5, which is larger than zero, so the call's intrinsic value is 5. At the same time, the put is out-of-the-money by 5, which can be viewed as another way of saying in-the-money by -5. So the put's intrinsic value is 0 since 0 is greater than -5.

The logic underlying intrinsic value is very intuitive. Suppose that a call option with a strike price of 55 is commanding a premium of less than $5 when the underlying asset is priced at 60. Suppose, for example, it is priced at $3. What will happen? Since we have assumed an American-type option, this call can be exercised at any time. Arbitragers will see a riskless profit opportunity and exploit it. In this case, the arbitrage strategy is to buy the call for $3 and exercise it immediately. This requires that the arbitrager pay the call writer $55 (the strike price) to get a unit of the underlying asset. The total cost of the underlying asset to the arbitrager is, therefore, $58: $3 for the option and $55 to exercise it. But, since the underlying asset is trading for $60, the arbitrager can immediately resell the underlying asset acquired through the exercise of the option. This sale brings $60. The "buy-to-exercise" strategy thus nets the arbitrager a $2 profit. This profit is the difference between the price at which the underlying asset is sold ($60) and the cost of acquiring the underlying asset ($3 + $55).

The buy-to-exercise strategy is a riskless strategy that requires no investment on the arbitrager's part. The arbitrage does not require any investment because the arbitrager pays for the option and pays the option writer the exercise price from the proceeds of a short sale of the underlying asset. A **short sale**, in this case, means that the arbitrager borrowed the underlying asset and used the borrowed asset to make delivery on his sale in the cash market. The short sale of the underlying asset is then covered by the underlying asset acquired through the exercise of the option. This type of sale is **covered** when the party that borrowed the asset returns it to the party that lent it. The strategy is riskless because all transactions are executed simultaneously at known prices.

Since the strategy is riskless and requires no investment (a classic **pure arbitrage**), many arbitragers will recognize the profit opportunity and behave similarly. Since the strategy requires the purchase of the call option, we can expect that the cumulative effect of this buying by arbitragers will bid up the price of the option until the option no longer affords an arbitrage profit. This of course happens at a price of $5. The option, therefore, must have a value of at least $5 and this is its intrinsic value. This is precisely the sum suggested by Equation 6.1.

Intrinsic value places a floor on the total value of an option. But can the option have a value greater than its intrinsic value and, if so, why? The answer is yes; the option can and usually will have a total value greater than its intrinsic value. The difference between the total value and the intrinsic value is called time value. Time value, like intrinsic value, is easily understood at an intuitive level.

Suppose that a call option has an intrinsic value of $5, as in the case we examined a moment ago. Next, suppose that the option has six months left before its expiration. What can happen in the next six months? If the price of the underlying asset declines, the intrinsic value will decline but cannot go lower than zero. Thus, the most one can lose in the form of intrinsic value from the purchase of this option is the amount by which it is in-the-money. If the price of the underlying asset declines by $5 (i.e., from $60 to $55), we lose the full intrinsic value. But if it declines by $10 (to $50), or $15 (to $45), or any other amount greater than $5, we still only lose the $5 intrinsic value. Suppose instead that the price of the underlying asset rises. If it rises by $5 our intrinsic value increases to $10. If it rises by $10, our intrinsic value increases to $15, and so on. We can readily see that there is an asymmetry here. The loss of intrinsic value from a downside price movement is strictly limited whereas there is no limit to the upside potential. It is this asymmetry between the up- and downsides that gives an option value beyond its intrinsic value.

How much in excess of intrinsic value will someone be willing to pay for this upside potential? This can be readily determined by looking at some actual option prices. Consider again Table 6.1. Notice that IBM was priced at $97.50 on 30 November 1989 and that the December 95 call was priced at $3.625 (3-5/8). Since this option was in-the-money by $2.50 but the option was commanding a premium of $3.625, the excess value was $1.125. Now look at the January 95 call. Notice that it was commanding a premium of $5.50 (5-1/2). Thus, it had excess value of $3.00. Finally look at the April 95 call. It was commanding a premium of $7.875 (7-7/8), which represented excess value in the amount of $5.375. These three call options were identical except for the time remaining until they expired. Clearly, the longer the time until expiration, the greater the excess value. But why? The

EXHIBIT 6.2.   Time Value Decay with Respect to Passage of Time

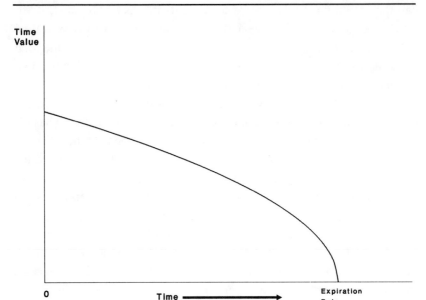

answer is simple. The excess value represents a monetary value placed on the option's potential to become more valuable before it expires. The longer the time until expiration, the greater this potential. It is not surprising then that the excess value we have been describing is called time value. The relationship between time value and time is depicted in Exhibit 6.2 and the relationship between the fair value of an option, the option's intrinsic value, and the option's time value is given by Equation 6.2.

Total Value (Premium) = Intrinsic Value + Time Value   **(6.2)**

Before moving on, the factors that influence an option's time value must be considered. Since time value is a price placed on potential, the question we need to ask is "what are the factors that influence potential?" Clearly, time remaining to expiration is one important factor, but it is not the only one. Suppose that the underlying asset's price has never changed over the last five or 10 years. Is it likely to change significantly over the near future? Probably not. Does the option have much potential to become more valuable? Clearly not. Would you be willing to pay a sizable sum for this potential? Certainly not. But suppose that the underlying asset's price has fluctuated dramatically over the last few years. Does the option have potential now? Clearly it does. The point then is that time value is a function not only of time but also of the volatility of the price of the underlying asset. We measure this volatility using a well-known statistical measure called **standard deviation**. We will call a standard deviation a "volatility unit" or a "unit of volatility" just as we did when we first introduced these terms in Chapter 4.

What other factors influence time value? One is the current price of the underlying asset itself. This price has two opposing impacts on time value. If the option is deep out-of-the-money, then there is very little potential for the underlying asset's price to change enough to put the option significantly in-the-money and we would not be willing to pay very much for time value. On the other hand, if the option is deep in-the-money then the intrinsic value is considerable and we will have to risk a large sum to get the potential we are after. This risk is an important factor and we will not be willing to pay very much beyond intrinsic value for the option. All other things being equal then, we would expect that time value is at a maximum when the option is at-the-money. And this is indeed the case. The relationship between time value and the price of the underlying asset is depicted in Exhibit 6.3.

There are two other factors that influence time value. One is the strike price of the option and the other is the current level of interest rates. The strike price of the option is obviously important because it, together with the price of the underlying asset, determines whether the option is "in-" or "out-of-the-money." The role played by interest rates is a bit more complicated. Call options can be viewed as a substitute for a long position in the underlying asset with the advantage that call options provide leverage. An investor can also get leverage, however, by borrowing some of the funds necessary for the direct purchase of the underlying asset. The higher the interest rate, the more attractive the call option alternative. Thus, we would expect the time value of call options to increase as interest rates increase. By the same

EXHIBIT 6.3.   Time Value as a Function of the Price of the Underlying Asset

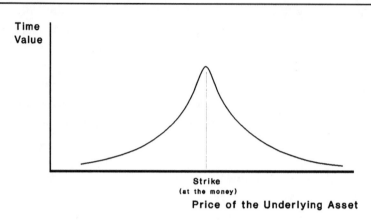

token, we would expect the value of put options to decrease as interest rates increase.

Option pricing models must capture all of the effects that have been described. The most widely used of the various option pricing models was first developed by Fischer Black and Myron Scholes and is referred to as the **Black/Scholes option pricing model** or OPM. This model was designed to determine the fair market value of a European-type call option on a non-payout asset. Many variants of the original model have been developed to fit special situations. Examples include European-type put options on non-payout assets, American-type options on non-payout assets, options on payout assets, options on futures contracts, and so on.

6.3   PAYOFF PROFILES

One of the best ways to understand the risk management uses of options and option-like instruments is to examine the payoff profiles associated with them. We discussed payoff profiles, also known as profit diagrams, in Chapter 4 and we used the concept to illustrate the outcomes of futures hedges in Chapter 5. A payoff profile depicts the profits and losses from a position in an instrument as of some specific point in time. In the case of call and put options, payoff profiles are usually depicted as of the time of the option's expiration. This is the last moment of the option's life before it expires. At that time, the option has no remaining time value and so the option's value is entirely explained by its intrinsic value.

Let's consider the payoff profile for a call option first. The first step in the construction of a payoff profile is the construction of a **value diagram**. Suppose that at some time prior to expiration, the call commands a premium of C dollars. This premium represents the sum the option purchaser pays for the option. At expiration the option will have a value of $A - S$ or zero, whichever is greater, where A denotes the value of the underlying asset and S denotes the strike price. For any value of A equal to or less than S, the option is worthless. For each $1 by which A exceeds S, the option's terminal value increases by $1. The value diagram then looks like that depicted in Exhibit 6.4.

Now recall that the option purchaser paid C dollars for this call option. The payoff profile is then the value diagram in Exhibit 6.4

EXHIBIT 6.4.   Value Diagram for a Long Call
(At expiration)

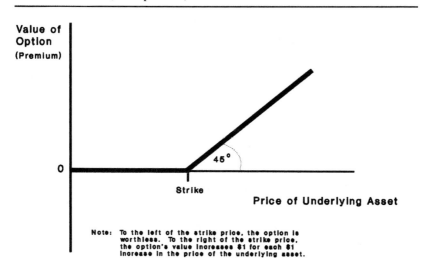

Value of Option (Premium)

0

Strike

Price of Underlying Asset

45°

Note: To the left of the strike price, the option is worthless. To the right of the strike price, the option's value increases $1 for each $1 increase in the price of the underlying asset.

EXHIBIT 6.5.   Payoff Profile for a Long Call
                 (At expiration)

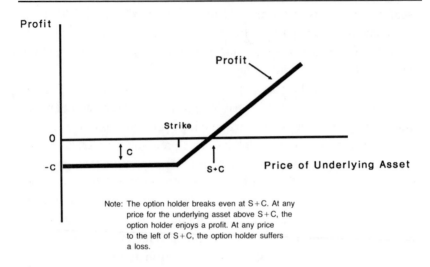

Note: The option holder breaks even at S+C. At any
      price for the underlying asset above S+C, the
      option holder enjoys a profit. At any price
      to the left of S+C, the option holder suffers
      a loss.

shifted down by the amount paid for the option. The profit function is given by Equation 6.3.

$$\text{Profit on long call} = \text{MAX}\{A - S, 0\} - C \qquad \textbf{(6.3)}$$

This profit is illustrated by the payoff profile depicted in Exhibit 6.5.

By the same process, we can construct the payoff profile for a put option. The profit function for a long put is given by Equation 6.4.

$$\text{Profit on long put} = \text{MAX}\{S - A, 0\} - P \qquad \textbf{(6.4)}$$

In Equation 6.4, P denotes the premium paid for the put. The payoff profile that corresponds to this profit function is depicted in Exhibit 6.6.

The payoff profiles for option writers are the mirror images of the payoff profiles for option purchasers. This symmetry is a reflection of the **zero-sum game** nature of options. That is, the profits to the winners exactly equal the losses to the losers. The payoff profiles for option writers are depicted in Exhibits 6.7 and 6.8.

EXHIBIT 6.6. Payoff Profile for a Long Put
(At expiration)

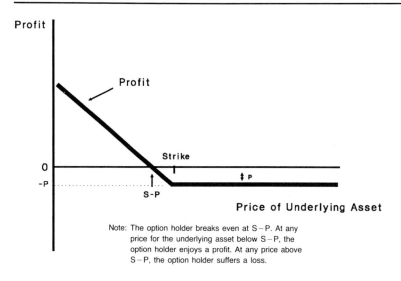

Note: The option holder breaks even at S − P. At any price for the underlying asset below S − P, the option holder enjoys a profit. At any price above S − P, the option holder suffers a loss.

EXHIBIT 6.7. Payoff Profile for a Short Call
(At expiration)

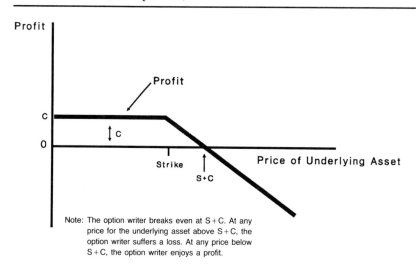

Note: The option writer breaks even at S + C. At any price for the underlying asset above S + C, the option writer suffers a loss. At any price below S + C, the option writer enjoys a profit.

EXHIBIT 6.8.   Payoff Profile for a Short Put
(At expiration)

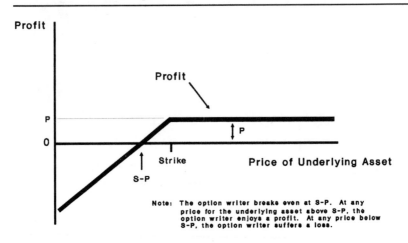

Note: The option writer breaks even at S-P. At any
price for the underlying asset above S-P, the
option writer enjoys a profit. At any price below
S-P, the option writer suffers a loss.

Options are very often combined to develop elaborate strategies. Most of these strategies are devised for speculative purposes but, quite often, special needs will make one of these strategies useful to a hedger.[3]

The most frequently used of the combination strategies are the straddle, the vertical spread, the horizontal spread, the diagonal spread, and the butterfly spread. In a **straddle**, the option purchaser buys (or sells) both a call and a put on the same underlying asset with the same strike price and the same expiration date. For this straddle, the option purchaser pays the option writer a sum equal to the cost of the two options, $C + P$. The payoff profile associated with this long-straddle strategy is depicted in Exhibit 6.9. The payoff profile for the short straddle is depicted in Exhibit 6.10.

Notice the peculiar "V" shape of a straddle. The payoff profile for a straddle suggests that such a strategy is useful for hedging volatility rather than direction. That is, the long straddle shows a positive payoff regardless of the direction of movement in the underlying asset's price. All that is required for a profit to be realized is that there be sufficient movement away from the strike price. The opposite is true for a short straddle. These strategies would be of interest to a firm with a volatility

EXHIBIT 6.9. Payoff Profile for a Long Straddle
(At expiration)

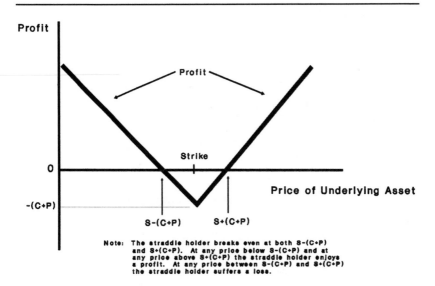

Note: The straddle holder breaks even at both S-(C+P) and S+(C+P). At any price below S-(C+P) and at any price above S+(C+P) the straddle holder enjoys a profit. At any price between S-(C+P) and S+(C+P) the straddle holder suffers a loss.

EXHIBIT 6.10. Payoff Profile for a Short Straddle
(At expiration)

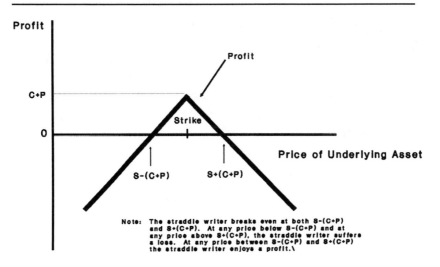

Note: The straddle writer breaks even at both S-(C+P) and S+(C+P). At any price below S-(C+P) and at any price above S+(C+P), the straddle writer suffers a loss. At any price between S-(C+P) and S+(C+P) the straddle writer enjoys a profit.\

235

exposure. A volatility exposure is an exposure in which the firm will suffer a negative result from any movement away from the current price level. A party with such an exposure can hedge it by purchasing a straddle with a strike price equal to the current price of the underlying asset.

Speculators also employ straddles. A speculator who purchases a straddle is sometimes said to be **long volatility** (or long **vols** in market parlance). The terminology stems from the fact that the speculator who is long a straddle will profit from an increase in volatility. Similarly, a speculator who is short a straddle is said to be **short volatility** (or short "vols").

A spread is a combination of options that involves the purchase of one option and the sale of another where both options are of the same class. That is, both options are calls or both options are puts. The payoff profiles associated with spreads are nearly identical whether we use calls or puts so we will not distinguish between them.

There are a number of different types of spreads. The **vertical spread** refers to a spread across strike prices. The term "vertical spread" comes from the traditional vertical listing of strike prices as we showed in Table 6.1. In the vertical spread, we buy a call (or a put) with one strike price and simultaneously sell a call (or a put) that has a different strike price. The expiration month and the underlying asset for the two options in the vertical spread are identical. If we buy the lower strike option and sell the higher strike option, the spread is called a vertical bull spread. For example, we could buy the Dec IBM 90 call for 8.375 and sell the Dec IBM 95 call for 3.625. The net premium paid is then 4.75. If we sell the lower strike option and buy the higher strike option, then the spread is called a **vertical bear spread**. A vertical bear spread with the same two IBM calls used to illustrate the **vertical bull spread** will result in a net premium received of 4.75. Payoff profiles for these two strategies are depicted in Exhibits 6.11 and 6.12.

A **horizontal spread** is a spread across expiration months. In this spread, we sell an option that has one expiration month and buy an option with a different expiration month. Both options have the same strike price and are written on the same underlying asset. The spread is

EXHIBIT 6.11. Payoff Profile for a Vertical Bull Spread
(At expiration)

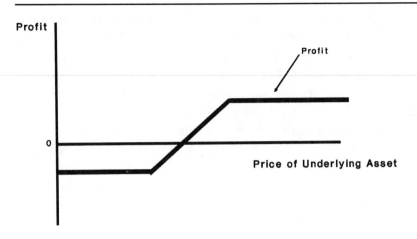

EXHIBIT 6.12. Payoff Profile for a Vertical Bear Spread
(At expiration)

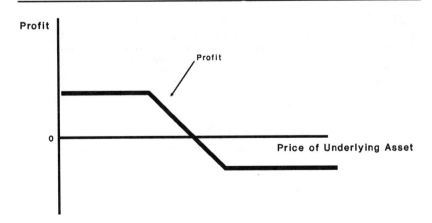

called a **horizontal bull spread** if we buy the back month and sell the front month. For example, we could buy the Jan IBM 95 call and sell the Dec IBM 95 call. The spread is called a **horizontal bear spread** if we buy the front month and sell the back month. Using the same two options and continuing the example, the horizontal bear spread would require that we buy the Dec IBM 95 call and sell the Jan IBM 95 call. The payoff profiles for these two horizontal spread strategies are depicted in Exhibits 6.13 and 6.14.

Notice the similarity of the payoff profile for the horizontal bull spread depicted in Exhibit 6.13 and the payoff profile for the short straddle depicted in Exhibit 6.10. Also notice the similarity of the payoff profile for the horizontal bear spread depicted in Exhibit 6.14 and the payoff profile for the long straddle depicted in Exhibit 6.9. These similarities suggest that horizontal spreads can be used in a fashion similar to straddles to hedge volatility exposures.

A **diagonal spread** is a spread across both the strike price and the expiration month. That is, it is vertical and horizontal at the same time. For example, we might buy the Dec IBM 95 call and sell the Jan IBM 100 call. A **butterfly spread** involves four options that are all calls or all puts. All four options have the same expiration month and are written on the same underlying asset. One option has a high strike

EXHIBIT 6.13.   Payoff Profile for a Horizontal Bull Spread
(At front month's expiration)

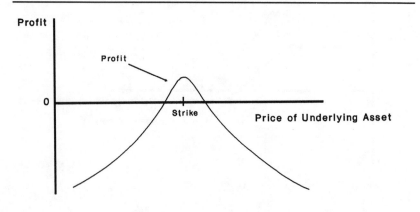

EXHIBIT 6.14.   Payoff Profile for a Horizontal Bear Spread
(At front month's expiration)

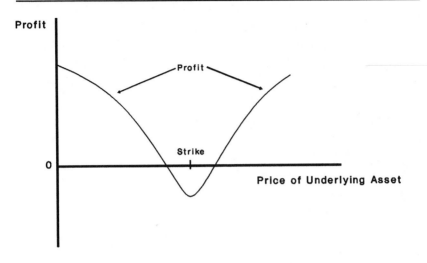

price, one has a low strike price, and two have the same strike price, which is between those of the high strike and low strike. The two middle strike options are sold and the two end options are purchased. For example, we might buy the Dec IBM 90 call and the Dec IBM 100 call and sell two Dec IBM 95 calls. This strategy can also be reversed. The reverse strategy, which consists of buying the two middle strikes and selling the two end strikes, is called a **reverse butterfly** or a **sandwich spread**. We will not draw the payoff profiles for either diagonal spreads or butterfly spreads.

6.4   HEDGING WITH OPTIONS

Having developed the payoff profiles for the more popular option strategies, let's consider the outcomes for a firm in need of a hedge that chooses to use an option as the hedging instrument. We will use the example of a CFO whose board has authorized the public offering of $50 million of 30-year bonds to fund the construction of a new production facility. This is the same example used to illustrate the use of interest-rate futures as hedging instruments in Chapter 5, Section 5.2. At the time the CFO received authorization, the corporate yield curve for investment grade bonds suggested that the firm could float an issue at par if it agreed to pay a coupon of 9.75 percent. But again, there is an estimated three-month lag between authorization by the board and the actual issuance of the securities. During these three months, the firm is exposed to the risk that yields might rise and the offering will have to be sold with a coupon above 9.75 percent.

In the last chapter, we examined how the firm's interest-rate risk could be hedged using interest-rate futures. The firm's risk profile, the payoff profile, and the residual risk profile (formed by combining the risk profile and the payoff profile) are repeated as Exhibits 6.15, 6.16, and 6.17, respectively.

As it happens, the CFO believes that interest rates are more likely to fall than rise in the coming months. Her past experience in predicting interest-rate movements has been reasonably good. She correctly predicted the subsequent direction of rates about 60 percent of the time. Nevertheless, the size of this offering is such that the interest-rate

EXHIBIT 6.15.   Risk Profile—Offering Lag

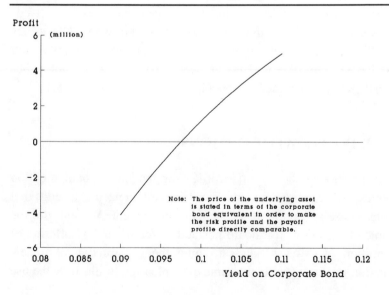

Note: The price of the underlying asset is stated in terms of the corporate bond equivalent in order to make the risk profile and the payoff profile directly comparable.

EXHIBIT 6.16. Payoff Profile—Short T-Bond Futures

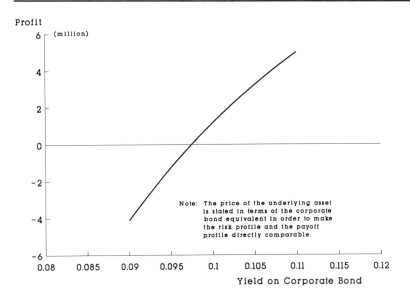

Note: The price of the underlying asset is stated in terms of the corporate bond equivalent in order to make the risk profile and the payoff profile directly comparable.

EXHIBIT 6.17. Residual Risk Profile—Futures Hedge
(Risk Profile + Payoff Profile)

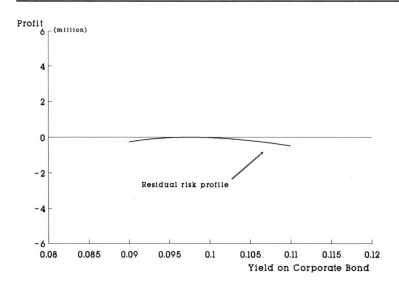

exposure must be hedged against an adverse upward movement in rates. She decides to hedge this offering in options.

Since the firm will suffer financially from any increase in rates, the CFO needs a hedge strategy that will produce positive profits if rates rise. The inverse relationship between yields and bond prices suggests that this is equivalent to a strategy that will prove profitable if bond prices decline. The appropriate strategy is to be long puts on a debt instrument. She decides to hedge by buying puts on T-bond futures. These puts have three months to expiration. She uses the same DVBP model used to determine the hedge ratio when she was hedging in futures. Thus, she concludes that she would need puts covering about $22 million of underlying T-bonds. As it happens, each option covers one T-bond futures contract and each futures contract covers $0.1 million; so she needs to buy 220 options. For these options, the CFO pays a premium of 1-1/4 per hundred dollars of face value (1.25 percent of par). The total cost of the options is therefore $275,000, which she pays up-front.

The payoff profile for these options, with the "price" of the underlying asset expressed as the "yield-equivalent on the *firm's* bonds*," rather than as a dollar price (horizontal axis), is depicted in Exhibit 6.18. This re-expression of the T-bond price as a corporate yield equivalent is necessary to allow us to combine the risk and payoff profiles. Notice that this re-expression makes the payoff profile of a long put look like the payoff profile of a long call. This is simply another reflection of the inverse relationship between prices and yields.

By combining the firm's risk profile, depicted in Exhibit 6.15, with the payoff profile from its long hedge in puts, depicted in Exhibit 6.18, we can quickly visualize the residual risk exposure from the hedged position. This is depicted in Exhibit 6.19.

Compare the residual risk profile from the option hedge (Exhibit 6.19) with the residual risk profile from the futures hedge (Exhibit 6.17). Notice that the futures hedge insulates the firm from any movement in interest rates whether that movement is favorable or unfavorable. The options hedge protects the firm from increases in interest rates but still allows the firm to benefit from decreases in

EXHIBIT 6.18. Payoff Profile—Long T-Bond Put

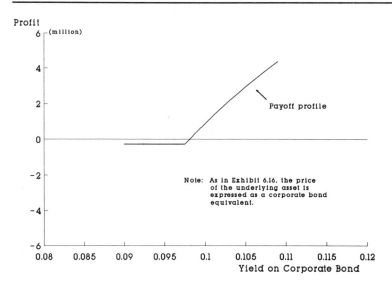

Payoff profile

Note: As in Exhibit 6.16, the price of the underlying asset is expressed as a corporate bond equivalent.

EXHIBIT 6.19. Residual Risk—Option Hedge

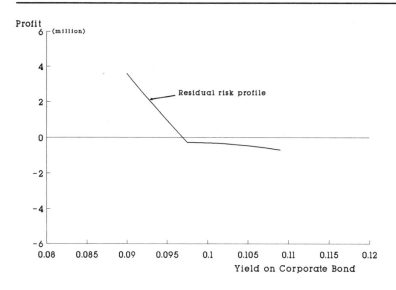

Residual risk profile

interest rates. Thus, if rates decline between the time the board authorizes the sale of new debt and the time of the actual public offering of that debt, the firm will enjoy lower financing costs than the current 9.75 percent. On the other hand, the preservation of the opportunity to benefit from a decline in rates has a cost to the firm. This cost is the up-front premium the firm pays to the option writer.

Notice the slight "dip" in the right side of the residual risk profile depicted in Exhibit 6.19. This dip reflects the fact that the size of this option hedge is not adjusted as the yield changes. The performance of the hedge can be improved by periodically adjusting the size of the hedge to take into account the changing DVBPs. This issue was discussed in Chapter 5 and we do not consider it further here.

The option hedging strategy employed above can just as easily be used to hedge exchange-rate risk, equity-price risk or commodity-price risk. The appropriate strategy (i.e., buying puts, buying calls, writing puts, writing calls, straddles, spreads, and so on) will depend on the nature of the firm's exposure. This is best visualized, as argued above, with graphic depictions of the firm's risk profile.

6.5   CASH SETTLEMENT OPTIONS

The original call and put options, like the original futures contracts, provided for the physical delivery of the underlying asset. In the case of futures, the delivery occurs during the contract's delivery month with the specific time of delivery left to the discretion of the contract seller. In the case of options, the delivery occurs only if the option holder, the long, elects to exercise the option. With American options, exercise can occur at any time. With European options, exercise is limited to the exercise period. However, just as deliverable futures contracts are rarely delivered, options are rarely exercised. Instead, parties with open positions in options make offsetting trades, called **closing trades**. That is, a party that had sold an option buys an identical option. He or she is now long and short an identical instrument. The clearing house then scratches one long and one short—thereby terminating the trader's position.

Shortly after the introduction of cash settlement futures on stock indexes, futures exchanges persuaded the CFTC to allow trading in **options on futures** on a trial basis. The experiment was successful and was later made permanent. Options on futures now trade on most futures exchanges. The purpose of an option on a futures contract is to allow the option writer (purchaser) in the case of a call (put) to deliver a standardized unit of underlying asset (the futures contract) should the long elect to exercise the option. But, with the introduction of options on stock-index futures, we had an option that, if exercised, resulted in the delivery of a futures contract that was then cash settled. It was a short step from this type of option to an option that was written directly on a stock index and that was itself settled in cash at the end of the option's life. Such options do not require an explicit decision on the part of the long to exercise the option. Instead, the option writer pays the option holder a sum equal to the amount that the option is "in-the-money" or "zero," whichever is greater, at the time of the option's expiration.

Cash settlement options written directly on stock indexes quickly supplanted options on stock-index futures. They also paved the way for other forms of cash settlement options including rate caps and rate floors, which we take up next.

6.6   INTEREST-RATE CAPS

From the perspective of the hedger, cash settlement options, like those written on stock indexes, are limited in their usefulness to those situations in which the hedger is concerned about fluctuations in prices over a short span of time. Think of this span as a single period. In other words, a single cash settlement will terminate the option on its expiration date. But suppose that the firm has a risk exposure that spans multiple periods, each of which succeeds the other. Such a situation might, for instance, occur if the firm is paying a semiannual floating rate of interest on its long-term debt and is concerned about a rise in rates.

Theoretically, this exposure can be hedged by stringing together a series of single-period interest-rate options—one expiring every six months. But this is impractical for two reasons. First, it assumes that each contract delivery month will be sufficiently liquid to enter a contract without substantial liquidity costs. Second, it assumes that options with every required delivery month into the very distant future are currently available. Both assumptions fail. In practice, only the front one or two contract months tend to be liquid—if indeed any are liquid—and conventional calls and puts are almost never written with expiration dates more than a year into the future.

The solution for this hedger is a special over-the-counter type of option traded in dealer-type markets. These options are called **interest rate caps** or simply **caps**. The writer (the seller) of a cap pays the cap holder (the purchaser) each time the contract's reference rate of interest is above the contract's ceiling rate of interest on a settlement date. By this structure, a cap provides a multi-period hedge against increases in interest rates. It is important to note that even though caps are multi-period options, the full premiums are ordinarily paid up-front.

The market makers for caps are commercial and investment banks. Market makers both buy and sell caps and they profit, as usual, from a spread between their bid price and their asked price. The rate cap premium takes the form of a percentage of the notional principal on which the cap will be written. For example, consider a dealer making a market in three-year six-month LIBOR caps with a strike price (cap) of 8 percent. The dealer might bid 1.28 percent and offer 1.34 percent. That is, the dealer will write a cap for a premium of 1.34 percent and buy a cap for a premium of 1.28 percent. The difference between the bid and asked, 0.06 percent (6 basis points), is the dealer's bid-ask spread.

Before considering the uses of caps, let's take a few moments to review the structure of a cap and the settlement procedure more carefully. The market-maker bank and the bank's customer enter an agreement in which they specify a "term" for the cap (such as two years or five years), a reference rate (such as three-month LIBOR, six-month LIBOR, or three-month T-bill), a contract **ceiling rate** that constitutes the cap's "strike" price and that is sometimes called the "cap rate," the cap's notional principal, and the settlement dates. On the first settlement date, the cap writer pays the cap holder a sum determined by Equation 6.5. This sum is recalculated on the calculation date that precedes each settlement date. If the bank is the cap writer, the bank will pay the customer any amount due. If the bank is the cap holder, the customer will pay the bank any amount due.

$$\text{Market Maker Pays} = D \times \text{MAX}\{\text{Reference} - \text{Ceiling, 0}\} \times NP \times LPP \qquad (6.5)$$

In Equation 6.5, D denotes a dummy variable that takes the value $+1$ if the market maker is the cap seller and -1 if the market maker is the cap purchaser; MAX denotes the "MAX function" described earlier, NP denotes the notional principal, and LPP denotes the length of the payment period. The value LPP will depend on the choice of reference rate and the frequency of payments. For example, LIBOR is quoted as actual over 360. Thus, LPP for a six-month LIBOR will typically be between 181 over 360 (181/360) and 184 over 360 (184/360). If the calculation results in a positive value (which can only happen if the bank is cap writer), then the bank pays the client. If the calculation results in negative value (which can only happen if the bank is the cap purchaser), then the client pays the bank. If the calculation produces the value zero, then no payments are made.

We can use Equation 6.5 to determine the payoff profile for a cap. The payoff profile is drawn for a single settlement date, but it looks the same for each settlement date covered by the cap. Such a payoff profile appears, from the cap purchaser's perspective, in Exhibit 6.20.

Notice that the cap's payoff profile looks identical to that for a long call. But this is actually misleading. A call option usually depicts "price" rather than "yield" on the horizontal axis. When yield is used on the horizontal axis, the payoff profile actually looks like that of a long put on a debt instrument. (This point was made earlier in Exhibit 6.18 and the discussion surrounding Exhibit 6.18.) This demonstrates that caps are indeed analogous to put options since price is inversely related to yield. There is one small difference however. Since the cap is a multi-period option and the premium for this option is paid in a single up-front lump sum, the payoff profile must amortize the premi-

EXHIBIT 6.20.   Payoff Profile for a Cap Purchaser
(Per settlement period)

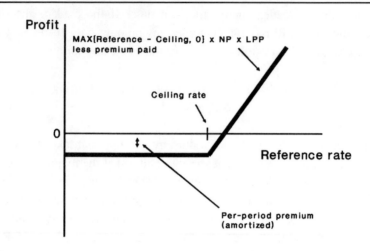

um to be truly representative. Suppose, for example, that a four-year semiannual cap can be purchased for 1.85 percent of the notional principal. Then the premium must be prorated by way of a standard amortization formula. We use Equation 6.6 for this purpose.

$$\text{Per period cost} = \text{Total Premium} \div PVAF \qquad \textbf{(6.6)}$$

where $PVAF$ denotes the **present value annuity** factor given by Equation 6.7.

$$PVAF = \frac{1 - (1 + k/m)^{-nm}}{k/m} \qquad \textbf{(6.7)}$$

In Equation 6.7, k is the annual discount rate, n is the term of the cap (in years), and m is the number of payment periods per year. For example, suppose that k is 8.00 percent. Then Equation 6.7 yields a $PVAF$ of 6.7327 and Equation 6.6 yields 0.2748. We conclude that the per period value of the premium is 0.2748 percent. This 0.2748 percent is the amortized single period premium for the cap depicted in Exhibit 6.20.

We have chosen here to express the rate cap premium on a per period basis—in this case a period is six months in length. It is also quite common to express the cap premium as **an effective annual percentage cost**. The per period cost can be re-expressed as an effective annual percentage cost using Equation 6.8.

$$\text{Effective Annual Percentage Cost} = (1 + PPC)^m - 1 \quad \textbf{(6.8)}$$

The "per period cost" is denoted PPC, which is obtained from Equation 6.6. In this example, the effective annual percentage cost is 0.55 percent. It is very useful to express the premium paid for the cap as an effective annual percentage cost, particularly when we are trying to compare alternative financing strategies. In such cases, we must reduce all costs to a single effective per-annum rate called "all-in-cost." We examine all-in-cost and consider a specific example in the next chapter.

The following example shows an interest rate cap at work. Suppose that it is currently 15 February 199X. A firm approaches a market maker bank in need of a five-year cap on six-month LIBOR. The firm and the bank agree to a "ceiling rate" of 10.00 percent, notional principal of $50 million, and settlement dates of 15 August and 15 February. The firm pays the bank the up-front fee for writing the cap. Assume the cap commences immediately and the calculation dates are some set number of days prior to each settlement date. The calculation date is simply the day on which the parties determine how much, if anything, is to be paid on the subsequent settlement date. The amount is determined by the spot value of the reference rate on the **fixing date**. The fixing date serves the same role in caps that the reset date serves in swaps.

Now suppose that the reference rate (six-month LIBOR) at the time of setting for the first payment is 10.48 percent. Since the reference rate exceeds the ceiling rate, the bank must make a payment to the firm. The amount of this payment is determined by Equation 6.5. Substituting the values $+1$ for D, 10.48 percent for the reference rate, 10.00 percent for the ceiling rate, $50 million for the notional principal, and 181/360 for the *LPP*, we obtain a payment of $120,667. The full set of payments to the firm on this particular cap might look something like that depicted in Table 6.3. (In Table 6.3, the indicated values for the reference rate are for illustration purposes only and do not represent actual rates on any specific dates.)

Since caps are multi-period options, the simplest way to price a cap is to decompose it into the actual series of single-period options to which it is equivalent. This series of single-period options is sometimes called a strip. The "fair value" of each of the options in the strip can then be determined by using an appropriate single-period option pricing model. The sum of these fair values is the fair value of the cap. The bank would then add (or subtract) a sum to this fair value to obtain the price at which it would sell (or buy) such a cap. As noted earlier, the difference between the bank's bid and asked prices is just another bid-ask spread.

The factors that influence the value of a cap are the same as the factors that influence the value of any option. They include the current level of interest rates, the ceiling rate (strike price) of the cap, the volatility of the reference rate, the current level of the reference rate, and the time to each cash settlement. With this special kind of option, however, we must also consider the term of the cap (sometimes called

TABLE 6.3
The Series of Payments On the Cap

Payment Date	Value of the Reference Rate	Value of the Ceiling Rate	LPP	Payment
15 Aug 199X	10.48	10.00	181/360	$120,667
15 Feb 199X + 1	9.89	10.00	184/360	0
15 Aug 199X + 1	9.24	10.00	181/360	0
15 Feb 199X + 2	8.56	10.00	184/360	0
15 Aug 199X + 2	9.78	10.00	181/360	0
15 Feb 199X + 3	10.18	10.00	184/360	46,000
15 Aug 199X + 3	10.94	10.00	182/360	237,611
15 Feb 199X + 4	12.34	10.00	184/360	598,000
15 Aug 199X + 4	11.08	10.00	181/360	271,500
15 Feb 199X + 5	9.67	10.00	184/360	0
				$1,273,778

the **tenor** of the cap)—that is, the number of payment periods it covers. The longer the term, the more valuable the cap.

Caps are priced as a percentage of the notional principal. Thus a cap, like the one above, that the bank priced at 1.85 would require an up-front payment by the bank's customer of $925,000. On this particular cap, the bank ultimately paid out a total of $1,273,778. There was no way, of course, to know in advance what the total payout would be. It could easily have been much less than $925,000 and it also could easily have been much more.

There are many uses for interest rate caps but the most common is to impose an upper limit to the cost of floating-rate debt. For example, suppose a firm raises debt capital by issuing a five-year floating rate note paying six-month LIBOR plus 80 basis points. The firm's management decides that it can handle an annual interest expense up to 10.8 percent but cannot afford to go above 10.8 percent. To limit the potential interest expense on this floating rate note, the firm buys the cap described above from the bank. Anytime six-month LIBOR exceeds 10 percent, the firm must pay more than 10.8 percent to its lenders. But, with the cap in place, the bank will pay the firm a sum equal to the excess over the firm's 10.8 percent cost and, therefore, the firm's net interest expense on its floating rate note is limited to a maximum of 10.8 percent. On the other hand, when LIBOR is below 10 percent, the firm is paying less than 10.8 percent to its lenders and so it does not need offsetting payments from the bank. These cash flows are illustrated in Exhibit 6.21.

Rate caps are often used in conjunction with swaps to produce "rate capped swaps." Consider a simple example. A firm wants rate-capped floating-rate debt but the firm has a comparative advantage in the fixed-rate market. It can thus reduce its borrowing cost if it borrows at a fixed rate, swaps its fixed-rate payments for floating-rate payments with a swap bank, and then caps its floating-rate payments to the swap bank with an interest-rate cap. The interest payment flows associated with these transactions are depicted in Exhibit 6.22. For obvious reasons, there are economies of scale for swap market makers to also make markets in rate caps.

Unlike swaps, which are generally not freely assignable, caps are

EXHIBIT 6.21.   Interest Flows: Cap Market Maker, Firm, and Lenders

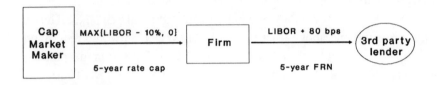

Note: This cash flow diagram only depicts interest
      flows. It does not show the principal flows
      between the firm and the third party lenders
      or the up-front fee for the cap paid to the
      cap market maker.

EXHIBIT 6.22.   Interest Flows on a Rate-Capped Swap

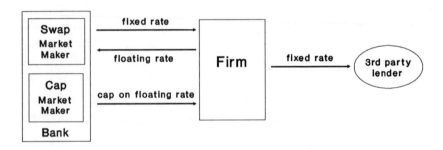

assignable by their holder. That is, the owner of a cap can sell or otherwise transfer the cap to another party. This assignability is important. It is not uncommon for a firm to plan an intermediate- to long-term floating-rate financing by engaging in a commercial paper rollover strategy. The firm may want to cap its floating rate, so it enters a rate cap with the six-month commercial paper rate as the reference rate. Then, after some time has elapsed, the firm decides it no longer needs the financing (perhaps it has disposed of the assets supported by the financing). In this case, it simply would not rollover its outstanding paper upon the paper's maturity. So, while the floating-rate financing has terminated, the cap for which the firm expended resources continues to exist despite the fact that the firm no longer has a need for it. A cap, like any option, will have at least some value until such time as it expires. By allowing the firm to assign the cap, the firm can recapture this value. As a practical matter, most cap market makers will buy back a cap at its current fair value less a small discount. We should note that caps are not assignable by the writer without the approval of the owner.

Before moving on to rate floors, let's examine one last issue involving interest rate caps that end users must consider: What ceiling rate should an end user purchase? That is, after the reference rate is decided, say six-month LIBOR, at what rate for six-month LIBOR should the ceiling (strike) be set? Should it be 9 percent, 10 percent, or 11 percent? The lower the ceiling, the greater the likelihood that the cap owner will receive payments from the bank and the greater these payments will be. Obviously, the lower the ceiling rate, the more attractive the cap from the purchaser's perspective. But, as usual, there is no "free lunch." The lower the ceiling rate, the greater the price the market maker is going to demand for the cap. The question then becomes, how much protection does the end user require and how much is the end user prepared to pay for this protection? We will not try to answer this question yet. As we will see shortly, there are other courses of action that can be pursued to reduce the cost of a cap. This brings us logically to the subject of interest-rate floors.

6.7 INTEREST-RATE FLOORS

An **interest-rate floor** is a multi-period interest-rate option identical to a rate cap except that the floor writer pays the floor purchaser when the reference rate drops below the floor rate. Let's again assume that the market maker bank is the seller of the option and a customer of the bank is the purchaser. In this case, the bank will pay the customer a cash sum, based on a settlement formula, whenever the reference rate falls below the floor rate. The cash settlement formula, which is repeated on each settlement date, is given by Equation 6.9.

$$\text{Market Maker Pays} = D \times \text{MAX}\{\text{Floor} - \text{Reference}, 0\} \times NP \times LPP \tag{6.9}$$

Notice that Equation 6.9 is almost identical to Equation 6.5 except that we have reversed the position of the strike price (ceiling in the case of the interest rate cap and floor in the case of the interest rate floor) in the formula. All other terms are identical. The payoff profiles associated with Equation 6.9 are depicted in Exhibit 6.23. Observe that the payoff profiles are identical to those for the call options that we described earlier in this chapter—but only after we recognize that we are using a ''rate'' in lieu of a ''price'' on the horizontal axis. Clearly, a floor is a multi-period call option.

The premium depicted in the single-period payoff profile for the rate floor, like the premium depicted in the single-period payoff profile for the rate cap, is an amortized single-period equivalent for the full premium paid up-front at the time of the floor purchase. The amortized value of this premium is found in an identical fashion to that for the rate cap by using Equations 6.6 and 6.7 and this per period cost can be converted to an effective annual percentage cost using Equation 6.8.

Interest-rate floors have been described as the ''mirror image'' of interest-rate caps. But this is technically not correct. The same kind of confusion often arises with calls and puts. The payoff profile for a long call is not the mirror image of the payoff profile for a long put. The mirror image of a long call is a short call and the mirror image of a long

EXHIBIT 6.23.   Payoff Profile for a Floor Purchaser
(Per settlement period)

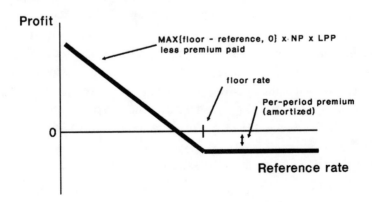

put is a short put. This is a direct result of the fact that option trading is, in the language of economics, a zero-sum game. That is, the profits to the winners are equal to the losses to the losers. The counterparty to a call purchaser is not a put purchaser. It is a call writer. Similarly, the counterparty to a put purchaser is a put writer. The final proof that long cap payoff profiles and long floor payoff profiles are not mirror images is the readily apparent fact that there is no theoretical limit to how high a reference rate can go, but there is an absolute limit to how low a reference rate can go.

Just as with interest-rate caps, there are many uses for interest-rate floors. The most common use is to place a floor on the interest income from a floating-rate asset. Let's consider a simple case: An insurance company has obtained funds by selling 7.00 percent 10-year fixed-rate annuities. These annuities constitute fixed-rate liabilities. Because the insurer's managers believe that interest rates are going to rise, they decide to invest the proceeds from the sale of the annuities in floating-rate assets (six-month T-bills) that are currently yielding 7.25 percent. Management's plan is to sell the floating-rate assets after rates rise and then invest the funds in fixed-rate assets.

While management's plan seems quite rational—"fix interest costs now by the sale of the annuities while interest rates are low, invest in floating-rate assets until rates rise, and then move to fixed-rate assets"—management still runs the risk that its interest-rate projections might prove wrong. It is this concern that drives management to purchase a floor. The firm buys a 10-year floor with a floor rate of 7.00 percent and the six-month T-bill as the reference rate. For this floor, the firm pays an up-front premium of 2.24 percent, which is equivalent to an annual percentage cost of 0.34 percent at a discount rate of 7 percent (compounded semiannually). The firm is now protected from declines in rates.

As it happened, management's interest-rate projections proved wrong—at least for a time. Rates declined and stayed below the floor rate for four years. During this time, the insurance company received payments from the bank. These payments made it possible for the insurer to meet its obligations to the holders of its annuity policies. About four-and-one-half years after the commencement of the floor, interest rates began to rise and about five years after the commencement of the floor, the insurer converted its floating-rate assets into five-year fixed-rate assets yielding 8.375 percent. At the same time, the insurer sold what remained of the floor back to the bank for 0.82 percent. While the firm held it, the floor performed exactly as required. It spared the insurance company serious financial damage by guaranteeing a minimum return on its floating-rate assets.

Like interest-rate caps, interest-rate floors can be, and often are, married to swaps. We won't illustrate a rate-floored swap with a cash flow diagram, but the logic parallels that used to depict the rate-capped swap in Exhibit 6.22.

The examples we used above to illustrate the cap and the floor both involved end users who were purchasers of these interest-rate options. Not all end users will be purchasers. One interesting situation, in which the end user is a floor seller, involves a combination of a cap and a floor known as a collar. We consider this type of interest-rate option in the next section.

6.8   INTEREST-RATE COLLARS

An **interest-rate collar** is a combination of a cap and a floor in which the purchaser of the collar buys a cap and simultaneously sells a floor. Collars can be constructed from two separate transactions (one involving a cap and one involving a floor) or they can be combined into a single transaction. A collar has the effect of locking the collar purchaser into a floating rate of interest that is bounded on both the high side and the low side. This is sometimes called "locking into a band" or "swapping into a band."

Consider an example: Suppose that a firm holds fixed-rate assets that are yielding 10 percent. These assets are funded with floating-rate liabilities tied to the prime rate. The current rate on these liabilities is 8 percent and the firm wants to cap the cost at 9.5 percent (called a **prime cap**). But, as it happens, the cap market maker wants an up-front premium, which translates into an effective annual percentage cost of 0.5 percent, for the prime cap. The firm feels that this is too high a price to pay. But, as it happens, the firm discovers that it can sell a prime floor with a floor rate of 7 percent for a premium equivalent to an effective annual percentage return of 0.45 percent. Since the firm is the seller of the floor it receives the premium. The firm decides to buy the cap and sell the floor—effectively purchasing a collar.

From the firm's perspective, its annual costs are now bounded between 7 percent and 9.5 percent. Since its interest revenue exceeds its interest cost, it has locked in a source of net revenue for the firm, although the amount of the revenue can vary within the bounds dictated by the collar. When prime rises above 9.5 percent, the bank pays the firm the difference. When prime falls below 7 percent, the firm pays the bank the difference. The payoff profile for the interest-rate collar is depicted in Exhibit 6.24.

By entering a collar, the firm is able to place a rate cap on its floating-rate liabilities while simultaneously reducing the cost of the cap with the premium received from the sale of the floor. The cost to the firm, of course, is the payouts the firm must make to the market maker bank should the reference rate fall below the floor rate. This

EXHIBIT 6.24.   Payoff Profile for a Collar Purchaser
(Per settlement period)

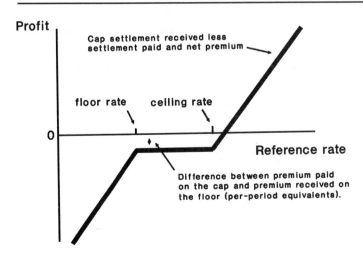

potential payout by the firm in a low-rate environment is often of less concern then its uncapped payouts in a high-rate environment and, consequently, the collar is considered an attractive way to cap floating-rate debt. Just as caps and floors can be combined with swaps, so can collars. As a general rule, however, collars are usually used alone.

A bank making markets (running a **book**) in caps, floors, and collars has an obvious interest in hedging the exposures associated with its positions in these instruments. The hedging of the these instruments is not, however, a primary focus of this book. We nevertheless address the issue indirectly when we consider the hedging of a swap book in Chapter 9.

6.9   MISCELLANEOUS INTEREST-RATE OPTIONS

In winding up this chapter, we need to briefly consider a few miscellaneous types of interest-rate options. In particular, we will discuss the "participating cap," the "Caption," and the "swaption."

A **participating cap** is structured for the end user who is in need of an interest-rate cap but who is unable or unwilling to pay the up-front cost of the cap. The end user could reduce the cost of the cap by entering into a collar, but the collar reduces the benefits from a decline in rates and the end user may not be willing to pay this price. The solution—the participating cap—is for the purchaser to pay the bank a portion of the difference between the reference rate and the ceiling rate when the reference rate is below the ceiling rate and for the cap seller to pay the cap purchaser the usual full difference between the reference rate and the ceiling rate when the reference rate is above the ceiling rate. The payment formula for the participating cap appears as Equation 6.10.

$$\text{Market Maker Pays} = D \times \{\text{MAX}(RR - CR, 0) + [-PF \times \text{MAX}(CR - RR, 0)]\} \times NP \times LLP \qquad \textbf{(6.10)}$$

The reference rate is denoted by RR, CR denotes the ceiling rate, and

PF denotes the percentage factor. All other notation is the same as that used earlier for caps and floors.

Let's consider a simple case. A firm approaches a market maker bank in need of a five-year cap on a floating-rate liability tied to one-year LIBOR. The firm wants its rate capped at 10 percent on notional principal of $40 million. The bank agrees to sell such a cap for an up-front premium of 2.75 percent. The firm cannot afford to pay such a large up-front fee. The bank then suggests a participating cap. The firm will pay the bank 30 percent of the difference between the reference rate and the ceiling rate (10 percent) whenever the reference rate is below the ceiling rate. In turn, the bank will pay the firm the full difference between the reference rate and the ceiling rate whenever the reference rate exceeds the ceiling rate. The firm agrees.

One year later, on the first settlement date, the reference rate (one-year LIBOR) stands at 9.42 percent. Plugging the values into Equation 6.10, we obtain the sum -$70,566.67. Since this value is negative, the firm is paying the bank. This calculation is repeated for each settlement period for five years.

$$
\begin{aligned}
\text{Market Maker Pays} = {} & 1 \times \{\text{MAX}(9.42\% - 10.00\%, 0) \\
& + [-30\% \times \text{MAX}(10.00\% \\
& - 9.42\%, 0)]\} \times \$40 \text{ million} \\
& \times 365/360 \\
= {} & -\$70,566.67
\end{aligned}
$$

The second special type of interest-rate option is actually an "option on an option." Technically, it is a call option on a cap. This type of option was first introduced in the mid-1980s. In 1987, Marine Midland Bank registered the service mark **caption** for its version of this instrument.

The question that immediately occurs is "why an option on an option?" The answer is surprisingly simple. Sometimes a firm wants to lock in the right to interest-rate risk protection but it is not really sure that it will need the protection or the firm may feel that a better alternative may become available if it waits a while.

Consider an example: The CFO of a firm is considering a seven-year floating-rate financing. He will be making a pitch to the firm's board for permission to go ahead. The CFO knows that the board will be concerned about the firm's exposure on a floating-rate financing and so the firm will need an interest-rate cap. The CFO approaches a market-maker bank that agrees to a 10.00 percent rate cap for an up-front premium of 2.25 percent if the firm will commit immediately. But, the CFO does not know if the board will approve his funding plans and so he cannot commit immediately. The board will decide in two weeks. But by the time the board does approve the plan, the cost of the cap may have risen. The market-maker bank solves the CFO's problem by offering him "an option on the cap" that is good for three weeks. For this option, the CFO might agree to pay the bank a premium of say 0.15 percent.

If the board approves the funding proposal, the CFO can notify the bank that he is exercising the firm's option on the cap. The bank then commits to a cap on the original terms (i.e., an up-front fee of 2.25 percent). If the board rejects the funding plan, the CFO lets the option on the cap expire.

To see the other use of an option on a cap, suppose that the board approves the funding plan but, in the intervening two weeks, the reference rate has declined considerably so that the same cap can be purchased for 1.95 percent. Should the CFO exercise the option on the cap? Clearly not. If he does, he will commit to an up-front fee of 2.25 percent. He can just as easily negotiate a new cap at an up-front premium of only 1.95 percent. Thus, even though the board approves the funding plan, the CFO lets the option expire while electing to buy a cap in the market.

Just as a bank can make a market in options on caps, so can the bank make a market in options on floors. These are not nearly as widely used as options on caps, however, and so we will not address them.

The final type of option we will consider is the **swaption**. A swaption is an option on a swap. Such options can be written on either interest-rate swaps or currency swaps. The concept is nearly identical to an option on a cap. The end user and the market-maker bank agree to the terms of a swap. The end user, however, cannot or does not want to make an immediate commitment to the terms of the swap. At the same time however, the end user cannot afford to take the chance that the market will evolve unfavorably between now and the time when the end user can commit. To lock in the terms of the swap, the end user agrees to purchase a swaption from the market-maker bank. Thus, the market-maker bank guarantees the terms of the swap for some period of time—perhaps one month, for example—during which the end user can choose to exercise the swaption or simply let it expire. As always, the end user will be required to pay a premium for the swaption. This premium is lost whether the end user chooses to exercise the swaption or not.

In closing this chapter on options, we will repeat again that there are very clear economies of scale for banks that make markets in swaps to also make markets in related risk-management tools. It is not surprising that swap market makers also make markets in forward contracts, caps, floors, collars, options on caps, options on floor, and swaptions.

6.10 SUMMARY

Options are contracts that grant their purchaser the right but not the obligation to do something. Most often this is the right to buy or sell some number of units of some underlying asset. In the case of cash settlement options, the ''right'' is the right to receive a cash payment. Options have limited lives. If not exercised by the end of its life, an option expires and is worthless. Options that can be exercised at any time are called American options and options that can only be exercised during a limited period are called European options.

Traditional options include calls and puts. Call options grant their holder the right to buy some number of units of the underlying asset as the option's strike price, while puts grant their holder the right to sell some number of units of the underlying asset at the option's strike price. For the right that an option conveys, the option purchaser pays the option writer an up-front fee called the option premium.

Options are attractive as speculative instruments because they provide the speculator with considerable leverage while strictly limiting downside risk. They are also attractive to hedgers because they provide a way to protect from adverse price movements while still preserving the opportunity to benefit from favorable price movements. The payoff profiles associated with options are somewhat more complex than those associated with futures and forward contracts. Further, these instruments can be combined in a great many ways to create a myriad assortment of unique profit structures.

Option valuation models are exceedingly complex. Most such models were derived as variants of the original Black/Scholes model. Even those that were not formulated as variants bear a strong resemblance to the Black/Scholes model. The value of an option consists of two parts. The first is called intrinsic value and it can be defined with the aid of a MAX function. In other words, the intrinsic value is the amount by which an option is in-the-money or zero, whichever is greater. The second component of option value is called time value. Time value represents the option's potential to acquire more intrinsic value before it expires.

Interest-rate caps and interest-rate floors are multi-period options that can be used for multi-period hedging. A similar result can be obtained using a strip of single-period puts or a strip of single-period calls. Recognition of this latter relationship is the key to understanding the pricing of caps and floors. The primary use of caps is to place a ceiling on the cost of floating-rate liabilities and the primary use of floors is to place a lower limit on revenue received from floating-rate assets.

Caps and floors can be combined to produce collars and other special configurations. They can also be combined with swaps to produce rate-capped swaps and rate-floored swaps. Sometimes, it is useful to buy an option on a cap, called a Caption, or an option on a swap, called a swaption.

Market makers in swaps find that there are economies of scale to be enjoyed if they also make markets in caps, floors, collars and other interest-rate options. It is not surprising then that such institutions try to maintain a broad line of risk management instruments.

REFERENCES AND SUGGESTED READINGS

Black, F. and M. Scholes "The Pricing of Options and Corporate Liabilities," *Journal of Political Economy*, pp. 637–59, May/June 1973.

Cox, J.C. and M. Rubinstein *Options Markets*, Englewood Cliffs, NJ: Prentice Hall, 1985.

Degler, W. "Selecting a Collar to Fit Your Expectations," *Futures Magazine*, 18(3), (March 1989).

Fall, W. "Caps vs. Swaps vs. Hybrids," *Risk*, 1(5), April 1988.

Haghani, V.J. and R.M Stavis "Interest Rate Caps and Floors: Tools for Asset/Liability Management," Bond Portfolio Analysis Group, Salomon Brothers, May 1986.

Jarrow, R.A. and A. Rudd *Option Pricing*, Homewood, IL: Irwin (1983).

Marshall, J.F. *Futures and Option Contracting: Theory and Practice*, Cincinnati, OH: South-Western (1989).

Ritchken, P. *Options: Theory, Strategy, and Applications*, Glenview, IL: Scott, Foresman (1987).

Tompkins, R. "The A-Z of Caps," *Risk*, 2(3) March 1989.

ENDNOTES

[1] The reader interested in the mathematics of option pricing models should consider several of the following: Marshall (1989), Ritchken (1987), Cox and Rubinstein (1985), and Jarrow and Rudd (1983).

[2] An excellent and inexpensive micro-based software package (IBM type) which is a virtual tool box of useful analytical techniques, including the Black/Scholes model for pricing European-type options on nonpayout assets, is available from MicroApplications (telephone: 1-516-821-9355). The package is called *A-Pack: An Analytical Package for Business*.

[3] For a more thorough development of each of these strategies as well as the formulae for the computation of their payoff profiles, see Marshall (1989), Chapters 17 through 20.

7

Corporate Objectives and the Structure of Swaps

7.1 OVERVIEW

The structure of a swap is governed by several factors. First and foremost among these is the objective of the end user of the swap product. For purposes of discussion and illustration, we assume throughout that the **end user** of the swap product is a for-profit commercial firm that we sometimes refer to as the **corporate user**.[1] We use the terms "end user" and "corporate user" rather loosely to include industrial corporations, financial corporations, banks, and thrifts.

Also important in determining the structure of a swap is the role played by the financial intermediary, which we will continue to refer to as the **bank** or as the **swap bank** but which we also sometimes refer to as the **swap dealer.** We use the term "bank" generically to include commercial banks, investment banks, merchant banks, and independent swap brokers and dealers. It is reasonable to expect that the bank does all it can to structure the swap so that the swap does, in fact, serve the objectives of its client—the corporate user. To the extent that meeting the client's needs necessitates a swap that has an unusually complicated structure or gives rise to a swap that is difficult for the bank to offset, the pricing of the swap will reflect a premium above that which is characteristic of the "plain vanilla" swaps we discussed in Chapter 1. The third major factor affecting the structure of a swap is the tax and accounting treatment of these instruments.

265

In this chapter, we concentrate on the objectives of the corporate end user of swaps and some of the many swap structures that have been developed by swap banks to meet these objectives. We are also going to use this chapter to take a brief look at a potentially important new breed of swaps called commodity swaps and we are going to consider the calculation of all-in cost. All-in cost, which we have alluded to in earlier chapters, is very important from the end user's perspective when choosing between alternative forms of financing that accomplish the same end result. Finally, we have included, as an appendix, a special section devoted to the use of swaps and futures for the hedging of a thrift's mortgage portfolio. This section will not be of interest to all readers and can be skipped without any break in the continuity of the text.

7.2 CORPORATE OBJECTIVES

As shown in Chapter 1, swaps evolved from back-to-back and parallel loans. Back-to-back and parallel loans involve two separate loan agreements together with a separate agreement addressing rights of set-off. These loans were conceived and first used as a mechanism to bypass foreign-exchange controls. While swaps are at least as useful as back-to-back and parallel loans for purposes of circumventing foreign-exchange controls, this is now not and really never has been, the primary objective of most corporate users of swap products. Far more important to today's corporate users of swaps are:

1. lowering financing costs;
2. hedging price risks (including both exchange-rate risk and interest-rate risk);
3. operating on a larger scale; and
4. gaining access to new markets.

7.2.1 Lowering Financing Costs

Imperfections in the world's capital markets and/or fixed-rate/floating-rate quality point differentials create a potential for the existence of comparative borrowing advantages that, in turn, make swap finance an attractive financing tool. The imperfections in the world's capital markets include controls on the movement of capital across national borders, unequal access to the world's capital markets due to differences in borrower size and market acceptance, government-granted loan guarantees, differing tax treatments of interest paid and/or received (both internationally and intranationally), and finally, different yield curve behaviors in different countries for both fixed-rate and floating-rate borrowings.

In addition to these obvious imperfections, there are less obvious ones as well. For example, a potential lender may have unequal access to, or knowledge of, legal protections afforded to lenders in the world's capital markets. Concern over the validity and enforceability of protective covenants can diminish a potential lender's willingness to lend to a nondomestic borrower. The end result is a higher cost of funds for the nondomestic borrower. Thus, domestic borrowers often enjoy a comparative borrowing advantage over nondomestic borrowers.

Swap finance can lower borrowing costs for both counterparties to a swap by exploiting these comparative advantages. We saw how this can be accomplished with the plain vanilla currency swap and the plain vanilla interest-rate swap in Chapter 1. With the rapid growth in swap finance and increasing competition among the banks that act as swap brokers and dealers, much of the potential cost-reducing benefits of swap finance have been arbitraged away and market efficiency has increased. It is for this reason that swap finance has served to integrate and internationalize the world's capital markets.

The substantial narrowing of bid-ask swap spreads, brought about by a general acceptance of swap finance and the standardization of the swap product, may not be beneficial for the less-efficient swap banks (who require more substantial spreads to ensure a profit from their intermediary role). However, it is a financial bonanza for the corporate users of swaps. Through the swap vehicle, such a user can be assured of obtaining funds at the lowest possible cost with minimal expense for the services of the swap banker.

7.2.2 Hedging Price Risks

Equally important to their use as a tool for lowering financing costs, swaps can be used to hedge financial price risks. Like futures contracts, swaps can be used very effectively to hedge both interest-rate risk and foreign-exchange rate risk. But, whereas futures contracts are best suited to hedging price risks of a relatively short term (typically less than one year), swaps are best suited to hedging price risks of a longer term. These often range from one to 10 years and can run considerably longer.

With the extreme volatility that has characterized interest rates and exchange rates, the importance of efficient hedging tools is difficult to overstate. We will illustrate by way of a simple example. Suppose a Swiss provider of retirement annuity contracts sells its policies worldwide. With its most popular policy, the Swiss firm provides fixed quarterly payments to its policyholder (payable at the end of each calendar quarter) for a period of 15 years in exchange for a single, immediate payment by the policyholder to the Swiss firm.[2] The Swiss firm does not necessarily invest the funds it receives from its policyholders in the policyholders' country. Rather, the firm looks worldwide for the most attractive investment opportunities it can find.

The Swiss firm is planning a policy offering in the United States. It determines that it can convert any dollars it receives to West German deutschemarks at the current spot exchange rate of 2.000 DM/USD and lend these deutschemarks to a German firm for an annual return of 10 percent (compounded quarterly). The loan would be a 15-year amortizing loan providing quarterly payments. On the strength of its knowledge of this investment opportunity, the Swiss firm offers its prospective U.S. policyholders a fixed annual rate of 9 percent (compounded quarterly). From the 1 percent receive/pay rate differential, the Swiss firm must cover its administrative costs and try to earn a reasonable profit for its shareholders. Suppose that the policy offering brings the Swiss firm a total of $50 million from 1,000 new policyholders.

The Swiss firm will receive quarterly revenues from its German investment in the amount of DM 3,235,340.[3] At an exchange rate of

2.000 DM/USD, this is equivalent to $1,617,670 for each of the next 60 quarters. At the same time, the Swiss firm must make aggregate quarterly payments to its U.S. policyholders in the amount of $1,526,767. The rate differential then translates, at the current spot exchange rate, to net quarterly revenue of $90,903 or an annual net revenue of $363,612. The Swiss firm estimates the annual administrative costs associated with providing these policies at $135,000. Thus, if all of its expectations are realized, the new policy offering should contribute $228,612 to the firm's annual profit.

Suppose, for the moment, that the Swiss firm does not hedge its currency commitments. If the deutschemark strengthens against the dollar, the Swiss firm will profit in excess of its expectations. On the other hand, it will suffer unexpected losses if the deutschemark weakens against the U.S. dollar. A small adverse change in the value of the deutschemark could easily wipe out all profit from this offering. For example, if the exchange rate were to rise to just 2.073 DM/USD, representing a weakened deutschemark, the annual profit contribution from the policy offering would be reduced to near zero. A more substantial weakening of the deutschemark could irreparably impair the financial integrity of the Swiss firm. The effects of an increase in the exchange rate are illustrated in Table 7.1.

TABLE 7.1
Illustration of Foreign-Exchange Exposure

		Exchange Rate (DM/USD)		
		2.000	2.073	2.146
Firm receives DM quarterly	DM	3,235,340	3,235,340	3,235,340
Converted to dollars	USD	1,617,670	1,560,704	1,507,614
Less USD payments to policyholders	USD	1,526,767	1,526,767	1,526,767
Gross quarterly profit (USD)	USD	90,903	33,937	(19,153)
Less quarterly administrative costs	USD	33,750	33,750	33,750
Net quarterly profit	USD	57,153	187	(52,903)
Net annual profit	USD	228,612	748	(211,612)

Note: The actual zero profit exchange rate occurs at 2.0732. For purposes of this example, we treat the second column net quarterly and net annual profits as approximately zero.

The Swiss firm cannot invest globally to earn the best rate possible unless it can hedge its exchange-rate risk. Without this capability, its activities are limited to matching its currency payment commitments by investing exclusively in assets that are denominated in the currency of its payment commitments (liabilities). Indeed, before the advent of currency swaps, this asset/liability management approach was the only risk management technique employed by this firm. This strategy is clearly suboptimal. It requires that potentially superior investment opportunities be ignored because of concern over foreign-exchange risk.

The Swiss firm is in the business of providing annuity contracts and not in the business of currency speculation and, so, it seeks to hedge its foreign-exchange exposure. The firm often hedges its short-term currency exposures in foreign-exchange forward and futures contracts. But these hedging instruments are not adequate to hedge this multi-year commitment.

The Swiss firm approaches a U.K.-based swap bank for a solution. The bank, which makes a market in both currency and interest-rate swaps, offers to pay the Swiss firm dollars at an annual rate of 9.85 percent in exchange for the Swiss firm paying the bank deutschemarks at a 10 percent annual rate. This involves a combination of a fixed-for-floating rate currency swap and a floating-for-fixed interest-rate swap. For both payment streams, we will assume quarterly compounding and a 15-year amortizing loan. The loan principal on the dollar side of the swap is $50 million, and the loan principal on the deutschemark side is DM 100 million. The latter is obtained by converting the dollar side to deutschemarks at the current spot exchange rate.

The Swiss firm now has two separate sets of cash flows. Exhibit 7.1 depicts the cash flows between the German firm, the Swiss firm, and the Swiss firm's U.S. policyholders. Exhibit 7.2 depicts the cash flows from the swap between the Swiss firm and the swap bank.

We can now combine the cash flows depicted in Exhibits 7.1 and 7.2. The *net* cash flows are depicted in Exhibit 7.3.

The Swiss firm is now fully hedged against fluctuations in the DM/USD exchange rate. Assuming that the Swiss firm's management has no reason to believe the DM/USD exchange rate is more likely to rise

EXHIBIT 7.1.   Quarterly Cash Flows from Commercial Transaction

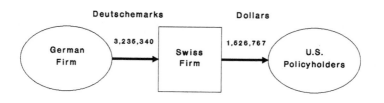

EXHIBIT 7.2.   Quarterly Cash Flows from Swap

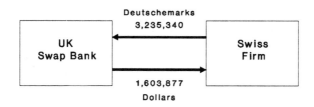

**EXHIBIT 7.3.   Combined Cash Flows from Commercial Transaction
and Swap**

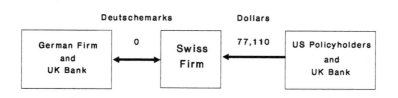

than fall in the coming years (that is, the current 2.000 spot DM/USD
exchange rate is an unbiased estimate of future spot DM/USD exchange rates), the firm's expected annual profit from the policy offering is reduced by the swap hedge to $173,440 [(4 × $77,110) −
$135,000].[4] The **cost of the hedge** to the Swiss firm is the amount by
which the expected annual profit from the policy offering is reduced as
a consequence of hedging. In this case, the annual cost of hedging is
$55,172 ($228,612 − $173,440).

It is premature to conclude that the positive hedging costs incurred when hedging with swaps would prevent the Swiss firm from hedging in this instrument. A **risk averse** firm enjoys a utility gain from the risk reduction that accompanies hedging. For this risk reduction, the swap hedger would likely be willing to pay a price—just as futures hedgers are willing to pay a price for the risk reduction made possible by hedging in futures.[5]

There are two ancillary benefits from hedging that are easily overlooked but that should be of considerable importance to the hedger. The first involves reduced financing costs and the second involves economies of scale.

By hedging, the corporate user of swaps reduces the uncertainty of its cash flows. This has implications for the firm's cost of funds completely separate from the reduced financing costs associated with swap finance itself. By reducing the uncertainty of its cash flows, the firm is viewed as more **creditworthy**. To the extent that the markets recognize this reduction in uncertainty, the firm's cost of debt and equity capital should decline. This, in turn, implies higher prices for the firm's stock.

The second ancillary benefit of hedging cash flows with swaps is associated with the scale on which the firm can operate. This benefit is addressed in the next section.

7.2.3 Exploiting Economies of Scale

Hedging of price risks, including financial price risks, makes it possible for a firm to operate on a larger scale. Consider again the case of the Swiss provider of annuity contracts. The annuity provider that does not hedge cannot operate on the same scale, for a given capital base, as the annuity provider that does hedge. Suppose that the prudent annuity provider holds $1 of equity capital for each $0.40 of annual profit volatility (however this might be defined). Next, suppose that, in the absence of hedging, each $1 of annuity policies gives rise to $0.05 of profit volatility. The unhedged annuity provider can then carry, at most, $8 of annuity policies for each $1 of equity capital it holds.

Now suppose that a complete swap hedge, like the one described for the Swiss firm above, reduces profit volatility by 90 percent. The residual risk, called basis risk, that remains is then 10 percent of the risk that existed in the absence of hedging. The same annuity provider can then carry $80 of annuity policies for each $1 of its equity capital. Thus, in this example, the hedged annuity provider can operate on a scale 10 times that of the unhedged annuity provider without bearing any greater risk.

Even when hedging is costly, as it is in the example of the Swiss firm above, the cost incurred from hedging may be a small price to pay for the increased scale at which the hedged firm can operate. The annuity provider that is capable of operating on a larger scale by hedging benefits from the greater profits associated with a larger policy base, but it may also benefit from **economies of scale**. That is, to the extent that the provision of annuity policies involves a high fixed cost and relatively little variable cost per policy, there may be significant cost savings to be enjoyed by annuity providers that can operate on a large scale. These savings alone may be sufficient in some cases to completely offset the costs of hedging.

7.2.4   Gaining Access to New Markets

There are many ways that swaps allow firms to access markets that they might otherwise be unable to profitably enter. Consider just one such possibility. Suppose the Swiss annuity provider would like to offer its annuity contracts to Italian citizens who require annuity payments in lira. In the absence of swap opportunities, the Swiss firm, which cannot afford to take foreign-exchange risk, is limited to finding investment opportunities in Italy. These opportunities might be inferior to other opportunities in other nations. In fact, given the investment opportunities in Italy, the Swiss firm might decide that it cannot currently invest in Italy (at a return sufficient to offer Italians an attractive annuity rate) and still earn a reasonable profit. Given this situation, the Swiss firm judges the Italian market to be closed to it at the current time.

By engaging a swap bank that makes a market in lira for dollar swaps, lira for deutschemark swaps, and so on, the annuity provider can seize an investment opportunity outside Italy and then transform this non-lira asset into a lira denominated asset. With lira assured, the annuity provider can obtain lira financing by offering its policies to Italian citizens in the same way that it offered its policies to U.S. citizens.

There are many other ways in which a firm can use swaps to access markets that would otherwise be closed to it or for which the cost of entering the market is judged to be prohibitive.

7.3 SWAP VARIANTS

Despite the usefulness of the swap for financing purposes, it is not always acceptable in its plain vanilla form. For example, in the plain vanilla fixed-for-floating interest-rate swap, the corporate user exploits its comparative advantage in the fixed (or floating) rate market by borrowing in this market and then swaps its payments on this obligation for a more desirable floating (or fixed) rate obligation. Suppose now that the corporate user can borrow at one floating rate (certificate of deposit rate or commercial paper rate) but prefers to have its liabilities denominated in another floating rate—T-bill or LIBOR, for example. In this case, we require a floating-for-floating rate swap. Or, suppose that the corporate user holds prepayable fixed-rate assets (home mortgages, for example) that are financed with floating-rate liabilities. We can use a swap to convert the fixed-rate assets to floating-rate assets, or we could use a swap to convert the floating-rate liabilities to fixed-rate liabilities. In both cases, we might require a termination option or an option to extend the swap.

One of the important functions that swap banks perform for their corporate clients is **financial engineering**. While the activities of financial engineers are not new, the explicit recognition of financial engineering as a professional field is quite new. Financial engineering encompasses a variety of overlapping areas. For our purposes, we are interested in only one of these areas—the design of customized solutions to the financing and risk management needs of clients.[6]

Financial engineering requires financial innovation. When a bank custom designs a new swap variant in order to meet the idiosyncratic needs of a particular client, the bank can charge a significant premium over its own costs for that custom design. This ''charge'' may take the form of a front-end fee or a wider than normal bid-ask spread on the swap. If the new product has wider appeal however, it will soon be transformed into a standardized high-volume item that will only be profitable for those banks that can deliver it in a very cost efficient manner. The front-end fee will disappear, and the bid-ask spread will narrow. Thus, banks compete against one another to deliver their swap products at the least possible cost; and they depend on a high volume of low margin swap transactions for the bulk of their profits. As a side note, the process of taking a custom solution to a financial problem and converting it to a widely-applicable tool for managing similar problems experienced by other clients is sometimes called **productizing**.

The point of this is that corporate users of swaps often require special features in their swap agreements. Many of these special features have been standardized and have given rise to swaps with special names. We will briefly review some of these special types of swaps in the several sections that follow. The variant forms of interest-rate swaps will be discussed first, and then the variant forms of currency swaps will be covered. All of the swap variants discussed originated as high-margin custom designs and have since been transformed into low-margin volume products.

7.3.1 Interest-Rate Swaps

Innovative banks have created a plethora of variants on the basic fixed-for-floating interest-rate swap in an effort to better serve the corporate user. These variants can be used individually or can be combined so that a given interest-rate swap has a number of variant features. Some of the variant forms of interest-rate swaps common today are zero coupon swaps; floating-for-floating swaps; callable, putable, and extendable swaps; forward swaps; delayed-rate-setting swaps; and rate-capped swaps. These and other variants are discussed below.

7.3.1.1 FIXED-FOR-FLOATING SWAPS

These are the basic or plain vanilla interest-rate swaps. The corporate user swaps a floating-rate obligation into a fixed-rate obligation or, alternatively, swaps a fixed-rate obligation into a floating-rate obligation. These were the first interest-rate swaps with standardized terms and the first to be offered as a mass market, low-margin product by swap dealers. The floating-rate side is typically pegged to LIBOR, and the fixed-rate side is typically priced at a spread over the yield on Treasury securities (notes and bonds). In its most common form, the counterparties to the swap make periodic interest payments to each other with the payments made at the same frequency; principal is not exchanged, and exchanges of interest are limited to an exchange of the interest differential—assuming the payment dates and frequencies are matched.

7.3.1.2 ZERO COUPON-FOR-FLOATING SWAP

This swap is a variant of the fixed-for-floating rate swap. Unlike the usual fixed-for-floating rate swap, in which each counterparty makes payments to the other with the same payment frequency, in the zero-coupon swap the fixed-rate payer makes a single payment at the termination of the swap agreement, with the interest calculated on a discount basis, while the floating-rate payer makes periodic payments. These swaps are attractive to corporate users who themselves hold zero-coupon assets but who pay a floating rate on their liabilities (or vice versa).

7.3.1.3 FLOATING-FOR-FLOATING SWAPS

These are also called **basis swaps**. Floating-for-floating swaps can be of several forms. In one form, the two sides of the swap are tied to different floating rates. For example, one side might be tied to six-month LIBOR while the other might be tied to a six-month certificate of deposit or a six-month commercial paper rate. In the second form, the two sides of the swap might be tied to the same pricing vehicle but with different payment frequencies. For example, one side might involve semiannual payments based on six-month LIBOR while the other might involve monthly payments based on one-month LIBOR. A third variant incorporates both of the first two. For example, one side might involve monthly payments priced on one-month LIBOR while the other side might involve semiannual payments calculated on six-month certificate of deposit rates. Other rates that have been used to index one side or the other of a floating-for-floating rate swap include prime rate, T-bill rate, and Fed funds rate.

7.3.1.4   CALLABLE SWAPS

A callable swap is a fixed-for-floating swap with a scheduled maturity date that gives the fixed-rate payer (floating-rate receiver) the right to terminate the swap prior to its maturity date. The fixed-rate payer may be regarded as having purchased a call option on the swap. For the call privilege, the fixed-rate payer typically pays a higher fixed rate than would be paid in a straight fixed-for-floating rate swap and may be required to pay a termination fee in the event the call privilege is exercised. Such a fee is calculated as a percentage of the swap's notional principal.

There is an important distinction to be drawn here. A callable swap is not the same thing as a swaption. Recall our discussion of swaptions in Chapter 6. A swaption is an option on a swap. If the option is not exercised, the swap never comes into existence. In a callable swap, the swap does come into existence no matter what, but the fixed-rate payer has the right to terminate the swap prior to its normal maturity date.

7.3.1.5   PUTABLE SWAPS

A putable swap is a fixed-for-floating swap with a scheduled maturity date that allows the floating-rate payer (fixed-rate receiver) to terminate the swap prior to the swap's maturity date. The floating-rate payer is regarded as having purchased a put option on the swap and pays for that privilege by accepting a fixed rate below that available on a straight fixed-for-floating swap. In addition, there may be an early termination fee payable by the floating-rate payer upon exercise of the option privilege. As with the call option, this fee is calculated as a percentage of the swap's notional principal. As with a callable swap, a putable swap should not be confused with a swaption.

7.3.1.6 EXTENDABLE SWAPS

An extendable swap is a fixed-for-floating swap in which one party has the right to extend the life of the swap beyond its scheduled maturity date. These swaps are economically equivalent to callable and putable swaps. For example, an extendable swap in which the fixed-rate payer can extend the scheduled maturity from two years to five years is equivalent to a callable swap with a five-year scheduled maturity that the fixed-rate payer can terminate after just two years. Like callable and putable swaps, the holder of an option to extend the maturity of the swap will typically have to pay for this valuable right and may have to pay a fee should that right be exercised. This can be seen clearly if we recognize the opportunity to synthesize an extendable swap from a swap and a swaption. For example, suppose we purchase a two-year swap and simultaneously purchase a swaption with a two-year life on a swap with a term of three years. That is, the swaption has a life of two years and the swap on which it is written has a term of three years. At the end of two years, we can elect to exercise the swaption and thus secure a swap with a three-year term; or, we can elect to let the swaption expire. The cash flows associated with this "swap plus swaption" strategy are identical to the cash flows associated with the extendable swap described earlier.

Note: Callable swaps, putable swaps, extendable swaps, and swaptions can be complimentary from the swap bank's perspective. We postpone discussion of swap complimentarity, however, to Chapter 9.

7.3.1.7 FORWARD SWAPS

A forward swap, also called a **deferred swap**, is a fixed-for-floating swap in which the swap rates are set immediately but the start of the swap is delayed. This type of swap can be attractive to a corporate user who does not require immediate swap financing but who feels that the prevailing fixed-for-floating rate opportunities are particularly attractive. Through the forward swap, the user "locks in" the current rate structure but delays the start of the swap until a specific future date.

7.3.1.8 DELAYED RATE-SETTING SWAPS

Delayed rate-setting swaps, also called **deferred rate-setting swaps**, are near mirror images of forward swaps. The corporate user is in need of immediate swap financing but considers the current fixed-for-floating rate structure unattractive. The corporate user agrees to enter the swap immediately with the rate to be determined later according to an agreed upon formula.[7] In this type of swap, the corporate user is usually granted the right to set the rates at the time of its choosing within some specified time frame.

7.3.1.9 RATE-CAPPED SWAPS

Rate-capped swaps are fixed-for-floating swaps in which ceilings are set on the floating rate. That is, the floating rate cannot rise above a certain "ceiling" level that constitutes the "cap." A rate cap affords the floating-rate payer an extra level of protection. For this protection, the floating-rate payer pays the fixed-rate payer a front-end fee. This type of swap is attractive to a corporate user with capped floating-rate assets and fixed-rate liabilities. A mortgage banker who holds a portfolio of rate-capped adjustable rate mortgages (ARMs) that are financed by fixed-rate long-term debt would constitute an example of this type of corporate user.[8]

Rate-capped swaps can be created in several ways. One way is to purchase a swap with a built-in rate cap. Another way, which we discussed in Chapter 6, is to enter a swap and to purchase separately an interest-rate cap. The cash flows from these strategies are identical and so we will not distinguish between them. Nevertheless, the user should consider the cost of all available alternatives before committing to one.

Closely related to the rate-capped swap is the **mini-max swap** that imposes both a floor and a ceiling to the floating-rate side of the swap. This same outcome can be achieved by using an appropriate combination of an interest-rate floor, an interest-rate cap, and a swap.

7.3.1.10 AMORTIZING SWAPS

In amortizing swaps, the notional principal on which the interest payments are based gradually declines, usually under a sinking-fund type schedule. The amortization may or may not provide for a grace period on the amortization of the notional principal. We will consider amortizing swaps in greater detail in Chapter 8.

7.3.1.11 ROLLER-COASTER SWAPS

In roller-coaster swaps, the notional principal on which the interest payments are calculated increases (**negative amortization**) for a time and then amortizes to zero over the remaining life of the swap. The schedule of changes in the notional principal is established at the outset. These swaps can be used by mortgage bankers to hedge portfolios of fixed-rate **graduated payment mortgages** (GPMs) when such mortgages are financed by floating-rate liabilities.

7.3.1.12 ASSET-BASED SWAPS

Most swaps are written to reduce the cost of financing or to hedge existing liabilities. Thus, interest-rate swaps were first designed as a tool for liability management. In recent years, these same swaps have been used to create synthetic instruments. A synthetic instrument is a combination of other instruments. Such an instrument behaves exactly like the real financial instrument (in terms of the amount, the timing, and the direction of the associated cash flows). These synthetic instruments can be used in arbitrage strategies to exploit price discrepancies between the real asset and the synthetic asset. Such swaps are sometimes called asset-based swaps. We will return to asset-based swaps later in this chapter.

7.3.2 Currency Swaps

Just as the plain vanilla interest-rate swap is not always adequate to meet the needs of an interest-rate swap end user, the plain vanilla currency swap can fail to meet the needs of a currency swap end user. To meet end users' needs, swap banks have created a number of currency swap variants. These variants can be used individually or can be combined with other variants to produce very effective solutions to financing and foreign-exchange risk management problems. We briefly examine the plain vanilla fixed-for-floating rate currency swap, fixed-for-fixed rate currency swaps, floating-for-floating currency swaps, circus swaps, and amortizing swaps. Unlike interest-rate swaps, which do not require an exchange of principals, currency swaps generally do require such an exchange. This is not an absolute, however; many currency swaps are structured in such a way that no principal exchanges are required. We consider the pricing of currency swaps with no initial exchange of principals in Chapter 8.

7.3.2.1 FIXED-FOR-FLOATING RATE NONAMORTIZING CURRENCY SWAPS

The fixed-for-floating rate nonamortizing currency swap is the plain vanilla form of currency swap. It is often called an exchange of borrowings. In this swap there is an initial exchange of principals at the outset and a re-exchange of principals at the swap's termination. Both exchanges are made at the same exchange rate—which is the spot exchange rate prevailing at the time the swap is negotiated. The re-exchange of principals at the swap's maturity constitutes a bullet transaction. During the life of the swap, the counterparties exchange periodic interest payments—each calculated on the principal it received from the other and denominated in the currency it received from the other. These payments are most often made annually or semiannually. One counterparty pays interest at a fixed rate, and the other pays at a floating rate with the payments made with equal frequency.

7.3.2.2 FIXED-FOR-FIXED RATE NONAMORTIZING CURRENCY SWAPS

The fixed-for-fixed rate nonamortizing currency swap is identical to the fixed-for-floating rate currency swap except that both counterparties pay a fixed rate of interest. This type of swap can be created via a single swap agreement or via two separate swap agreements. In the latter case, a fixed-for-floating rate currency swap can be used for the initial exchange of currencies with the corporate user paying the floating rate. A fixed-for-floating rate interest-rate swap can then be used to convert the floating-rate side to a fixed rate. The end result is a cash flow pattern identical to a fixed-for-fixed rate currency swap.

7.3.2.3 FLOATING-FOR-FLOATING RATE NONAMORTIZING CURRENCY SWAPS

The floating-for-floating rate nonamortizing currency swap is identical to the fixed-for-floating rate currency swap except that both counterparties pay a floating rate of interest. This type of swap can be created via a single swap agreement or via two separate swap agreements. In the latter case, a fixed-for-floating rate currency swap can be used for the initial transaction with the corporate user paying the fixed rate. A fixed-for-floating rate interest-rate swap can then be used to convert the fixed-rate side to a floating rate. The end result is a cash flow pattern identical to a floating-for-floating rate currency swap.

Circus Swaps.   When a transaction consists of both a currency swap and an interest-rate swap with LIBOR-based pricing for the floating-rate side of each, the swap is called a **circus swap**. The examples offered above in which a fixed-for-floating rate currency swap is converted to either a fixed-for-fixed or floating-for-floating rate currency swap via a fixed-for-floating interest-rate swap would constitute a circus swap if the floating-rate side of each swap is LIBOR-based.

7.3.2.4 AMORTIZING CURRENCY SWAPS

Unlike the single re-exchange of principals associated with swaps that take the form of bullet transactions, amortizing currency swaps are re-exchanged in stages. That is, the principals amortize over the life of the swap. These currency swaps can be fixed-for-floating, fixed-for-fixed, or floating-for-floating.

This look at swap variants is not meant to be exhaustive nor detailed. Other types of interest-rate and currency swaps exist, and new ones are evolving all the time. Our cursory examination of these products is sufficient, however, to provide an appreciation of the versatility associated with these instruments. It is also sufficient to appreciate the complexities associated with pricing these products and the difficulties encountered by swap banks in managing their swap portfolios.

7.4 A CLOSER LOOK AT ASSET-BASED SWAPS

We have already indicated that asset-based swaps are swaps that are used to create synthetic instruments. In order to understand this use of swaps, a better understanding of the notion of a synthetic instrument is needed.

Any financial instrument gives rise to a series of cash flows. These cash flows may be known with a high degree of certainty—as in the case of a fixed-rate instrument—or they may be very uncertain—as in the case of a floating-rate instrument. The series of cash flows, which we will call the "pattern" of cash flows, associated with a "real instrument" can often be exactly duplicated by using a combination of other instruments. For example, the sale of a put option on a futures contract coupled with the purchase of a call option on the same futures contract (in which both options have the same strike price and the same expiration date) will give rise to a cash flow pattern that exactly duplicates that associated with a straight long position in the futures contract itself. Given this, we can view the *combination* of the short put and the long call as a synthetic futures. Similarly, a strip of zero coupon bonds, if properly selected, can be used to exactly duplicate a conventional bond. The strip of zeros can be regarded as a synthetic conventional bond.

Swaps are well suited to the manipulation of cash flow patterns in order to create synthetic instruments. Let's consider a few examples. Suppose that a firm has an opportunity to purchase a seven-year zero coupon corporate bond (zero) for $20 million (current cost) and it offers a very attractive return (yield) for the risks involved. Suppose that this is 13.5 percent (semiannual bond equivalent yield). That is, the firm would buy the zero now for $20 million and collect $49.91 million in seven years. The firm can obtain nonamortizing funding for the purchase of this zero from third party lenders at an annual cost of 9 percent with quarterly interest payments.

As it happens, the firm's sales and, consequently, its profitability are very interest-rate sensitive.[9] That is, when interest rates rise, the firm's profitability declines and when interest rates decline, the firm's profitability rises. Management's studies have shown that the firm's quarterly operating profit tends to increase (or decrease) by $0.3 million for each 1 percent decrease (or increase) in interest rates. This interest-rate sensitivity increases the volatility of the firm's **earnings per share** (EPS) and, as management is acutely aware, the firm's shareholders prefer less EPS volatility to more (all other things being equal).

Management feels it would be foolish to pass up the zero coupon bond opportunity but it would prefer an asset that provides a cash flow pattern that offsets the volatility of its profits from operations. This kind of cash flow pattern can be achieved, for instance, by holding a floating-rate asset tied to three-month LIBOR. A floating-rate note (FRN) issue of another corporation is an example of such an asset.

Management decides to buy the zero and to use a zero coupon-for-floating interest-rate swap to convert the zero's yield into a floating rate of interest. The swap is structured as follows: The swap bank agrees to pay the firm three-month LIBOR plus 3.5 percent on notional principal of $20 million in exchange for the firm's agreement to pay the bank $29.91 million in seven years. This swap was priced off-market as the firm wanted to be sure it matched its terminal cash flow

EXHIBIT 7.4.   Asset-Based Swap—Zero Coupon Bond to Floating-Rate Note Conversion
(Interest flows)

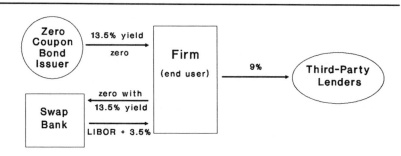

End result: Floating rate asset supported by fixed rate liability.

of $49.91 million. This explains why the floating rate, which the bank agrees to pay, is three-month LIBOR plus 3.5 percent rather than three-month LIBOR flat. We will consider off-market pricing of swaps in Chapter 8. The full set of interest flows from these transactions is depicted in Exhibit 7.4.

Notice that after all the cash flows are taken into consideration, the firm has the equivalent of a floating-rate note that will return LIBOR plus 3.5 percent. Thus, this zero coupon-for-floating interest-rate swap has been combined with a zero coupon bond to create a synthetic floating-rate note that the firm holds as an asset.

The advantages of holding a floating-rate note rather than a zero coupon bond can now be considered. The firm is going to make quarterly payments at the annual rate of 9 percent to its third-party lenders. By holding a floating-rate asset funded by a fixed-rate liability, the firm has created an interest-rate sensitive financial structure. The sensitivity is such that a 1 percent rise in interest rates will result in an additional $0.05 million of net interest revenue. This offsets a portion of the firm's interest-rate sensitivity from its operations. The firm's EPS volatility with and without the swap position is depicted in Exhibit 7.5. It is obvious that the firm has benefited from this swap.

EXHIBIT 7.5.   Quarterly EPS—Comparative Outcomes

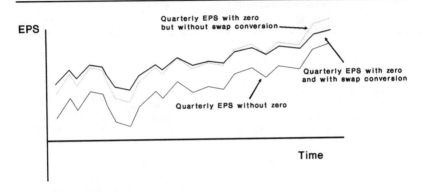

While EPS would have been enhanced by the purchase of the zero, with or without the transformation made possible by the zero coupon-for-floating interest-rate swap, by employing the latter, the asset also reduces EPS volatility.

Now consider one more example. An interest-rate sensitive firm, similar to the one above, would like to make some investments that have a floating-rate character. This firm, however, has fully written off its fixed assets and has little remaining ability to shelter its income from taxes. As a result, the firm is paying effective average tax rates of nearly 44 percent on its income. As it happens, the firm identifies another firm, in a much lower tax bracket, that is in need of financing. Our firm agrees to purchase, via a private placement, a convertible-preferred stock issue of the second firm. As it happens, this preferred stock issue is callable at par after five years with a mandatory call at the end of 10 years. The preferred stock pays a fixed rate of 10 percent in semi-annual installments. Under current U.S. law, preferred dividends received by a corporation are largely exempt from taxes at the level of the recipient corporation.

The purchase of the convertible issue provides the first firm with fixed-rate tax-sheltered income. However, as previously noted, the firm prefers floating-rate assets because of the interest-rate sensitivity of its own operations. To solve the problem, the firm enters a fixed-for-floating interest-rate swap as fixed-rate payer (floating-rate receiver). It elects a 10-year callable swap. This swap is callable (terminable) by the fixed-rate payer after five years. The end result is that the firm has created a tax-sheltered revenue source that has a floating-rate character. This asset-based swap has allowed the firm to create a synthetic tax-sheltered convertible floating-rate note from a combination of convertible/callable preferred stock and a fixed-for-floating callable swap. The full set of interest and dividend flows is depicted in Exhibit 7.6.

The latter example of the use of asset-based swaps is particularly instructive because it demonstrates the importance that tax asymmetries play in motivating many swaps. Indeed, a large segment of the swap business is **tax driven**. Tax driven swaps are, of course, just one of many manifestations of the modern practice of financial engineering.

The examples provided above are only meant to be suggestive of the hundreds of possible uses for asset-based swaps in the creation of synthetic instruments. The key to understanding synthetic instruments and the uses of swaps in creating them, is the appreciation of the role played by individual cash flows. For most purposes, if we can duplicate the cash flows of a real instrument, we have the opportunity to create a viable synthetic instrument.

EXHIBIT 7.6.   Asset-Based Swap—Fixed-Rate Tax-Sheltered Dividends to Floating-Rate Tax-Sheltered Interest

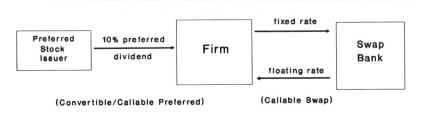

(Convertible/Callable Preferred)   (Callable Swap)

End result: The firm has converted a convertible/callable issue of preferred stock to a convertible/ callable tax-sheltered floating rate note.

This look at synthetic instruments has ignored "qualitative differences" between real and synthetic instruments. Qualitative differences can be important, but we do not consider them here.

7.5   COMMODITY SWAPS

In 1986, The Chase Manhattan Bank pioneered the first **commodity swaps**. Commodity swaps have a structure that is very similar to interest-rate swaps. After their initial introduction, several large banks saw an opportunity in commodity swaps and immediately set up market making operations. As of early 1990, it was generally recognized that the leaders in this field, besides Chase, were Bankers Trust and Banque Paribas.

Despite the potential uses for commodity swaps, a cloud was cast over the commodity swap market almost immediately when the **Commodity Futures Trading Commission** (CFTC), which is responsible for the regulation of trading in futures and commodity options, voiced concerns about the legality of the contracts. The intervention of the CFTC brought it into direct confrontation with the industry's trade group, the International Swap Dealers' Association (ISDA), which sought to protect the interests of its members. At the same time, those banks already involved in commodity swaps moved the bulk of their business overseas.

In July of 1989, the CFTC issued a favorable policy statement on commodity swaps. The agency decided to grant these off-exchange transactions a "safe harbor" provided that five specific criteria were met. For the most part, the CFTC's criteria reflected current practice and established the legitimacy of most existing contracts. Specifically, commodity swaps do not fall into the CFTC's regulatory jurisdiction if:

1. they can not be terminated by one counterparty—barring default—without the other counterparty's consent;
2. they do not require credit support—such as margin or other collateral;

3. they do not use a mark-to-market process with accompanying transfers of variation margin;

4. parties entering the contracts do so as a part of their general line of business; and

5. they are strictly institutional transactions and not offered to the retail public.

In order to offer swap alternatives to less creditworthy clients, many banks had been employing a mark-to-market system for their financial swaps (interest rate and currency). It seemed a logical step to do the same for commodity swaps. The CFTC's policy statement, however, seems to have closed the door, at least temporarily, on this method of eliminating credit risk. With the exception of the restriction on marking-to-market with accompanying transfers of variation margin, the CFTC's conditions posed little problem for the involved market-making banks. Unless the mark-to-market prohibition is lifted, banks will simply have to limit their activities to good credits.

The volume of commodity swap activity increased considerably after the CFTC's favorable policy statement. Nevertheless, by year-end 1989, the volume of outstanding commodity swaps was still estimated to be under $8 billion. Despite this, the increasing volume of activity suggests that commodity swaps have the potential to become an important risk management vehicle.

Commodity swaps are structured in very much the same way as interest-rate swaps. One party pays a floating price for a commodity and the other pays a fixed price for the commodity. The physical commodity is not actually exchanged. Payment flows are limited to the difference between the floating price and the fixed price. Commodity swaps can be used to fix the price that a user of a commodity will pay for the commodity or to fix the price that a producer will receive from sales of the commodity.

To better understand the commodity swap process, the following example provides a detailed illustration. A crude oil producer that operates a number of fields in the southwest United States has been repeatedly burned by dramatic fluctuations in the price of crude. When

EXHIBIT 7.7.   Oil Producer's Transactions in the Spot Market

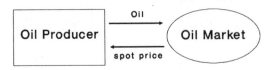

Monthly production averages ▪ 20,000 barrels

the price of crude rose sharply in the 1970s, he leveraged his firm in order to expand his operations. A subsequent drop in the price of oil in the 1980s made it extremely difficult for him to meet his financial obligations. A recent rise in the price of oil has made him financially sound once again, but he wants to avoid a repetition of his earlier experience. At present, his production is sold directly in the spot market for oil. These transactions are depicted in Exhibit 7.7.

This producer always sells his crude oil in the open market. At his current size, he can produce 20,000 barrels a month. He occasionally hedges his short-term production in oil futures, but he finds futures to be inadequate for long-term hedging. He recently heard about commodity swaps and has approached a swap dealer for a better explanation. The swap dealer offers a commodity swap priced around the producer's grade of crude. The dealer offers to pay the producer the fixed sum of $18.65 per barrel on 20,000 barrels at the end of each month for the next five years. This is $0.10 below the current spot price for his grade. In exchange, the producer will pay the swap dealer the average weekly price of spot crude (for his grade) as reported by some specific source—such as Platt's Oilgram Price Report. This payment will also cover 20,000 barrels. At the end of each month, the producer and the swap dealer will exchange the difference between $18.65 and the average spot price for crude. This is depicted in Exhibit 7.8.

For a swap bank to make a market in commodity swaps, it must be able to offset its swaps with matched swaps with other counterparties or to hedge its swaps in some other instrument. The simplest solution is a matched swap with another counterparty. For example, suppose

EXHIBIT 7.8. **Commodity Swap: Crude Oil**

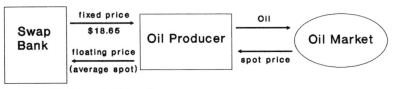

that the swap bank is approached by an oil refiner that would like to fix the cost of its oil purchases for the next five years. The swap bank offers to pay the refiner a floating price for oil in exchange for the refiner paying the bank a fixed price of $18.85 a barrel. This is $0.10 a barrel above the current spot price. The swap bank's complete set of cash flows with its two counterparties is depicted in Exhibit 7.9.

Notice the "oil market" in Exhibit 7.9. The oil market plays the same role in a commodity swap that the third-party lender plays in interest-rate swaps. There is, of course, no reason to limit commodity swaps to oil. The market could just as easily have been copper, corn, wheat, lumber, or any of hundreds of other commodities that expose their producers and users to significant levels of price risk. The commodity swap business has many possibilities. The structures of

EXHIBIT 7.9. **Matched Commodity Swaps with Swap Bank**

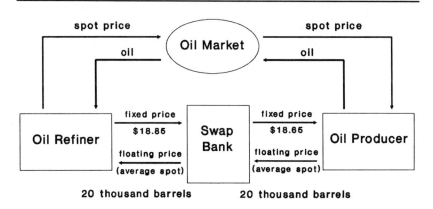

swaps, as we have already seen, are only limited by the imagination and ingenuity of those bankers and commercial interests with a use for them.

This brief look at commodity swaps is not meant to be exhaustive. But it should give the reader some feeling for this new product line and it uses. The logic of commodity swaps is a mirror of that for financial swaps. Consequently, an understanding of the latter will take us a long way toward an understanding of the former.

7.6 CHOOSING BETWEEN FINANCING ALTERNATIVES—THE ALL-IN COST

We have repeatedly referred to the all-in cost associated with financing opportunities. Before closing this chapter, it will be worth our while to consider the concept of all-in cost and its uses from the corporate end user's perspective.

It can be extremely difficult for a financial manager presented with multiple financing alternatives to choose among them without first having a conceptual tool with which to reduce the costs to some common denominator. There are a number of approaches that have been suggested over the years, but none has proven superior to the concept of all-in cost (also called effective annual percentage cost). The term all-in cost implies that this calculation considers *all* costs associated with a financing, not just the explicit interest costs. Other, less obvious, costs include such things as flotation costs (underwriters' fees, and so on) and miscellaneous administrative expenses.

The concept is much easier for the beginner to understand if he or she is already familiar with the concept of **internal rate of return**. An all-in cost is the cost-side equivalent of the revenue-side notion of internal rate of return. Internal rate of return, often denoted IRR, is a concept familiar to most modern financial managers. It is defined as the discount rate that equates the present value of all the future cash flows from an investment with the investment's initial cost. In equation form, the IRR is the value k, which solves Equation 7.1. In

Equation 7.1, $CF(t)$ denotes the cash flow at time t, n is the number of periods of cash flow involved, and k is the discount rate.

$$\text{Cost} = \sum_{t=1}^{n} CF(t) \cdot (1 + k)^{-t} \qquad \textbf{(7.1)}$$

Internal rate of return is used to convert cash flow revenue streams to a percentage return basis. The technique assumes each cash flow received can be reinvested to earn the same rate. While this assumption may in practice be violated, it does not, in the authors' opinion detract from the usefulness of the approach.

Let's consider first the concept of internal rate of return. Suppose that, for an initial cash outlay (cost) of $500, we can receive positive cash flows (revenues) each year for the next three years. Each cash flow is received at the end of the year involved. The first cash flow will be $200, the second will be $300, and the third will be $150. We will represent these cash flows two ways. The first is the simple tabular form that appears as Table 7.2. The second is a payment time line. This is Exhibit 7.10.

The solution to the IRR equation is found using an iterative approach. That is, we select a value for k and plug it into Equation 7.1. If the right-hand side (the sum of the present values) is greater than the left-hand side (the cost), then the discount rate was too low. If the right-hand side is less than the left-hand side, then the discount rate was too high. By successively trying different values for k, we can determine the IRR to any degree of accuracy we desire. The IRR

TABLE 7.2
Cash Flow Stream

Time	Cash Flow	Type
0	($500)	Cost
1	200	Revenue
2	300	Revenue
3	150	Revenue

EXHIBIT 7.10.   Payment Time Line

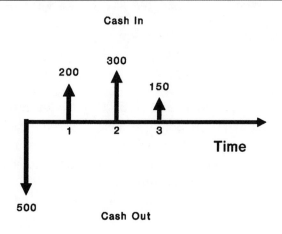

calculation is available on most modern financial calculators and many spreadsheet packages, but we prefer to use the same software package we employed for our previous "number crunching" requirements.[10] In this particular case, the value of k that satisfies the equation is 14.923 percent. We, therefore, conclude that the investment's internal rate of return is 14.923 percent.

The only difference between an internal rate of return and an all-in cost is that in an internal rate of return, the "cost" of an investment precedes the "revenues" from the investment, whereas in an all-in cost, the "revenue" from a financing precedes the "cost" of the financing. But, since one party's liability is another party's asset, it follows that one party's internal rate of return is another party's all-in cost. With this understanding, the solution is simple. First, calculate the firm's initial proceeds from a financing (the revenue) and then calculate each subsequent cash outlay (cost). When all the "cash flows" have been generated, we simply reverse all the signs, that is, we treat the initial proceeds as the initial cost and we treat the subsequent cash outflows as cash inflows (revenues). Once the signs have been changed, we can compute the internal rate of return in the usual manner and call it an all-in cost. It would certainly help to consider an example.

7.6.1   All-In Cost: An Example

The Gremlin Corporation needs to raise $20 million of seven-year debt capital. The firm's financial managers would like a fixed rate of interest and they are considering two financing alternatives. Management has no strong preference for the structure of the financing. Consequently, the sole objective is to minimize the firm's cost of funds as measured by the "all-in cost."

ALTERNATIVE 1

The firm would issue a straight fixed-rate note (nonamortizing). The firm's investment bank has told the firm that the note can be sold at par if the firm is willing to pay a semiannual coupon of 12-¾ percent. The investment bank would offer the note to the public at par (100) with 97-½ going to the firm. The difference represents the flotation costs of the issue. The firm would also bear the administrative costs of servicing the issue. These costs amount to $41,000 every six months payable at the same time as the coupon.

ALTERNATIVE 2

The firm would issue $20 million of six-month commercial paper through a commercial paper dealer. Every six months new paper would be sold and the proceeds used to pay off the maturing paper. This strategy would involve an initial issue and then 13 rollovers (refundings). The paper dealer would charge one-sixteenth of a point for each issue to handle the distribution.[11] This would be payable at the time of issue. The firm has an excellent credit rating and would pay the going rate on investment-grade paper. For purposes of this example, we will suppose that the commercial paper rate for investment-grade paper has averaged one-half point (50 basis points) above LIBOR. To convert this floating-rate liability to a fixed-rate liability, the firm would enter a fixed-for-floating interest rate swap. The commercial paper dealer, who also makes a market in interest-rate swaps, has offered a seven-year interest-rate swap with the bank as floating-rate payer. The firm would pay the bank a semiannual rate of 12 percent and the bank would pay the firm six-month LIBOR. Administrative costs will total $18,000 every six months payable at the time the paper is redeemed by the firm. There are no other costs.

The key to calculating the all-in costs of these two financing alternatives is to generate the full set of net cash flows. To generate the set of net cash flows, the precise amount and time of each cash inflow and each cash outflow must be determined. Once the full set of cash flows has been obtained the all-in cost can be determined by using an internal rate of return program. There are, however, two special considerations: First, the cash flows are stated on a semiannual basis. Thus, the IRR generated will be a half-year IRR. The rate must still be annualized. Second, if we designate cash inflows as positive (+) values and cash outflows as negative (−) values, all the flows will have the opposite sign from that ordinarily used to generate an IRR. As noted earlier, this problem is solved by simply reversing the signs when entering the cash flows into the IRR program.

The first thing to do is to list all sources of "cash in" and all sources of "cash out." For alternative 1, the "cash in" includes the proceeds from the sale of the seven-year fixed rate note. The "cash out" includes the underwriting fee (paid only once), the interest coupon paid semiannually, the administrative costs paid semiannually, and the final redemption. These individual flows together with the resultant "net flows" are depicted in Table 7.3.

The flows for alternative 2 are a bit more complex than the flows for alternative 1. First, there is a new issue every six months and a redemption every six months. Second, there are two sets of interest flows—the interest flows on the paper and the interest flows on the swap. It is important that we don't need to concern ourselves with the unknown value "LIBOR" since the firm will pay LIBOR plus one-half percent (the approximate paper rate) and receive LIBOR. The LIBORs cancel leaving a net cost of one-half percentage point per year (25 basis points every six months). The swap coupon is 12 percent paid in two semiannual installments ($1.2 million each). The full set of cash flows are depicted in Table 7.4.

We are now ready to determine the all-in cost of the two financing

TABLE 7.3
Cash Flows for Alternative 1
Cash Flows

Period	Proceeds	Underwriting Costs	Interest	Adm	Redemp	Net Flow
0	20,000,000	− 500,000				19,500,000
1			− 1,275,000	− 41,000		− 1,316,000
2			− 1,275,000	− 41,000		− 1,316,000
3			− 1,275,000	− 41,000		− 1,316,000
.			.	.		.
.			.	.		.
.			.	.		.
13			− 1,275,000	− 41,000		− 1,316,000
14			− 1,275,000	− 41,000	− 20,000,000	− 21,316,000

TABLE 7.4
Cash Flows for Alternative 2
Cash Flows

Period	Proceeds	Underwriting Costs	25 bps Interest	Swap Coupon Interest	Adm	Redemp	Net Flow
0	20,000,000	-12,500					19,987,500
1	20,000,000	-12,500	-50,000	-1,200,000	-18,000	-20,000,000	-1,280,500
2	20,000,000	-12,500	-50,000	-1,200,000	-18,000	-20,000,000	-1,280,500
3	20,000,000	-12,500	-50,000	-1,200,000	-18,000	-20,000,000	-1,280,500
.	.	.	.	.	.	.	.
.	.	.	.	.	.	.	.
.	.	.	.	.	.	.	.
13	20,000,000	-12,500	-50,000	-1,200,000	-18,000	-20,000,000	-1,280,500
14			-50,000	-1,200,000	-18,000	-20,000,000	-21,268,000

alternatives. We reverse the signs of all the net cash flows above and then calculate the internal rate of returns. These internal rates of return are the all-in costs. Alternative 1 is found to have a half-year all-in cost of 6.863 percent. This half-year IRR can be translated to an effective annual percentage rate using Equation 7.2. This translation yields an all-in cost of about 14.20 percent. The same procedure applied to alternative 2 produces an annual all-in cost of 13.22 percent.

$$\text{Effective annual percentage cost} = (1 + IRR)^2 - 1 \quad \textbf{(7.2)}$$

The all-in cost calculations suggest that alternative 2 is the better financing alternative. It accomplishes the same end result as alternative 1 but saves the firm 98 basis points a year. It is important to note that we have ignored any qualitative differences between the two alternatives. We would be remiss if we failed to point out that qualitative differences will sometimes influence the financing decision.

While commercial paper is, by definition, short-term debt, the strategy of rolling the paper over every six months for a period of seven years coupled with an interest-rate swap gives the strategy a long-term fixed-rate character and it is, therefore, best viewed as long-term debt.

The all-in cost approach discussed above is particularly useful when the firm is considering capping a floating rate liability, placing a floor under a floating-rate asset, or wrapping a collar around a floating-rate liability. The reader should recall that the premiums paid to acquire interest-rate caps, interest-rate floors, and interest-rate collars can be amortized to obtain their percentage annual cost equivalents. For example, suppose that a firm has priced a floating rate financing and determined that the all-in cost is LIBOR + 1.25 percent. The firm would like to place a 10 percent cap on the floating rate so it also prices a 8.75 percent interest rate cap. Suppose that the cap has an annual percentage cost equivalence of 0.25 percent. We can now obtain the all-in cost of the capped floating rate financing by simply adding the 0.25 percent cost of the cap to the LIBOR + 1.25 percent cost of the financing to get an all-in cost of LIBOR + 1.50 percent but capped at 10.25 percent (10 percent plus cost of cap). The point, once again, is that the merits of alternative forms of financing can only be intelligently compared if we reduce all costs to a common denominator.

Before closing this chapter, we remind the reader that the appendix to this chapter considers the swap and futures alternatives to hedging a mortgage portfolio. This appendix should be of some interest to those involved in the thrift industry but may be skipped without any loss of continuity by other readers.

7.7 SUMMARY

Swaps can be used to:

1. lower financing costs;
2. hedge interest-rate and exchange-rate exposures;
3. operate on a larger volume in order to exploit economies of scale; and
4. gain access to new markets.

The intense utilization of the swap product has significantly reduced, through arbitrage, the potential cost-reducing benefits once obtainable with swap finance, but the other uses of swaps remain. Many of the largest firms are only beginning to understand the uses to which they may put swaps. The use of swaps for these latter purposes continues to expand rapidly.

The uses of swaps discussed in this chapter highlight the versatility of this financing and risk-management tool. Two of the other uses of swaps, which have not been discussed in this chapter, include the protection of overseas trading profits by multinationals and gap management by banks.[12]

Different end user objectives necessitate different swap variants or combinations of variants. For example, swaps can be written to swap fixed rates into floating rates, to swap zero coupons into floating rates, to swap floating rates into other floating rates, to amortize notional principals, with options to call or put the swap, or to extend the term of the swap, with provisions to delay the commencement of the swap or begin the swap but delay the rate setting, to convert assets rather than liabilities, with rate ceilings and/or rate floors, and so on.

Asset-based swaps are often used to create synthetic instruments. A synthetic instrument is a combination of other instruments that have a combined cash flow stream identical to that of some real instrument. Very often, these swaps are driven by tax asymmetries in the markets.

A potentially important variety of swaps are commodity swaps. These swaps are structured exactly the same way as an interest-rate swap. The counterparties to a commodity swap exchange fixed prices for floating prices of the underlying commodity but do not actually exchange the physical commodity itself.

In the final analysis, the selection of a financing structure from among the many alternatives available must depend on three factors:

1. the form of the outcome desired;
2. the cost of each alternative, as measured by some common denominator such as all-in cost; and
3. any qualitative differences that might apply.

REFERENCES AND SUGGESTED READING

Angrist, S.W. "Big Stakes Hedge Starts Branching Out: Commodity Swaps Grow for Oil, Metals," *The Wall Street Journal*, September 26, 1989.

Brown, K.C. and D.J. Smith, "Recent Innovations in Interest Rate Risk Management and the Reintermediation of Commercial Bank Lending," *Financial Management*, *17* (4), Winter 1988.

Finnerty, J.D., "Financial Engineering in Corporate Finance: An Overview," *Financial Management*, *17* (4), Winter 1988.

Grant, C. "Swedish Lessons for the French," *Euromoney*, 107–114 (Jan 1985).

Hume, J.G. "Remaining Calm in Troubled Markets: The Growth of Risk Hedging Vehicles," *Journal of Commercial Bank Lending*, 7:7 36–44 (Dec 1984).

Krzyzak, K. "Copper Bottomed Hedge," *Risk*, 2(8), September 1989.

Loeys, J. "Interest Rate Swaps: A New Tool for Managing Risk," *Business Review* (Federal Reserve Bank of Philadelphia) (May/June 1985).

Lota-Gerd, P.E. "Forward Foreign Exchange: Protecting Overseas Trading Profits," *Credit and Financial Management*, 87:5, 31–38 (June 1985).

Madura, J. and C. Williams, "Hedging Mortgages with Interest Rate Swaps vs Caps: How to Choose," *Real Estate Finance Journal*, 3:1, 90–96 (Summer 1987).

Mahajan, A. and D. Mehta, "Strong Form Efficiency of the Foreign Exchange Market and Bank Positions," *Journal of Financial Research*, 7:3, 197–207 (Fall 1984).

Marshall, J.F. *Futures and Option Contracting: Theory and Practice*, Cincinnati: South-Western (1989).

Simonson, D.G. "Asset/Liability: A Time for Swaps," *United States Banker*, 98:2, 51052 (Feb 1987).

Smith, C.W., C.W. Smithson, and L.W. Wakeman, "The Market for Interest Rate Swaps," *Financial Management*, *17* (4) Winter 1988.

Wade, R.E. "Managing a Negative Gap in a Rising Interest Rate Environment," *Financial Managers' Statement*, 9:4, 33–37 (July 1987).

Wallich, C.I. "The World Bank's Currency Swaps," *Finance and Development*, 2:1, 15–19 (June 1984).

ENDNOTES

[1]The end user of the swap need not be, and often is not, a for-profit commercial firm. Many swaps have been arranged to provide reduced-cost financing for sovereign nations and international organizations. The Kingdom of Sweden is a leading user of swap finance and thus an example of the former (see Grant (1985)). The World Bank, discussed in Chapter 1, is a leading user and excellent example of the latter (see Wallich (1984)).

[2]An annuity is a series of equal-sized payments spread out at equal intervals in time. They are valued with the aid of present value annuity arithmetic.

[3]This sum is determined with the aid of present value arithmetic. In particular, 60 quarterly payments of DM 3,235,340 have a present value of DM 100 million at an annual discount rate (interest rate) of 10 percent (compounded quarterly). Each payment represents interest and a partial repayment of principal.

[4]The assumption that the current spot exchange rate of deutschemarks for dollars is an unbiased estimate of all future spot exchange rates of deutschemarks for dollars is made for simplicity of illustration only. In fact, the current spot exchange rate of one currency for another will generally not be an unbiased estimate of the future spot exchange rates for those two currencies. In efficient capital and currency markets, the relationship between these forward exchange rates and the respective countries' nominal interest rates is explained by the interest-rate parity theorem discussed in Chapter 2.

[5]For a detailed discussion of the behavior of the firm hedging in futures in the presence of positive hedging costs, see Marshall (1989), Chapter 7. The arguments presented there are directly extendable to a swap hedge.

[6]For a discussion of the many areas encompassed by financial engineering, see Finnerty (1988).

[7]Most often, this "formula" simply specifies the spread over Treasury which will be used to fix the rate at the time the swap coupon is set.

[8]Rate-capped swaps are not the only means by which rate-capped mortgages can be hedged. Other instruments useful for this purpose include interest-rate options and rated-capped floating rate notes.

[9]Any firm involved in the sale of durable goods, which most consumers finance, will tend to have interest-sensitive sales and profits.

[10]We use *A-Pack: An Analytical Package for Business*, a fuller description of A-Pack can be found in the footnotes to Chapter 2.

[11]The standard dealer fee for placing commercial paper is one-eighth of a percentage point per dollar per year. This fee translates to one-sixteenth of a percentage point for six-month paper.

[12]For a discussion of the use of swaps and related instruments to protect overseas trading profits, see Lota-Gerd (1985). For a discussion of the use of swaps in gap management by banks and other depository institutions, see Wade (1987), and Brown and Smith (1989).

CHAPTER 7:

APPENDIX

Futures Versus Swaps:
Some Considerations for the Thrift Industry*

John F. Marshall

INTRODUCTION

Studies have shown that financial managers often lack an understanding of the mechanics of hedging, lack the expertise to construct and manage hedges, or simply fail to appreciate the benefits of hedging.[1] Thrift managers are not an exception and, historically, thrifts have been reluctant to hedge. The experiences of the industry over the last decade, however, have forced thrifts to re-examine their risk-management practices and many are now struggling to understand hedging concepts and hedging tools.[2]

Prior to the introduction of swaps, the principal instruments for hedging interest-rate risk were interest-rate futures contracts. Thrifts were never big users of futures. The studies noted above have shown that managers mistakenly regard futures as "speculative" in nature or only suitable for hedging short-term risk exposures. Swaps, on the other hand, have been widely embraced during the last few years as an effective long-term risk management tool.

In this paper, I examine the source of a thrift's long-term interest-rate risk, and I compare swaps and futures hedging strategies for the management of this risk. I argue that, while swap hedges can be very effective, they are not necessarily superior to futures hedges when cost is considered.

---

*This article is reprinted, with minor changes, from *Review of Business*, *12*(3), Winter 1990.

I. THRIFTS AND INTEREST-RATE RISK: THE PROBLEM

Consider the case of a thrift institution that acquires (either by origination or assignment) conventional fixed-rate mortgages using funds obtained from the sale of three-month certificates of deposit (CDs). To make the example concrete, let's suppose the thrift purchases $25 million of newly originated 20-year mortgage debt having a coupon of 10 percent and yielding 10 percent (thus the mortgages are priced at par). The mortgagors will make payments to the thrift on a quarterly basis.[3] The thrift funds the mortgages by selling $25 million of three-month (90 day) CDs. The plan is to refund the mortgage assets every three months by selling replacement CDs. This process would be continued until the mortgages mature. At the time of the initial CD sale, the three-month CD rate is 8 percent.

The example is complicated a bit by the amortizing nature of mortgage debt. At each refunding, fewer CDs need to be sold to carry the mortgage assets. Consider the first three and the last three payments in the amortization schedule. These are depicted in Table 7.A.1.[4] Notice that, after the first CD cycle matures, the thrift only needs to raise $24.9 million from the sale of replacement CDs. After the seventy-eighth cycle matures, the thrift will only need to raise $1.4 million from the sale of replacement CDs.

TABLE 7.A.1
Mortgage Amortization Schedule
(all values are in thousands)

Payment Number	Payment	Principal Component	(Book Value) Principal Remaining
1	725.65	100.65	24,899.35
2	725.65	103.17	24,796.18
3	725.65	105.75	24,690.44
.			
78	725.65	673.84	1,398.71
79	725.65	690.68	708.03
80	725.73	708.03	0.00

EXHIBIT 7.A.1. Mortgage Finance by a Thrift

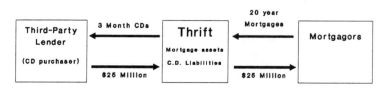

Initial Exchange of Principals and Documents

In a stable interest-rate environment, the thrift would simply carry the mortgages unhedged and enjoy a rate spread of 2 percent (the difference between the 10 percent the thrift receives on its mortgage assets and the 8 percent the thrift pays on its CD liabilities). The first set of cash flows is illustrated in Exhibit 7.A.1. The exhibit depicts the initial exchange of principals between the thrift and the mortgagors on the one hand and the thrift and the third-party lenders (CD purchasers) on the other.

The CDs mature at the time the first mortgage payment is made and the thrift must refund its mortgage assets with the sale of replacement CDs. The thrift will receive a payment of $725,650 from the mortgagors, will pay $25,500,000 to the third-party lenders to retire its matured CDs, and will receive $24,899,350 from the sale of new CDs to third-party lenders. The cash flows between the thrift and the mortgagors and the thrift and the third-party lenders are depicted in Exhibit 7.A.2.

These cash flows provide the thrift with a net inflow of $125,000. This is, of course, one quarter's rate spread on $25 million: 0.25 · (10

EXHIBIT 7.A.2. Mortgage Finance by a Thrift

Cash Flows at Time of First Mortgage Payment
Net Cash Inflow to the Thrift: $0.125 Million

percent − 8 percent) × $25 million. Barring any premature repayment of principal by the mortgagors, the cash flows depicted in Exhibit 7.A.2 are known with certainty since the pay/receive rates were locked in at the time the mortgages were funded. However, it cannot be known at the time of the initial mortgage funding what the three-month CD rate will be at the time of the first refunding; nor can it be known at the time of the initial mortgage funding what the refunding rate will be for any of the subsequent 78 refundings. It is evident, that the liabilities side of the thrift's mortgage business involves a floating rate of interest (reset once every three months) while the asset side involves a fixed rate of interest (10 percent). This floating/fixed rate mismatch is the source of the thrift's interest-rate risk.

If three-month CD rates do not change from their 8 percent level and no mortgagors prepay, the second cash flow stream will produce net revenues of $124,490: The thrift will receive $725,650 from the mortgagors, will pay $25,397,340 to the third-party lenders to retire the second CD financing, and will receive $24,796,180 from third-party lenders on the sale of replacement CDs. Of course, there is no guarantee that the three-month CD rate will not change. Nevertheless, we can calculate the expected present value of the mortgage lending as a function of the expected rate spread. This is given by:

$$E[PV] = \sum_{t=1}^{80} \{E[D(t)] \div 4) \cdot PR(t) \cdot (1 + (k \div 4)\}^{-t} \textbf{ (7.A.1)}$$

Where $E[D(t)]$ denotes the expected rate spread at time t, $PR(t)$ denotes the principal remaining at time t (i.e., the portion of the principal that has not yet amortized), and k denotes the thrift's discount rate— presumably its risk-adjusted cost of funds. If we assume that $D(t) = 2$ percent for all t, that k is 10 percent (the current mortgage rate), and that there are no mortgage principal prepayments, then the expected present value of the mortgages to the thrift is $3,428,900.

If the CD rate rises, the refunding becomes more expensive and the thrift's revenue declines accordingly. The rise in the CD rate reduces the rate spread $D(t)$ and thus reduces the present value of the mortgage assets.

II. THE SWAP HEDGE

The thrift described in the preceding section can hedge its interest-rate risk by becoming a counterparty to a fixed-for-floating interest-rate swap. In such a swap, the thrift would agree to make quarterly fixed-rate payments on $25 million of amortizing debt to a swap dealer in exchange for the swap dealer's quarterly floating-rate payments to the thrift. The floating-rate side of a fixed-for-floating rate swap is usually tied to LIBOR but can just as easily be tied to some other rate such as the T-bill rate or a commercial paper rate. In this case, it would be tied to the three-month CD rate.

Swap dealers routinely price the fixed-rate side of an interest-rate swap as a spread over U.S. Treasuries of a similar average life.[5] In this particular case, the mortgage debt has an average life of 13.22 years. Thus, the swap dealer would take the T-bond with a maturity closest to 13.22 years and add a premium. The size of the premium will depend on whether the swap dealer is paying or receiving fixed rate. Suppose, for purposes of this example, that the swap dealer is currently offering to pay the 13.22 year T-bond yield plus 38 basis points and is offering to receive fixed-rate for the 13.22 year T-bond yield plus 54 basis points. Both rates are quoted against the three-month CD rate. Suppose further that the 13.22 year T-bond yield is currently 8.40 percent.[6]

In this case, the thrift is looking to convert its floating-rate liabilities to fixed-rate liabilities. Thus, the thrift is the fixed-rate payer (floating-rate receiver) and will pay a quarterly rate of 8.94 percent (8.40 percent plus 0.54 percent). The cash flows between the thrift and the swap dealer are depicted in Exhibit 7.A.3.

EXHIBIT 7.A.3.   Interest-Rate Swap with Swap Dealer

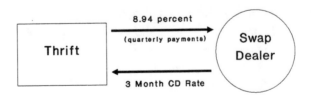

EXHIBIT 7.A.4.   Mortgage Lending with Swap Hedge

Now, by combining the cash flows between the thrift and the mortgagors and the thrift and the third-party lenders (Exhibit 7.A.1) with the cash flows between the thrift and the swap dealer (Exhibit 7.A.3), we get the completely hedged set of cash flows depicted in Exhibit 7.A.4. Notice that there is no longer any interest-rate uncertainty in the thrift's position. The thrift is now both paying and receiving the three-month CD rate (so they fully offset one another). The thrift is receiving 10 percent from the mortgagors and paying 8.94 percent to the swap dealer. The end result is a fixed-rate spread of 1.06 percent for the life of the mortgages.

This example illustrates the standard hedge using interest-rate swaps and it is the precise type of situation for which swap dealers market their services. The swap hedge is very effective. But notice that the swap hedge is not costless. The 2 percent rate spread that the mortgage-assets/CD-liabilities were expected to generate has been reduced to 1.06 percent. The reduction in the rate spread represents the cost of the hedge.[7] An alternative, but equivalent, way to appreciate this cost is to look at the change in the present value of the rate spread. In this case, the present value of the rate spread declines from $3,625,300 to $1,921,400. The difference, $1,703,900, is the cost of the hedge.

III. THE FUTURES HEDGE

The futures alternative to the swap hedge is a little more complicated than a simple short hedge. The thrift is concerned that interest rates might rise. A rise in rates would result in an increase in the thrift's cost of CD funding for its mortgage assets. The appropriate strategy is to sell a sufficient number of interest-rate futures. We could use either T-bond futures or mortgage futures. The Chicago Board of Trade (CBOT) discontinued its GNMA futures contract, but new mortgage-based futures are being introduced. For simplicity, let's suppose that a futures contract on 30-year mortgages exists. This is the ''contract'' we will use to illustrate the futures hedge. The goal is to determine the appropriate number of futures to sell short so as to precisely offset any change in rates and preserve the present value of the asset/liability rate spread.

There are a number of difficulties in determining the appropriate number of mortgage futures to sell. First, if changes in the CD rate are not perfectly correlated with changes in the mortgage rate, hedging will be inexact at best. Second, the hedge ratio is not stable over time—as the mortgages age, the hedge ratio will need to be recalculated. We'll address the latter problem first.

The hedge ratio can be estimated using any of the various hedge ratio models—depending on the analyst's preferences. The most versatile approach is the dollar value basis point (DVBP) model. The ''dollar value of a basis point'' is defined as the change in the market value of $100 of face value debt for a one basis point change in the instrument's yield. We begin by dividing the DVBP of the debt instrument to be hedged by the DVBP of the instrument underlying the futures (regarded as the futures DVBP). This ratio is then multiplied by the yield beta. The yield beta is the ratio of the change in the yield of the instrument to be hedged and the change in the yield of the hedging instrument. This yield beta is found by simple linear regression.[8] The product of the DVBP ratio and the yield beta is then the hedge ratio. The dollar size of the hedge is given by Equation 7.A.2.

$$FV_{hedge} = FV_{cash} \times \frac{DVBP_{cash}}{DVBP_{futures}} \times \beta_y \qquad \textbf{(7.A.2)}$$

The dollar size of the hedge is then translated into a specific number of futures contracts by dividing by the face value of a single futures contract. Assume that $FV_{futures}$ equals $0.1 million.

$$NF = \frac{FV_{hedge}}{FV_{futures}} \qquad \textbf{(7.A.3)}$$

To continue with our example, we would first calculate the DVBP of the mortgages held in the mortgage portfolio which, as it happens, is $0.06848. We would then calculate the DVBP of the futures. Let's suppose the futures DVBP is $0.08500. Next, we estimate the yield beta between the 20-year mortgage rate (the mortgages held by the thrift) and the rate on the mortgages underlying the futures. Let's suppose the yield beta is 1.06. That is, for each 1 basis point change in the yield of the futures, we expect a 1.06 basis point change in the yield of the thrift's mortgages.

The initial hedge for the thrift's position is then given:

$$FV_{hedge} = \$25 \text{ million} \times \frac{\$0.06848}{\$0.08500} \times 1.06$$

$$= \$21.35 \text{ million}$$

$$\approx 214 \text{ futures}$$

At the time of the first refunding, the thrift would recalculate the size of the hedge based on its new level of mortgage principal, the new values of the DVBPs, and the yield beta for 19.75-year mortgages (as opposed to the earlier 20-year mortgages). This process would be repeated every three months and the size of the futures hedge adjusted accordingly.

The hedge is very effective provided that all yield changes in the CD rate are matched by identical changes in the mortgage yield. That is, if three-month CD yields rise by 1 basis point, the 20-year mortgage yield must also rise by 1 basis point. Later, after the first refunding, a 1 basis point change in CD yields must be matched by a 1 basis point change in 19.75-year mortgage yields. Although this is not a realistic scenario, consider the outcome if it were: Suppose that, immediately after the mortgages were acquired (while the mortgages still have a 20-year life), rates rise by 1 basis point. The next CD refunding is then expected to cost 8.01 percent (up from 8 percent). The present value of the mortgage/CD rate spread declines by $17,100. This is completely offset, however, by a $17,100 profit on the futures hedge.

There is, however, an inconsistency in our assumptions. We have assumed that, on average, the yield on 20-year mortgages changes by more than the yield on 30-year mortgage futures (yield beta was 1.06). Yet, we have also assumed parallel shifts in three-month CD and 20-year mortgage yields (and every mortgage maturity less than 20 years). The reality, of course, is that short-term rates and long-term rates are not equally volatile. We must adjust the size of the hedge to account for this difference in volatilities.

The first step in the adjustment is to calculate, what I will call, an "adjustment beta." The adjustment beta (β_a) is the ratio of the change in the three-month CD rate to the change in the 20-year mortgage rate. This is estimated in the same manner as the yield beta. To continue our example, suppose that the adjustment beta is found to be 1.35. This suggests that, for each basis point change in the 20-year mortgage rate, the CD rate can be expected to change by 1.35 basis points (typical of the greater volatility of short-term rates).

The final step is to adjust the size of the hedge to reflect the difference in yield volatilities. This is accomplished by multiplying the face value of the hedge obtained with the DVBP model by the adjustment beta. The full hedge model is given by Equation 7.A.4.

$$FV_{hedge} = FV_{cash} \times \frac{DVBP_{cash}}{DVBP_{futures}} \times \beta_y \times \beta_a \qquad \text{(7.A.4)}$$

In this case, the calculation is:

$$
\begin{aligned}
FV_{hedge} &= \$21.35 \text{ million} \times 1.35 \\
&= \$28.82 \text{ million} \\
&\approx 288 \text{ futures}
\end{aligned}
$$

Thus, we find that the thrift can hedge by selling 288 mortgage futures at the time the mortgages are acquired. The full set of cash flows (excluding principal flows) associated with this strategy is depicted in Exhibit 7.A.5.

At the time of each refunding, the thrift would recalculate all five of the variables that enter into the determination of the optimal hedge: FV_{cash}, $DVBP_{cash}$, $DVBP_{futures}$, β_y, and β_a. All other things being equal, FV_{cash}, $DVBP_{cash}$, and β_a will decline with the passage of time; β_y will rise; and $DVBP_{futures}$ will not change. The combined effect is such that the size of the hedge decreases with each refunding. Of course, the futures used in the hedge are of limited term so the thrift will need to periodically roll forward into later delivery futures. The strategy requires a balancing of the frequency of rollover against the liquidity of the instrument. The near delivery futures will typically be more liquid and thus involve less liquidity cost, but, at the same time, necessitate more frequent rollover and thus involve greater transaction costs.

The hedge strategy presented here is neither perfectly effective nor costless. Like most futures hedging, there will be some basis risk as the various yields involved in the hedging model fluctuate in a less than perfectly predictable manner. The futures hedge is, therefore, less effective than the nearly perfectly effective swap hedge. Nevertheless, the futures hedge may still be preferable. We have seen that the swap

EXHIBIT 7.A.5.   Mortgage Lending with Futures Hedge

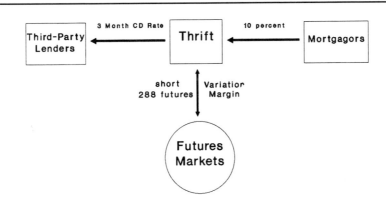

hedge is quite costly—resulting in a considerable forfeiture of present value. The futures hedge may be less costly.[9] If so, the trade-off is one of efficacy against cost. The comparative efficacies and costs of the swap hedge and the futures hedge are empirical issues. I make no effort to address these issues here, but this is clearly an area ripe for study.

IV. PREPAYMENT ADJUSTMENTS AND OTHER CONSIDERATIONS IN THE CHOICE OF THE OPTIMAL HEDGE

There are two other considerations in the choice of the hedging instrument. The first involves intermediate cash flows engendered by the hedge. The second involves mortgage prepayments.

Daily marking-to-market of futures will necessitate the regular transfer of variation margin to and from the margin account of the thrift. There are no comparable intermediate transfers of funds with a swap hedge. This would seem to suggest a preference for the swap hedge. This conclusion, however, is premature. Assuming the futures hedge behaves perfectly, the precise amount of the margin transfer out (in) of the thrift's account will be matched by an increase (decrease) in the present value of its rate spread. Suppose, for example, that interest rates decline. Margin will be transferred from the thrift's margin account (since it is short futures). At the same time, the decline in the cost of the thrift's CD liabilities will result in an increase in the value of the rate spread. Thus, as long as the thrift has sufficient liquidity to meet its margin requirements, these intermediate cash flows should not be an overriding consideration.

The second, and far more significant, consideration is mortgage prepayment by mortgagors. Conventional mortgage indentures typically allow the mortgagor to prepay the mortgage principal without penalty after some initial period. Mortgages are prepaid for a variety of reasons.[10] The more unpredictable the prepayment rate, the greater the advantage of futures hedging over swap hedging.

Suppose that, immediately after acquiring the mortgages and entering into a swap with a swap dealer, interest rates decline and $2 million of mortgage debt is prepaid. The thrift can easily adjust its liabilities by simply refunding $2 million less in the next sale of CDs. The swap hedge, however, is not so easily adjusted. In fact, unless very special provisions have been included in the swap agreement to allow the thrift to amortize the swap more quickly, the thrift will, quite likely, be locked into the swap. In such a situation, the portion of the swap no longer covering actual mortgages becomes a speculation and exposes the thrift to precisely the kind of interest-rate risk the thrift entered the swap to avoid. One solution is to negotiate a cancellation of a portion of the swap principal with the swap dealer. As a general rule, the swap dealer will oblige but only if adequately compensated. Alternatively, the thrift could default on the swap. A default would bring the swap default provisions into play. These provisions require the thrift to indemnify the swap dealer for the cost of securing a replacement swap.[11] A default will, of course, damage the reputation of the thrift and make subsequent hedging more difficult.

A swap can be written with a provision granting the thrift the option to accelerate the amortization of the swap principal. This option has value, however, and the swap dealer will not grant it without compensation—which, in turn, further reduces the profitability of holding a mortgage portfolio.

The prepayment problem is minimized with the futures hedge. The thrift can simply lift a sufficient portion of its futures hedge to offset the portion of the mortgages that have been prepaid. However, since the greatest number of prepayments is likely to occur when interest rates decline, and the mortgagors can prepay without penalty, the mortgage principal received may not be sufficient to cover the loss on the futures hedge. Nevertheless, the ability to easily offset the futures hedge, in whole or in part, allows the thrift to minimize this source of uncertainty. To protect against a decline in rates and accelerated prepayments, the thrift might couple the futures hedge with an appropriate position in interest-rate options. Several forms of interest-rate options could be used for this purpose including call options on interest-rate futures, call options on a debt instrument, and over-the-counter interest-rate floors.[12]

An alternative solution to the prepayment problem is to use a mixed hedge—part swap and part futures. The swap portion can be used to cover that amount of mortgage debt not likely to be prepaid and the futures hedge can cover the rest.

REFERENCES

Belongia, M.T. and G.J. Santoni, "Hedging Interest Rate Risk with Financial Futures: Some Basic Principles," *Review*, Federal Reserve Bank of St. Louis, December 1984. Reprinted in *Current Reading on Money, Banking, and Financial Markets*, J.A. Wilcox, ed.

Block, S.B. and T.J. Gallagher, "The Use of Interest Rate Futures and Options by Corporate Financial Managers," *Financial Management*, Autumn 1986.

Booth, J.R., R.L. Smith, and R.W. Stolz, "The Use of Interest Futures by Financial Institutions," *Journal of Bank Research*, Spring 1984.

Gardner, M.J. and D.L. Mills, "Asset/Liability Management: Current Perspectives for Small Banks," *The Journal of Commercial Bank Lending*, December 1981.

Kaufman, G., "Measuring and Managing Interest Rate Risk: A Primer," *Economic Perspectives*, Federal Reserve Bank of Chicago, January/February 1984.

Loeys, J.G., "Interest Rate Swaps: A New Tool for Managing Risk," *Business Review*, Federal Reserve Bank of Philadelphia, May/June 1985. Reprinted in *Current Reading on Money, Banking, and Financial Markets*, J.A. Wilcox, ed.

Marshall, J.F., *Futures and Option Contracting: Theory and Practice*, Cincinnati: South-Western, 1989.

McNulty, J.E., "Measuring Interest Rate Risk: What Do We Really Know?" *Journal of Retail Banking*, Spring/Summer 1986. Reprinted in *Current Reading on Money, Banking, and Financial Markets*, J.A. Wilcox, ed.

Quinn, L.R., "How Corporate America Views Financial Risk Management," *Futures*, January 1989.

Sinkey, J., *Commercial Bank Financial Management*, New York: Macmillan, 1983.

Toevs, A., "Gap Management: Managing Interest Rate Risk in Banks and Thrifts," *Economic Review*, Federal Reserve Bank of San Francisco, Spring 1983.

ENDNOTES

[1]See Block and Gallagher [2], Quinn [9], and Booth, Smith, and Stolz [3].

[2]Thrifts are also candidates for asset/liability management strategies on which much has been written. Examples include McNulty [8], Kaufman [5], Toevs [11], and Gardner and Mills [4]. For an extensive bibliography on gap analysis through 1983, see Sinkey [10]. For a discussion of the relationship between gap analysis and futures hedging see Belongia and Santoni [1]. Nevertheless, the nature of the thrift's core business renders asset/liability management solutions inadequate at best.

[3]In most cases, residential mortgage debt of the type held by thrifts will involve monthly rather than quarterly payments. However, little is lost by the quarterly-payment assumption. The cash flow diagrams and analysis are simplified a bit by this assumption without any fundamental damage to the realism of the example.

[4]The amortization schedule was generated using *A-Pack: An Analytical Package for Business*, from MicroApplications.

[5]Average life is used by swap dealers to equate the maturities of nonamortizing Treasury debt and amortizing mortgage debt. Average life is discussed in Chapter 8.

[6]The T-bond rate is a semiannual rate while this particular example involves quarterly payments and thus a quarterly compounded rate. This necessitates a conversion from semiannual rate to its quarterly compounded equivalent. For purposes of this example, however, we will ignore this adjustment. The adjustment process is discussed in Chapter 8.

[7]For a fuller discussion of this point, see Loeys [6].

[8]For a fuller discussion of the estimation of the yield beta, see Marshall [7], Chapter 12.

[9]Ibid

[10]The prepayment rate is the percentage of the mortgages on which the mortgagors elect to prepay the principal during some defined period of time. Some of the factors that cause prepayment are highly predictable. These include such things as the death of the home owner, the sale of the home, and foreclosure. Other components of the prepayment rate are far less predictable. The most important of these less predictable factors is the general level of interest rates. A decline in rates will lead to some refinancings. Thus, the greater the decline in interest rates the higher the prepayment rate.

[11]For a discussion of indemnification of a counterparty in the event of a default on a swap, see Chapter 9.

[12]These different forms of interest-rate options are discussed in Chapter 6.

8

The Pricing
of Swaps

8.1 OVERVIEW

In this chapter, we consider how swap banks price swaps. (We assume that the swap bank is acting as a dealer in swaps and hence as a counterparty to the swap rather than as a swap broker.) The pricing of the swap is important for both the swap bank and the corporate user. The corporate user might want to compare the pricing of swaps offered by several swap banks and compare the all-in cost of these swap alternatives to the all-in cost of other financing and/or other risk-management opportunities available to it.

The bank's pricing will hinge on a number of things. These include:

1. the maturity of the swap;
2. the structure of the swap;
3. the availability of other counterparties with whom the bank can offset the swap;
4. the creditworthiness of the client counterparty;
5. the demand and supply conditions for credit generally and for swaps in particular in all countries whose currencies are involved in the swap; and
6. any regulatory constraints on the flow of capital that influence the efficiency of the markets.

The market for swaps consists of short-dated swaps—those under two years—and long-dated swaps—those over two years. The market for short-dated swaps is largely an interbank market and of little interest to corporate end users. To the degree that corporate end users have a need for short-term hedges, they can usually construct very efficient hedges by using interest-rate and exchange-rate futures and/or FRAs. In addition, since short-dated swaps can easily be replicated from FRAs and Eurodollar futures, it is not surprising that short-dated swaps are usually priced off a futures strip. A **futures strip**, the reader will recall, is a sequence of futures contracts. The most important group of futures for pricing short-dated swaps are the Eurodollar futures that are traded on the International Monetary Market (IMM). Short-dated swaps priced off IMM Eurodollar futures contract and that use IMM settlement dates are called **IMM swaps**. The logic of pricing short-dated swaps off the IMM strip parallels the pricing of FRAs as it was discussed in Chapter 5 and we do not take it up again. Instead, this chapter concentrates on long-dated swaps.

The pricing of interest-rate swaps is the chapter's first topic and starts with the plain vanilla fixed-for-floating rate swap based on bullet transactions. The analysis then progresses slightly by introducing amortization and payment frequency considerations. The examples assume that the swap bank offsets its swaps in the U.S. Treasury and/or Eurodollar markets until such time as it can offset the swaps with other counterparties. After completing a look at the pricing of interest-rate swaps, the pricing of currency swaps is discussed. The plain vanilla currency swap, which is called an exchange of borrowings, is examined first and is followed by **amortizing currency swaps** and pricing complications introduced by off-market transactions. Finally, the pricing of fixed-for-fixed rate currency swaps created through a combination of a fixed-for-floating interest rate swap and a fixed-for-floating exchange of borrowings (currency swap) is considered.

It is important to understand that in the discussion of swap pricing that follows, bid-ask spreads that range to 25 basis points are employed. Swap spreads of this magnitude were typical in swap bank pricing in the mid 1980s, but have narrowed considerably during the last few years. Spreads of 10 basis points or less are more realistic today. In any case, the actual size of the spread used in our examples is not very important to understanding the principles involved.

For the corporate reader interested in discussing a swap with a swap bank, we have included the membership list of the International Swap Dealers Association as an appendix to this chapter. This is the most complete list currently available of firms actively involved in making markets in swaps. For each swap bank, we have included the firm's name and address. We have deliberately left out phone numbers and contact points because these change from time to time.

8.2 INDICATION PRICING SCHEDULES: THE INTEREST-RATE SWAP

Swap banks regularly prepare indication pricing schedules for use by their capital market personnel. These schedules provide swap dealers with guidelines for pricing swaps and they are updated frequently to take account of changing market conditions. Prices take the form of interest rates and are stated in terms of basis points (bps). Each basis point is one-one hundredth of one percent. In the case of dollar-based interest rates, the fixed-rate side of the swap is usually stated as a spread over prevailing yields on on the run U.S. Treasury securities. On the runs are the securities of a given maturity that were most recently auctioned. For example, five years ago the Treasury auctioned 10-year notes. With the passage of time, these 10-year notes have become five-year notes. If the Treasury was now to auction a new issue of five-year notes, then there would be at least two five-year T-note issues simultaneously trading. The most recent issues (the on the runs) have the more current coupon and tend to be more liquid then the older issues. The floating-rate side is most often taken to be LIBOR flat. The pricing structure assumes bullet transactions. That is, as with Treasury securities, it is assumed that the principal is repaid in a lump sum at maturity.

A minor complication introduced by this pricing scheme is that the interest rate on the fixed-rate side of a swap is quoted as a semiannual **bond equivalent yield**. Bond equivalent yields are based on a 365-day year. The floating-rate side is usually tied to LIBOR. LIBOR is quoted as an annual money market yield. Money market yields are based on a 360-day year. This difference in yield conventions often necessitates some conversions to make the rates more directly comparable. This issue will be addressed shortly.

In the early days of swaps, it was quite common for the swap bank to require a front-end fee for arranging the swap. The front-end fee was negotiable and could run as much as one-half of a percentage point. The justification for the front-end fee was the time it took to write the swap documentation and the time it took to work with the client to design a swap that would accomplish the client's objectives. With the increasing standardization of swaps, front-end fees have all but disappeared. Today, a front-end fee will only be imposed when some fancy financial engineering is required or when the client is purchasing a special option-like feature. Front-end fees have never been common on interbank swaps.[1]

Consider a typical indication pricing schedule for swaps with various maturities as depicted in Table 8.1. The prices indicated are for fixed-for-floating interest-rate swaps and assume semiannual compounding (sa). Although we always state interest rates on an annual basis, it is customary to call an annual rate of interest compounded semiannually a semiannual rate. For example, the phrase "a semiannual rate of 8 percent" means an annual interest rate of 8 percent that is compounded semiannually. The phrase "an annual rate of 8 percent" means an annual interest rate of 8 percent that is compounded annually.

Let us consider a simple example: A corporation has determined that it can sell $25 million of five-year nonamortizing debt at par by offering a semiannual coupon of 9.675 percent.[2] It prefers floating-rate liabilities to fixed-rate liabilities and approaches the capital markets group of our swap bank to arrange an interest-rate swap. Call this corporate client Counterparty 1.

The swap bank has been asked to pay fixed rate and receive floating rate. Since the bank has been asked to pay fixed rate, the bank offers to pay 9.26 percent (five-year TN rate + 34 bps) in exchange for six-month LIBOR flat. The corporate client's net cost of funds,

TABLE 8.1
Indication Pricing for Interest Rate Swaps

Maturity	Bank Pays Fixed Rate	Bank Receives Fixed Rate	Current TN Rate
2 years	2-yr TN sa + 20 bps	2-yr TN sa + 45 bps	8.55 percent
3 years	3-yr TN sa + 25 bps	3-yr TN sa + 52 bps	8.72 percent
4 years	4-yr TN sa + 28 bps	4-yr TN sa + 58 bps	8.85 percent
5 years	5-yr TN sa + 34 bps	5-yr TN sa + 60 bps	8.92 percent
6 years	6-yr TN sa + 38 bps	6-yr TN sa + 66 bps	8.96 percent
7 years	7-yr TN sa + 40 bps	7-yr TN sa + 70 bps	9.00 percent
10 years	10-yr TN sa + 50 bps	10-yr TN sa + 84 bps	9.08 percent

Note: The schedule assumes semiannual rates and bullet transactions.
TN denotes the Treasury note rate.

after the interest-rate swap, appears to be LIBOR + 0.415 percent (9.675% + LIBOR − 9.260%). This is not, however, quite correct. Because the fixed-rate sides are bond equivalent yields, the difference between them, 0.415 percent, is also a bond equivalent. This difference cannot be added directly to LIBOR without first converting it to a money market yield equivalent. Remember, six-month LIBOR is quoted as a semiannual money market yield (MMY) and based on the assumption of a 360-day year, while the fixed-rate side of a fixed-for-floating rate swap is quoted as a semiannual bond equivalent yield (BEY) and based on the assumption of a 365-day year. (We discussed the differences in yield conventions in Chapters 2 and 3.) The importance of the difference in yield conventions when pricing swaps now becomes apparent. For this reason, we will reiterate some of what has already been said on this subject—but now in the context of swap pricing.

To combine these values correctly, we must transform the fixed-rate differential, 0.415 percent, to its money market yield equivalent. The conversion formula appears as Equation 8.1.[3] This conversion is simple because both six-month LIBOR and the swap coupon are semiannual rates. When the payment frequencies are mismatched (annual versus semiannual, for example) the conversions are somewhat more complex.

$$\text{MMY differential} = \text{BEY differential} \times \frac{360}{365} \qquad \textbf{(8.1)}$$

$$= 0.415 \text{ percent} \times \frac{360}{365}$$

$$= 0.409 \text{ percent}$$

The final floating-rate cost of funding for this corporate client is then LIBOR + 0.409 percent. The cash flows associated with this swap are depicted in Exhibit 8.1. As it happens, had this corporate client borrowed directly in the floating-rate market, it would have been required to pay LIBOR plus 1.25 percent. The client thus enjoyed a cost savings by engaging in the swap.

The swap bank above would look for an opportunity to offset this swap with another swap. Until it can do so, however, the bank will hedge in T-notes and Eurodollars (or T-bills). For example, since the swap bank has agreed to pay fixed rate and receive floating rate, it might short $25 million (market value) six-month Treasury bills and use the proceeds from this sale to purchase $25 million (market value) of five-year Treasury notes.[4] The bank can obtain the securities for the short sale by a reverse repurchase agreement (reverse) with another institution. In a reverse, the bank "purchases" a security from another party and agrees to "sell" the security back to this same party at a specific later date for a specific price. (The repo/reverse market is discussed more fully in Chapter 3.)

An alternative way to obtain securities for a short sale exists when the swap bank holds a portfolio of Treasuries separate and distinct

EXHIBIT 8.1. Cash Flows Between Counterparty 1 and Swap Bank

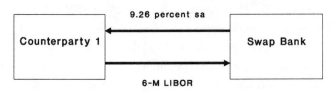

($25 million notional principal)

from its swap operations. For example, the portfolio might represent an investment portfolio that the bank manages either for itself or for its clients, or the swap bank might be a market maker in Treasuries (known as a government securities dealer). These portfolios can serve as the source of the securities that the swap bank sells short. The swap desk will pay other departments of the bank for these securities. The cost of these intrabank borrowings is called the **transfer pricing rate** (TPR). The transaction may be viewed as equivalent to a reverse repurchase agreement between departments within the bank. For purposes of this text, we assume that the TPR is the prevailing rate on Treasuries of the maturity borrowed. In practice, the TPR will usually be at a premium to Treasuries. The cash flows for the swap bank are depicted in Exhibit 8.2.

The swap bank prefers to offset the swaps to which it is a counterparty with matching swaps with other counterparties. The Treasury/ Eurodollar positions represent hedges placed only until such time as a matched swap can be arranged. It is important to note that if the swap bank hedges in T-bills, as opposed to Eurodollars, it will have a residual basis risk because LIBOR and the T-bill rate are not perfectly correlated. This point is addressed more fully in the next chapter.

Suppose now that another corporate client approaches the swap bank in need of $30 million of fixed-rate dollar financing. This firm has a comparative advantage in the floating-rate (LIBOR) market. It can sell semiannual five-year nonamortizing floating rate notes (FRNs) at par by paying six-month LIBOR plus 150 basis points. Through the

EXHIBIT 8.2. Cash Flows After Offset in Government Securities Market

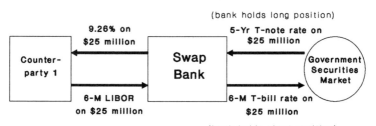

vehicle of the swap, the corporate client would like to convert this floating-rate liability into a fixed-rate liability. The swap bank is asked to receive fixed rate and pay floating rate. Call this corporate client Counterparty 2.

The swap bank has been asked to receive fixed rate and pay floating rate. Assume that the indication pricing schedule depicted in Table 8.1 is still in effect. Since the bank has been asked to receive fixed rate, it would require that Counterparty 2 pay 9.52 percent (five-year TN rate + 60 bps) in exchange for the bank paying six-month LIBOR flat. To calculate Counterparty 2's net cost of funds, we must first convert the floating-rate spread over LIBOR (1.5 percent), which is stated on a money market basis, to a bond equivalent basis. Equation 8.1 allowed us to move from a bond equivalent yield to a money market yield; in this case, we need to move in the opposite direction. Equation 8.2 allows us to move from a money market yield to a bond equivalent yield. Again, this conversion is simple because both rates are already stated on a semiannual basis. If the payment frequencies were mismatched, the conversions would be more complex.

$$\text{BEY differential} = \text{MMY differential} \times \frac{365}{360} \qquad \textbf{(8.2)}$$

$$= 1.5 \text{ percent} \times \frac{365}{360}$$

$$= 1.521 \text{ percent}$$

The conversion renders the value 1.521 percent. Counterparty 2's net cost of funds, after the interest-rate swap, is then 11.041 percent (LIBOR + 1.521 percent − LIBOR + 9.52 percent). As it happens, this firm could have borrowed fixed-rate funds directly at a cost of 11.375 percent. Thus, this client has also enjoyed a benefit from its swap.

The cash flows between the bank and Counterparty 2 are depicted in Exhibit 8.3. The swap bank could offset its position with Counter-

EXHIBIT 8.3. Cash Flows Between Counterparty 2 and Swap Bank

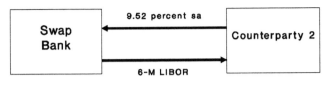

($30 million notional principal)

party 2 by selling $30 million (market value) of five-year Treasury notes short and by using the proceeds from this short sale to purchase $30 million (market value) of six-month T-bills.

Notice that the bank's cash flows with Counterparty 2 are very nearly the mirror image of the bank's cash flows with Counterparty 1. In fact, if the swap bank lifts its Treasury market positions which it is using to hedge its swap with Counterparty 1, it will only require a $5 million position in Treasuries/Eurodollars to hedge the interest-rate exposure that stems from its swap with Counterparty 2. The flows, from the swap bank's perspective, are depicted in Exhibit 8.4.

EXHIBIT 8.4. Cash Flows Between Counterparties and Swap Bank with Residual Position in Government Securities

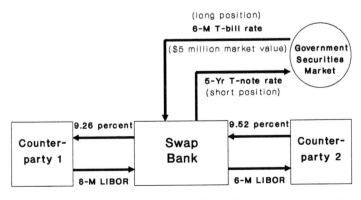

($25 million notional principal)   ($30 million notional principal)

The indication pricing schedule used to price the swaps made between the swap bank and Counterparties 1 and 2 assumes that the swaps are of the plain vanilla fixed-for-floating rate variety and that the counterparties have a satisfactory credit standing in the eyes of the swap bank. Thus, the indication pricing schedule provides starting prices only. To the extent that the swap will require a special structure, or that a counterparty's credit standing is not first rate, or that the swap exposes the bank to special risks, the swap pricing will have to be adjusted to reflect these factors. Price adjustments can take the forms of a wider swap bid-ask spread or a front-end fee or both. Front-end fees, however, are no longer typical except when special financial engineering is required or when the swap incorporates an option-like feature. In the latter case, the front-end fees are best viewed as option premiums.

For example, if Counterparty 1, who is paying the equivalent of LIBOR plus 0.409 percent, desired a rate cap of 12.5 percent, the swap bank would likely oblige; but it would add a front-end fee and/or raise the floating rate payment. Suppose this particular swap bank will oblige Counterparty 1's request for a rate cap, but it will require a front-end fee of one-quarter point (25 basis points) and increase the counterparty's rate to LIBOR plus 0.550 percent. Similar fees and adjustments would be made if the counterparty required a call feature, a put feature, a rate floor, and so on.

8.3 ADJUSTMENTS TO INDICATION PRICING

The indication pricing schedule assumes that payments are to be made semiannually and that all transactions are bullet transactions. It is not unusual for one or both of these assumptions to fail. When this happens, an adjustment in pricing must be made.

We will first consider the pricing adjustments necessitated by a failure of the nonamortizing bullet-transaction assumption. Following this, we will consider the adjustments necessitated by a failure of the semiannual payment assumption.

8.3.1 Amortizing Loans: Duration versus Average Life

The indication pricing schedule assumes that the swap is nonamortizing so that the interest payments are calculated on the same notional principal throughout the term of the swap. Suppose instead that the swap bank's client requires a swap that is based upon amortizing principal. Any number of amortizing schedules are possible. For example, the client might require:

1. that the notional principal underlying the swap be reduced by a fixed dollar amount each year (often called a sinking fund schedule);

2. that the notional principal be reduced by a fixed dollar amount each year beginning after some defined **grace period** during which no amortization of notional principal occurs; or

3. that the principal amortize at an increasing rate as is customary with mortgage-type amortization schedules (perhaps the client is a savings and loan looking to hedge the interest-rate risk associated with its mortgage portfolio).

As already described, most swap banks price the fixed-rate side of an interest-rate swap as a spread over Treasury securities. Treasury debt is always nonamortizing. That is, the Treasury pays periodic (semiannual) interest but does not repay any principal on a Treasury note or bond until such time as the note or bond matures. At maturity, the Treasury repays all principal in a single transaction. Given the nonamortizing nature of Treasury securities, it is not appropriate to base the price of an N-year amortizing swap on the prevailing yield of an N-year nonamortizing Treasury security.

Operatives in the debt markets, including commercial banks, investment banks, and government securities dealers, know that, all other things being equal, the longer the maturity associated with a given debt instrument, the more price sensitive the debt instrument will be to fluctuations in yield levels. It is partly for this reason that long-term debt instruments are regarded as more risky than short-term debt instruments. This fact forms the foundation for one well-known, though not universally accepted, explanation for the shape of the Treasury yield curve—the liquidity preference theory—which holds that the yield on a debt instrument is directly related to its price sensitivity to interest-rate fluctuations.[5] However, it has also long been known that maturity alone is not the sole determinant of a debt instrument's price sensitivity to changes in interest rates. A second, and very important, determinant is the speed with which the debt principal amortizes. Other less important factors include the size of the coupon payments, the frequency of the coupon payments, and the yield presently afforded by the instrument.

In 1938, Frederick Macaulay developed a measure of price sensitivity to yield changes that incorporates all five of the factors that influence price sensitivity. This measure is known as duration. Some of the uses of duration were discussed in Chapters 2 and 4 but we have not yet attempted to apply the concept to the pricing of swaps.

Assuming equal basis point changes in yield, two debt instruments with identical durations will have identical interest-rate sensitivities. In addition, the ratio of two debt instruments' durations is an accurate measure of their relative price sensitivities to equivalent yield changes when such price sensitivity is stated on a percentage basis. Duration, which is measured in years and denoted here by D, is a weighted-average time to the maturity of the instrument. The weights are the ratios of the present values of the future cash flows (including both interest and principal) to the current market price of the instrument. The current price of the instrument is, of course, the sum of the present value of all future cash flows associated with the instrument.

The duration formula from Chapter 2 is repeated here as Equation 8.3.

$$D = \sum_{t}^{m \cdot T} W_t \cdot (t/m) \tag{8.3}$$

where $W_t = \dfrac{CF(t/m) \cdot (1 + y/m)^{-t}}{\sum_t CF(t/m) \cdot (1 + y/m)^{-t}}$

$$t = 1, 2, 3, \ldots m \cdot T$$

$CF(t/m)$ = Cash flow at time t/m (time measured in years).
$\quad\quad y$ = Present yield on instrument.
$\quad\quad m$ = The number of payment periods per year.

Because of its long-standing role as a measure of a debt instrument's price sensitivity to fluctuations in yield (interest-rate risk), it seems logical to use duration in the pricing of the fixed-rate side of interest-rate and currency swaps. Unfortunately, duration has proven unsatisfactory for this purpose. The duration equation allows one to determine an instrument's duration if one knows its yield. A problem occurs when the instrument's duration and the appropriate yield— which is the fixed rate of interest used for the swap coupon—are both not known.

One widely used solution to pricing the fixed-rate side of a swap is to use a weighted-average measure of the times at which notional principal is amortized where the weights are formed without reference to yield. **Average life** is such a measure.[6]

The average life of an instrument is found by forming the product of the principal repayment and the time at which that principal repayment will be made. These products are then added and the sum is divided by the notional principal at the start of the swap. The average life formula appears as Equation 8.4.

$$AL = \frac{\Sigma P(t) \cdot t}{IP} \qquad\qquad (8.4)$$

AL = average life.
$P(t)$ = principal repaid (or cancelled) at time t.
IP = initial principal (principal at start of swap).

It is important to remember that in interest-rate swaps the principal repayments are only notional. The notional nature of the principal, however, does not affect the calculation of the average life.

Let's consider a simple example: Suppose a firm requires an amortizing swap with an initial notional principal of $9.5 million and a term of nine and one-half years with semiannual payments. The principal will amortize under a semiannual sinking-fund type schedule with notional principal payments of $0.5 million each.[7] Thus, the first payment is due at time 0.5, the second is due at time 1.0, and so on until the last—which is due at time 9.5. The first product is formed by multiplying $0.5 million by 0.5; the second is formed by multiplying $0.5 million by 1; and so on.

These products are then added to get 47.5 million. Finally, this sum is divided by the initial notional principal of 9.5 million to get an average life of five years. Thus, the swap has an average life of five years. The calculation of this average life is repeated below.

Time		Principal Repaid			Product
0.5	×	$0.5 M	=		$0.25 M
1.0	×	$0.5 M	=		$0.50 M
.	.	.	.		.
.	.	.	.		.
.	.	.	.		.
9.5	.	$0.5 M	.		$4.75 M
				Sum	47.50 M

$$AL = 47.5 \div 9.5 = 5 \text{ years}$$

Once the average life has been determined, the swap is treated as though it is equivalent to a T-note that has a maturity equal to the swap's average life. The next step is to look at the indication pricing schedule for the pricing of swaps of this term. This particular swap would be priced from the five-year T-note. While the average life of an amortizing instrument is not the same as its term to maturity, the average life of a nonamortizing instrument, such as a T-note, is identical to its term to maturity.

Suppose the five-year T-note is currently yielding 8.75 percent. Using the duration formula, we find that the five-year T-note has a duration of 3.98. Using the same yield to calculate the duration of the amortizing swap, we find that the swap has a duration of 3.93. Thus, the duration of the swap and the duration of the T-note with the same average life are nearly the same—although not necessarily identical.

When pricing swaps, an important argument in favor of the use of average life, as opposed to duration, lies in the treatment of interest. With a typical debt instrument, interest payments flow only one way. With a swap, interest payments flow two ways and are therefore largely offsetting. The offsetting nature of the interest payments suggests a strong argument for focusing on the principal alone—which is precisely what average life does.

With the widespread stripping of coupon-bearing Treasury securities to create zero coupon Treasury products, sufficient liquidity has developed in zero coupon Treasuries for the emergence of a well-defined zero coupon yield curve. The zero coupon yield curve depicts the relationship between the yields on zero coupon Treasuries and their respective maturities. Zero coupon securities are unique in that their duration, average life, and maturity are identical.

At present, many swap banks use the zero coupon yield curve as the basis of their swap hedging operations but continue to price their swap products off the conventional yield curve. It is likely that in time swap banks may switch to pricing their swap products off the zero coupon yield curve. Some already do. In keeping with common practice, however, we will continue to use coupon-bearing Treasuries for our pricing discussion.

8.3.2 Semiannual Rates versus Other Payment Frequencies

Interest-rate swaps priced as a spread over Treasuries assume semiannual interest payments. When the bank's client requires annual payments, as opposed to semiannual payments, the bank must adjust the fixed rate of interest to reflect this difference.

Consider again the case of Counterparty 2, which had approached the swap bank for a five-year fixed-for-floating interest-rate swap. This party would pay fixed rate and receive floating rate. The bank quotes a semiannual fixed rate of 9.52 percent (five-year TN + 60 bps). Counterparty 2 now indicates that it prefers annual fixed-rate payments although it still wishes to receive semiannual floating-rate payments based on six-month LIBOR.

The swap bank is agreeable but must now determine the annual rate that is equivalent to a semiannual rate of 9.52 percent. The procedure for determining the equivalent annual rate is founded on basic time value arithmetic. That is, we calculate the annual interest rate that would provide the same future value, for a given starting sum, as would the semiannual rate. This calculation appears as Equation 8.5.

$$r_{an} = \left(1 + \frac{r_{sa}}{2} \right)^2 - 1 \qquad (8.5)$$

In Equation 8.5, r_{an} denotes the annual interest rate and r_{sa} denotes the semiannual interest rate. More generally, an interest rate stated on one payment frequency can be converted into an interest rate stated on another payment frequency by using the relationship given in Equation 8.6.

$$r_m = m \cdot \left[(1 + \frac{r_z}{z})^{z/m} - 1 \right] \qquad (8.6)$$

r_m = Annual rate of interest assuming m compoundings per year.
r_z = Annual rate of interest assuming z compoundings per year.

In this more general formulation, m would be 1 if the rate r_m were annual; z would be 2 if the rate r_z were semiannual; and so on. These conversions ignore the issue of reinvestment risk. Reinvestment risk is the risk that income received from an investment will be reinvested at a rate that differs from the rate that prevailed at the time the investment was acquired. The swap bank can be expected to attach a premium to its swap pricing when the swap structure gives rise to reinvestment risk. This risk, however, is small in comparison to other risks that are discussed shortly and so we will ignore it.

Now let's return to Counterparty 2. Counterparty 2 requires a payment schedule that provides for annual, rather than semiannual, payments of fixed-rate interest. The bank calculates the annual interest rate using Equation 8.6.

$$r_1 = 1 \cdot [(1 + .0952/2)^{2/1} - 1] = 9.747\%$$

The swap bank now offers its client a fixed-for-floating rate swap in which the bank would pay semiannual interest to the client at the rate of six-month LIBOR in exchange for the client's annual payments to the bank at the rate of 9.747 percent.

There is one additional problem with this swap from the swap bank's perspective. Since the bank pays the client semiannually but the client only pays the bank annually, there is a payment mismatch that exposes the bank to considerable credit risk. For example, suppose that the floating-rate side is initially set at 8.5 percent and that six months after the swap documents are executed, the bank pays its counterparty client $1.275 million—calculated as one-half of 8.5% on $30 million. Next, suppose that, six months later, the counterparty client defaults at the time the counterparty is due to make its first payment to the bank. While the counterparty's default frees the bank from its obligation to make the current and future interest payments, as per the rights of set-off contained in the terms and conditions of the swap agreement, the bank has already made its first payment to the counterparty. It must now utilize the swap's default provisions to try to recover its losses.

This example illustrates the extra level of risk associated with entering into swaps that have payment timing mismatches. We will consider this problem again, and the steps the swap bank might take to alleviate it, in Chapter 9. One final point is, however, in order. Because payment timing mismatches increase the risk exposure of the swap bank, we might expect that the swap bank will insist on additional compensation from its counterparty client. For example, the bank might add a few basis points to the fixed rate its counterparty client is required to pay.

It is important to note that there is almost always some credit risk to the swap bank from its swap activities. While the rights of set-off relieve the swap bank from making payments to its counterparty should the counterparty default, the default does not relieve the swap bank of its commitments to other counterparties—including those with whom the bank has matched the defaulted swap. Thus, credit risk is very real even when the timing of the payments are perfectly matched. Clearly, however, mismatched timing of payments amplifies credit risk.

8.4   MARKET IMBALANCES AND PAY/RECEIVE RATE ADJUSTMENTS

The difference between the fixed rate a swap bank must receive and the fixed rate it is willing to pay at any given average life is its bid-ask spread for swaps with that average life. In preparing its indication pricing schedules and implied spreads, the swap bank must take several things into consideration. Of major importance, of course, are the competitive pressures of the market. The swap bank must offer competitive swap pricing if it is to attract rate-conscious corporate clients.

Suppose that the swap bank using the indication pricing schedule appearing in Table 8.1 finds that it is attracting considerable five-year average life fixed-for-floating swap activity on the bank-pays-fixed-rate side but very little swap activity on the other side. The swap bank prefers to offset its swaps with other swaps rather than resorting to hedging in the cash market for Treasury securities. Looking again at the bank's current pricing for five-year average life swaps, it can be seen that the bank needs to attract additional swap activity on the bank-receives-fixed-rate side. At present, the bank's base pricing requires the Treasury note rate plus 60 basis points (TN + 60 bps) from fixed-rate payers. The bank can attract additional activity on the bank-receives-fixed-rate side by lowering the fixed rate it requires of fixed-rate paying counterparties. For example, it could lower its price on five-year average life swaps to the Treasury note rate plus 58 basis points. At the same time, it might lower the rate that it will pay so as to discourage new swaps on the bank-pays-fixed-rate side until such time as it can fully offset its existing portfolio of swaps. For example, it might lower its bank-pays rate to the Treasury note rate plus 31 basis points. These pricing adjustments are summarized in Table 8.2.

By frequently adjusting its pay/receive rates, the swap bank is able to attract additional counterparties on the side of the market it prefers and to thereby correct market imbalances. In more extreme cases, the swap bank might find that some of the counterparties attracted to its prevailing rate are themselves swap banks who have developed imbalances on the other side of the fixed-for-floating-rate market.

TABLE 8.2
Pay/Receive Pricing Adjustments to
Correct Market Imbalances

	Maturity	Bank-Pays Fixed Rate	Bank-Receives Fixed Rate	Current TN Rate
Old	5 years	5-yr TN sa + 34 bps	5 yr TN sa + 60 bps	8.92 percent
New	5 years	5-yr TN sa + 31 bps	5 yr TN sa + 58 bps	8.92 percent

8.5 INDICATION PRICING SCHEDULES: CURRENCY SWAPS

In the plain vanilla currency swap, the counterparty client wants to swap a fixed-rate obligation in one currency for a floating-rate obligation in another currency. By using a currency swap in conjunction with an interest-rate swap, we can convert a fixed-rate obligation in one currency to a fixed-rate obligation in another currency or, alternatively, we can use a currency swap in conjunction with an interest-rate swap to convert a floating-rate obligation in one currency to a floating-rate obligation in another currency.

This section concentrates on the pricing of fixed-for-floating-rate currency swaps. The swap bank's international capital markets team will estimate appropriate pay and receive fixed rates for all of the currencies in which the bank makes a market. All rates are against six-month LIBOR flat. The fixed rates may be stated on an annual or a semiannual basis and the adjustment from annual to semiannual or vice versa is exactly the same as that described in our discussion of rate adjustments for interest-rate swaps. Assume that the rates in the following examples are all stated on a semiannual basis.

In the case of currency swaps, indication pricings are often stated as a mid-rate to which some number of basis points is added or subtracted depending on whether the swap bank is to receive or pay fixed rate. Such a schedule is depicted for deutschemark-to-dollar rates in Table 8.3.

The structure of the DM-to-USD indication pricing schedule in

TABLE 8.3
Indication Pricing for
Deutschemark-to-Dollar Swaps

Maturity	Mid-Rate
2 years	6.25% sa
3 years	6.48% sa
4 years	6.65% sa
5 years	6.78% sa
6 years	6.88% sa
7 years	6.96% sa
10 years	7.10% sa

Note: The rates above are mid-rates. To these rates, deduct one-eighth percent (12.5 bps) if the bank is paying fixed rate. Add one-eighth percent (12.5 bps) if the bank is receiving fixed rate. All principal transactions are assumed to be bullet transactions.

Table 8.3 is typical of currency swaps, although the size of the bid-ask spread (25 basis points) is excessive by current standards. The swap bank would likely offer similar schedules for the other major hard currencies including the Swiss franc, French franc, British pound, Canadian dollar, and Japanese yen.

As already mentioned, the rates in Table 8.3 are mid-rates. The actual pay/receive rates are found by deducting/adding the appropriate premium to the mid-rate. For straight U.S. dollar interest-rate swaps, the indication pricing schedule depicted in Table 8.1 lists both the bank's pay and receive rates. Nevertheless, we can obtain a mid-rate for interest-rate swaps by simply taking the average of the pay and receive rates. For example, for the five-year interest-rate swap the mid-rate is 9.39 percent—calculated as (9.26 + 9.52) ÷ 2.

Consider now a simple example: A German firm approaches our swap bank looking to convert a DM 35 million five-year semiannual fixed-rate liability into a floating-rate dollar liability. The swap bank offers an exchange of borrowings (straight currency swap) at the current spot exchange rate of 1.75 DM/USD. At the current exchange rate, the principal is $20 million. Since the bank will be paying fixed rate, the rate is found by taking the five-year mid-rate and deducting one-eighth of one percent. This calculation produces a rate of 6.655 percent (6.78 − 0.125). Thus, the German counterparty client would pay the swap bank six-month LIBOR on principal of $20 million and the swap bank would pay the German firm 6.655 percent sa on DM 35 million.

Unlike an interest-rate swap, in which there is no exchange of principals, there is often an exchange of principals in the straight currency swap. That is, at the commencement of the swap, the German firm would exchange its DM 35 million for the bank's $20 million. For the next five years, the two parties would pay each other interest at the rates indicated. After five years, the two parties would re-exchange principals at the same exchange rate used for the initial exchange of principals (i.e., 1.75 DM/USD). The straight currency swap clearly involves three separate cash flows:

1. the initial exchange of principals;
2. the interest payments; and
3. the re-exchange of principals.

These are depicted in Exhibits 8.5, 8.6, and 8.7.

As with interest-rate swaps, the swap bank makes its profit on currency swaps from its bid-ask spread. For this swap bank, the spread is currently one-quarter point (25 basis points) since the bank is adding and subtracting one-eighth point from its mid-rate. The bank is, of course, looking to offset its exchange-rate and interest-rate exposures. These exposures are most easily offset by finding another counterparty client with matching needs. Such a client would be looking to exchange 20 million five-year floating-rate dollars for fixed-rate deut-

EXHIBIT 8.5.   Currency Swap (Exchange of Borrowings)
Initial Exchange of Principals

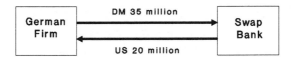

EXHIBIT 8.6.   Currency Swap (Exchange of Borrowings)
Interest Flows Between Exchanges of Principals

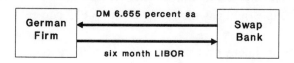

EXHIBIT 8.7.   Currency Swap (Exchange of Borrowings)
Reexchange of Principals

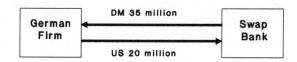

schemarks. Assuming the bank has such a client immediately available, the bank would offer to swap the currencies at the current spot exchange rate of 1.75 DM/USD. The bank would pay this second counterparty six-month LIBOR flat in exchange for the second counterparty client paying the bank DM 6.905 percent sa.

By offsetting the currency and interest exchanges with a second counterparty with cash flow needs that match those of the first, the bank is fully hedged against fluctuations in both exchange rates and interest rates. Of course, the bank may not be able to immediately identify a counterparty with matching needs. In this case, the bank might want to construct temporary hedges by using other instruments such as FRAs, FXAs, DIFFs, currency futures, and/or positions in Treasuries and foreign debt. We address these considerations more fully in Chapter 9.

In the event that the bank experiences a demand imbalance on one side of the currency swap market, the bank will have to raise or lower its mid-rate. For example, suppose that the bank experiences a surge in demand for currency swaps by clients who want to pay five-year fixed-rate deutschemarks and receive floating-rate dollars. To discourage this side of the market and encourage the other, the bank will raise its five-year mid-rate from 6.78 percent to say 6.85 percent.

Determining the correct mid-rates to serve as the basis of swap pricing is typically a function of a swap bank's international capital markets group. **Capital markets groups** operate with an international perspective and continuously monitor the capital markets worldwide. They watch their own banks' swap portfolios closely and adjust rates quickly when they suspect that an imbalance is developing. A capital markets group may find, for instance, that they must lower the bank's four-year mid-rate while simultaneously raising the bank's five-year mid-rate.

8.6   CURRENCY SWAPS WITH NO INITIAL EXCHANGE OF BORROWING

The straight currency swap involves an initial exchange of principals and an eventual re-exchange of principals. Not all currency swaps involve two exchanges of principals. Let us consider such a case.

Suppose it is now 1 February 1989. As a consequence of an earlier financing, a firm is committed to making semiannual floating-rate (six-month LIBOR) dollar payments on an amortizing loan for four more years. The payment dates are 1 August and 1 February. By the nature of the firm's business, the firm receives revenue in deutschemarks. The firm's current payment schedule is depicted in Table 8.4.

Recent fluctuations in the DM/USD exchange rate and U.S. interest rates have caused the firm's management to become increasingly concerned about its dollar liabilities and have led the firm to look for a way to convert its floating-rate dollar liabilities to fixed-rate deutsche-mark liabilities. At the same time, it would like to lock in the current DM/USD exchange rate (1.75 DM/USD) for all future exchanges. The swap bank offers a currency swap with no initial exchange of principals. The bank offers to pay LIBOR on the amortizing balance and to pay $0.5 million every six months. The swap has an average life of two and one-half years, and the bank's current mid-rate for two and one-half year deutschemarks is 6.365 percent. In exchange for the bank's paying LIBOR, the bank requires the firm to pay the bank 6.49

TABLE 8.4
Amortization Schedule of Dollar Loan

Date	Loan Balance Before Payment	Loan Balance After Payment	Payment Amount
1 Feb 1989	–	$4.0 million	—
1 Aug 1989	$4.0 million	$3.5 million	$0.5 million + LIBOR
1 Feb 1990	$3.5 million	$3.0 million	$0.5 million + LIBOR
1 Aug 1990	$3.0 million	$2.5 million	$0.5 million + LIBOR
1 Feb 1991	$2.5 million	$2.0 million	$0.5 million + LIBOR
1 Aug 1991	$2.0 million	$1.5 million	$0.5 million + LIBOR
1 Feb 1992	$1.5 million	$1.0 million	$0.5 million + LIBOR
1 Aug 1992	$1.0 million	$0.5 million	$0.5 million + LIBOR
1 Feb 1993	$0.5 million	$0.0	$0.5 million + LIBOR

percent (mid-rate plus 12.5 basis points). In addition, the bank will pay the firm $0.5 million every six months in exchange for the firm's payments to the bank of 0.875 million deutschemarks every six months. This latter sum reflects principal translations at a DM/USD exchange rate of 1.75. These payments are depicted in Table 8.5.

The counterparty client's dollar commitments to its earlier financing source (third-party lender) are now assured. The bank will pay its counterparty client $0.5 million + LIBOR flat every six months and the counterparty client will then pay this identical sum to its creditor.

TABLE 8.5
Currency Swap Payment Schedule

Date	Bank Pays Counterparty Client	Counterparty Client Pays Bank
1 Feb 89	—	—
1 Aug 89	$0.5 million + LIBOR	DM 0.875 million + 6.49 percent
1 Feb 90	$0.5 million + LIBOR	DM 0.875 million + 6.49 percent
1 Aug 90	$0.5 million + LIBOR	DM 0.875 million + 6.49 percent
1 Feb 91	$0.5 million + LIBOR	DM 0.875 million + 6.49 percent
1 Aug 91	$0.5 million + LIBOR	DM 0.875 million + 6.49 percent
1 Feb 92	$0.5 million + LIBOR	DM 0.875 million + 6.49 percent
1 Aug 92	$0.5 million + LIBOR	DM 0.875 million + 6.49 percent
1 Feb 93	$0.5 million + LIBOR	DM 0.875 million + 6.49 percent

The client's net liability is now to pay DM 0.875 million plus 6.49 percent sa. That is, it has a fixed-rate deutschemark commitment— exactly what it was looking for. It is now fully hedged with respect to exchange rates and interest rates.

Unlike the straight currency swap, which is best understood as an exchange of borrowings, this currency swap is best viewed as a series of forward contracts all made at the current spot rate of 1.75 DM/USD with the normal forward-spot exchange-rate differential incorporated in the interest payments made by the counterparties.

8.7 OFF-MARKET PRICING

Just as it is frequently necessary to make pricing adjustments to interest-rate swaps for payment frequencies that differ from those assumed in the indication pricing schedules and for amortization schedules that differ from those assumed in the indication pricing schedules, it is also frequently necessary to make pricing adjustments for variations in currency swap requirements. The straight currency swap assumes semiannual payments and bullet transactions. If the currency swap requires annual fixed-rate payments instead of semiannual payments, the annual equivalent rate for the semiannual rate would be determined again by using Equation 8.6. If the swap is an amortizing one, the appropriate rate would be found employing average life rather than maturity (as with the currency swap in the preceding example). There is one additional adjustment that is often necessary in the case of currency swaps. This occurs when the swap is **off-market**.

The need for an off-market swap arises when a firm has an existing liability at a rate that differs from that which is currently prevailing in the market. Consider the following case: A U.S. firm is committed to making semiannual interest payments to holders of its deutschemark bonds that were issued five years ago. The bond principal covers DM 18 million, all of which will be repaid at maturity in 10 more years. The bond carries a fixed coupon of 9.50 percent. The U.S. firm wants to swap this liability for a floating-rate dollar liability. Its purpose is to eliminate exchange-rate risk. Note that this swap requires no initial exchange of principals and is similar in this regard to the case discussed in the preceding section.

The swap bank's current indication pricing schedule (Table 8.3) calls for the bank to pay a fixed rate of DM 6.975 percent sa (mid-rate less 12.5 basis points) against six-month LIBOR flat. However, the counterparty client, which is the U.S. firm in this case, requires the bank to pay DM 9.50 percent. Any rate other than DM 9.50 percent will leave a residual exchange-rate risk for the U.S. firm. This swap calls for off-market pricing.

The trick to pricing off-market swaps is to create cash flow patterns with equivalent present values. This requires that we exploit our knowledge of the 10-year U.S. fixed rate and the 10-year DM fixed rate. We use mid-rates for this purpose. The latter is 7.10 percent (Table 8.3) and the former is 9.75 percent (Table 8.1).

The first step is to determine the rate differential between that which the bank's counterparty client requires and that which the bank would ordinarily pay. The differential, in this case, is 2.525 percent— calculated as 9.50 percent less 6.975 percent. That is, the client requires that the bank pay a premium of 2.525 percent on the DM fixed-rate side.

The next step is to determine the dollar-rate premium that has the same present value as this 2.525 percent DM premium. Since this DM payment takes the form of an annuity, we can compute the present value of the payment using present value annuity arithmetic. The necessary relationship is given by Equation 8.7.[8]

$$PVA = PMT \times \{[1 - (1 + R/m)^{-m \cdot n}] \div R/m\} \qquad (8.7)$$

PVA = Present value of the annuity.
PMT = Annuity payment.
   R = Mid-rate (for deutschemarks).
   n = Term of swap (number of years to maturity of swap).
   m = Frequency of interest payments.

The values of PMT, R, m, and n are, in this case, 2.525, 7.10

percent, 2, and 10, respectively. Plugging these values into Equation 8.7 provides a present value of 35.725.

Now use this present value to determine the dollar-interest premium. To obtain the dollar-interest premium Equation 8.7 is again employed but this time the current mid-rate for dollars is used for R (9.75 percent). Substitute the value 35.725 for PVA and solve for PMT. The value of PMT that solves this particular case is 2.836. This value is interpreted as the dollar-rate premium on this off-market transaction. However, this rate premium was derived from fixed-rate bond equivalent yields and, consequently, cannot be added directly to LIBOR. An adjustment must first be made. Use Equation 8.1 to make the necessary adjustment. The adjustment provides a yield premium of 2.797 percent that can be added directly to LIBOR. The swap will then call for the bank to pay its counterparty client deutschemarks at the semiannual fixed rate of 9.50 percent in exchange for the counterparty client paying the bank dollars at the rate of six-month LIBOR plus 2.797 percent. At maturity, the parties will exchange principals at an exchange rate of 1.75 DM/USD (the spot rate at the time the swap is negotiated). The cash flows associated with this swap are depicted in Exhibits 8.8 and 8.9. The bank may also look to collect a front-end fee if any special financial engineering is required in designing the swap or evaluating the client's needs.

The client firm is now fully hedged against exchange-rate fluctuations. The deutschemark payments, including both interest and principal, that it must make to its creditor (the third-party lender) are perfectly matched by the bank's payments to its client firm. The client firm's net position consists of its LIBOR plus 2.797 percent payments to the bank. It need no longer concern itself at all with the DM/USD exchange rate.

EXHIBIT 8.8. Off-Market Pricing of Currency Swap
Interest Flows Between Counterparty and Bank

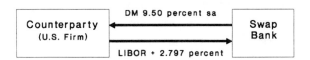

EXHIBIT 8.9.   Off-Market Pricing of Currency Swap
Terminal Exchange of Principals

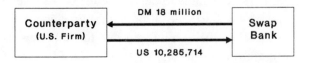

Note: In this swap, the only exchange of principals
occurs at the termination of the swap agreement.
This exchange takes place at the spot rate which
prevailed at the time the swap was negotiated,
i.e., 1.75 DM/US.

8.8   A NOTE ON THE PRICING OF CIRCUS SWAPS

The swap pricing discussed in this chapter has provided for the pricing of fixed-for-floating interest-rate swaps and fixed-for-floating currency swaps. The corporate user, however, might require a swap to convert fixed-rate payments in one currency to fixed-rate payments in another currency or, alternatively, to convert floating-rate payments in one currency to floating-rate payments in another currency. As mentioned in Chapter 7, fixed-for-fixed rate and floating-for-floating rate currency swaps can be engineered by combining a fixed-for-floating interest-rate swap with a fixed-for-floating currency swap. When both of the floating rates are LIBOR, these combinations are often called **circus swaps**.

The pricing of circus swaps directly follows from the mechanics of the two swap components. Consider one last time the off-market swap discussed in the previous section. The U.S. firm has swapped a 9.50 percent fixed-rate deutschemark commitment for LIBOR plus 2.797 percent. This same client can now convert its dollar floating-rate payments to fixed-rate payments using the rates in Table 8.1. That is, the bank will pay its counterparty client LIBOR + 2.797 percent in exchange for the client paying the bank the "bank-receives" rate of 9.92 percent plus 2.836 percent. The end result for the counterparty client is a fixed-rate semiannual payment of 12.756 percent USD.

No additional adjustments for principal are required since the principal in an interest-rate swap is purely notional. The interest flows

EXHIBIT 8.10.   Off-Market Circus Swap
Currency Swap Component

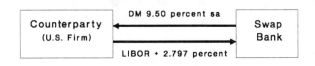

EXHIBIT 8.11.   Off-Market Circus Swap
Interest-Rate Swap Component

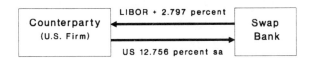

EXHIBIT 8.12.   Off-Market Circus Swap
Net Interest Flows

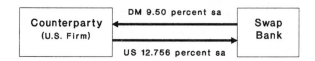

from the currency portion of this off-market circus swap are depicted in Exhibit 8.10 (this repeats Exhibit 8.8). The interest flows from the interest-rate portion of the circus swap are depicted in Exhibit 8.11. The net cash flows from the combined components of the circus swap are depicted in Exhibit 8.12.

8.9   SUMMARY

The pricing of swaps is a complex undertaking. Typically, a swap bank's capital markets group is charged with developing and periodically revising indicative swap pricing schedules for both the interest-rate and the currency swaps in which the bank makes a market.

These schedules provide base rates. The base rates are adjusted to reflect any special features the client requires, the creditworthiness of the client, the frequency of interest payments, and whether the swap will be at-market or off-market. The arithmetic of swap pricing depends heavily on the mathematics of the time value of money.

Short-dated swaps are usually priced off a futures strip. When the pricing vehicle is the IMM's Eurodollar contract and the swap uses IMM settlement dates, the swap is called an IMM swap. Dollar-based long-dated swaps are usually priced as a spread over Treasuries of similar maturity. This assumes that the swap is nonamortizing. When the swap involves amortization of principal, an alternative measure of the swap term must be used. The most frequently used of such measures is the average life of the swap.

The swap banker must monitor the bank's swap portfolio on a continuous basis. While temporary hedges are often constructed through positioning in the Government securities market, futures, and other hedging media, the optimal long-term goal is to match all swaps. This matching is often achieved by writing a swap with a second counterparty or by writing a swap with another swap bank on an interbank basis. When one side of the bank's swap portfolio becomes out of line with the other side, the bank can adjust its bid and asked prices to attract activity to the deficient side and/or make the surplus side less attractive.

A need for off-market pricing arises whenever a client of the bank requires a swap to be written at a rate that differs from the prevailing swap rates. This situation is most likely to arise when a firm seeks to transform the type of interest rate or the currency associated with an existing obligation. The off-market pricing adjustments are made with the aid of present value arithmetic.

Circus swaps, by combining interest-rate and currency swaps, allow the end-user to convert fixed-rate debt in one currency to fixed-rate debt in a different currency, or to convert floating-rate debt in one currency to floating-rate debt in another currency. These swaps are priced in exactly the same fashion as other swaps but the pricing is a two-stage process.

REFERENCES AND SUGGESTED READING

Arak, M., L. S. Goodman, and J. Snailer. "Duration Equivalent Bond Swaps: A New Tool," *Journal of Portfolio Management*, 26-32 (Summer 1986).

Fage, P., *Yield Calculations*, London: Credit Swiss First Boston, October 1986.

Gay, G. D. and R. W. Kolb. "Removing Bias in Duration Based Hedging Models: A Note," *Journal of Futures Markets*, 4:2, 225-228 (Summer 1984).

Kopprasch, R., J. Macfarlane, D. Ross, and J. Showers. "The Interest Rate Swap Market: Yield Mathematics, Terminology and Conventions," in *The Handbook of Fixed Income Securities* (2d ed), edited by F. Fabozzi and I. Pollock.

Leibowitz, M. L. "The Dedicated Bond Portfolio in Pension Funds—Part II: Immunization, Horizon Matching and Contingent Procedures," *Financial Analysts Journal*, 47-57 (Mar/Apr 1986).

Macaulay, F. R. *Some Theoretical Problems Suggested by the Movement of Interest Rates, Bond Yields, and Stock Prices in the United States since 1856*, New York: Columbia University Press for the National Bureau of Economic Research, (1938).

Nadler, D. "Eurodollar Futures/Interest Rate Swap Arbitrage," Quantitative Strategies Group, Shearson Lehman Hutton, April 1989.

Weston J. F. and T. E. Copeland. *Managerial Finance*, 8th ed., New York: Dryden Press, (1986).

ENDNOTES

[1] Interbank swaps are swaps made between swap banks. Banks enter into interbank swaps for a variety of purposes including:

1. to hedge other bank positions;

2. to close a gap;

3. to speculate on the direction of interest rates and exchange rate; and

4. to better manage their own swap portfolios.

[2] The corporation will, of course, also encounter some flotation costs in the form of underwriting fees. While these flotation costs must be factored in to obtain the firm's all-in cost in any actual financing, we ignore them here in order to concentrate on the pricing of swaps.

[3] For a fuller discussion of yield conversions and yield conventions, see Chapters 2 and 3. For more detail, see Fage (1986).

[4] When the swap bank's objective is simply to hedge a swap until a matched swap can be booked or until the swap can be assigned to another party, the bank will often hedge the swap in T-note and Eurodollar (or T-bill) futures. This is important as futures hedges, like swaps themselves, are off-balance sheet positions while cash

market positions are on-balance sheet positions. This use of futures to hedge un-matched swaps is discussed more fully in Chapter 9.

[5]The liquidity premium theory explains the shape of the yield curve in terms of ever greater interest-rate risk associated with ever greater maturities on U.S. Treasury securities. Greater risk requires higher levels of interest as compensation.

[6]For an examination of the relationship between duration and average life, see Leibowitz (1986).

[7]A sinking fund is a program involving the periodic set aside of a fixed sum to provide for the eventual retirement of an outstanding debt or preferred stock issue.

[8]For a discussion of the arithmetic of annuities, see Chapter 2. For a more detailed discussion, see Weston and Copeland (1986).

CHAPTER 8

APPENDIX

Who's Who Among
Swap Dealers
(International Swap Dealers
Association Membership—1990)

AIG Financial Products Corp.
667 Madison Avenue,
  21st Floor
New York, NY 10021
USA

Algemene Bank Nederland NV
335 Madison Avenue
New York, NY 10017
USA

Allied Irish Banks plc
12 Old Jewry
London EC2R 8DP
UK

Amsterdam-Rotterdam Bank
  NV
Capital Markets Group
Foppingadreef 22 P.O. Box
  283
1000 EA Amsterdam
The Netherlands

Australia and New Zealand
  Banking Group
Minerva House
Montague Close
London SE1 AD4
UK

Banca Commerciale Italiana
Piazza della Scala, 6
Milan 20121
Italy

Banca Commerciale Italiana
  (Suisse)
Lowenstrasse 60
8001 Zurich
Switzerland

Banca del Gottardo
via S. Franscini 8
Lugano 6901
Switzerland

Bank Mees & Hope NV
Herengracht 548
P.O. Box 293
1017 CG/1000 Amsterdam
The Netherlands

Bank of America
555 California Street
10th Floor #3269
San Francisco, CA 94104
USA

Bank of Boston
100 Federal Street
Boston, MA 02110
USA

The Bank of Ireland
Group Treasury Ltd.
91 Pembroke Rd.
Dublin, 4
Ireland

Bank of Montreal
Off-Balance Sheet Trading
One First Canadian Place,
   17th Floor
Toronto, Ontario M5X 1A1
Canada

Bank of New England NA
28 State Street (S35MMK)
Boston, MA 02109
USA

Bank of New York
48 Wall Street,
   11th Floor
New York, NY 10015
USA

The Bank of Nova Scotia
44 King Street West
Toronto, Ontario M5H 1H1
Canada

The Bank of Tokyo, Ltd.
Capital Markets Division
3-2 Nihombashi Hongokucho,
   1-chome
Chiyoda-ku, Tokyo
Japan

Bankers Trust Company
One Bankers Trust Plaza,
   32nd Floor
130 Liberty Street
New York, NY 10015
USA

Banque de L'Union Europeene
4, rue Gaillon
Paris cedex 02 75107
France

Banque Indosuez
44 Rue de Courcelles
Paris F75008
France

Banque Nationale de Paris
8-13 King William Street
London EC4N 7DN
UK

Barclays de Zoete Wedd Ltd.
Ebbgate House
2 Swan Lane
London EC4R 3TS
UK

Baring Brothers & Co., Ltd.
8 Bishopsgate
London EC2N 4AE
UK

Bayerische Hypotheken
und Wechsel Bank
Theatinerstr. 11
D8000 Munchen 2
Federal Republic of Germany

Bayerische Vereinsbank AG
Bleidenstr. 12
Frankfurt/M. 1 D-6000
Federal Republic of Germany

Bear Stearns Capital Markets
Inc.
245 Park Avenue, 4th Floor
New York, NY 10167
USA

Berliner Bank
Aktiengesellschaft
Treasury Department
Hardenbergstrasse 32
1000 Berlin 12
West Germany

BHF-Berliner Handels-und
Frankfurter Bank
Bockenheimer Landstr. 10
6000 Frankfurt/Main 1
West Germany

Bierbaum Martin Inc.
Wall Street Plaza,
7th Floor
New York, NY 10005
USA

BSI-Banca Della Svizzera
Italiana
65 East 55th Street,
25th Floor
New York, NY 10022
USA

Canadian Imperial Bank
of Commerce
30 North LaSalle Street
Suite 4100
Chicago, IL 60602
USA

The Charterhouse Bank
    Limited
1 Paternoster Row
St. Paul's
London EC4M 7DH
UK

Chase Manhattan Capital
    Markets Corporation
One Chase Manhattan Plaza,
    21st Floor
New York, NY 10081
USA

Chemical Bank
277 Park Avenue, 9th Floor
New York, NY 10172
USA

Christiania Bank
P.O. Box 1166 Sentrum
0107, Oslo 1
Norway

Citicorp
55 Water Street, 47th Floor
New York, NY 10043
USA

Commerzbank
    Aktiengesellschaft
Mainzer Landstrasse 32-36
D-6000 Frankfurt am Main
Federal Republic of Germany

Commonwealth Bank of
    Australia
Corner Pitt St & Martin Pl.
Sydney NSW 2000
Australia

Continental Bank, NA
231 South LaSalle Street,
    17th Floor
Chicago, IL 60697
USA

Credit Commercial de France
115-117 Avenue des Champs
    Elysees
Paris 75008
France

Credit Lyonnais
DCMC/DMF
19 Boulevard des Italiens
75002 Paris
France

Credit Suisse
Paradeplatz 8
Zurich 8001
Switzerland

Dai-Ichi Kangyo Bank, Ltd.
One World Trade Center
Suite 4911
New York, NY 10048
USA

Daiwa Europe Bank plc
Level 19, City Tower
40 Basinghall St.
London EC2V 5DE
UK

De Nationale Investeringsbank
  NV
P.O. Box 380
The Hague
2501 BH
The Netherlands

Den Danske Bank
af 1871, Aktieselskab
12 Holmens Kanal
DK-1092 K
Denmark

Deutsche Bank Capital
  Markets Ltd.
150 Leadenhall Street
P.O Box 126
London EC3V 4RJ
UK

DG Bank-Deutsche
  Genossenschaftsbank
AM Platz der Republik
D-6000 Frankfurt (Main) 1
West Germany

Dresdner AG
Jurgen-Ponto-Platz 1
Frankfurt/Main D-6000
West Germany

Drexel Burnham Lambert
60 Broad Street, 5th Floor
New York, NY 10004
USA

Elders Securities UK Limited
73 Cornhill
London EC3V 3QQ
UK

First Boston Corporation
Park Avenue Plaza, 6th Floor
New York, NY 10055
USA

First Interstate Capital Markets
  Ltd.
707 Wilshire Blvd.
Los Angeles, CA 90017
USA

First National Bank of
  Chicago
1 First National Plaza
Law Department—
  Suite 0287, 11th Floor
Chicago, IL 60670
USA

Fuji Bank Ltd.
1-5-5 Otemachi
Chiyoda-ku
Tokyo 100
Japan

Garvin GuyButler Corp.
120 Broadway, 20th Floor
Room 2023
New York, NY 10271
USA

Goldman Sachs & Co.
85 Broad Street, 27th Floor
New York, NY 10004
USA

Hill Samuel Bank Ltd.
100 Wood Street
London EC2P 2AJ
UK

HongkongBank
99 Bishopgate
London EC2P 2LA
UK

IBJ International
Bucklersbury House
3 Queen Victoria Street
London EC4N 8HR

The Industrial Bank of Japan,
   Ltd.
3-3, Marunouchi
1-chome, Chiyoda-ku
Tokyo 100
Japan

Industriekreditbank AG-
   Deutsche Indust
P.O. Box 771
L-2017 Luxembourg
Luxembourg L-2017
Federal Republic of Germany

Istituto Bancario San Paolo
   di Torino
9 St. Paul's Churchyard
London EC2V 6DD
UK

Istituto Mobiliare Italiano
Viale Dell'Arte, 25
Rome 00144
Italy

J. Henry Schroder Wagg &
   Co. Ltd.
120 Cheapside
London EC2V 6DS
UK

Kidder, Peabody & Co.
   Incorporated
20 Exchange Place
New York, NY 10005
USA

Kleinwort Benson Ltd.
20 Fenchurch Street
London EC3P 3DB
UK

Koch Refining International
P.O. Box 2256
Wichita, Kansas 67201
USA

Kredietbank (Suisse) SA
7, Boulevard Georges-Favon
Geneva, CH 1204
Switzerland

Lloyds Bank plc
199 Water Street
One Seaport Plaza
New York, NY 10038
USA

Long-Term Credit Bank of
    Japan, Ltd.
2-4 Otemachi 1-chome
Chiyoda-ku
Tokyo 100
Japan

Louis Dreyfus Energy Corp.
10 Westport Road
Wilton, CT 06897
USA

Manufacturers Hanover Trust
    Company
270 Park Avenue, 7th Floor
New York, NY 10017
USA

Maryland National Bank
10 Light Street
Baltimore, MD 21202
USA

Mellon Bank, N.A.
One Mellon Bank Center
Room 400
Pittsburgh, PA 15258
USA

Merrill Lynch Capital Markets
World Financial Center
North Tower, 7th Floor
New York, NY 10281-1218
USA

Midland Montagu
10 Lower Thames Street
London EC3R 6AE
UK

Mitsubishi Bank Ltd.
International Capital Markets
    Division
7-1, Marunouchi 2-chome
Chiyoda-ku, Tokyo 100
Japan

The Mitsubishi Trust and
    Banking Corp.
4-5 Marunouchi 1-chome
Chiyoda-ku, Tokyo 100
Japan

The Mitsui Bank, Ltd.
1-2 Yurakucho, 1-chome
Chiyoda-ku, Tokyo 100
Japan

The Mitsui Trust & Banking
  Co. Ltd.
International Money Market &
  Swap Group
1-1, Nihonbashi-Muromachi,
  2-chome
Chuo-ku, Tokyo 103
Japan

Morgan Grenfell & Co. Ltd.
23 Great Winchester Street
London EC2P 2AX
UK

Morgan Guaranty Trust
  Company of NY
23 Wall Street, 8th Floor
New York, NY 10015
USA

Morgan Stanley & Co. Inc.
1221 Avenue of the Americas
McGraw-Hill Building, 4th
  Floor
New York, NY 10020
USA

National Australia Bank
  Limited
500 Bourke Street, 31st Floor
Melbourne, Victoria 3000
Australia

National Bank of Canada
600 de la Gauchetiere West
6th floor-T9165-1
Montreal, Quebec H3B 4L8
Canada

NatWest Capital Markets
100 Wall Street
New York, NY 10005
USA

Nederlandsche
  Middenstandsbank NV
P.O. Box 1800
Amsterdam 1000 BV
The Netherlands

Nikko Capital Securities, Co.,
  Inc.
One World Financial Center
Tower A200 Liberty Street
New York, NY 10281
USA

The Nippon Credit Bank, Ltd.
13-10, Kudan-kita, 1-chome
Chiyoda-ku, Tokyo 102
Japan

Nomura Capital Services Inc.
180 Maiden Lane
The Continental Center
New York, NY 10038
USA

The Norinchukin Bank
8-3 Ohtemachi, Chiyoda-ku
1-chome
Tokyo 100
Japan

Paribas Corporation
787 Seventh Avenue
Equitable Tower, 30th Floor
New York, NY 10019
USA

Phibro Energy, Inc.
600 Steamboat Road
Greenwich, CT 06830
USA

Prudential Bache Capital
  Markets
One Seaport Plaza
199 Water Street
New York, NY 10292
USA

Rabobank Nederland
P.O. Box 17100
Utrecht 3500 HG
The Netherlands

Republic National Bank of
  New York
452 Fifth Avenue
New York, NY 10018
USA

The Royal Bank of Canada
Royal Bank Plaza
16th Floor, South Tower
Toronto, Ontario M5J 2J5
Canada

The Royal Bank of Scotland
67 Lombard Street, 3rd Floor
London EC3P 3D
UK

S.G. Warburg & Co. Ltd.
1 Finsbury Avenue
London EC2M 2PA
UK

The Saitama Bank Ltd.
1-2-6 Nihombashi
Muromachi, Chuo-ku
Tokyo 103
Japan

Salomon Brothers Inc.
One New York Plaza,
  41st Floor
New York, NY 10004
USA

The Sanwa Bank, Ltd.
55 East 52nd Street,
  25th Floor
New York, NY 10055
USA

Saudi International Bank
99 Bishopsgate
London EC2M 3TB
UK

Scandinavian Bank Group PLC
Scandinavian House
2/6 Cannon Street
London EC4M 6XX
UK

Security Pacific Hoare Govett,
 Inc.
40 East 52nd Street, 5th Floor
New York, NY 10022
USA

Shearson Lehman Hutton
 Special Financing, Inc.
American Express Tower
World Financial Center
New York, NY 10285-1240
USA

Skandinaviska Enskilda
 Banken Co.
245 Park Avenue, 33rd Floor
New York, NY 10167
USA

Societe Generale
3 Rue Lafayette
Paris 75009
France

State Bank of Victoria
Level 14
385 Bourke Street
Melbourne Victoria 3000
Australia

Sumitomo Bank Capital
 Markets, Inc.
1 World Trade Center
Suite 9651
New York, NY 10048
USA

The Sumitomo Bank, Ltd.
3-2, Marunouchi 1-chome
Chiyoda-ku, Tokyo 100
Japan

The Sumitomo Trust and
 Banking Co., Ltd
527 Madison Avenue, 2nd
 Floor
New York, NY 10022
USA

Svenska Handelsbanken/
 Svenska Int'l PLC
3 Newgate Street
London EC1A 7DA
UK

Swiss Bank Corporation
Swiss Bank House
1 High Timber Street
London EC4V 3SB
UK

Swiss Volksbank
Bahnhofstr. 53
Zurich 8001
Switzerland

The Tokai Bank, Limited
6-1, Otemachi 2-chome
Chiyoda-ku, Tokyo 100
Japan

The Toronto Dominion Bank
55 King Street West & Bay,
    10th Floor
P.O. 1 Toronto M5K 1AZ
Canada

Tradition Berisford L.P.
61 Broadway, 4th Floor
New York, NY 10006
USA

UBS Securities
299 Park Avenue
New York, NY 10171
USA

Union Bank of Finland Ltd.
Aleksanterinkatu 30
Helsinki 00100
Finland

Westdeutsche Landesbank
    Girozentrale
450 Park Avenue
New York, NY 10022
USA

Westpac Banking Corporation
Westpac House
75 King William Street
London EC4N 7HA
UK

Wood Gundy Inc.
Royal Trust Tower, P.O. Box
    274,
44th Floor, Toronto Dominion
    Center
Toronto, Ontario M5K 1M7
Canada

Yamaichi Securities Co., Ltd.
4-1, Yaesu 2-chome
Chuo-ku, Tokyo
Japan

The Yasuda Trust & Banking
    Co., Ltd.
Foreign Exchange & Money
    Market Dept
2-1, Yaesu, 1-chome Chuo-ku
Tokyo 103
Japan

9

Managing a Swap Portfolio

9.1 OVERVIEW

The swap market was not very liquid until swap banks, acting in the capacity of brokers, transformed themselves into dealers. As dealers, swap banks stand ready to enter swaps as a counterparty—without regard to the timeliness with which matched swaps can be arranged. This process of making markets in swaps is often called "warehousing." The portfolio of swaps so warehoused is often called a swap "book." Running a swap book requires a considerable appreciation of the risks involved and the ways in which these risks can be managed.

In this chapter, we consider the management of a swap portfolio from the perspective of a market-making swap bank. In the examination of the pricing of swaps in Chapter 8, we discussed the swap bank's sources of revenue from intermediating in swap finance. These included the bank's bid-ask spread and, to a lesser degree, front-end fees (for financial engineering and special features) that are charged to the counterparty client. While these revenue sources are of considerable importance in the management of a swap portfolio, further discussion of them would be largely redundant. Consequently, we will concentrate our discussion in this chapter on the other key considerations in running a swap portfolio—identifying and quantifying the various risks to which the swap bank is exposed from its swap activity. This leads logically to a discussion of the hedging of swaps individually and the hedging of a swap portfolio.

The management of the risks associated with a swap portfolio is considerably more complex than is the management of the risks associated with a stock portfolio. While swap risks, like stock risks, contain both systematic and unsystematic components, the former are not easily managed by simple diversification. In addition, the nondiversifiable risks cannot be measured by simple criteria, such as beta coefficients, which are often used to measure the systematic risk associates with common stock portfolios.[1] First, there are many different types of risks and these risks are related in complex ways. Second, the optimal hedge for a portfolio of booked swaps can and usually does change over time, even if no changes are made to the swap portfolio. Third, the legal rights of the counterparties to swaps vary from country to country. Finally, the tax and accounting treatment of swaps are not uniform from country to country, although considerable progress toward uniformity in bank accounting and capital requirements has been made recently. We will address all of these issues in this chapter.

9.2 RISK EXPOSURE FOR THE SWAP BANK

Throughout this chapter, it is assumed that the swap bank is a swap dealer and not a speculator in swaps. That is, the bank looks to profit from its market-making activities alone. As a market maker, the bank does not take naked positions in swaps and it looks to be fully hedged at all times. Thus, to the extent that the bank makes an effort to forecast interest rates and exchange rates, it does so as a service to its clients and to more accurately quantify the risks associated with its swap portfolio. In reality, however, swap dealers do use swaps to speculate (within narrow bounds set down by senior management and/ or the bank's asset/liability committee) on the direction of interest rates and exchange rates.

The swap bank actually has two separate portfolio management problems. First, it must manage the risks associated with newly negotiated swaps until such time as those swaps can be matched against swaps with other counterparties. Second, the bank must manage the risks associated with its portfolio of matched swaps. Some risks are specific to the first portfolio problem and some to the second. Still other risks are important in the management of both portfolios. Swap risks are more interrelated than the risks that characterize most other types of asset portfolios. We will first discuss the different sources of risk and then discuss the relationships of these risks to each other. The risks we examine include:

interest-rate risk;

exchange-rate risk;

credit risk;

market risk;

default risk;

mismatch risk;

basis risk;

spread risk;

sovereign risk;

and delivery risk.

We should point out that there is some inconsistency in the usage of these terms. For example, as we will point out again later, what we have called "default risk" in this text is called "credit risk" by some swap dealers.

9.2.1 Interest-Rate Risk

The inverse relationship between debt instrument yields and the prices of fixed-rate debt instruments is the source of interest-rate risk. All other things being equal, a change in the level of interest rates for debt of a given maturity will necessitate an equivalent change in the yield of all existing debt instruments of that same maturity.[2] This yield adjustment must take the form of a change in the instrument's price since the coupon on a fixed-rate instrument is, by definition, fixed. This is, of course, also true for the swap coupon. Thus, a swap with a given term exposes the counterparties, who are paying and receiving at a fixed-rate, to an interest-rate risk. The extent of the risk for the bank, the focus of this discussion, will depend on the degree to which the bank has offset the risk in other swaps or, alternatively, offset the risk in temporary hedges while looking for matched swaps.

The floating-rate side of a swap will periodically adjust to the prevailing interest rate. This adjustment is called a **reset** and it occurs at discrete intervals, usually semiannually. The **reset dates** are specified in the terms of the swap agreement. Because the floating rate adjusts to prevailing market conditions, the floating-rate side of a swap is characterized by significantly less interest-rate risk than the fixed-rate side. This is not to imply that there is no interest-rate risk on the floating-rate side. As long as there is a lag between resets, there is some interest-rate risk. Nevertheless, the risk is small. For this reason, we concentrate our discussion on the management of the interest-rate risk associated with the fixed-rate side.

Consider a simple example in the context of an interest-rate swap: A swap bank enters a $100 million 10-year fixed-for-floating swap as receiver of the semiannual swap coupon. At the time, the bank's 10-year mid-rate is 10.50 percent. The bank will pay six-month LIBOR to Counterparty A. The bank's commitment is depicted in Exhibit 9.1. Immediately after negotiating the first swap, the bank begins the search for a second counterparty with matching needs with whom the bank will negotiate a mirror-image commitment. A matched swap would have the cash flows depicted in Exhibit 9.2. The bank expects to earn one-eighth point on each side for a total of 25 basis points on the combined swaps. This is depicted in Exhibit 9.3.

Consider the bank's expected revenue from the matched swaps depicted in Exhibit 9.3 (we will ignore any front-end fees as these are increasingly rare). For purposes of the calculations, assume that Counterparty B is identified and signed without any lag and that the swaps are perfect matches. The bank earns 12.5 basis points every six months (25 basis points annually) on $100 million. This is equivalent to $125,000. The present value of this cash-flow stream is calculated using present value annuity arithmetic. (The present value annuity

EXHIBIT 9.1.   Matched Swaps
Initial Swap with Counterparty A

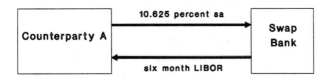

($100 million notional principal)

EXHIBIT 9.2.   Matched Swaps
Goal: A Matched Swap with Counterparty B

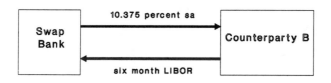

($100 million notional principal)

EXHIBIT 9.3.   Combined Cash Flows from Matched Swaps

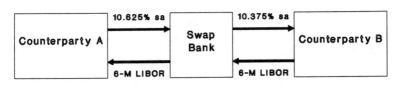

($100 million notional principal)   ($100 million notional principal)

formula was given in Chapter 2, Equation 2.2). Recall that only interest is exchanged. There is no exchange of notional principals on interest-rate swaps.

$$PVA = 125,000 \times (\{1 - [1 + (0.105 \div 2)]^{-2 \cdot 10}\} \div$$
$$(0.105 \div 2))$$
$$= 1,525,278$$

Thus, the pair of swaps should earn the bank $1,525,278 in a present value sense before the bank's administrative and other overhead costs. Suppose now that the bank does not hedge its interest-rate exposure while searching for the second counterparty and, while the bank is looking, interest rates change, forcing the bank to revise its 10-year mid-rate. Consider what happens to the present value of the bank's revenues if the rate were to rise and also if the rate were to fall before counterparty B is booked. These scenarios are depicted in

EXHIBIT 9.4. Present Value of Paired (Matched) Swaps
(Bank Is Fixed-Rate Receiver on Initial Swap)

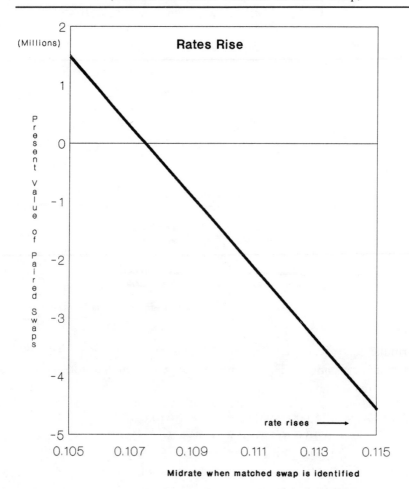

EXHIBIT 9.5.   Present Value of Paired (Matched) Swaps
(Bank Is Fixed-Rate Receiver on Initial Swap)

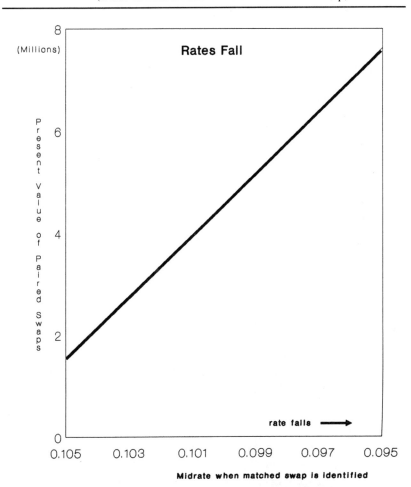

Exhibits 9.4 and 9.5, respectively, and illustrate the present value of the matched swap after the movement in the midrate. The present value of these outcomes is also depicted in the first line of Table 9.1 on the assumption that the mid-rate rises by 50 basis points. The second line of Table 9.1 indicates what the present value would be had the initial swap called for the swap bank to *pay* fixed rate rather than *receive* fixed rate. These present values are calculated using the prevailing 10.5 percent mid-rate as the discount rate.

One can think of the bid-ask spread as a kind of cushion against

TABLE 9.1
Sensitivity Analysis
Present Value of Cash Flows

	No Change	Mid-rate	
		Rises 50 bps	Falls 50 bps
Bank Receives Fixed Rate	$1,525,278	−$1,525,278	$4,575,834
Bank Pays Fixed Rate	$1,525,278	$4,575,834	−$1,525,278

interest-rate risk. For example, if the spread is 25 basis points, as it is in the preceding example, the mid-rate could move 25 basis points against the bank before the profit from the paired swaps would be completely eliminated. It follows then that a narrower bid-ask spread means a smaller cushion. As the liquidity of the swap market has grown, there has been a substantial narrowing of the bid-ask spread and a concomitant decrease in the size of the interest-rate risk cushion.[3]

9.2.2 Exchange-Rate Risk

Just as there is an interest-rate risk whenever there is an unhedged fixed-rate commitment, there is also an exchange-rate risk whenever there is an exchange-rate commitment. Consider an example: A U.S.-based swap bank agrees to a nonamortizing five-year exchange of borrowings with a French firm. The swap bank would provide the French firm with $25 million, and the firm would provide the bank with 100 million French francs (FF). The spot exchange rate at the time the swap is written is 4.000 FF/USD. This can be stated equivalently as 0.2500 USD/FF. We employ the latter in this example. The bank's five-year mid-rate is FF 11.375 percent. The French firm agrees to pay six-month LIBOR and the bank agrees to pay the French firm a semiannual rate of FF 11.25 percent. The swap coupon is found by deducting one-eighth point from the mid-rate. Now suppose that the bank carries the swap unhedged while it looks for a matched swap.

The swap bank runs the risk that the exchange rate of dollars for francs will change unfavorably while it is looking for a counterparty with matching needs. Suppose now that, within a few days, the bank is able to locate a counterparty with matched needs. In the interim, the spot exchange rate has declined to 0.2375 USD/FF. Thus, on the matched swap, the bank's counterparty provides the bank with $23.75 million and the bank provides this second counterparty with FF 100 million. The bank must now secure the additional $1.25 million elsewhere. There is a cost to the bank associated with obtaining the required funds. Most likely, the bank's swap division will obtain funds from other divisions of the bank at a price. The price for funds for intrabank transfers is called the transfer pricing rate (TPR) or, sometimes, the **cost of carry**.

In this particular case, there is both an exchange-rate risk and an interest-rate risk. To make matters worse, these risks tend to be positively correlated. All other things being equal, higher interest rates generally mean stronger currencies, and lower interest rates generally mean weaker currencies. Since the franc fell vis-à-vis the dollar, it is highly likely that French interest rates also fell relative to the dollar. Suppose that, at the time the second swap is written, the bank's five-year semiannual mid-rate is FF 10.375 percent. The second counterparty agrees to pay the bank FF 10.50 percent in exchange for the bank paying the second counterparty six-month LIBOR. Thus, the net result is that the bank is receiving FF 10.50 percent and paying FF 11.25 percent. The bank has lost on both the exchange-rate and the interest-rate fronts.

9.2.3 Credit Risk

Different swap banks define credit risk differently. For example, in the following discussion we define credit risk as the probability that a counterparty client will default. We then multiply this probability by **market risk** (which is defined in the next section) to obtain a dollar value called **default risk** (this will be discussed in Section 9.2.5). Many swap banks use the term credit risk to mean what we have called default risk. These usage differences of the terms "credit risk" and "default risk" are less important than the concepts involved and the methods of measurement employed. Nevertheless, the student of swaps should be aware of these differences in usage.

Credit risk is the risk that the bank's counterparty to a swap will be unable to fulfill its obligations due to bankruptcy, supervening illegality, change in the tax or accounting laws relative to those applicable at the time the swap was originated, and so on. As an intermediary between two matched swaps, the swap bank is independently obligated to both counterparties. That is, while the termination provisions of its swap with Counterparty A will release the bank from its obligation to make payments to Counterparty A, should Counterparty A default on its obligation to the bank, the termination provisions with A do not release the bank from its obligations to Counterparty B.

Credit risk is generally regarded as the single, most-significant risk for swap banks. Fortunately, it is a risk that can be significantly reduced by diversification and other portfolio management strategies.

Credit risk is closely related to two other forms of risk: market risk and mismatch risk. For the moment, we assume that the default on the part of one of the bank's counterparties will force the bank to seek a **replacement swap**. Ideally, a replacement swap would have terms identical to those of the defaulted swap. Unfortunately, it is highly probable that market conditions will have changed since the time the defaulted swap was originated. The bank, therefore, must seek a replacement swap that involves off-market pricing. The bank may have to pay (or receive) a front-end fee for such a swap. Calculating the size of the monetary inducement necessary to obtain a replacement swap on the same terms as the defaulted swap is called marking-to-market. Banks have routinely marked their swaps to market in an effort to assess their default exposure. Marking-to-market is now required as part of recently enacted bank capital adequacy rules. We will address these rules later.

9.2.4 Market Risk

Market risk refers to the difficulty of finding a counterparty with matched needs. Generally, the longer the maturity, the thinner the market and the greater the market risk. When a market is thin, the bank can demand a greater spread from a counterparty client. On the other hand, when the bank does a swap with one counterparty in a thin market, it may have to make concessions to attract another swap counterparty for an offsetting swap. As with credit risk, there are usage differences in terminology with market risk. Some swap dealers regard these risks as manifestations of mismatch risks. We define mismatch risk more specifically later.

Because markets tend to be thinnest in the longer-maturity swaps, the swaps with the greatest market risk also tend to exhibit the greatest interest-rate risk. Thus market risk and interest-rate risk are closely related. Indeed, many swap practitioners do not make a distinction between these forms of risk.

Market risk is related to credit risk. Should a counterparty default on its obligations to the bank, the bank must seek a replacement swap. The financial injury to the bank from such a default will depend on market conditions at the time. For example, suppose that three years into a seven-year $40 million nonamortizing fixed-for-floating interest-rate swap, Counterparty A, which is paying a semiannual swap coupon of 10.35 percent against the bank's six-month LIBOR, defaults. The bank had matched this swap with a swap to another counterparty on which the bank is paying a swap coupon of 10.15 percent. Consequently, the bank is forced to find a replacement swap with terms similar to those of the defaulted swap. Since the original swap was written, interest rates have declined. Current market conditions dictate a mid-rate for a four-year fixed-for-floating-rate swap of 8.75 percent. With the bank's one-eighth point premium, the counterparty would pay the bank a semiannual coupon of 8.875 percent against the bank's paying six-month LIBOR.

The bank should be able to induce a counterparty to accept the swap on the same terms as the defaulted swap if the bank pays the replacement counterparty a sum equal to the present value of the difference between the initial swap coupon and the prevailing swap rate. This is a semiannual rate differential of 1.475 percent (10.35 − 8.875) on $40 million of notional principal. This sum would be discounted at the current mid-rate of 8.75 percent sa. The present value of this sum is $1,955,762, and is the extent of the financial injury to the bank caused by the default of Counterparty A. This is a simple application of the off-market pricing discussed in Chapter 8. The sum that has to be paid to induce a fixed-rate paying counterparty to enter a swap at a coupon above the prevailing market rate is sometimes called a **buy-up**. (If the swap bank requires a fixed-rate paying client to pay a rate below the market rate, the swap bank can expect to receive an up-front payment called a **buy-down**.)

9.2.5 Default Risk

Default risk measures the bank's combined exposure from credit risk and market risk. For example, suppose that, at the time a given swap is contemplated, the swap bank estimates that there is a 4 percent probability that a specific prospective counterparty will default on a $20 million three-year nonamortizing fixed-for-floating interest-rate swap. The bank also estimates the economic harm to the bank, based on various projected future market conditions, should the counterparty default after one year, two years, or three years. The combination of credit risk (probability of default) and market risk (financial injury in the event of default) determines the bank's default risk.

9.2.6 Mismatch Risk

Swap banks make markets in swaps by accommodating their clients' needs. If a swap bank insisted on matching every provision of every pair of swaps to which it serves as an intermediary, it would have a very difficult time finding counterparties. Furthermore, even if it can induce a prospective counterparty to take a swap on the bank's terms, the bank will likely find that it must agree to pricing concessions in the form of a front-end fee paid to the second counterparty client.

For these reasons, swap banks generally do not insist on exact pairing of swap provisions. Instead, the swap bank running a swap portfolio will focus on the overall character of the portfolio rather than the character of the individual swaps.

Mismatches, which can include mismatches with respect to notional principal, maturity, the swap coupon, the floating index, the reset dates for the floating index, the payment frequencies, or the payment dates, expose the bank to some additional risk—especially if a counterparty defaults. Consider the following possibility: Suppose that a bank agrees to pay a counterparty a six-month LIBOR on a notional principal of $30 million. Payment dates are 30 January and 30 July. The counterparty will pay the bank a single annual payment at a rate of 9.80 percent. This payment is to be made each year on 30 July. When payment dates on an interest-rate swap are matched, the counterparties only need pay, or receive, the interest differential. But, when the payment dates are mismatched, as they are in this example, the full interest payment must be made, at least on the unmatched dates. Suppose now that the bank pays $1.2 million in interest to the counterparty on 30 January. The counterparty is not due to make any payments to the bank before 30 July. Now suppose that the counterparty defaults on its obligation to the bank at the time it is to make its first payment on 30 July. The counterparty's default releases the bank from its obligation to make its second payment to the counterparty; but, the bank must now resort to legal channels to recover its earlier payment to the counterparty. The bank will likely find itself in the position of a general creditor in the proceedings that follow.

As a second example of mismatch risk, consider mismatched reset dates. Suppose the initial swap is made when LIBOR is 6.5 percent. Several days elapse before a matched swap can be arranged. In the interim, LIBOR has risen to 7.20 percent. The bank is now locked into a significant payment mismatch until, at least, the next reset date.

9.2.7 Basis Risk

The basis is the difference between two prices. In the case of interest-rate swaps, the basis is the difference between two different floating-rate indexes. Basis risk is the risk that the two indexes might fluctuate relative to one another. Basis risk can arise in two ways. In the first way, the counterparty requires a floating-for-floating rate swap but the two sides of the swap are pegged to different indexes. This scenario is depicted in Exhibit 9.6 for a floating-for-floating interest-rate swap involving three-month LIBOR and six-month LIBOR. In the second, two separate counterparties do a fixed-for-floating rate swap with the bank but the floating rates are pegged to different indexes. This is depicted in Exhibit 9.7 for fixed-for-floating interest-rate swaps involving the six-month T-bill rate and six-month LIBOR.

This particular combination is quite common—both in the context of swaps and in other forms of financial spreading. Indeed, many of

EXHIBIT 9.6.   Basis Risk
Single Floating-for-Floating Rate Swap

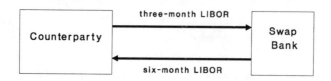

these spreads are so common, they have been given special names. For example, the spread between the T-bill rate and LIBOR for the same maturities is called, in market parlance, the **TED spread**. The term is derived from *T*-bills and *E*urodollars, since LIBOR is the interest rate paid on Eurodollar deposits.

Suppose that, initially, LIBOR is 9.5 percent and the T-bill rate is 8.5 percent. If the 1 percent (100 basis points) rate differential was absolutely fixed, there would be no basis risk to the bank. However, the differential is not absolutely fixed. The rate differential between LIBOR and the T-bill rate could have been as small as 10 basis points and as large as 140 basis points in recent years. These fluctuations are the source of basis risk. In this particular case, basis risk is measured as the variance of the TED spread.

In the language of statistics, basis risk exists when the two indexes are less than **perfectly correlated**. It is for this reason that the effectiveness of a hedge is routinely measured in terms of the degree of correlation (or its squared value—the coefficient of determination—as discussed in Chapter 4).

EXHIBIT 9.7.   Basis Risk
Two Fixed-for-Floating Rate Swaps

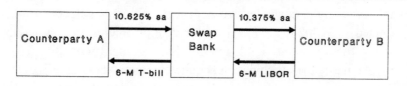

9.2.8   Sovereign Risk

Sovereign risk arises in currency swaps. It is a reflection of a country's financial standing in the world community and, to some degree, it is a function of the country's political stability and historic performance in meeting its international financial obligations. The greater the probability that a government may impose foreign-exchange controls, thus making it impossible for a counterparty to honor its commitments, the greater is the sovereign risk. This is one form of a condition called **supervening illegality**.

In the event that an illegality should arise, the counterparties to a swap have the right to terminate the swap subject to an attempt by the affected party to assign the swap to a branch or an affiliate located in another jurisdiction. Should the nature of the illegality, or the terms of the contract prevent such a change of jurisdiction, or should the assignment be unacceptable to the other party, then the swap contract provides for the early termination of the swap on a two-way payment basis. Early termination provisions and settlement options are discussed in more detail in Section 9.4.2.

Because the existence of sovereign risk affects a counterparty's creditworthiness, many analysts simply regard it as another aspect of credit risk. This is a mistake. Credit risk is counterparty specific, while sovereign risk is country specific. Thus, all swaps made with counterparties in the same country share sovereign risk. Routine diversification, which can substantially reduce credit risk, will do little to reduce sovereign risk unless an extra step is taken to ensure that the diversification is also across countries.

Most banks set strict limits to their allowable exposure by country. These can be set in terms of the total notional principal or some other criteria. Importantly, the limits usually encompass more than just the swap exposure. They may also embody country specific exposures to the bank from its positions in FRAs, FXAs, general credit, and so on. This is important because the bank's exposures to sovereign risk (and foreign-exchange risk) are correlated across all its positions in any one country or any one currency.[4]

9.2.9   Spread Risk

Spread risk is the risk that during the time between the origination of one swap and the subsequent origination of a matched swap the bank's spread over the relevant Treasury maturity will change. This should not be confused with interest-rate risk. To make the difference clear, let's suppose that at the time the bank originates the first swap, the bank prices the "bank-pays-fixed-rate-side" of a five-year swap at the five-year T-note rate plus 74 basis points. By the time the bank originates the matched swap, it has changed its pricing on the bank-receives-fixed-rate-side to the five-year T-note rate plus 70 basis points. Even if there were no change in the T-note rate, there has been a change in the bank's cost. It is this possibility that constitutes spread risk. On the other hand, a change in the T-note rate would be a manifestation of interest-rate risk.

9.2.10   Delivery Risk

The final risk we discuss is **delivery risk**, also called **settlement risk**. This risk exists when payments are made between counterparties who must affect their payments to each other at different times of the day owing to different settlement hours between the capital markets of the two parties. This most often occurs when the payments are made between counterparties in two different countries. For example, the Japanese capital markets close for the day before the U.S. markets open.

Delivery risk is greatest in currency swaps at the time the principals are exchanged. Though this risk can be considerable, it can be managed. For example, many banks place a limit on the size of the allowable daily settlement with any one party. In some cases, banks make their exchanges through a neutral third party that does not make payment to either involved party until payments have been received from both parties. When the currencies are the same, delivery risk is considerably less than it first appears because the swap agreement usually requires the counterparties to make net payments rather than gross payments. That is, only the difference in the value of the payments needs to be exchanged with the higher value-paying party making a payment to the lower value-paying party equal to the difference in the values to be exchanged. Thus, **netting** payments significantly reduces the delivery exposure of both parties to a swap. Because it is so easily managed, we do not discuss this risk any further.

9.3 QUANTIFYING THE EXPOSURE

It is not enough to simply *identify* the risks to which the bank is exposed when it books a swap. It is also important to *quantify* the exposure associated with swaps for at least four reasons. First, the greater the collective risks associated with booking a swap, the greater the compensation the swap bank should require from its counterparty client. This compensation may take the form of a front-end fee but will usually take the form of a larger coupon (if the bank is receiving fixed rate) or smaller coupon (if the bank is paying fixed rate). Second, the bank will need to hedge the hedgeable risks (including interest-rate risk, exchange-rate risk, and possibly basis risk) until such time as matched swaps can be negotiated. Formulation of the optimal hedge requires a quantification of the risks that are the subject of the hedge. Third, as suggested by portfolio theory, many risks will be, at least to some degree, offsetting so that the total risk associated with the bank's portfolio will be substantially less than the sum of the risks individually. This tendency for certain risks to be coincidentally offsetting is sometimes called a **natural hedge**. Accurate assessment of these risks requires quantification. Finally, the bank's internal policy, as well as regulatory compliance, will likely require some objective assessment of the risks and some explicit limitation to the risks that can be taken with respect to a single counterparty or a group of related counterparties.

As a general rule, management teams set the maximum allowable risk that the firm can bear. These risk levels have several dimensions. Risk limits are set by individual counterparties, maturities, types of exposure, and as noted earlier, by country—to mention a few. Most swap banks assign the measurement of risk exposures to risk management specialists. These experts monitor both the absolute size of the individual exposures and the portfolio implications of the risks. They then make pricing recommendations, devise and execute hedging strategies, and formulate policies to encourage or discourage specific swaps in order to bring about a better portfolio balance.

We considered the quantification of interest-rate risk in the context of a simple example in Section 9.2.1. Exchange-rate risk can be quantified in a similar fashion. These issues will be taken up again in Section 9.4.1 when we discuss the hedging of these risks. For now, we concentrate on quantifying default risk (encompassing both credit and market risks) and mismatch risk.

9.3.1 Quantifying Default Risk

As mentioned earlier, default risk encompasses both credit risk and market risk. Credit risk is an objective assessment of the likelihood that a prospective counterparty will default. Market risk is a quantitative estimate of the financial injury that will be experienced should the client default. The quantification of credit risk and market risk will be examined individually and then combined to obtain the default risk exposure.

A bank with a long history in the credit markets has considerable experience estimating the likelihood that potential clients will default on their financial obligations. All such banks have extensive training programs for credit managers. The assessment of credit risks includes an examination of the potential counterparty's financial statements, financial history, its management's track record, collateralization of the obligation, and other pertinent factors. Some banks rely heavily on point scoring systems. Others use regression and discriminant analysis.[5] Some banks take a much more subjective approach, relying heavily on their own managers' personal knowledge of the client firm and its management.

All banks with substantial involvement in the swap markets devote considerable resources to economic forecasting. This will always include the forecasting of interest rates and exchange rates and will usually involve the forecasting of economic trends generally and industry trends more narrowly.

Assume, for purposes of an example, that a client has approached the swap bank for a $30 million three-year nonamortizing fixed-for-floating interest-rate swap. The client firm would pay an annual fixed-rate coupon and the bank would pay one-year LIBOR. Using its credit expertise, management determines that the probability of the client defaulting within a year is negligible, but that there is a 1.25 percent probability that this client will default after one year (but before two years), and a 2 percent probability that the client will default after two years (but before three years). The bank's current mid-rate for an interest-rate swap of this maturity is 9.73 percent. To this, the bank adds or subtracts one-eighth point depending on whether the client is paying or receiving the fixed rate.

The bank next attempts to determine what the market risk is. This requires some assumptions as to the course of future interest rates. Some banks simply assume some number of basis points above and below the current mid-rate for each year forward that rates must be projected (method 1 below). Other banks make more complex estimates of the rates that might prevail and the probabilities associated with each of the possible rates (method 2 below). These two methods are contrasted in Table 9.2.

For purposes of this example, we assume the simpler of the two methods—method 1. The market risk is measured as the present value

TABLE 9.2
Comparison of Interest Rate Forecasting Techniques

| | Method I | | | Method II | |
| | | | | Probability (%) | |
	Decrease	Increase	Rate Change	Yr 1	Yr 2
Year 1	70 bps	70 bps	− 250 bps	0.5	2.5
			− 200 bps	2.5	4.5
Year 2	110 bps	110 bps	− 150 bps	5.0	8.0
			− 100 bps	9.5	12.0
			− 50 bps	20.0	15.0
			0 bps	25.0	16.0
			50 bps	20.0	15.0
			100 bps	9.5	12.0
			150 bps	5.0	8.0
			200 bps	2.5	4.5
			250 bps	0.5	2.5

of the rate differential encountered in negotiating a replacement swap should the counterparty client default. We use the current mid-rate to discount the rate differential. The present value is determined using the present value annuity formula (remembering that the payments are made annually in this specific case).

$$PVA = \$30 \text{ million} \times \text{rate change} \times \{[1 - (1.0973)^{-Y}] \div .0973\}$$

where Y = the years remaining on this swap at the time of default.

The resultant values are summarized in Table 9.3. These values represent the *change in revenue relative to the expected revenue* from the swap under each interest-rate scenario.

We interpret Table 9.3 as follows: If rates fall and the client defaults after making its first swap payment, the bank will suffer a loss of $365,788. This is the amount the bank would have to pay a replacement counterparty to enter a swap on the same terms as the defaulted swap. If rates rise *and* the client defaults after making its first swap payment, the bank enjoys a windfall gain of $365,788. This is the amount the bank could ask of a replacement counterparty to accept a swap on the same terms as the defaulted swap. The values for the second year are interpreted similarly. Don't be misled, however. Swap indemnification provisions will generally not allow the nondefaulting party to reap a windfall profit from the other party's default.

Remember that the losses and gains in Table 9.3 only occur if the

TABLE 9.3
Market Exposure in the Event of Default

If Default Occurs After	Profit ($+$) or Loss ($-$) (Market Risk) from Interest-Rate Change	
	Rates Decrease	Rates Increase
1 Year (Y = 2)	$-\$365,788$ (-70 bps)	$+\$365,788$ ($+70$ bps)
2 Years (Y = 1)	$-\$300,738$ (-110 bps)	$+\$300,738$ ($+110$ bps)

TABLE 9.4
Default Risk Exposure

If Default Occurs After	Default Risk Exposure from an Interest-Rate Change	
	Rates Decrease	Rates Increase
1 Year	− $4,572	+ $4,572
2 Years	− $6,015	+ $6,015

counterparty defaults. As mentioned earlier, the swap bank has estimated the likelihood of such an occurrence. The estimate is that the
probability of a default after one year is 1.25 percent and the probability of a default after two years is 2 percent.[6] The default exposure is
then found by multiplying the market risk by the probability of default.
This appears in Table 9.4.

Notice that the default exposure is considerably less than the
market exposure for the simple reason that the bank does not expect its
counterparty to default. On the basis of the default exposure, the bank
can be expected to adjust its pricing by adding a risk premium. As
discussed elsewhere in this book, financial risk is usually measured in
terms of **volatility** of an outcome around an expected outcome. Volatility, in turn, is usually measured as the standard deviation of the
outcome. Using this logic, the size of the risk premium would be
determined on the basis of the volatility of the default exposure. Some
banks prefer to consider only downside risk (i.e., the financial harm
resulting from a default if interest rates have moved in an unfavorable
direction). They argue that a counterparty client is unlikely to default
on a swap on which it has a positive mark-to-market value even if it is
bankrupt. To do so would be to knowingly discard value. On the other
hand, swap contracts typically include a specification of **termination
events** and **events of default**. The occurrence of such an event will
generally bring the contract's default provisions into play. One such
event would be bankruptcy. For these reasons, we will assume equal
likelihood of a default on a swap with positive mark-to-market value as
on one having a negative mark-to-market value.[7]

All other things being equal, the larger the swap bank's default exposure, the greater the spread the bank will quote. For purposes of the example, we assume the bank measures its exposure in terms of volatility. Assuming equal likelihood of an increase and a decrease in interest rates, the standard deviation of the exposures are depicted in Table 9.5.

It is important to appreciate the portfolio implications of default risks. Default risks are not highly correlated. This is not to suggest that they are completely uncorrelated. Most firms will be affected, to some degree, by economic conditions. But the correlations are likely to be quite low. Further, because the bank is a fixed-rate payer on half the swaps and a fixed-rate receiver on half the swaps, collectively the default risks may be viewed as uncorrelated.[8]

For purposes of continuing the example, assume that the swap bank writes N identical matched swaps ($\frac{1}{2} \cdot N$ pairs of swaps). The bank has the same default exposure (standard deviation, σ) to each counterparty. From a portfolio perspective, the per-swap default risk (standard error of the mean, σ_μ) declines as the number of swaps in the swap portfolio increases. The relationship is given by Equation 9.1.

$$\sigma_\mu = \frac{\sigma}{\sqrt{n}} \qquad\qquad \textbf{(9.1)}$$

The per-swap default exposure can now be seen to decline as the size of the portfolio grows. This is depicted in Exhibit 9.8. The behavior of the default risk makes it clear that default risk is largely **unsystematic**.

TABLE 9.5
Volatility of Exposure (Standard Deviation)

If Default Occurs After	Standard Deviation
1 Year	4,572
2 Years	6,015

Variance = Σ Prob[Exposure] $\times$ (Exposure $-$ Mean)^2
Standard Deviation = Variance$^{1/2}$

EXHIBIT 9.8.   Behavior Per-Swap Default Risk

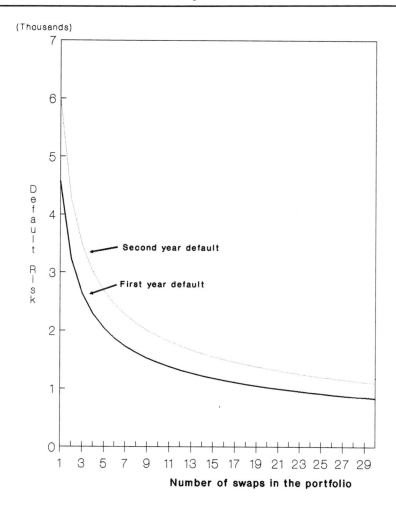

It is important to realize that, while default risk on a swap is small for a swap dealer, there is still considerable default risk exposure to the third-party lenders (investors) who provide the underlying funds used by the counterparties to a swap. The default risk for these parties is separate from the default risk to the swap dealer. At the same time, however, to the degree that the swap hedges other financial risks of a firm, the swap should enhance the creditworthiness of the firm in the eyes of its lenders (investors). This credit enhancement may afford some benefits for the firm.

9.3.2 Quantifying Mismatch Risk

As already argued, mismatch risk arises from the bank's efforts to accommodate its clients. Potential counterparties to swaps rarely have identical needs. This leads to mismatches in notional principals, payment frequencies, rate reset dates, payment dates, and so on.

A swap that is perfectly matched in all its provisions does not expose the bank to any mismatch risk. Every provision of a swap that is not perfectly matched increases the mismatch risk. The greater the degree to which a provision is mismatched, the more that that provision contributes to mismatch risk. This risk is difficult to quantify because mismatched swap provisions interact in a myriad of ways. Some mismatched provisions may interact in such a way as to amplify the risks produced by the individual ones. Other mismatched provisions may interact in such a way as to mollify one another. The remainder of this section examines some of the swap provisions that are often mismatched and the kinds of risk they engender.

A mismatch of notional principal exposes the bank to interest-rate risk on the principal discrepancy. The amount of this exposure can be calculated using the same procedure employed in Section 9.2.1. The only difference is that the calculation is applied to the principal discrepancy rather than the full notional principal. Mismatched maturities also create an exposure to interest-rate risk. In this case, however, the exposure is measured only on those payments that follow the termination of the swap with the shorter maturity.

A mismatch of the indexes that are used to calculate the floating rates creates basis risk. The exposure to this basis risk depends on the degree of correlation between the two indexes. Floating-rate indexes can differ in either of two ways: the rates can be tied to different instruments (e.g., six-month LIBOR and six-month CD rate) or they can be tied to the same index but with different reset frequencies (e.g., six-month LIBOR and three-month LIBOR). Careful study of historic spread relationships, spread volatility, and a forecast of the future spread can be used to quantify this risk. Payment frequency mismatches create an exposure in the event of default. The quantification of this exposure has been addressed in Section 9.3.1.

For plain vanilla swaps, the final consideration is the floating-rate reset dates. These are the dates the floating rate is set for the next payment period. A difference of only one day introduces some interest-rate risk. The greater the number of days by which the reset dates differ, the greater the interest-rate risk. Fortunately, this form of risk is easily diversified away. As a swap portfolio gets larger, it becomes increasingly less **date sensitive**.

Specialty swaps, including callable swaps, putable swaps, extendable swaps, amortizing swaps with grace periods, forward swaps, delayed rate-setting swaps, rate-capped swaps, and so on introduce a great many mismatch complications. To some degree these problems can be solved by matching a provision in one swap with a provision in a different swap that is not part of the first pair of swaps. Alternatively, the swap bank can buy the necessary offsetting provisions from the counterparty to the matched swap. The cost of this purchase should be passed on to the party who desires the specialty feature. For example, suppose Counterparty A wants the right to extend a four-year swap for another three years at Counterparty A's discretion. Counterparty B has a matched need, but Counterparty B has no desire to have its swap extended. The bank can offer to purchase the right to extend the swap with Counterparty B for an additional three years. Suppose that Counterparty B agrees to provide such an option for a front-end payment of $0.5 million. The bank would then provide Counterparty A with the right to extend its swap with the bank for an additional front-end fee of at least $0.5 million. The value that Counterparty B and other potential counterparties place on the specialty provision affords some insight into the value of that provision. In an efficient market, this value should be representative of the exposure.

9.4 MANAGING SWAP RISKS

We have argued that certain risks associated with managing a swap portfolio are considerable when the swaps are viewed individually. Yet, when viewed collectively these same risks can be negligible. This is typical of default risk. In the language of traditional portfolio theory, we say such risks are unsystematic. Diversification of the swap portfolio dramatically reduces unsystematic risks as the size of the portfolio becomes large. Other unsystematic risks include the reset-date risk component of mismatch risk and the basis risk when floating rates are tied to different indexes.

9.4.1   Hedging Interest-Rate Risk

The preceding discussion serves to emphasize the importance of the character of the portfolio as a whole in assessing and measuring risk exposures. Ideally, each and every swap should be matched individually. But, from a pragmatic perspective, this is not possible. Risks that are not offset by matched swaps should be hedged whenever possible. It is not necessary, and it is not cost effective, to hedge unmatched swaps individually. It is more efficient to consider the degree to which the unmatched individual swap exposures are offsetting and then to hedge only the residual risk. It should be noted that hedging an individual swap or a portfolio of swaps exposes the swap bank to another kind of risk. In the language of hedging theory, this risk is called basis risk. The term basis risk, as used in hedging theory, is more broadly interpreted than the narrow usage employed here to describe the risk associated with tying two floating-rate swaps to different indexes.[9]

A bank can hedge residual interest-rate risk in Treasury securities, as discussed in Chapter 8, or in interest-rate futures. Hedging in Treasury securities is attractive when the Treasury positions will serve as an intermediate-term to long-term substitute for a matched swap. When the objective is a very short-term hedge, interest-rate futures, including Treasury bond, note, and bill futures and Eurodollar futures, may be a better, more cost-effective hedge. The following example illustrates the hedging process from an operational perspective.

Consider a bank that negotiates new swap deals throughout the day. (For simplicity, we only consider plain vanilla interest-rate swaps.) The swaps are priced as a spread over Treasuries. The risk management department uses a **duration-based hedging model**.[10] The hedge ratio is found by first dividing the swap's duration D_s (using the swap's coupon as the yield) by the duration of the hedging instrument D_h. This duration ratio is then multiplied by the ratio of the current price of the swap as a percentage of its notional principal P_s (this is $1 for all new swaps written "at market") and the current market price of $1 face value of the hedging instrument P_h. That is, the hedge ratio is given by Equation 9.2.

$$HR = \frac{D_s}{D_h} \times \frac{P_s}{P_h} \qquad (9.2)$$

The size of the hedge is then calculated by multiplying the swap's notional principal by the hedge ratio. This is translated into a given number of futures by dividing by the face value of the futures instrument. In the case of T-notes and T-bond futures, this face value is $0.1 million. In the case of Eurodollar and T-bill futures, this face value is $1 million. Suppose that T-note futures are currently priced at 95 percent of par. While the bank hedges both the fixed-rate side (in T-note and/or T-bond futures) and the floating-rate side (in Eurodollar and/or T-bill futures), we illustrate the hedging program for the fixed-rate side only.

Suppose, also for simplicity, that the bank starts the current day with no unmatched swaps. The first swap is finalized at 9:15 AM. The risk management department is immediately notified that the swap has a maturity of five years and a notional principal of $30 million. The bank is the fixed-rate receiver. The risk management department determines that the swap has a duration of 3.15 years. The T-note futures, which the bank uses to hedge all swaps with average lives of two years to 12 years, have a duration of 6.54 years.[11] Using the procedure outlined above, the risk management department determines that the $30 million notional principal can be hedged by selling 152 T-note futures. This calculation is:

$$\text{Face Value of Hedge} = \frac{3.15}{6.54} \times \frac{1.00}{0.95} \times \$30 \text{ million}$$

$$= \$15.21 \text{ million}$$

Number of Futures $= \$15.21$ million $\div$ $0.1 million ≈ 152

The risk management group immediately makes the necessary transactions. The bank is now hedged until a matched swap can be arranged. At 9:48 AM, the risk management department is notified that a second swap has been negotiated. The swap is for $15 million for three years. Like the first, the bank is again the fixed-rate receiver. The risk managers determine that this second swap can be hedged by selling 43 T-note futures. This is done immediately and the bank is now short 195 T-note futures. At 10:23 AM, the risk management group is notified that a third swap has been negotiated. This one is a $25 million six-year swap and the bank is the fixed-rate payer. Because the maturity of this swap is different from the first two, it is not regarded as a matched swap. All three swaps are thus carried as unmatched. The risk managers determine that this swap can be hedged by purchasing 153 futures and the transactions are effected immediately. The bank's futures position is thus reduced to a short position of 42 T-note futures. At 10:52 AM, the risk management group is notified that a $20 million four-year swap with the bank as fixed-rate payer has been negotiated. This swap is regarded as a partial match for the first swap. The hedge for the fourth swap requires the purchase of 102 futures. The transactions are effected immediately and the bank is now long 60 T-note futures. These trades are summarized in Table 9.6, which shows a small portion of the bank's daily risk management report.

A swap bank that makes a market in currency swaps might hedge its foreign-exchange risk using currency futures in a fashion similar to

TABLE 9.6
Risk Management Report

Time	Bank is Fixed-Rate Payer (−) Receiver (+) Notional Principal	Maturity	Short (−) Long (+) Futures Hedge	Net Futures Position
09:15 AM	+ 30.0 million	4 years	− 152	− 152
09:48 AM	+ 15.0 million	3 years	− 43	− 195
10:23 AM	− 25.0 million	6 years	+ 153	− 42
10:52 AM	− 20.0 million	4 years	+ 102	+ 60

that used by the swap bank above to hedge its interest-rate risk. Other instruments that can be used to hedge interest-rate and currency exposures include options, forward contracts, forward rate agreements (FRAs), and forward exchange agreements (FXAs). (These instruments were discussed in Chapters 5 and 6.)

9.4.2 Managing Credit Risk

Credit risk is not a hedgeable risk. Fortunately, as we discussed in Section 9.3.1, it is easily reduced through diversification. Nevertheless, the swap bank must include provisions to protect itself from individual defaults. Failure to do so would increase the likelihood of defaults that are in the financial interests of the bank's counterparties. For credit risk to be fully diversified away, the likelihood of defaults that injure the bank and the likelihood of defaults that benefit the bank must equal.

There are a number of ways that banks can protect themselves from credit risk. These include:

1. incorporating "events of default" provisions that provide for appropriate payments to cover damages resulting from early termination of the swap into the swap document;
2. improving the creditworthiness of the counterparty through credit enhancements;
3. reducing the size of the credit risk by set-off with existing counterparties; and
4. passing the credit risk to another party by assignment of the swap.

We consider each of these briefly in turn.

All swap contracts include **termination clauses** that provide for the assessment of damages in the event that one party to a swap should default. These clauses detail the various "events of default" and "termination events" and the process for "measuring damages." The latter is one of the most important clauses in a swap agreement and it is not surprising that the ISDA's code of swaps devotes more space to detailing the available options for measuring and assessing damages in the event of a default or early termination than it does to almost any other single issue.

In the early days of swap contracting, swap banks employed a variety of ad hoc methods for measuring and assessing damages. In 1985, the ISDA introduced its first code of swaps, which helped standardize swap contracts and which provided several detailed methods for assessing damages in the event of a default or early termination. This standardization process continued with a 1986 revision of the code and culminated in 1987 with the publication of the ISDA's standard form agreements. The ISDA's standards provide several alternative methods for determining settlement payments upon early termination. Critical to each of these methods are the concepts of **defaulting party** and **affected party**. A defaulting party is a counterparty that has committed an event of default. An affected party is a counterparty that has suffered a termination event. Events of default and termination events are discussed in Chapter 10.

The ISDA's 1986 code provided three basic methods for measuring and assessing damages from defaults and early terminations: **agreement value method**, **indemnification method**, and **formula method**. The agreement value method provides for damages to be determined on the basis of ''market quotations'' obtained by the nondefaulting party. The market quotation is an amount (which may be negative) determined on the basis of quotations from reference swap market makers equal to the replacement cost of the swap. The indemnification method provides for the assessment of damages on the basis of the ''loss'' resulting from the default or early termination. The code provides details for determining the amount of ''loss.''

The formula method provides for the calculation of a lump-sum payment based on a hypothetical series of borrowings and investings in short-term instruments so as to replicate the cash flows associated with the swap. The calculation produces a ''formula settlement amount.'' The payment is then equal to the excess, if any, of the formula settlement amount of the defaulting party over the formula settlement amount of the nondefaulting party.

The formula settlement method is rarely used today and only then in certain special situations. In the years since the 1986 code was released, the agreement value method has become nearly universal.

Under all three damage assessment methods the parties may select options to provide for one-way payments, two-way payments, or limited two-way payments. In the one-way payment option, the defaulting or affected party makes payment to the nondefaulting party of the amount required (based on the assessment method selected) if that sum is greater than zero. No payment is made if the sum is less than zero. In the two-way payment option, each party is required to make payment to the other irrespective of which party has defaulted or been affected. These payments are based on the extent to which the assessment amounts exceed zero. In the limited two-way payment option, the one-way payment method applies in cases of an event of default while the two-way payment method applies in the event of a termination event. Thus, a termination clause may require payments in either direction (from the party who is benefited to the party who is injured by early termination) regardless of which party is responsible for the default, or, the clause may specify that only the defaulting party shall be required to make a close-out payment.

The principal problem with payments required under termination provisions is that this protection is likely to fail if the default is associated with a counterparty's bankruptcy. In such an event, the counterparty may not be in a position to pay the required indemnity and, indeed, may be stayed from making payment by the bankruptcy laws of its country. Furthermore, even when payment is effected, it will likely be at less than full face value.

The second way to manage credit risk is to improve the creditworthiness of the counterparty through credit enhancements. The simplest form of credit enhancement is for the bank to require that the counterparty pledge collateral. The value of the collateral should be at least equal to the bank's "market" exposure. This exposure will change over time as market conditions evolve. The posting of collateral equal to the mark-to-market replacement cost of the swap contract is the most appealing of such approaches. A variation of this same approach is for the swap agreement to call for the posting of collateral in the event that the counterparty's creditworthiness deteriorates.

The third way to manage credit risk is to reduce the exposure by reversing existing swaps. This is most easily accomplished if the existing counterparty is a swap bank. There are a number of ways to structure a reversal, and which one works best in a given situation will depend on the surrounding circumstances. A counterparty may have reasons other than exposure reduction for wanting to reverse a swap:

1. the underlying debt may have been prepaid;
2. the expectation of the parties responsible for the swap may have changed;
3. a very attractive replacement swap has become available; or
4. the swap may have a positive mark-to market value and the firm would like to reverse the swap to enhance current earnings.

The two basic ways to reverse a swap are to:

1. enter a new swap with opposite terms to the original; and
2. effect a cancellation by buy out.

The first approach may be made at-market or off-market depending on the behavior of interest rates since the original swap was negotiated. Such a reversal may be effected with the existing counterparty or with an altogether different counterparty. As discussed in Chapter 8, writing an off-market swap will usually involve a buy-up or a buy-down. The payments on these swaps can then be netted and the exposure reduced. If the two swaps have been made with the same counterparty, the counterparties may find it convenient to cancel the swaps based on their off-setting nature. The second approach, to engage in a simple buy-out cancellation, involves requesting the counterparty to cancel the swap based on a close-out payment. Swap banks will generally accommodate these requests near replacement cost. Other counterparties may not be so willing because their existing swap is designed to serve some specific corporate purpose.

Consider the following example: A swap bank enters a five-year interest-rate swap as fixed-rate payer with Counterparty A and then matches this commitment as fixed-rate receiver with a swap with Counterparty B. The swap bank records a credit exposure on both swaps. Later, the swap bank enters a five-year interest-rate swap as fixed-rate receiver with Counterparty C and would, normally, look to match this swap with a swap with another counterparty, whom we will call Counterparty D. In the swap with Counterparty D, the bank would be the fixed-rate payer. If the bank does this, it would then have a recorded exposure on four separate swaps. Now, suppose that instead of doing the final swap with Counterparty D, the bank again approaches Counterparty B. Recall that in its first swap with Counterparty B, the bank is the fixed-rate receiver. Since the bank now needs a swap to match its obligation to Counterparty C, in which the bank is the fixed-rate payer, the bank offers such a swap to Counterparty B. At the same time, the bank requests that the two opposing swaps between the swap bank and Counterparty B cancel one another. As it happens, Counterparty B is amenable to this cancellation. By writing off-setting swaps in this way, the bank reduces its swap exposure from four swaps to two swaps.

Of course, it is highly unlikely that market conditions have remained unchanged since the time the first swap with Counterparty B was written. Thus, the off-setting swaps will not have identical terms or identical values. This will necessitate a netting of economic values that results in a profit or loss for the swap bank (and, of course, a loss or profit for Counterparty B). This closeout will be effected with a single payment from the bank to Counterparty B or by a single payment from Counterparty B to the bank. The value of this closeout payment is approximately the value of writing an off-market swap, as discussed in Chapter 8.

Swap banks often engage in multiple swaps with the same counterparties but not always for the purpose of reversing existing swaps. It is common today for banks that frequently engage in swaps with one another (interbank swaps) to have a **master swap agreement**. Such an agreement is simply a document that governs all swaps between the parties with each new swap representing a supplement to the master agreement. Such a master agreement provides for a netting of obligations. Thus, payment flows between the parties are limited to the payment differentials. Banks generally maintain that this netting of obligations reduces their exposure on their swap portfolios and, for internal risk-management purposes, swap banks typically calculate a net exposure to each final institution with which they transact. For purposes of bank regulation of credit exposures however, it has not yet been decided whether this netting of exposures under master swap agreements will affect bank capital requirements. The recently adopted Federal Reserve rules governing capital requirements and credit exposures are covered later in this chapter.

The final approach to the management of credit risk is to assign the swap to another party. That is, a booked swap can, theoretically, be **assigned** and the credit risk transferred in the process. This approach is difficult because it requires the approval of both counterparties to the swap. The uninvolved counterparty may be unwilling to allow its swap to be transferred since that party derives no benefit from the transfer. A solution is to include an assignment clause at the time the swap is written, thus permitting the bank to make such a transfer. These assignments, however, are quite complicated. As a general matter, permissive assignments are not allowed under most swap agreements. Most often assignment is a matter left to subsequent negotiation should interest in an assignment arise.

9.4.3   Miscellaneous Portfolio Management Considerations

There are a great many other considerations in the management of the risks associated with swaps. Many of these arise only when specialty swaps are created. For example, a bank may have a difficult time finding a match for a putable or a callable swap. Or, it may find that such a swap can only be matched if the bank buys the necessary provisions from a second counterparty. But different features of different speciality swaps can, sometimes, be offsetting. For example, if the bank grants a floating-rate payer the right to terminate a seven-year swap after four years (a putable swap), the bank might be able to offset the risk by entering a second swap with a four-year maturity as a floating-rate payer while reserving the right to extend the life of the swap for three additional years (an extendable swap).

If the first counterparty elects to ''put'' its swap with the bank, the bank would not extend its swap with the second counterparty. If the first counterparty elects not to ''put'' its swap with the bank, the bank would extend its swap with the second counterparty.

We have assumed throughout that the bank looks to minimize its risk exposure. This is not necessarily a realistic assumption. Some swap banks take speculative positions in swaps. That is, they carry a portion of their swap portfolio unhedged, or they deliberately mismatch specific swap provisions in an effort to exploit their expectations as to the likely course of interest rates, spreads between different rate indexes, the future shape of the yield curve, and so on. These decisions are typically made by experienced management teams backed up by the bank's research department.

9.5 TREATMENT OF SWAPS UNDER THE NEW INTERNATIONAL CAPITAL STANDARDS

Many of the institutions that act as market makers in swaps are commercial banks. These banks were attracted to the swap market because swaps allow them to enhance their return on equity. This opportunity to increase profitability is possible because swaps are off-balance sheet transactions. That is, swaps do not appear on either the asset side or the liability side of a balance sheet.

Despite the considerable amount of deregulation in the banking industry over the past 10 years, banking is still one of the most highly regulated of all industries. There is a public interest in maintaining the soundness of the banking system. For this reason, banks are subject to a great number of regulatory controls. One of the most important of these controls is the requirement that banks and bank holding companies maintain satisfactory levels of bank capital. All other things being equal, banks would prefer to count both long-term debt and equity as capital, while bank regulators would prefer to count only equity. Debt allows the firm to leverage itself and, in so doing, increase the return to its shareholders.

Capital provides a cushion for depositors in the event that the bank suffers operating losses and/or some of the bank's assets lose value. Historically, the capital requirement was determined as a percentage of bank assets. But, because swaps provide a source of earnings for banks without increasing bank assets, swap activity did not increase capital requirements. Thus, swaps were seen as a way to enhance shareholder returns. As swaps and other off-balance sheet activity became a progressively larger portion of bank business, bank regulators became increasingly concerned about the adequacy of bank capital under the existing capital requirements. They believed that swaps exposed the banks to risks which conventional risk measures ignored.

On several occasions, bank regulators made capital adequacy proposals to correct what they perceived to be a dangerous situation. Many of the proposals were extreme. For example, some early proposals would have imposed capital requirements on notional swap principal equal to the requirements imposed on a straight loan. Such proposals demonstrated a lack of understanding of the swap product. As we have shown in this chapter, the default risk on a swap (in which cash flows pass in two directions) is considerably less than the default risk on a straight loan that has an equal principal (in which cash flows pass in only one direction).

A second argument made by U.S. banks against the imposition of new capital requirements focused on the global nature of the swap market. Banks maintained that stiff capital requirements on swaps would force them to increase their bid-ask spread on the swaps in which they make a market in order to cover their increased costs. This increase in the bid-ask spread for domestic swap banks would place them at a competitive disadvantage to nondomestic swap banks. The swap business would then simply move overseas—mostly to London. The banks further argued that if the United States was to remain a leader in international finance it could not afford to surrender to its foreign competition.

These arguments proved persuasive. As a first step, the Federal Reserve, together with the Bank of England, issued proposals that called for risk-based capital requirement. These were put out for public comment during 1986 and 1987. Subsequently, the Fed sent representatives to Basle, Switzerland, to work with representatives of the central banking authorities of the Group of Ten plus Luxembourg.[12] This group became known as the **Basle Supervisors' Committee**, and, in December of 1987, it agreed to a set of principles that dealt with the definition of bank capital and new risk-based capital requirements.

This set of principles became known as the **Basle Accord**. The Basle Accord standardized bank capital requirements across nations and removed the argument that stiffer swap capital requirements would unfairly impact U.S. banks.

After a period of public comment, the Federal Reserve issued final guidelines on 19 January 1989. These guidelines were designed to achieve several important goals:[13]

Establishment of a uniform capital framework, applicable to all federally supervised banking organizations.

Encouragement of international banking organizations to strengthen their capital positions.

Reduction of a source of competitive inequality arising from differences in supervisory requirements among nations.

The Fed's new guidelines encompass more than just swap activity. Indeed, the guidelines impose risk-adjusted capital requirements based on all off-balance sheet and on-balance sheet activities that contribute to a bank's risk exposure.

The procedure for assessing capital requirements for a swap is a four-step process: The first step is to determine the notional principal on the swap. Based on this notional principal, the swap coupon, and the prevailing level of interest rates, the swap is marked-to-market and the replacement cost of the swap is ascertained. To this replacement cost, an additional amount is added on to account for future volatility. This **add-on factor** ranges from 0 to 5 percent depending on the type of swap and the term of the swap. The result of these calculations is called the **credit risk equivalent**. Ascertaining this value constitutes the second step. The third step involves a risk weighting. This requires a simple multiplication of the credit risk equivalent by a fixed percentage. The percentage itself depends on the general quality of the creditor.

For example, a swap with a central government within the **Organization of Economic Cooperation and Development** (OECD) involves a risk-weighting factor of 0. At the other extreme is a swap with a bank incorporated outside of the OECD. For swaps with these institutions, the risk-weighting factor is 100 percent. In between these extremes are swaps with domestic corporations and swaps with banks incorporated within the OECD. This multiplication yields a value called the **risk-weighted asset**. The final step is to determine the capital requirement by multiplying the risk-weighted asset by the **capital ratio**. The Basle Accord set this at 8 percent and this ratio was later adopted by the Federal Reserve.

Suppose a swap bank negotiates a four-year interest-rate swap with a domestic corporation having a notional principal of $50 million. Because the swap has a term of more than one year, the add-on factor will be 0.5 percent of the notional principal. When the swap is first written, the swap is at market and has a mark-to-market value of $0. When the "add on" of $0.25 million (0.005 × $50 million) is included, the swap is found to have a credit risk equivalent of $0.25 million. The risk weight for this swap is 50 percent, so the risk weighted asset is $0.125 million. Since the capital ratio is 8 percent, the capital requirement is $10,000. Thus, the bank must keep $10,000 of capital to support this particular swap. As interest rates change, the swap will be repeatedly marked-to-market with the result that the capital requirement will continuously change. Suppose, for example that interest rates rise and the swap is found to have a replacement cost of $50,000. The bank's capital requirement for this swap would rise to $12,000. These calculations are depicted in Exhibit 9.9.

The Fed's guidelines have had a very positive effect on the market. The guidelines reflect the realities of swap risks to market-making banks. They also eliminate a cloud that has hung over the swap market from the outset. Since the Fed's new guidelines were announced, the rate of growth of the market has accelerated. A subtle but interesting implication of the new guidelines is that in the future, bank analysts will, in all likelihood, judge bank performance on the basis of **return on risk adjusted assets** (RORA) rather than the traditional **return on assets** (ROA).

For those readers interested in a more detailed analysis of the Federal Reserve's new capital guidelines, we have included, as an appendix to this chapter, a more comprehensive summary of the guidelines and their implications for U.S. banks and bank holding companies. This summary was prepared by Robert Bench and Harold Schuler of the Regulatory Advisory Practice of Price Waterhouse.

EXHIBIT 9.9. **Determination of Capital Requirements Under New Guidelines for Off-Balance Sheet Activity**

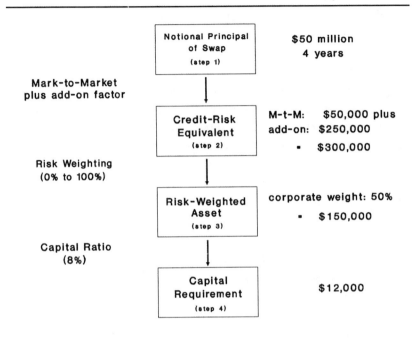

9.6 SUMMARY

A swap bank holds a portfolio of swaps so it can earn a return from its bid-ask spread and, to a lesser degree, from front-end fees. While a front-end fee provides an immediate reward, the return from the bid-ask spread is realized over an extended period of time. To profit from its swap activity, the swap bank must bear risk. A fundamental premise of financial theory is that economic entities (including both individuals and firms) are risk averse. Thus, a key ingredient in successfully running a swap portfolio (swap book) is controlling the various risk exposures associated with the portfolio.

Ideally, the swap bank would perfectly match each swap to which it becomes a counterparty with an offsetting swap with another counterparty. If both swaps could be entered simultaneously and if all of the bank's counterparties were completely free of credit risk, then the bank's portfolio would be riskless. In such a perfect environment, the swap bank would best be viewed as a pure arbitrager—taking riskless positions with no investment and earning a profit by helping end users exploit their respective comparative advantages. Unfortunately, the real world is not nearly so perfect. Swaps are custom designed to meet the end users' needs and potential counterparties with matching needs are not always easily found. When found, they often require special swap features that result in a mismatching of at least some swap provisions. Finally, very few potential counterparties are perfect credits. As a consequence of these realities, there are a great many different risks associated with running a swap portfolio. These include interest-rate risk, exchange-rate risk, credit risk, market risk, default risk, mismatch risk, basis risk, spread risk, sovereign risk, and delivery risk. The risks must be identified, measured, and managed.

The risks associated with a swap portfolio are related in complex ways. To some degree, the risks are often offsetting—in the sense of natural hedges. Thus, the risk manager must consider the risk character of the overall portfolio rather than the risk character of the swaps individually. Some risks can be hedged. Others cannot be. When hedging is possible, the risk manager will hedge in futures, options, the Treasury and Eurodollar markets, FRAs, FXAs, and other risk management vehicles. Hedges of this type must be managed dynamically—placed and lifted as the portfolio evolves over time. The risks that are not hedgeable should be managed in other ways. Some risks, such as credit risks, are unsystematic by nature and can be dramatically reduced by simple diversification. Nevertheless, the bank should reduce these risks as much as possible by providing for replacement compensation in the event of default and by credit enhancements when possible. Other risks, like sovereign risk, are systematic by nature and can best be managed by limiting the firm's exposure in markets where this risk is deemed to be more substantial.

Identifying, measuring, and managing the risks associated with running a swap portfolio are clearly complicated undertakings. Most swap banks maintain a staff of risk management specialists who are often consulted prior to the writing of a swap. This is particularly important when the swap is complicated by novel provisions with which the bank has little experience.

REFERENCES AND SUGGESTED READINGS

Altman, E. I. *Corporate Financial Distress*, New York: John Wiley and Sons, Inc., (1983).

Chen, K. H. and T. A. Shimerda. "An Empirical Analysis of Useful Financial Ratios," *Financial Management* (Spring 1981).

Commins, K. "Risk Management: The Eight Best Hedges," *Intermarket*, 4:8, 17-23 (Aug 1987).

Cooper, D. F. and Watson, I. R. "How to Assess Credit Risks in Swaps," *Banker*, 137:732, 28-31 (Feb 1987).

Felgran, S. D. "Interest Rate Swaps: Use, Risk, and Prices," *New England Economic Review* (Federal Reserve Bank of Boston), 22-32 (Nov/Dec 1987).

Foster, G. *Financial Statement Analysis*, 2d ed., Englewood Cliffs, N.J.: Prentice-Hall (1986).

Gay, G. D. and R. W. Kolb "Removing Bias in Duration Based Hedging Models: A Note," *Journal of Futures Markets*, 4:2, 225-228 (Summer 1984).

Haugen, R. A. *Modern Investment Theory*, Englewood Cliffs, N.J.: Prentice-Hall, (1986).

Henderson, S. K. "Termination Provisions of Swap Agreements," *International Financial Law Review* (UK), 22-27 (Sep 1983).

Hyde, J. H. "A Swap Torpedo," *United States Banker*, 98:10 36-40 (Oct 1987).

Marshall, J. F. *Futures and Option Contracting*, Cincinnati: South-Western (1989).

Miller, G. "When Swaps Unwind," *Institutional Investor*, 20:11, 165-178 (Nov 1986).

Smith, D. J. "Measuring the Gains from Arbitraging the Swap Market," *Financial Executive*, 4:2, 46-49 (Mar/Apr 1988).

Stoakes, C. "How to Terminate A Swap," *Euromoney*, (Apr 1985).

Winder, R. "The Art of Exposure Management," *Euromoney*, 51-54, (Apr 1986).

ENDNOTES

[1] In the context of modern portfolio theory, the risk associated with holding an investment portfolio can be divided into two types: **systematic** and **unsystematic**. Unsystematic risk is that risk which is unique to the individual asset. This risk is easily diversified away. Systematic risk is that portion of the asset's risk which is correlated to the behavior of the general market. Systematic risk is measured with the aid of beta coefficients. An asset's beta is the ratio of its covariance of return with the market to the variance of the rate of return on the market as a whole. A fuller discussion of systematic risk, unsystematic risk, and beta measurement can be found in Haugen (1986). In the context of hedging theory with futures, a fuller discussion can be found in Marshall (1989, Chapters 6 and 7).

[2] More precisely, the yield level is a function of duration. However, since maturity is the primary determinant of duration, we adopt the standard convention of discussing

yields relative to maturities rather than yields relative to durations. For a more complete discussion of this point, see Chapter 2.

[3]When swaps were first introduced, the market maker's bid-ask spread would often run to 100 basis points or more. Intense competition has reduced the spreads to no more than 20 basis points and usually substantially less.

[4]This issue has been examined by Winder (1986).

[5]**Regression analysis** and **discriminant analysis** are multivariate forecasting techniques which have been used to determine which financial ratios or combinations of financial ratios are most reliable at predicting business failure. As such, these tools are useful for assessing the creditworthiness of a client firm. For a more detailed discussion of these techniques and their application in measuring creditworthiness, see Foster (1986) and Altman (1983). Factor analysis has also been used for this purpose. For a discussion of this technique, see Chen and Shimerda (1981). For a discussion of the measurement of credit risk in the context of swap finance, see Cooper (1987).

[6]The credit risks (probabilities of default) used in this example are considerably higher than those typical in actual practice. For example, a 1987–88 survey by the ISDA of 71 swap dealers showed that only 11 had ever experienced any write-offs of notional principal. These write-offs amounted to $33.0 million on aggregate portfolios of $283.0 billion— equivalent to about one-one-hundredth of 1 percent.

[7]Some swap banks have attempted to mark their swaps to market (i.e., determining replacement cost) and requiring the counterparties to post collateral equal to this mark-to-market value. The First Boston Corporation was the first swap dealer to adopt a mutual mark-to-market collateral provision in its swap master agreements.

[8]This assumes that there is equal likelihood of a counterparty's default whether interest rates rise or fall. This assumption would be violated if the fixed-rate paying counterparties become increasingly likely to default when interest rates fall or if fixed-rate receiving counterparties become increasingly likely to default when interest rates rise. The violation of the assumption however, does not alter the conclusion. It only mitigates, to some degree, the strength of the conclusion.

[9]The term "basis" is used in hedging theory to mean the difference between two prices. These prices need not be interest rates. They can just as easily be exchange rates, commodity prices, and so on. Basis risk is the risk that the two prices will evolve differently. Basis risk is measured as the variance of the basis. A hedge is considered effective if the basis risk is less than the price risk. For a more thorough discussion of basis risk, see Chapter 4. For a very thorough discussion of basis risk in the context of futures hedging, see Marshall (1989) Chapter 7.

[10]Many swap banks prefer the dollar value basis point model to hedging interest-rate exposure. It can be shown, however, that, if properly used, a duration-based hedging model, adjusted for yield-change differences, and the dollar value basis point hedging model will produce the same hedge outcomes. For a derivation and discussion of the dollar value basis point model and its relationship to the duration model, see Marshall (1989), Chapter 12.

[11]Futures themselves have no duration, but they behave exactly as though they have a duration identical to that of the underlying instrument. For this reason, we

calculate the duration of the T-note on which the futures is written and then treat this duration as the duration of the T-note futures. The same would apply if we were using T-bill or T-bond futures as the hedging instrument. Importantly, the underlying instrument must be taken to be the "cheapest-to-deliver" alternative permissible on the futures. For a further discussion of this point, see Gay and Kolb (1984).

[12]The Group of Ten is Belgium, Canada, France, Germany, Italy, Japan, the Netherlands, Sweden, Switzerland, and the United Kingdom.

[13]See Federal Reserve Press Release dated January 19, 1989 to accompany Risk-Based Capital Guidelines.

CHAPTER 9:

APPENDIX

Risk Based Capital Guidelines for U.S. Banks and Bank Holding Companies*

Robert R. Bench and Harold D. Schuler
Price Waterhouse

---

*Price Waterhouse delivers expertise in accounting and auditing services for the financial services industry. Among the services provided is its Regulatory Advisory Practice which is based in Washington and London. Robert Bench is Managing Partner of the Regulatory Advisory Practice. He formerly served as Deputy Comptroller of the Currency. Harold Schuler is Senior Manager of the Regulatory Advisory Practice.

OVERVIEW

The U.S. Federal banking agencies ("Agencies"), the Federal Deposit Insurance Corporation, the Federal Reserve, and the Comptroller of the Currency, have been supervising capital adequacy on a joint basis since 1980.

They have done so by requiring that all banks continuously meet a minimum ratio of total capital to total assets. Since 1985, banks have been required to maintain a ratio of 6 percent of total capital to total assets. However, using this simple test alone has implicitly penalized banks for holding low-risk, low-earning, liquid assets. This test has also tacitly encouraged banks to limit total assets on their balance sheets and to promote various off-balance sheet instruments.

In contrast, the new guidelines focus on relating bank capital to the risk characteristics of a bank's activities, regardless of whether a bank accounts for those activities on or off its balance sheet.

INTERNATIONAL REGULATION OF BANK CAPITAL

In July, 1988, the Bank for International Settlements ("BIS") through its Committee on Banking Regulations and Supervisory Practices issued a framework for measuring capital adequacy and setting minimum capital standards for internationally active banks.

The Committee has two prime goals:

- to strengthen the soundness and stability of the international banking system; and

- to remove an important source of competitive inequality arising from differences in the definition and calculation of capital adequacy among the world's banking supervisors.

The framework emphasizes a minimum standard and a general evaluative approach based upon the credit risk of each banking activity as well as other factors considered in a comprehensive evaluation of capital adequacy. These would include an assessment of a bank's liquidity position, management quality, asset quality, and earnings capacity.

Central bankers and supervisors from Belgium, Canada, France, West Germany, Italy, Japan, Luxembourg, Netherlands, Sweden, Switzerland, the United Kingdom, and the United States serve on the Committee. All members have begun to implement the standards in their respective national jurisdictions. In addition, non-member countries have begun to look at adoption of the common framework.

The framework has four broad features:

- a common international definition of "Core Capital" or "Tier I Capital" and a list of items which can constitute "Supplementary Capital" or "Tier II Capital";

- a general framework for assigning banking activities to risk categories or pools and procedures for calculating a risk-based capital ratio;

- a schedule for achieving the minimum ratio; and

- transition rules through 1992.

The Committee incorporated flexibility into the framework so that each country's unique accounting conventions and market conditions could be accommodated.

APPLICATION

The Agencies apply these guidelines to all U.S. banks.

The guidelines also apply on a consolidated basis to bank holding companies with consolidated assets of $150 million or more. For those companies with less than $150 million in consolidated assets, the guidelines generally apply on a bank-only basis.

IMPLEMENTATION

The Agencies are phasing these guidelines in over time with full implementation scheduled for December 31, 1992. The guidelines contain specific transitional arrangements. Existing capital to assets ratios will remain in effect until at least 1990.

CAPITAL TARGETS AND STANDARDS

1993 STANDARD

After December 31, 1992, all banks will be expected to meet a minimum ratio of qualifying total capital to weighted risk assets of 8%. At least half of this amount (4%) should be in the form of core capital (Tier I) net of goodwill. The maximum amount of supplementary capital or Tier II capital that will count towards meeting the total capital standard will be equal to the total amount of core capital less any goodwill which the bank has. In addition, the combined maximum amount of subordinated debt and intermediate-term preferred stock qualifying as Tier II capital will be limited to 50% of Tier I capital.

In calculating Tier II capital, the allowance for loan and lease losses will be limited to 1.25% of risk weighted assets.

Qualifying total capital is calculated by adding Tier I and Tier II capital together and deducting from this sum certain investments in banking or finance subsidiaries that are not consolidated for accounting or supervisory purposes, reciprocal holdings of banking organization capital securities, or other items at the direction of the banking regulators.

TRANSITION AND IMPLEMENTING ARRANGEMENTS

No formal risk-based capital standard or minimum level has been set for the period from the issuance date of these guidelines until December 31, 1990. However, banks are expected to move toward the capital targets during this period.

By December 31, 1990, all banks and bank holding companies will be expected to maintain total capital equal to 7.25% of total risk weighted assets. Of this amount, 3.25% must be in the form of core capital.

Between December 31, 1990 and December 31, 1992, banks will be able to include supplementary capital elements in amounts up to 10% of core capital (before deducting goodwill and disallowed intangibles) to meet the interim 7.25% target. In addition, the maximum amount of the allowance for loan losses which will qualify as Tier II capital will be 1.5% of total risk weighted assets.

DEFINITION OF CAPITAL

Under the guidelines, capital is divided into two components: Core Capital (Tier I), and Supplementary Capital (Tier II).

CORE CAPITAL - TIER I

Tier I Capital is defined as the sum of core capital elements less goodwill.

Core capital consists of common stockholders' equity (common stock, surplus, and retained earnings). All capital reserves that represent an appropriation of retained earnings, minority interests in the common stockholders' equity accounts of consolidated subsidiaries are also included. Supplementary capital elements are only included during transition period.

Preferred stock will be treated differently for banks versus bank holding companies. *For banks,* non-cumulative perpetual preferred stock is allowed as a component of core capital, but may not be the dominant core capital element. Any other forms of preferred stock or excess amounts of qualifying non-cumulative preferred stock will be considered Tier II capital. *For bank holding companies,* total preferred stock (no distinction is made between cumulative and noncumulative) counted as Tier I capital may not exceed 25% of total core capital.

For banks, any goodwill on the books will immediately be deducted from core capital to determine Tier I capital. *For bank holding companies,* goodwill in existence prior to March 12, 1988 will not be deducted from core capital until full phase-in of the guidelines after December 31, 1992.

SUPPLEMENTARY CAPITAL - TIER II

Tier II or Supplementary Capital includes general loan loss reserves, cumulative perpetual preferred stock, long-term preferred stock, hybrid capital instruments, subordinated debt and intermediate preferred stock subject to the qualifying tests, limits and deductions explained below.

Supplementary Capital includes the *general loan loss reserves* established against future, but unidentified losses. Over the transition period, the amount of the reserve for loan losses which will qualify as supplementary capital will diminish. From enactment until December 31, 1990, the entire amount of the reserve will be considered supplementary capital. From January 1, 1991 to December 31, 1992, the maximum amount permitted in the calculation will be 1.5% of total risk weighted assets. After December 31, 1992, the maximum amount permitted will be 1.25% of total risk weighted assets. Individual bank loan portfolios may require higher reserves, but these additional reserves for loan losses will not count towards meeting the regulatory capital standard. Any allocated transfer risk reserves are deducted from the reserve component.

Supplementary Capital also includes *cumulative perpetual preferred stock* (having no fixed maturity date and not redeemable at the option of the holder) and *long-term preferred stock* (with an original maturity of 20 years or more).

Another significant element of Supplementary Capital is *hybrid capital instruments* (long-term debt instruments) which meet the following criteria:

- the instrument must be unsecured, fully paid-up, subordinated to general creditors and depositors, and be capable of absorbing losses;

- the instrument must not be redeemable at the option of the holder before maturity, except with the prior approval of the primary Federal regulator;

- the instrument must convert to common stock or perpetual or long-term preferred stock if the sum of the retained earnings and surplus becomes negative; and,

- the instrument must disclose that the issuer has the option of deferring interest payments if the issuer does not report a profit in the most recent four quarters taken together, and the issuer eliminates cash dividends on common and preferred stock.

Also qualifying as Supplementary Capital are *subordinated debt* and *intermediate-term preferred stock* (with an original maturity of less than 20 years) with an original weighted average maturity of at least five years. In each of the last five years to maturity, the value of the instrument will be discounted 20 percent per year. Consistent with current regulatory requirements, subordinated debt must be unsecured, subordinated to the interests of the depositors and must clearly state on its face that it is not a deposit and is not insured by a Federal agency.

Finally, the guidelines limit the sum of subordinated debt and intermediate-term preferred stock which may be considered as Supplementary Capital to 50% of Tier I Capital (net of Goodwill).

DEDUCTIONS FROM CAPITAL

Aside from goodwill (see page 5), other deductions from Tier I Capital include other intangible assets (e.g. mortgage servicing rights, leaseholds and core deposit value) in excess of 25% of Tier I Capital less goodwill as determined by the Agencies on a case-by-case basis. Investments in unconsolidated banking and financial subsidiaries, and reciprocal holdings of capital instruments of banking organizations are deducted from Tier I or Tier II or both based on the tier with which the corresponding instrument(s) would comply.

SUMMARY OF CAPITAL ELEMENTS

	TIER I	TIER II
COMMON STOCKHOLDERS EQUITY	x	None
PERPETUAL PREFERRED STOCK		
Banks:		
• Non-Cumulative	**Up to 50% of**	**Any Excess of**
• Market Rate Adjustable Non-Cumulative	**Tier I capital**	**Tier I guideline**
• Cumulative	**None**	**x**
• Auction Rate	**None**	**x**
Bank Holding Companies:		
• Non-Cumulative	**Up to 25% of**	**Any Excess of**
• Market Rate Adjustable Non-Cumulative	**Tier I capital**	**Tier I guideline**
• Cumulative		
• Auction Rate		
MINORITY INTERESTS IN CONSOLIDATED SUBSIDIARIES	x	**Any Excess of**
• Less than dominant in relation to equity		**Tier I guideline**
ALLOWANCE FOR LOAN LOSSES		
• Until 1990	**None**	**No limit**
• 12/31/90 to 12/31/92 *	**None**	**1.50%**
• 01/01/93 and beyond *	**None**	**1.25%**
HYBRID CAPITAL INSTRUMENTS AND LONG TERM PREFERRED STOCK	**None**	**No limit**
SUBORDINATED DEBT AND INTERMEDIATE TERM PREFERRED STOCK	**None**	**Up to 50% of Tier I capital (less goodwill)**

DEDUCTIONS FROM ASSETS AND CAPITAL

	TIER I	TIER II
INVESTMENTS IN UNCONSOLIDATED BANKING AND FINANCE SUBSIDIARIES	**less 50%**	**less 50%**
RECIPROCAL HOLDINGS OF CAPITAL INSTRUMENTS OF BANKING ORGANIZATIONS	**less 50%**	**less 50%**
GOODWILL	**less 100%**	**None**
OTHER INTANGIBLE ASSETS	**Agency determination on a case-by-case basis**	**None**

* As a percentage of risk-weighted assets

MEASUREMENT OF CAPITAL RATIO

RISK WEIGHTS FOR BALANCE SHEET ASSETS

Risk weighted assets are determined by assigning assets and off-balance sheet credit equivalent amounts to one of four risk categories ranging from 0 to 100 percent.

CATEGORY I (0% Weighting)

The assets assigned a 0% weight are: cash (both domestic and foreign) owned and held in all offices of a bank or in transit; claims on and balances due from Federal Reserve banks; securities issued by the U.S. Government or its agencies; and, claims on or unconditional guarantees by member governments of the Organization for Economic Cooperation and Development (OECD).

> Specifically included in the definition of "U.S. Agency" are: Government National Mortgage Association (**GNMA**), the Veterans Administration (**VA**), the Federal Housing Administration (**FHA**), the Export-Import Bank (**Exim Bank**), The Overseas Private Investment Corporation (**OPIC**), the Commodity Credit Corporation (**CCC**), and the Small Business Administration (**SBA**).

CATEGORY II (20% Weighting)

Category II includes: all claims on domestic depository institutions and foreign banks headquartered in OECD countries; cash items in process of collection; and short-term (original maturity of less than one year) claims on non-OECD banks. Included as well are claims on and guarantees of U.S. Government- sponsored Agencies.

> The term "U.S. Government-sponsored Agency" includes: the Federal Home Loan Mortgage Corporation (**FHLMC**), the Federal National Mortgage Association (**FNMA**), the Farm Credit System (**FCS**), the Federal Home Loan Bank System (**FHLBB**) and the Student Loan Marketing Association (**SLMA**).

In addition, this category includes: general obligation claims on, or portions of claims guaranteed by the full faith and credit of U.S. and OECD country, state and local governments; local currency claims on foreign central governments to the extent the bank has local currency liabilities in the foreign country; and, claims on *official multilateral lending institutions or regional development institutions* in which the U.S. Government is a shareholder or a contributing member. Specific examples are the World Bank and the regional development banks.

Category II also includes those portions of loans or other assets guaranteed by, or backed by the guarantee of a domestic depository institution. This would include instruments supported by a standby letter of credit (e.g. commercial paper, tax-exempt or asset-backed securities). In addition, those assets which are collateralized by cash, U.S. Treasury securities and guarantees, securities of U.S. Government-sponsored Agencies, and securities issued by multilateral lending institutions and regional development banks mentioned above are also assigned to Category II.

CATEGORY III (50% Weighting)

This includes all accruing loans fully secured by first liens on 1 to 4 family residences and all mortgage-backed securities backed by pools of *conventional mortgages* (except stripped securities which are included in Category IV).

Category III also includes revenue bonds or similar obligations (including loans and leases) of the U.S. or state or local governments, where the *source of repayment is revenue from the facilities financed rather than from general tax funds*.

CATEGORY IV (100% Weighting)

Category IV captures all the assets which are not included in any of the other categories.

This comprises the majority of a bank's loan portfolio including industrial development bonds and similar obligations issued by U.S., state or local governments where the benefiting private party or enterprise is committed to pay the principal and interest, and no government guarantee has been given.

This category also encompasses all claims (remaining maturity exceeding one year) on non-OECD banks; **all** non-local currency claims on non-OECD governments; local currency claims on a non-OECD central government *that exceed local currency liabilities owed by the bank* (claims that entail an element of transfer risk); claims on foreign and domestic private sector obligors not included in Categories I-III (customer liabilities to the bank on acceptances outstanding involving standard risk claims); and claims on commercial firms owned by the public sector.

All stripped mortgage- and asset-backed securities including all interest only and principal only securities are assigned to the 100% risk pool regardless of issuer or guarantor.

Full risk weighting is also given investments in fixed assets, premises, and other real estate owned; investments in unconsolidated companies, joint ventures or associated companies that have not been deducted from capital; instruments that qualify as capital issued by other banking organizations; and, common and preferred stock of other corporations including any stock acquired for debts previously contracted.

QUALIFYING ADJUSTMENTS TO RISK WEIGHTS FOR BALANCE SHEET ASSETS

Lower risk weights are assigned to weighted assets under the conditions described below involving collateral, guarantees and bank-issued standby letters of credit. Risk-weightings are reduced only for the portions of assets covered by such instruments.

Only certain types of *collateral* held by the bank reduce the risk weighting of the related asset. Such collateral, generally limited to cash on deposit in the bank, securities issued by, or guaranteed by the U.S. Government or its agencies, securities issued by, or guaranteed by U.S. Government-sponsored agencies, securities issued by or guaranteed by the central governments of OECD countries, and securities issued by multilateral lending institutions or regional development banks, reduces the risk weighting to Category II (20%).

Guarantees which impact on risk weightings include guarantees or guarantee-type instruments of: the U.S. Government or its agencies; U.S. Government-sponsored agencies; domestic state and local governments; and domestic depository institutions. All unconditional guarantees of the central governments of OECD countries and the U.S. government and its agencies, and unconditional local currency guarantees of non-OECD central governments will lower the risk weighting to Category I (0%). The other guarantees mentioned above will reduce the risk weighting to Category II (20%).

Also, customer's liability on *acceptances* executed, own acceptances discounted and held in portfolio, and purchased risk participation in other banks' acceptances are assigned the weight applicable to the obligor. However, acceptances or portions of acceptances in which risk participations have been sold to other depository institutions, as well as bankers acceptances of other banks purchased in the market are assigned the weight applicable to the relevant (purchasing or executing) bank.

WEIGHTING RISKS FOR OFF-BALANCE SHEET ACTIVITIES

Treatment for **all off-balance sheet items** follows a two-step process. First, the principal or face value amount of the off-balance sheet item is multiplied by a credit conversion factor to derive a balance sheet "credit equivalent amount". Then, the credit equivalent amount is assigned to the appropriate risk category by obligor, guarantor or type of collateral.

- **100% Conversion Factor**

    Direct credit substitutes - any irrevocable off-balance sheet obligation in which a bank has essentially the same credit risk as if it made a direct loan to the obligor. Examples are guarantees or guarantee-type instruments backing financial claims such as outstanding securities, loans and other financial liabilities; standby letters of credit; surety arrangements that back or guarantee repayment of commercial paper, tax-exempt securities, and commercial or individual loans or debt obligations.

    Participations acquired, sale and repurchase agreements and asset sales with recourse not already included on the balance sheet are treated as direct credit substitutes and are converted at 100 percent.

    Forward agreements (forward purchases, forward deposits accepted, partly-paid shares and securities) convert at 100 percent of the principal amount of the assets to be purchased.

- **50% Conversion Factor**

    Transaction-related contingencies (e.g. bid bonds, performance bonds, performance standby letters of credit, warranties, and standby letters of credit related to particular transactions) are converted at 50%.

    Also covered by this conversion factor are unused commitments with an **original** maturity exceeding one year   (commercial and consumer credit commitments), and revolving underwriting facilities (RUFs) and note issuance facilities (NIFs) where a borrower can issue short-term paper in its own name on a revolving basis and the underwriting banks have a legally binding commitment to either purchase any notes the borrower is unable to sell by the roll-over date or to advance funds to the borrower.

- **20% Conversion Factor**

    This factor covers short-term, self-liquidating trade-related contingencies which arise from the movement of goods including commercial letters of credit and other documentary letters of credit collateralized by the underlying shipments.

• **0% Conversion Factor**

These include unused commitments with an original maturity of one year or less or which are unconditionally cancellable at any time. *Unused retail credit card lines* are included if the bank has the unconditional option to cancel the card at any time.

INTEREST RATE AND FOREIGN EXCHANGE RATE CONTRACTS

Risk weights for interest rate and exchange rate contracts are determined using a two-step process like that applied to other off-balance sheet items. While the BIS framework discusses two valuation approaches, the Agencies require that U.S. banks follow the current exposure method.

CURRENT EXPOSURE METHOD

The current exposure method requires banks to calculate the credit equivalent amount by:

1. determining the current replacement cost of contracts having positive value on the reporting date by *marking them to market*; and,

2. adding to that amount an estimate (the *"add-on"*) of the potential increase in credit exposure over the remaining life of all such contracts by multiplying the face value of all contracts by the conversion factors.

CREDIT CONVERSION FACTORS		
Remaining Maturity	**Interest Rate**	**Exchange Rate**
Less than 1 year	-0-	1.0%
One year and over	0.5%	5.0%

Higher conversion factors are required for foreign exchange instruments than for interest rate contracts because exchange rate contracts involve an exchange of principal upon maturity and are deemed more volatile than interest rate contracts.

Credit equivalent amounts must be computed for the following:

I.   Interest Rate Contracts

    A.   Single currency interest rate swaps
    B.   Basis swaps
    C.   Forward rate agreements
    D.   Interest rate options purchased
    E.   Any other instrument that gives rise to similar
        credit risk

II.   Exchange Rate Contracts

    A.   Cross-currency interest rate swaps
    B.   Forward foreign exchange contracts
    C.   Currency options purchased
    D.   Any other instrument that gives rise to similar
        credit risk

Once the credit equivalent amount for interest rate and exchange rate instruments has been determined, that amount will be weighted within the overall framework according to the category of the counterparty and the nature of any underlying collateral or guarantees. ***Regardless of counterparty, the maximum credit equivalent applied to foreign exchange and interest rate swaps is 50 percent.***

        Exchange rate contracts with original maturities of 14 calendar days or less will be excluded. Instruments (including futures and options) traded on exchanges that require daily payment of variation margin are also excluded. However, all such instruments not traded on an exchange are subject to capital requirements and are to be treated in the same way as other interest rate and exchange rate contracts.

No potential future credit exposure is calculated for basis swaps (i.e. single currency interest rate swaps in which payments are based upon two floating rate indices). Their credit exposure is evaluated solely on the basis of their mark-to-market value.

        Swaps and similar contracts must be considered on a gross basis.

In those cases where the credit exposure on interest rate and foreign exchange rate contracts is already reflected on the balance sheet, counterparty exposures will be deducted from balance sheet assets to avoid double counting.

BALANCE SHEET ASSET RISK WEIGHTINGS

Type of Asset:	Risk Weight

Cash (Domestic and Foreign)
Deposit Reserves and Balances at
  Federal Reserve Banks
Securities Issued by the U.S. Government
Claims on Central Governments of OECD Countries
Portions of Securities and Loans Unconditionally
  Guaranteed by the U.S. Government
Book Value of Paid-In Stock of a Federal
  Reserve Bank
	0%

Cash Items in Process of Collection
Claims on Domestic Depository Institutions
  and OECD Banks
Claims on Non-OECD Banks Maturing in
  Less Than One Year
Claims Guaranteed by Domestic Depository
  Institutions
Local Currency Claims on Foreign Central
  Governments to the Extent of Local
  Currency Liabilities in the Foreign Country
Securities and Other Claims on or Guaranteed
  by U.S. Government-Sponsored Agencies
Portions of Loans and Other Assets Collateralized
  by Securities Issued by or Guaranteed by U.S.
  Government-Sponsored Agencies,
  U.S. Treasury, OECD Countries or Cash
General Obligation Claims on and Guaranteed by
  U.S. State and Local Governments Secured
  by the Full Faith and Credit of the State or
  Local Taxing Authority
Claims on Official Multilateral Lending Institutions
  or Regional Development Institutions in
  which the U.S. Government is a Shareholder
  or a Contributing Member
Privately-Issued Mortgage-Backed Securities
  Representing Indirect Ownership or
  Mortgage-Related U.S. Government Agency
  or U.S. Government-Sponsored Agency
  Securities
Portions of Securities and Loans Conditionally
  Guaranteed by the U.S. Government
	20%

U.S. State or Local Government Revenue Bonds
  or Similar Obligations Where Debt is Repaid
  Out of Revenues from Financed Facilities
Residential Real Estate Mortgages Representing
  First Liens on 1-4 Family Dwellings
Credit Equivalent Amounts of Interest Rate and
  Foreign Exchange Rate Related Contracts
  Unless Assigned to a Lower Risk Weight
	50%

All Claims on Private Obligors Unless Assigned
  to a Lower Risk Weight
Claims on Non-OECD Foreign Banks with a
  Remaining Maturity Exceeding One Year
Claims on Foreign Central Governments
  Not Included Above
Obligations Issued by State or Local Governments
  Repayable Solely by a Private Party or
  Enterprise
Premises, Plant and Equipment, Other Fixed
  Assets and Other Real Estate Owned
Investments in Unconsolidated Subsidiaries, Joint
  Ventures, or Associated Companies (If Not
  Deducted from Capital)
Instruments Issued by Other Banking
  Organizations that Qualify as Capital
All Other Assets (Including Claims on Commercial
  Firms Owned by the Public Sector) and Any
  Intangible Asset Not Deducted from Capital
	100%

OFF-BALANCE SHEET ASSET RISK WEIGHTINGS

Type of Asset:	Conversion Factor

Direct Credit Substitutes
Sales and Repurchase Agreements and Asset
  Sales with Recourse Not Already on the
  Balance Sheet
Principal Amount of Assets to be Purchased
  of Forward Agreements
Securities Lent Where the Bank is at Risk
	100%

Transaction-Related Contingencies
Unused Commercial and Consumer Credit
  Commitments with an Original Maturity
  Exceeding One Year
Revolving Underwriting Facilities (RUFs) and
  Note Issuance Facilities (NIFs) Where the
  Borrower Can Issue Short-Term Paper in its
  Own Name on a Revolving Basis and the
  Underwriting Banks Have a Legally Binding
  Commitment to Either Purchase Any Notes
  the Borrower is Unable to Sell by the Roll-
  Over Date or to Advance Funds to the
  Borrower
	50% 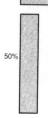

Short-Term, Self-Liquidating, Trade-Related
  Contingencies Which Arise from the
  Movement of Goods
	20%

Unused Commitments with an Original
  Maturity of One Year or Less
Unused Commitments Which are
  Unconditionally Cancellable at Any Time
	0%

ISSUES FOR SENIOR MANAGEMENT

Strategic Issues

Who should be responsible for coordinating and implementing capital adequacy requirements?

How will the bank communicate to its various operations the impact of the capital guidelines on its overall capital position?

Who is going to develop and present training programs as well as provide ongoing communications on the capital guidelines appropriate to the different levels of the bank's staff?

How do the capital guidelines affect the bank's internal accounting and disclosure policies?

Does the bank allocate capital by business unit, line of business, or function? Will this change?

Which existing products should be retained and/or strengthened? Which should be abandoned?

Have the capital guidelines been introduced into the bank's product development methodology?

How will the guidelines affect pricing decisions?

Within the 100% weight category, individual assets exhibit different credit risk characteristics. What pricing differentials, if any, should be adopted?

How will the new guidelines affect the bank's main competitors, both locally and internationally?

What areas of competitive advantage should be exploited?

Can the bank refocus its marketing efforts to lower the risk weighting on higher-weighted assets in each of its lines of business?

Is the bank fully aware of the differences between the U.S. guidelines and those abroad as they may impact on the bank's global capital position?

Do Tier I or Tier II capital need to be increased?

What are the potential implications for return on equity due to increasing Tier I and Tier II capital?

ISSUES FOR SENIOR MANAGEMENT

Operational Issues

Overall, what procedures are in place to ensure all input data correctly identifies counterparty and security type by risk weight category?

There is the probability that certain guarantee and commitment transactions will be open to differing interpretations regarding their classification and subsequent risk weighting. Does the bank know that all of the different types of guarantees and commitments are completely recorded, properly classified and, therefore, correctly weighted?

Can the bank properly aggregate counterparty information across all of its different transaction systems?

Are the bank's systems capable of classifying off-balance sheet exposures by counterparty risk weight?

Can the bank's systems distinguish between the different types of collateral held on loans or off-balance sheet exposures?

Do the bank's systems include the consideration of residual maturities of off-balance sheet instruments to assign risk weighting?

Can the bank's systems identify all "in the money" off-balance sheet exposures requiring capital allocations on a deal by deal basis?

Can the bank's systems measure required mark-to-market revaluations for capital allocations purposes?

ISSUES FOR SENIOR MANAGEMENT

Monitoring Issues

What changes are necessary in the bank's systems to comprehensively monitor capital adequacy?

Who will be internally responsible for monitoring compliance with the guidelines?

Is there risk-based capital expertise on the Asset/Liability Committee?

Is the bank positioned to monitor the interaction of the capital guidelines with other regulations such as Expedited Funds Availability, Reg CC?

What plans have been put in place for the bank's holding company, branches and subsidiaries, both domestic and international, to supply the necessary consolidated information on a timely basis?

Can the bank improve the way in which it monitors its exposure and residual maturities to each counterparty on forward foreign exchange contracts, currency options, swaps, and other similar instruments?

Who will independently check any proposed systems to ensure that they fully meet all of the new requirements?

What procedures exist to ensure that when individual business units exceed their capital allocation, even temporarily, management is informed promptly of the impact on the individual unit as well as the consolidated entity?

ILLUSTRATIVE CALCULATION OF RISK-BASED CAPITAL RATIO FOR BANKS*

Example of a bank with $6,000 in total capital and the following assets and off-balance sheet items:

Balance Sheet Assets:	
Cash	5,000
U.S. Treasuries	20,000
Balances at domestic banks	5,000
Loans secured by first liens on 1-4 family residential properties	5,000
Loans to private corporations	65,000
Total Balance Sheet Assets	100,000

Off-Balance Sheet Items:	
Standby letters of credit ("SLCs") backing general obligation debt issues of US municipalities ("GOs")	10,000
Long-term legally binding commitments to private corporations	20,000
Interest rate swaps and foreign exchange contracts	51,000
Total Off-Balance Sheet Items	81,000

This bank's total capital to total assets (leverage) ratio would be 6% ($6,000/$100,000).

To compute the bank's risk weighted assets:

1 Compute the credit equivalent amount of each off-balance sheet (OBS) item.

Off-Balance Sheet Item	Face Value		Conversion Factor		Credit Equivalent Amount
SLCs backing municipal GOs	10,000	X	1.00	=	10,000
Long-term commitments to private corporations	20,000	X	0.50	=	10,000
Interest rate swaps and foreign exchange contracts	(See page 19 for calculation of credit equivalent amounts.)				

2 Multiply each balance sheet asset and the credit equivalent amount of each OBS item by the appropriate risk weight.

0% Category:						
Cash	5,000					
US Treasuries	20,000					
Credit equivalent amounts of foreign exchange contracts	210					
	25,210	X	0.00	=		0
20% Category:						
Balances at domestic banks	5,000					
Credit equivalent amounts of SLCs backing GOs of US municipalities	10,000					
Credit equivalent amounts of interest rate swaps	1,300					
	16,300	X	0.20	=		3,260
50% Category:						
Loans secured by first liens on 1-4 family residential properties	5,000	X	0.50	=		2,500
100% Category:						
Loans to private corporations	65,000					
Credit equivalent amounts of long-term commitments to private corporations	10,000					
	75,000	X	1.00	=		75,000
Total Risk-weighted Assets						**80,760**

This bank's ratio of total capital to risk weighted assets (risk-based capital ratio) would be 7.43% ($6,000/$80,760). Although this bank meets the current regulatory capital requirements, under the full phased-in risk-based capital guidelines, the bank would be undercapitalized.

This example has been taken from Appendix A of Regulation Y of the Federal Reserve Capital Adequacy Guidelines for Bank Holding Companies and State Member Banks.

CALCULATION OF CREDIT EQUIVALENT AMOUNTS FOR INTEREST RATE AND FOREIGN EXCHANGE RELATED TRANSACTIONS*

Type of contract (remaining maturity)	Potential exposure					Current exposure			Credit equivalent amount (dollars)
	Notional principal (dollars)	x	Potential exposure conversion factor	=	Potential exposure (dollars)	Replacement cost (1)	Current exposure (dollars) (2)	=	
1 120-day forward foreign exchange	5,000,000		0.01		50,000	100,000	100,000		150,000
2 120-day forward foreign exchange	6,000,000		0.01		60,000	-120,000	0		60,000
FOREIGN EXCHANGE CONTRACTS	11,000,000								210,000
3 3-year single-currency fixed/ floating interest rate swap	10,000,000		0.005		50,000	200,000	200,000		250,000
4 3-year single-currency fixed/ floating interest rate swap	10,000,000		0.005		50,000	-250,000	0		50,000
5 7-year cross-currency floating/ floating interest rate swap	20,000,000		0.05		1,000,000	-1,300,000	0		1,000,000
INTEREST RATE SWAPS	40,000,000								1,300,000
TOTAL	51,000,000								1,510,000

Once the credit equivalent amounts have been determined, they will be risk weighted by counterparty and nature of the underlying collateral or guarantees.

In our example, all foreign exchange contracts are denominated in OECD currencies. All interest rate swaps are floating rate instruments of OECD banks.

(1) These numbers are purely for illustration.
(2) The larger of zero or a positive mark-to-market value.

* This example has been taken from Appendix A of Regulation Y of the Federal Reserve Capital Adequacy Guidelines for Bank Holding Companies and State Member Banks.

10

Swap Documentation

10.1 OVERVIEW

Swaps are typically initiated through telephone conversations. The initial agreement usually hinges on a few key economic issues such as the swap coupon, the floating rate, the payment frequency, and the maturity. The verbal agreement is confirmed by a TELEX, Fax, or letter (called the **confirmation**), usually within 24 hours. While both parties are legally bound by the initial agreement, it is still far from complete. Complete documentation, which is extensive, is exchanged later. The swap documentation must cover all terms agreed to in the initial exchange and must also cover a great many incidental issues, including many indirect economic issues and some noneconomic issues, that bear on the relationship between the counterparties. These include such things as events of default, methods of computing damages on an early termination, jurisdiction governing disputes, and so forth.

In the early days of swap finance each swap bank chose its own wording for all of its swap contract documentation. Variations in the phrasing of this documentation and differing definitions of certain terms necessitated careful review by each counterparty's legal counsel. As a consequence, the lack of standardization introduced potentially injurious delays in the approval of the contracts as well as unnecessarily large legal expenses. Lack of standardization also made it potentially difficult for swap banks to match swaps, and it limited the swap market participants' ability to trade swaps in a well-defined secondary market and to reverse swaps with existing counterparties.

A limited amount of standardized wording began to emerge as banks found it efficient and economical to reuse the same (or similar) clauses in swaps that had similar terms. Banks also found it convenient to pirate one another's clauses as new features found their way into swap contracts. Despite this evolution, however, standardization remained elusive.

Most of the operatives in the swap banking industry eventually came to recognize that it was in the interests of all participants to work toward standardization. As a first effort, a small group of representatives from some of the leading swap banks began working on standardization of documentation in 1984. In March of 1985, this group, now expanded, organized itself as the New York-based International Swap Dealer's Association (ISDA). Then, in June of 1985, the ISDA released its first code of swaps: *The Code of Standard Wording, Assumptions and Provisions for Swaps, 1985 Edition*. The 1985 Code addressed two key issues:

1.   the cash flows of a rate swap, including the specification and calculation of the fixed- and floating-rate sides; and

2.   the amounts payable upon an early termination of the swap. The ISDA code proved appealing and was soon adopted, in whole or in part, by most U.S. swap dealers.

During this same period, the London-based British Bankers' Association (BBA) was working on its own code of swaps; and in August of 1985 the BBA introduced its documentation guidelines—the *British Bankers' Associations Interest Rate Swaps* or *BBAIRS*. This code was intended primarily as a documentation aid for interbank swaps. While the BBA's code is important, particularly for British banks, this chapter focuses on the more successful standardization efforts of the ISDA.

The ISDA's 1985 Code was only the first step in that organization's efforts at standardizing the language and provisions of swap documentation. In 1986, the ISDA released a revised and expanded version of the code (**1986 Code**). Like the 1985 version, this version devotes considerable attention to defining the cash flows associated with rate swaps and the amounts payable upon early termination. But the 1986 Code refines these provisions to facilitate the development of integrated master swap agreements. The 1986 Code also addresses a number of other issues to which the 1985 Code had been silent. In particular, the 1986 Code devotes considerable attention to the subjects of "events of default" and "termination events." The 1986 Code also provides a list of representations made by the parties to the swap, a list of agreements pertaining to information to be furnished on an ongoing basis, definitions pertaining to specific entities when a swap is guaranteed or supported by an entity other than the actual counterparty, cross border provisions, and withholding tax provisions.

In 1987, the ISDA took another giant step toward standardization of documentation by introducing standard form agreements. There are two versions of the standard form agreements. The first is a code-based form called the **Interest Rate Swap Agreement**. It is an agreement for U.S. dollar denominated swaps and incorporates the 1986 Code by reference, with certain modifications. The second is a multicurrency form called the **Interest Rate and Currency Exchange Agreement**. This covers interest-rate swaps in any currency as well as currency swaps and cross-currency interest-rate swaps. The Interest Rate and Currency Exchange Agreement does not reference the code directly but incorporates provisions that are virtually identical to those in the 1986 Code. Certain provisions of the code, Articles 2 through 8, which describe how fixed and floating payments are to be calculated and which provide various floating-rate options, are not included in this standard form. These issues are, instead, addressed through separate confirmations. To assist in the addressing of these issues, the ISDA also released in 1987 a document called the *1987 Interest Rate and Currency Exchange Definitions*.

In this chapter, we provide an overview of the standard form agreements and we introduce a number of terms defined in the 1986 Code, many of which have not been used elsewhere in this book. The reader is cautioned that many of the terms have subtle legal meanings that we have made no attempt to capture in this brief review. Documentation is a complex legal affair and any party to it should consult expert counsel. The full text of the ISDA's 1986 Code is included as an appendix to this chapter. The appendix does not include certain historical and explanatory material that accompanies the 1986 Code. The reader interested in this explanatory material, the Standard Form Agreements, and the *1987 Interest Rate and Currency Exchange Definitions* may obtain these documents, at modest cost, directly from the ISDA. The ISDA can also provide empirical data to assist those interested in studying the swap markets in greater depth. The ISDA's address appears below.

International Swap Dealers Association
1270 Avenue of the Americas
Rockefeller Plaza
Suite 2118
New York, NY 10020
USA

10.2   STANDARD FORM AGREEMENTS

While the 1985 and 1986 ISDA codes greatly enhanced the standard-ization of swap documentation, neither is, in and of itself, a contract. The codes simply provide standard definitions, presumptions that apply unless specifically overridden, and a menu of options for dealing with certain matters. The existence of the code does not eliminate the need for the counterparties to a swap to develop and execute contracts, although the contracts they develop should, logically, reference the ISDA code.

As already noted, the ISDA introduced two types of standard form agreements in 1987. These are structured as master swap agreements. As such, each agreement consists of a set of standard terms applicable to any swap transaction together with an accompanying schedule that allows the parties to tailor the agreement by listing terms specific to swaps between the two parties.

As master agreements, the swap documentation governs all subse-quent swaps between the parties by simple reference to the master agreement. Each new swap becomes a supplement to the existing master agreement and, consequently, the swap parties can limit their negotiation on each new swap to those matters of economic impor-tance. This minimizes the likelihood that disagreements over the terms of the swap will develop later and greatly speeds execution for parties that frequently transact swaps with one another. As discussed in the last chapter, master agreements can provide for a netting of exposures and, hence, the recording of exposures on a net basis. The agreements provide that all swap transactions governed by the master agreement are simultaneously terminated if either party defaults on any swap transaction that is governed by the master agreement. This prevents a bankruptcy trustee from selectively enforcing those swaps that have a positive mark-to-market value, while discarding those swaps with negative mark-to-market value. As of this writing, however, the Federal Reserve has not yet taken a final position on whether this netting of exposures will be applicable to the determination of bank capital requirements under its new capital guidelines.

The two versions of the standard form agreements (i.e., the code-based U.S. dollar version and the multicurrency version) employ the same basic ordering of provisions and, for the most part, the same numbering of their sections. The first section provides for the identification of the parties to the swap. This is followed by sections dealing with payments, representations, agreements, events of default and termination events, early termination, transfer, multibranch provisions, notices, tax matters, credit support documentation, governing law and jurisdiction, definitions, and confirmations.

10.2.1 Payments

Most payment terms are specific to the swap and, therefore, are specified in the accompanying schedule. The standard terms provide for the netting of payments on a given swap when payments between the parties are to be made on the same date and in the same currency. As an extension, the agreement provides that the parties net payments on all swaps governed by the same master agreement when those payments are to be made on the same date and in the same currency.

10.2.2 Representations

This section contains representations and warranties that each party to the swap makes to the other. The representations and warranties are deemed to be repeated with each new swap that is governed by the master agreement. The **basic representations** concern corporate authority to enter into the swap agreement and the validity of the agreement. Other representations include the **absence of certain events**, such as the occurrence of an event of default or a termination event, the **absence of litigation** that might threaten the legality, validity, or enforceability of the contract, the **accuracy of financial information**, and the **accuracy of specific information** that is furnished in writing by one party to the other.

10.2.3   Agreements

This section provides for supplemental agreements to furnish documents, excluding tax covenants in the code-based form, as detailed by the parties in the accompanying schedule to the master agreement. These might include such things as the periodic furnishing of financial statements or legal opinions, the provision of "credit support documentation," or other documents.

10.2.4   Events of Default and Termination Events

Events of default indicate that a credit problem has arisen and entitle the nondefaulting party to terminate all swaps governed by the master agreement. Termination events are due to occurrences other than credit problems and allow for the termination of those swaps directly affected by the termination event.

The agreements provide for seven specific events of default, but the parties may specify others if they like. The specific events of default, most of which apply to both parties, are: failure to pay, breach of covenant, credit support default, misrepresentation, default under specified swaps, cross default, and bankruptcy.

Failure to pay refers to any failure by either party to pay an amount that is required under the agreement. A **breach of covenant**, as an event of default, refers to a failure to comply with any covenant of the swap agreement other than the making of a required payment, a tax-related matter, or a failure to give notice that a termination event has occurred. **Credit support default** refers to any default under an applicable credit support document. It only applies to a party if a credit support document is required by that party or on behalf of that party. **Misrepresentation** refers to breach of any representation (other than a tax representation) made in the swap agreement or credit support documentation. **Default under specified swaps** refers to a default that results in the designation or occurrence of a termination event under another swap. **Cross default** refers to a default on some other indebtedness. This event of default can be applied to both parties, only one party, or excluded entirely from the swap agreement by so indicating in the accompanying schedule. The **bankruptcy** event of default is broadly defined to allow for significant variations in the bankruptcy and insolvency laws of the countries covered by the swap agreement.

The agreement specifies certain termination events. These are illegality, a tax event, a tax event upon merger, and a credit event upon merger. An **illegality** is deemed to have occurred if a change in law or regulation makes it impossible for either party to perform its obligations. A **tax event** occurs if a withholding tax is imposed on a swap transaction. In this event, the party required to pay the tax may opt to terminate the swap. A **tax event upon merger** occurs if a merger results in the imposition of a withholding tax on one or more swaps. Only those affected swaps may be terminated. A **credit event upon merger** occurs if a merger results in a deterioration of the creditworthiness of one of the parties. In such an event, the other party may elect to terminate all swaps governed by the master agreement.

10.2.5 Early Termination

Upon the occurrence of an event of default, the nondefaulting party has the right to designate an **early termination date**. In the case of bankruptcy, the termination is automatic. With the exception of bankruptcy, the nondefaulting party must provide notice to the defaulting party as to the early termination date.

In the case of the occurrence of a terminating event, the party that is entitled to designate an early termination date varies with the nature of the terminating event.

As previously mentioned, in the case of an event of default, all swaps governed by the same master agreement are terminated. In the case of a termination event, only the affected swaps are terminated.

Once a notice of early termination has become effective, each party to a terminated swap is released from its obligation to make its required payments under the swap. The parties must then calculate **termination payments**. (The options available to the parties were discussed in Chapter 9.) These termination payment options include the agreement value method, the indemnification method, and the formula method. As also mentioned in Chapter 9, the agreement value method has become nearly universal. The payments may be made on a one-way basis, a two-way basis, or a limited two-way basis.

10.2.6   Transfer

This section of the agreements provides a general prohibition against the **transfer** of rights and obligations under the agreement to other parties. Allowance is made for specifying exceptions to this general prohibition. These exceptions must be detailed in the accompanying schedule. This is the general prohibition against permissive assignment discussed in Chapter 9.

10.2.7   Multibranch Provisions

This section of the agreements allows institutions with multiple branches that operate from several locations to govern all swaps with a single master agreement.

10.2.8   Notices

This section requires that addresses and TELEX and/or Fax numbers for purposes of providing required **notices** be specified in the accompanying schedule. All notices provided must be in writing and sent to the required address, TELEX, or Fax.

10.2.9   Tax Matters

The tax section of the agreements deals with three tax issues: gross up, tax representation, and tax covenants. As a general rule, counterparties are required to make their payments without any withholding or deductions for taxes. However, if a party making a payment is legally required to withhold taxes from the payment, that party is required to gross up the amount of the payment for any amount withheld on account of "indemnifiable taxes." The party is, however, released from its **tax gross up** obligation if the withholding is the result of a breach of a tax-related representation or covenant made by the other party. The parties must specify all applicable tax representations in the accompanying schedule and must agree to give notice of breaches of tax representation (tax covenants).

10.2.10   Credit Support Documentation

The parties should identify in the accompanying schedule all required **credit support documents**. These include guarantees, security agreements, and letters of credit.

10.2.11   Governing Law and Jurisdiction

The agreements require that the parties must specify in the accompanying schedule whether New York law or English law will govern the agreements.

10.2.12   Definitions

This section of the agreements defines the following terms: business day, default rate, interest on unpaid amounts, interest on termination payments, and specified entities. We will define the term "business day" in the next section of this chapter. The **default rate** is the rate of interest, compounded daily, paid by a defaulting party to a nondefaulting party on any unpaid amounts. The nondefaulting party pays a lower rate of interest on any unpaid amounts. In the case of a terminating event, both parties pay a rate of interest lower than the default rate on the amount of their respective termination payments from the early termination date to the due date. The term **specified entities** means different things in different contexts. In each of the contexts in which it is used, the parties must specify the term's meaning in the accompanying schedule.

10.2.13   Confirmations

The agreements require the exchange of **confirmations** that detail the
terms of each new swap entered under the master agreement. In the
code-based form, intended for U.S. dollar interest-rate swaps only,
these confirmations must specify the notional amount, the trade date,
the effective date, the termination date, the fixed-rate payer, the fixed-
rate payment dates, the fixed amount of each payment, the floating-
rate payer, the floating-rate payment dates, the floating rate for the
initial calculation period, the floating-rate option, the designated maturity, the spread (plus or minus), the floating-rate day-count fraction,
the reset dates, compounding (if applicable), and certain other terms as
appropriate.

In the multicurrency form, all of this same information must be
provided, but other information is required as well. This includes the
relevant currencies, initial exchange, final exchange, and so forth.

10.3   MISCELLANEOUS 1986 CODE DEFINITIONS

The 1986 Code defines a great many terms used in swap documentation. Some of the more important of these terms, including many not
used elsewhere in this text, are briefly defined in this section. The
definitions below are not necessarily meant to be precise or complete.
The reader requiring more precision should refer to the ISDA documents listed in the references to this chapter, or to the Code itself,
which forms an appendix to this chapter.

Bond equivalent yield and money market equivalent yield	Yield measures used to standardize rate measures on instruments ordinarily quoted on a bank discount basis.
Business day	Any day other than a Saturday, Sunday, or a day on which commercial banks are required or authorized to be closed in the city of reference. If no city of reference is specified, New York is assumed.

Calculation agent	The swap party (or a third party) designated to determine the applicable floating rate and the corresponding floating- and fixed-rate payments due on the payment dates.
Calculation date	The earliest date for any calculation period for which it is practical for the calculating agent to calculate the payments due on the subsequent payment date.
Calculation period	The period beginning on one period end date and ending on the day just prior to the next period end date.
Designated maturity	The period of time specified as such.
Dollar	A unit of lawful U.S. currency.
Early termination date	A business day on which the parties to a swap will settle via a lump-sum payment following an event of default or a termination event.
Effective date	The date specified as the first date of the term of the swap (i.e., interest begins accruing).
Eurodollar convention	The process for determining payment dates for each payment period. This determination of dates requires allowance for non-banking days in New York and London.
Fixed amount	The amount payable by a fixed-rate payer on a payment date.
Floating amount	The amount payable by a floating-rate payer on a payment date.
Gross payment	The full amount of any required payment. When gross payments are specified, each party is required to make full payment of all amounts due to the other party.

London banking day Any day in which dealings in dollars are transacted in the London interbank market.

Net payment The difference between the payments made by the counterparties to a swap. When net payments are specified, only the higher paying counterparty is required to make a payment. The paying party's payment is equal to the difference between the two parties' gross payments. In the absence of any specification, net payments are assumed.

New York banking day Any day, other than a Saturday, Sunday, or other day on which commercial banks in New York are required or authorized to be closed.

Notional amount The amount specified as such for purposes of calculating the floating- and fixed-rate payments.

Payment date A date that a payment is due. Options allow for delayed payment and early payment. In the event that a payment date would otherwise fall on a nonbanking day in either New York or London, options can be included to allow for payments to be made on a "following banking day," a "modified following banking day," or a "preceding day" basis.

Period end dates Dates on which payment periods end. These may or may not correspond to the payment dates.

Rate cut-off date The last date used in the determination of the relevant rate. The rate cut-off date must precede the period end date for a payment period.

Reference amount

An amount that is representative for a single transaction in the relevant market at the relevant time.

Reference banks

Banks, selected by the calculation agent, in either the London interbank market or New York City, as appropriate, from which rate quotations are obtained in arriving at the relevant rate. Reference banks are used to obtain rates when the floating rate involves LIBOR or prime.

Reference dealers

Dealers selected by the calculation agent for purposes of determining the relevant rate when the floating rate is Treasury bill, certificate of deposit, commercial paper, Federal funds, or bankers acceptances.

Relevant rate

The applicable value for the floating-rate side of a rate swap. The relevant rate is always stated on an annual basis and is determined by prevailing rates on one or more reset dates. The relevant rate may involve a spread over (or under) the prevailing rate.

Reset dates

Specified dates on which the relevant rate is set for the next payment period. When more than one reset date is specified, an averaging of the prevailing rates may be required.

Spread

An amount added to (if positive) or subtracted from (if negative) the prevailing rate to arrive at the relevant rate.

Term

The length of time from the effective date of the swap transaction to the termination date of the swap.

Termination date   The date specified that serves as the last date of the swap agreement.

Trade date   The date on which the parties enter into the rate swap transaction.

10.4 SUMMARY

This chapter has provided a general review of the efforts made to standardize swap documentation and language. Standardization has been greatly enhanced by the efforts of the New York-based ISDA and the London-based BBA. This standardization has greatly reduced the time it takes to finalize a swap transaction by treating each new swap as a supplement to a master agreement. Further, this standardization has reduced the cost of contracting, and enhanced the liquidity of the secondary market in swaps.

The ISDA's efforts began with the publication of the 1985 *Code of Standard Wording, Assumptions and Provisions for Swaps*. This effort continued with a 1986 revision of the Code and eventually led to the 1987 publication of standard form agreements and accompanying support material. The full text of the ISDA's 1986 Code appears as an appendix to this chapter.

REFERENCES AND SUGGESTED READING

Cunningham, D.P. and J.B. Golden, "A Practitioner's Guide to the 1986 Code of Swaps," in *Swap Finance Update*, ed., Boris Antl, London: Euromoney, 1987.

Genova, G. and D. Thompson, "A Guide to Standard Swap Documentation," *Commercial Lending Review*, 3(2), pp. 44-49, Spring, 1988.

ISDA, *1986 Code of Standard Wording, Assumptions and Provisions for Swaps*, International Swap Dealers Association, 1986.

ISDA, *1987 Interest Rate and Currency Exchange Definitions*, International Swap Dealers Association, 1987.

ISDA, *User's Guide to the Standard Form Agreements*, 1987 Edition, International Swap Dealers Association, 1987.

Stoakes, C. "Standards Make Swaps Faster," *Euromoney*, November 1985.

CHAPTER 10

APPENDIX

Code of Standard Wording, Assumptions, and Provisions for Swaps: 1986 Edition*

CODE OF STANDARD WORDING, ASSUMPTIONS
AND PROVISIONS FOR SWAPS, 1986 EDITION

Any or all provisions of this Code may be incorporated into a document by wording in the document indicating that, or the extent to which, the document is subject to the Code of Standard Wording, Assumptions and Provisions for Swaps, 1986 Edition (as published by the International Swap Dealers Association, Inc.). All provisions of this Code so incorporated in a document will be applicable to that document unless otherwise provided in that document, and all terms defined in this Code and used in provisions of this Code that are incorporated by reference in a document will have the respective meanings set forth in this Code unless otherwise provided in that document. Any term used in a document will, when combined with the name of a party, have meaning in respect of the named party only.

The parties to a Rate Swap Agreement may, but need not, include in the Rate Swap Agreement any of the matters or terms covered by this Code, and a Rate Swap Agreement need not be limited to the matters or terms covered by this Code.

ARTICLE 1
CERTAIN GENERAL DEFINITIONS

Section 1.1. Rate Swap Agreement. "Rate Swap Agreement" means an agreement (however designated) governing one or more Rate Swap Transactions.

Section 1.2. Rate Swap Transaction. "Rate Swap Transaction" means a rate exchange or swap transaction.

Section 1.3. Dollar. "Dollar" and "$" each means the lawful currency of the United States of America.

Section 1.4. New York Banking Day. "New York Banking Day" means any day other than a Saturday, a Sunday or a day on which commercial banks in New York City are required or authorized to be closed.

Section 1.5. London Banking Day. "London Banking Day" means any day on which dealings in deposits in Dollars are transacted in the London interbank market.

Section 1.6. Business Day. "Business Day" means any day other than a Saturday, a Sunday or a day on which commercial banks in the city specified by the parties (or, if a city is not specified, New York City) are required or authorized to be closed.

ARTICLE 2
PARTIES

Section 2.1. Fixed Rate Payor. "Fixed Rate Payor" means, in respect of a Rate Swap Transaction, a party obligated to make payments from time to time during the Term of the Rate Swap Transaction of amounts calculated by reference to a fixed per annum rate.

Section 2.2. Floating Rate Payor. "Floating Rate Payor" means, in respect of a Rate Swap Transaction, a party obligated to make payments from time to time during the Term of the Rate Swap Transaction of amounts calculated by reference to a floating per annum rate.

ARTICLE 3
TERM

Section 3.1. Term. "Term" means the period commencing on the Effective Date of a Rate Swap Transaction and ending on the Termination Date of the Rate Swap Transaction.

Section 3.2. Effective Date. "Effective Date" means the date specified as such for a Rate Swap Transaction, which date is the first day of the Term of the Rate Swap Transaction.

Section 3.3. Termination Date. "Termination Date" means the date specified as such for a Rate Swap Transaction, which date is the last day of the Term of the Rate Swap Transaction.

Section 3.4. Trade Date. "Trade Date" means, in respect of a Rate Swap Transaction, the date on which the parties enter into the Rate Swap Transaction.

ARTICLE 4
CERTAIN DEFINITIONS RELATING TO PAYMENTS

Section 4.1. Fixed Amount. "Fixed Amount" means, in respect of a Rate Swap Transaction, an amount that, subject to Sections 9.2, 9.3 and 10.2 of this Code, is payable by a Fixed Rate Payor on an applicable Payment Date and determined by reference to a Calculation Period as provided in Article 5 of this Code.

Section 4.2. Floating Amount. "Floating Amount" means, in respect of a Rate Swap Transaction, an amount that, subject to Sections 9.2, 9.3 and 10.2 of this Code, is payable by a Floating Rate Payor on an applicable Payment Date and determined by reference to a Floating Rate Option and a Calculation Period as provided in Article 6 of this Code.

Section 4.3. Notional Amount. "Notional Amount" means, in respect of any Calculation Period for a Rate Swap Transaction, the amount specified as such for the Rate Swap Transaction.

Section 4.4. Eurodollar Convention. "Eurodollar Convention" means, with respect to either Payment Dates or Period End Dates for a Rate Swap Transaction, that such Payment Dates or Period End Dates will be each day during the Term of the Rate Swap Transaction that numerically corresponds to the preceding applicable Payment Date or Period End Date, as the case may be, in the calendar month that is the specified number of months after the month in which the preceding applicable Payment Date or Period End Date occurred (or, in the case of the first applicable Payment Date or Period End Date, the day that numerically corresponds to the Effective Date in the calendar month that is the specified number of months after the month in which the Effective Date occurred), except that (a) if there is not any such numerically corresponding day in the calendar month in which a Payment Date or Period End Date, as the case may be, should occur, then the Payment Date or Period

End Date will be the last day that is a New York Banking Day and a London Banking Day in that month, (b) if a Payment Date or Period End Date, as the case may be, would otherwise fall on a day that is not a New York Banking Day and a London Banking Day, then the Payment Date or Period End Date will be the first following day that is a New York Banking Day and a London Banking Day unless that day falls in the next calendar month, in which case the Payment Date or Period End Date will be the first preceding day that is a New York Banking Day and a London Banking Day and (c) if the preceding applicable Payment Date or Period End Date, as the case may be, occurred on the last day in a calendar month that was a New York Banking Day and a London Banking Day, then all subsequent applicable Payment Dates or Period End Dates, as the case may be, prior to the Termination Date will be the last day that is a New York Banking Day and a London Banking Day in the month that is the specified number of months after the month in which the preceding applicable Payment Date or Period End Date occurred.

Section 4.5. Payment Date. "Payment Date" means, in respect of a Rate Swap Transaction,

(a) if "Delayed Payment" or "Early Payment" is not specified for the Rate Swap Transaction and Payment Dates are specified or otherwise predetermined for the Rate Swap Transaction, each day during the Term of the Rate Swap Transaction so specified or predetermined and the Termination Date;

(b) if "Delayed Payment" or "Early Payment" is not specified for the Rate Swap Transaction and the parties specify that Payment Dates will occur in accordance with the Eurodollar Convention at a specified interval of calendar months, each day during the Term of the Rate Swap Transaction at the specified interval, determined in accordance with the Eurodollar Convention, and the Termination Date;

(c) if "Delayed Payment" is specified for the Rate Swap Transaction and Period End Dates are established for the Rate Swap Transaction, each day that is five New York Banking Days after an applicable Period End Date or after the Termination Date; or

(d) if "Early Payment" and a period of days are specified for the Rate Swap Transaction and Period End Dates are established for the Rate Swap Transaction, each day that is the specified number of days before an applicable Period End Date or before the Termination Date;

except that, in the case of subsections (a), (c) and (d) above, an adjustment will be made if any Payment Date would otherwise fall on a day that is not a New York Banking Day (or, if a party to the Rate Swap Transaction is obligated to pay Floating Amounts calculated by reference to any "LIBOR" Floating Rate Option, any Payment Date would otherwise fall on a day that is not a New York Banking Day and a London Banking Day), so that

(e) if (i) the "Following Banking Day" convention is specified for the Rate Swap Transaction or (ii) an applicable convention is not specified, the Payment Date will be the first following day that is a New York Banking Day (and, if any "LIBOR" Floating Rate Option applies to the Rate Swap Transaction, a London Banking Day);

(f) if the "Modified Following Banking Day" convention is specified for the Rate Swap Transaction, the Payment Date will be the first following day that is a

New York Banking Day (and, if any "LIBOR" Floating Rate Option applies to the Rate Swap Transaction, a London Banking Day) unless that day falls in the next calendar month, in which case the Payment Date will be the first preceding day that is a New York Banking Day (and, if any "LIBOR" Floating Rate Option applies to the Rate Swap Transaction, a London Banking Day); or

(g) if the "Preceding Banking Day" convention is specified for the Rate Swap Transaction, the Payment Date will be the first preceding day that is a New York Banking Day (and, if any "LIBOR" Floating Rate Option applies to the Rate Swap Transaction, a London Banking Day).

Section 4.6. Period End Date. "Period End Date" means, in respect of a Rate Swap Transaction,

(a) if Period End Dates are not established for the Rate Swap Transaction, each Payment Date during the Term of the Rate Swap Transaction;

(b) if Period End Dates are specified or otherwise predetermined for the Rate Swap Transaction, each day during the Term so specified or predetermined; or

(c) if it is specified for the Rate Swap Transaction that Period End Dates will occur in accordance with the Eurodollar Convention and an interval of calendar months is specified, and if "Delayed Payment" or "Early Payment" is specified for the Rate Swap Transaction, each day during the Term at the specified interval, determined in accordance with the Eurodollar Convention;

except that, in the case of subsection (b) above, an adjustment may be made if any Period End Date would otherwise fall on a day that is not a New York Banking Day (or, if a party to the Rate Swap Transaction is obligated to pay Floating Amounts calculated by reference to any "LIBOR" Floating Rate Option, any Period End Date would otherwise fall on a day that is not a New York Banking Day and a London Banking Day), so that

(d) if "No Adjustment of Period End Dates" is specified for the Rate Swap Transaction, an adjustment will not be made, notwithstanding that the Period End Date occurs on a day that is not a New York Banking Day (or a London Banking Day);

(e) if (i) the "Following Banking Day" convention is specified for the Rate Swap Transaction or (ii) an applicable convention is not specified, the Period End Date will be the first following day that is a New York Banking Day (and, if any "LIBOR" Floating Rate Option applies to the Rate Swap Transaction, a London Banking Day);

(f) if the "Modified Following Banking Day" convention is specified for the Rate Swap Transaction, the Period End Date will be the first following day that is a New York Banking Day (and, if any "LIBOR" Floating Rate Option applies to the Rate Swap Transaction, a London Banking Day) unless that day falls in the next calendar month, in which case the Period End Date will be the first preceding day that is a New York Banking Day (and, if any "LIBOR" Floating Rate Option applies to the Rate Swap Transaction, a London Banking Day); or

(g) if the "Preceding Banking Day" convention is specified for the Rate Swap Transaction, the Period End Date will be the first preceding day that is a

New York Banking Day (and, if any "LIBOR" Floating Rate Option applies to the Rate Swap Transaction, a London Banking Day).

Section 4.7. Calculation Period. "Calculation Period" means, in respect of a Rate Swap Transaction, each period from, and including, one Period End Date to, but excluding, the next following applicable Period End Date during the Term of the Rate Swap Transaction, except that (a) the initial Calculation Period for each party to the Rate Swap Transaction will commence on, and include, the Effective Date, and (b) the final Calculation Period for each party to the Rate Swap Transaction will end on, but exclude, the Termination Date.

Section 4.8. Calculation Agent. "Calculation Agent" means the party to a Rate Swap Transaction (or a third party) designated as such for the Rate Swap Transaction and responsible for (a) calculating the applicable Floating Rate, if any, for each Calculation Period or Compounding Period, (b) calculating any Floating Amount payable in respect of each Calculation Period, (c) calculating any Fixed Amount payable in respect of each Calculation Period, (d) giving notice to the parties to the Rate Swap Transaction on the Calculation Date for each Calculation Period, specifying (i) the date for payment in respect of such Calculation Period, (ii) the party or parties required to make the payment or payments then due, (iii) the amount or amounts of the payment or payments then due and (iv) reasonable details as to how such amount or amounts were determined and (e) if, after such notice is given, there is a change in the number of days in the relevant Calculation Period and the amount or amounts of the payment or payments due in respect of that period, promptly giving the parties to the Rate Swap Transaction notice of such changes, with reasonable details as to how such changes were determined. Whenever the Calculation Agent is required to select banks or dealers for the purpose of calculating a Floating Rate, the Calculation Agent will make such selection in good faith for the purpose of obtaining a representative rate that will reasonably reflect conditions prevailing at the time in the relevant market.

Section 4.9. Calculation Date. "Calculation Date" means, for any Calculation Period, the earliest day on which it is practicable to provide the notice that the Calculation Agent is required to give in respect of that Calculation Period, and in no event later than the close of business on the Business Day next preceding the Payment Date in respect of that Calculation Period.

ARTICLE 5
FIXED AMOUNTS

Section 5.1. Calculation of a Fixed Amount. The Fixed Amount for each applicable Payment Date in respect of any Calculation Period will be

(a) if an amount is specified for the Rate Swap Transaction as the Fixed Amount payable in respect of that Calculation Period, such amount; or

(b) if an amount is not specified for the Rate Swap Transaction as the Fixed Amount payable in respect of that Calculation Period, an amount calculated on a formula basis in respect of that Calculation Period as follows:

$$\begin{matrix} \text{Fixed} \\ \text{Amount} \end{matrix} = \begin{matrix} \text{Notional} \\ \text{Amount} \end{matrix} \times \begin{matrix} \text{Fixed} \\ \text{Rate} \end{matrix} \times \begin{matrix} \text{Fixed Rate} \\ \text{Day Count} \\ \text{Fraction} \end{matrix}$$

Section 5.2. Certain Definitions Relating to Fixed Amounts. For purposes of the calculation of a Fixed Amount:

(a) "Fixed Rate" means the per annum rate specified as such for the Rate Swap Transaction, expressed as a decimal.

(b) "Fixed Rate Day Count Fraction" means

(i) if (A) "Actual/365" is specified for a Rate Swap Transaction as the applicable Fixed Rate Day Count Fraction or (B) an applicable Fixed Rate Day Count Fraction is not specified, the actual number of days in the Calculation Period in respect of which payment is being made divided by 365 (or, if any portion of that Calculation Period falls in a leap year, the sum of (X) the actual number of days in that portion of the Calculation Period falling in a leap year divided by 366 plus (Y) the actual number of days in that portion of the Calculation Period falling in a nonleap year divided by 365);

(ii) if "Actual/360" is specified for a Rate Swap Transaction as the applicable Fixed Rate Day Count Fraction, the actual number of days in the Calculation Period in respect of which payment is being made divided by 360; or

(iii) if "30/360" or "360/360" is specified for a Rate Swap Transaction as the applicable Fixed Rate Day Count Fraction, the number of days in the Calculation Period in respect of which payment is being made (calculated on the basis of a year of 360 days with 12 30-day months) divided by 360.

ARTICLE 6

FLOATING AMOUNTS

Section 6.1. Calculation of a Floating Amount. The Floating Amount for each applicable Payment Date in respect of any Calculation Period for a Rate Swap Transaction will be

(a) if Compounding is specified, an amount equal to the sum of the Compounding Period Amounts for each of the Compounding Periods in that Calculation Period; or

(b) if Compounding is not specified, an amount calculated on a formula basis in respect of that Calculation Period as follows:

$$
\begin{array}{c}
\text{Floating} \\
\text{Amount}
\end{array}
=
\begin{array}{c}
\text{Notional} \\
\text{Amount}
\end{array}
\times
\begin{array}{c}
\text{Floating} \\
\text{Rate} \\
\pm \text{ Spread}
\end{array}
\times
\begin{array}{c}
\text{Floating} \\
\text{Rate} \\
\text{Day Count} \\
\text{Fraction}
\end{array}
$$

Section 6.2. Calculation of a Compounding Period Amount. The Compounding Period Amount for any Compounding Period for a Rate Swap Transaction will be an amount calculated on a formula basis in respect of that Compounding Period as follows:

$$
\begin{array}{c}
\text{Compounding} \\
\text{Period} \\
\text{Amount}
\end{array}
=
\begin{array}{c}
\text{Adjusted} \\
\text{Notional} \\
\text{Amount}
\end{array}
\times
\begin{array}{c}
\text{Floating} \\
\text{Rate} \\
\pm \text{ Spread}
\end{array}
\times
\begin{array}{c}
\text{Floating} \\
\text{Rate} \\
\text{Day Count} \\
\text{Fraction}
\end{array}
$$

Section 6.3. Certain Definitions Relating to Floating Amounts. For purposes of the calculation of a Floating Amount:

(a) "Floating Rate" means, in respect of any Calculation Period or Compounding Period for a Rate Swap Transaction, a per annum rate, expressed as a decimal, equal to

(i) if a per annum rate is specified for the Rate Swap Transaction as the Floating Rate applicable in respect of that Calculation Period or Compounding Period, the Floating Rate so specified;

(ii) if only one Reset Date is established for the Rate Swap Transaction during (or with respect to) that Calculation Period or Compounding Period, the Relevant Rate for that Reset Date;

(iii) if more than one Reset Date is established for the Rate Swap Transaction during (or with respect to) that Calculation Period or Compounding Period and the "Unweighted Average Rate" method of calculation is specified, the arithmetic mean of the Relevant Rates for each of these Reset Dates;

(iv) if more than one Reset Date is established for the Rate Swap Transaction during (or with respect to) that Calculation Period or Compounding Period and the "Weighted Average Rate" method of calculation is specified, the arithmetic mean of the Relevant Rates in effect for each day in that Calculation Period or Compounding Period, calculated by multiplying each Relevant Rate by the number of days such Relevant Rate is in effect, determining the sum of such products and dividing such sum by the number of days in the Calculation Period or Compounding Period; or

(v) if more than one Reset Date is established for the Rate Swap Transaction during (or with respect to) that Calculation Period or Compounding Period and neither the "Unweighted Average Rate" nor the "Weighted Average Rate" method of calculation is specified, a Floating Rate determined (A) as if "Weighted Average Rate" had been specified as the applicable method of calculation if the applicable Floating Rate Option is a "Prime" or "Federal Funds" Floating Rate Option and (B) as if "Unweighted Average Rate" had been specified as the applicable method of calculation if any other Floating Rate Option is applicable.

(b) "Reset Date" means each day specified as such (or determined pursuant to a method specified for such purpose) for the Rate Swap Transaction, except that an adjustment will be made if any Reset Date would fall on a day that is not a New York Banking Day (or, if the Floating Amount is being calculated by reference to any "LIBOR" Floating Rate Option, any Reset Date would fall on a day that is not a New York Banking Day and a London Banking Day), so that the Reset Date will be the first preceding day that is a New York Banking Day (and, if the Floating Amount is being calculated by reference to any "LIBOR" Floating Rate Option, a London Banking Day).

(c) "Relevant Rate" means (subject to the effect of any applicable Rate Cut-off Date), for any day, a per annum rate, expressed as a decimal, equal to

(i) if such day is a Reset Date, the rate determined with respect to that day for the specified Floating Rate Option as provided in Article 7 of this Code; or

(ii) if such day is not a Reset Date, the Relevant Rate determined pursuant to clause (i) above for the next preceding Reset Date.

(d) "Rate Cut-off Date" means each day specified as such (or determined pursuant to a method specified for such purpose) for the Rate Swap Transaction. The Relevant Rate for each Reset Date in the period from, and including, a Rate Cut-off Date to, but excluding, the next applicable Period End Date (or, in the case of the last Calculation Period, the Termination Date) will (solely for purposes of calculating the Floating Amount payable on the next applicable Payment Date) be deemed to be the Relevant Rate in effect on that Rate Cut-off Date.

(e) "Spread" means the per annum rate, if any, specified as such for the Rate Swap Transaction (expressed as a decimal). For purposes of determining a Floating Amount or a Compounding Period Amount , if positive the Spread will be added to the Floating Rate and if negative the Spread will be subtracted from the Floating Rate.

(f) "Floating Rate Day Count Fraction" means, in respect of any Calculation Period or Compounding Period, (i) if any "Treasury Bill" Floating Rate Option is specified as the applicable Floating Rate Option, the actual number of days in that Calculation Period or Compounding Period divided by 365 (or, if any portion of that Calculation Period or Compounding Period falls in a leap year, the sum of (A) the actual number of days in that portion of the Calculation Period or Compounding Period falling in a leap year divided by 366 plus (B) the actual number of days in that portion of the Calculation Period or Compounding Period falling in a nonleap year divided by 365) and (ii) in all other cases, the actual number of days in that Calculation Period or Compounding Period divided by 360.

Section 6.4.   Certain Additional Definitions Relating to Compounding.   For purposes of the calculation of a Floating Amount where "Compounding" is specified:

(a) "Compounding Period" means, in respect of a Calculation Period, each period from, and including, one Compounding Date to, but excluding, the next following applicable Compounding Date during that Calculation Period, except that (i) each initial Compounding Period for a Rate Swap Transaction will commence on, and include, the Effective Date and (ii) each final Compounding Period for a Rate Swap Transaction will end on, but exclude, the Termination Date.

(b) "Compounding Date" means each day during the Term of a Rate Swap Transaction specified as such (or determined pursuant to a method specified for such purpose) for the Rate Swap Transaction, except that, if the Period End Date for any Calculation Period is subject to adjustment in accordance with Section 4.6 of this Code, each applicable Compounding Date in that Calculation Period will be subject to adjustment in the same manner as such Period End Date.

(c) "Adjusted Notional Amount" means (i) in respect of the first Compounding Period in any Calculation Period, the Notional Amount for that Calculation Period and (ii) in respect of each succeeding Compounding Period in that Calculation Period, an amount equal to the sum of the Notional Amount for that Calculation Period and the Compounding Period Amounts for each of the previous Compounding Periods in that Calculation Period.

ARTICLE 7

CALCULATION OF RATES FOR CERTAIN FLOATING RATE OPTIONS

Section 7.1.   Floating Rate Options.   For purposes of determining a Relevant Rate:

(a) "LIBOR" means that the rate in respect of a Reset Date will be determined on the basis of the offered rates for deposits in Dollars for a period of the Designated Maturity commencing on that Reset Date which appear on the Reuters Screen LIBO Page as of 11:00 a.m., London time, on the day that is two London Banking Days preceding that Reset Date. If at least two such offered rates appear on the Reuters Screen LIBO Page, the rate in respect of that Reset Date will be the arithmetic mean of such offered rates. If fewer than two offered rates appear, the rate in respect of that Reset Date will be determined as if the parties had specified "LIBOR (Reference Banks)" as the applicable Floating Rate Option.

(b) "LIBOR (Reference Banks)" means that the rate in respect of a Reset Date will be determined on the basis of the rates at which deposits in Dollars are offered by the Reference Banks at approximately 11:00 a.m., London time, on the day that is two London Banking Days preceding that Reset Date to prime banks in the London interbank market for a period of the Designated Maturity commencing on that Reset Date and in a Representative Amount. The Calculation Agent will request the principal London office of each of the Reference Banks to provide a quotation of its rate. If at least two such quotations are provided, the rate in respect of that Reset Date will be the arithmetic mean of the quotations. If fewer than two quotations are provided as requested, the rate in respect of that Reset Date will be the arithmetic mean of the rates quoted by major banks in New York City, selected by the Calculation Agent, at approximately 11:00 a.m., New York City time, on that Reset Date for loans in Dollars to leading European banks for a period of the Designated Maturity commencing on that Reset Date and in a Representative Amount.

(c) "Prime" means that the rate for a Reset Date will be the rate set forth in H.15(519) for that day opposite the caption "Bank Prime Loan". If on the Calculation Date for a Calculation Period such rate for a Reset Date in that Calculation Period is not yet published in H.15(519), the rate for that Reset Date will be the arithmetic mean of the rates of interest publicly announced by each bank that appears on the Reuters Screen NYMF Page as such bank's prime rate or base lending rate as in effect for that Reset Date as quoted on the Reuters Screen NYMF Page on that Reset Date or, if fewer than four such rates appear on the Reuters Screen NYMF Page for that Reset Date, the rate determined as if the parties had specified "Prime (Reference Banks)" as the applicable Floating Rate Option.

(d) "Prime (Reference Banks)" means that the rate for a Reset Date will be the arithmetic mean of the rates of interest publicly announced by each Reference Bank as its prime rate or base lending rate as in effect for that day. Each change in the prime rate or base lending rate of any bank so announced by such bank will be effective as of the effective date of the announcement or, if no effective date is specified, as of the date of the announcement.

(e) "Treasury Bill" means that the rate for a Reset Date on which United States Treasury bills are auctioned will be the rate set forth in H.15(519) for that day opposite the Designated Maturity under the caption "U.S. Government Securities/Treasury Bills/Auction Average (Investment)". If on the Calculation Date for a Calculation Period United States Treasury bills of the Designated Maturity have been auctioned on a Reset Date during that Calculation Period but such rate for such Reset Date is not yet published in H.15(519), the rate for that Reset Date will be the Bond Equivalent Yield of the auction average rate for these Treasury bills as announced by the United States Department of the Treasury. If United States Treasury bills of the Designated Maturity are not auctioned during any period of seven consecutive calendar days ending on and including any Friday and a Reset Date would have occurred if such Treasury bills had been auctioned during that seven-day period, a Reset Date will be deemed to have occurred on the day during that seven-day period on which such Treasury bills would have been auctioned in accordance with the usual practices of the United States Department of the Treasury, and the rate for that Reset Date will be determined as if the parties had specified "Treasury Bill (Secondary Market)" as the applicable Floating Rate Option (unless it is indicated for the Rate Swap Transaction that weeks in which United States Treasury bills of the Designated Maturity are not auctioned will be ignored, in which case there will not be any Reset Date during that seven-day period).

(f) "Treasury Bill (Secondary Market)" means that the rate for a Reset Date will be the Bond Equivalent Yield of the rate set forth in H.15(519) for that day opposite the Designated Maturity under the caption "U.S. Government Securities/Treasury Bills/Secondary Market". If on the Calculation Date for a Calculation Period such rate for a Reset Date in that Calculation Period is not yet published in H.15(519), the rate for that Reset Date will be the Bond Equivalent Yield of the arithmetic mean of the secondary market bid rates of the Reference Dealers as of approximately 3:30 p.m., New York City time, on that day for the issue of United States Treasury bills with a remaining maturity closest to the Designated Maturity.

(g) "CD" means that the rate for a Reset Date will be the rate set forth in H.15(519) for that day opposite the Designated Maturity under the caption "CDs (Secondary Market)". If on the Calculation Date for a Calculation Period such rate for a Reset Date in that Calculation Period is not yet published in H.15(519), the rate for that Reset Date will be the rate set forth in Composite 3:30 P.M. Quotations for U.S. Government Securities for that day in respect of the Designated Maturity under the caption "Certificates of Deposit". If on the Calculation Date for a Calculation Period the appropriate rate for a Reset Date in that Calculation Period is not yet published in either H.15(519) or Composite 3:30 P.M. Quotations for U.S. Government Securities, the rate for that Reset Date will be determined as if the parties had specified "CD (Reference Dealers)" as the applicable Floating Rate Option.

(h) "CD (Reference Dealers)" means that the rate for a Reset Date will be the arithmetic mean of the secondary market offered rates of the Reference Dealers as of 10:00 a.m., New York City time, on that day for negotiable certificates of deposit of major United States money market banks with a remaining maturity closest to the Designated Maturity and in a Representative Amount.

(i) "Commercial Paper" means that the rate for a Reset Date will be the Money Market Yield of the rate set forth in H.15(519) for that day opposite the Designated Maturity under the caption "Commercial Paper". If on the Calculation Date for a Calculation Period such rate for a Reset Date in that Calculation Period is not yet published in H.15(519), the rate for that Reset Date will be the Money Market Yield of the rate set forth in Composite 3:30 P.M. Quotations for U.S. Government Securities for that day in respect of the Designated Maturity under the caption "Commercial Paper" (with a Designated Maturity of one month or three months being deemed to be equivalent to a Designated Maturity of 30 days or 90 days, respectively). If on the Calculation Date for a Calculation Period the appropriate rate for a Reset Date in that Calculation Period is not yet published in either H.15(519) or Composite 3:30 P.M. Quotations for U.S. Government Securities, the rate for that Reset Date will be determined as if the parties had specified "Commercial Paper (Reference Dealers)" as the applicable Floating Rate Option.

(j) "Commercial Paper (Reference Dealers)" means that the rate for a Reset Date will be the Money Market Yield of the arithmetic mean of the offered rates of the Reference Dealers as of 11:00 a.m., New York City time, on that day for commercial paper of the Designated Maturity placed for industrial issuers whose bond rating is "Aa" or the equivalent from a nationally recognized rating agency.

(k) "Federal Funds" means that the rate for a Reset Date will be the rate set forth in H.15(519) for that day opposite the caption "Federal Funds (Effective)". If on the Calculation Date for a Calculation Period such rate for a

Reset Date in that Calculation Period is not yet published in H.15 (519), the rate for that Reset Date will be the rate set forth in Composite 3:30 P.M. Quotations for U.S. Government Securities for that day under the caption "Federal Funds/ Effective Rate". If on the Calculation Date for a Calculation Period the appropriate rate for a Reset Date in that Calculation Period is not yet published in either H.15 (519) or Composite 3:30 P.M. Quotations for U.S. Government Securities, the rate for that Reset Date will be determined as if the parties had specified "Federal Funds (Reference Dealers)" as the applicable Floating Rate Option.

(l) "Federal Funds (Reference Dealers)" means that the rate for a Reset Date will be the arithmetic mean of the rates for the last transaction in overnight Federal funds arranged by each Reference Dealer prior to 9:00 a.m., New York City time, on that day.

(m) "Bankers Acceptance" means that the rate for a Reset Date will be the Money Market Yield of the rate set forth in H.15 (519) for that day opposite the Designated Maturity under the caption "Bankers Acceptances (Top Rated)". If on the Calculation Date for a Calculation Period such rate for a Reset Date in that Calculation Period is not yet published in H.15 (519), the rate for that Reset Date will be determined as if the parties had specified "Bankers Acceptance (Reference Dealers)" as the applicable Floating Rate Option.

(n) "Bankers Acceptance (Reference Dealers)" means that the rate for a Reset Date will be the Money Market Yield of the arithmetic mean of the offered rates of the Reference Dealers as of the close of business in New York City on that day for top-rated bankers acceptances of the Designated Maturity and in a Representative Amount.

Section 7.2. Certain Published and Displayed Sources.

(a) "H.15 (519)" means the weekly statistical release designated as such, or any successor publication, published by the Board of Governors of the Federal Reserve System.

(b) "Composite 3:30 P.M. Quotations for U.S. Government Securities" means the daily statistical release designated as such, or any successor publication, published by the Federal Reserve Bank of New York.

(c) "Reuters Screen LIBO Page" means the display designated as page "LIBO" on the Reuter Monitor Money Rates Service (or such other page as may replace the LIBO page on that service for the purpose of displaying London interbank offered rates of major banks).

(d) "Reuters Screen NYMF Page" means the display designated as page "NYMF" on the Reuter Monitor Money Rates Service (or such other page as may replace the NYMF page on that service for the purpose of displaying prime rates or base lending rates of major United States banks).

Section 7.3. Certain General Definitions Relating to Floating Rate Options.

(a) "Representative Amount" means, for purposes of any Floating Rate Option for which a Representative Amount is relevant, an amount that is representative for a single transaction in the relevant market at the relevant time.

(b) "Designated Maturity" means the period of time specified as such for a Rate Swap Transaction.

(c) "Reference Banks" means (i) for purposes of the "LIBOR (Reference Banks)" Floating Rate Option, four major banks in the London interbank market and (ii) for purposes of the "Prime (Reference Banks)" Floating Rate Option, three major banks in New York City, in each case selected by the Calculation Agent.

(d) "Reference Dealers" means (i) for purposes of the "Treasury Bill (Secondary Market)" Floating Rate Option, three primary United States Government securities dealers in New York City, (ii) for purposes of the "CD (Reference Dealers)" Floating Rate Option, three leading nonbank dealers in negotiable Dollar certificates of deposit in New York City, (iii) for purposes of the "Commercial Paper (Reference Dealers)" Floating Rate Option, three leading dealers of commercial paper in New York City, (iv) for purposes of the "Federal Funds (Reference Dealers)" Floating Rate Option, three leading brokers of Federal funds transactions in New York City and (v) for purposes of the "Bankers Acceptance (Reference Dealers)" Floating Rate Option, three leading dealers of bankers acceptances in New York City, in each case selected by the Calculation Agent.

(e) "Bond Equivalent Yield" means, in respect of any security with a maturity of six months or less, the rate for which is quoted on a bank discount basis, a yield (expressed as a percentage) calculated in accordance with the following formula:

$$\text{Bond Equivalent Yield} = \frac{D \times N}{360 - (D \times M)} \times 100$$

where "D" refers to the per annum rate for the security, quoted on a bank discount basis and expressed as a decimal; "N" refers to 365 or 366, as the case may be; and "M" refers to, if the Designated Maturity approximately corresponds to the length of the Calculation Period in respect of which the Bond Equivalent Yield is being calculated, the actual number of days in that Calculation Period and, otherwise, the actual number of days in the period from, and including, the applicable Reset Date to, but excluding, the day that numerically corresponds to that Reset Date (or, if there is not any such numerically corresponding day, the last day) in the calendar month that is the number of months corresponding to the Designated Maturity after the month in which that Reset Date occurred.

(f) "Money Market Yield" means, in respect of any security with a maturity of six months or less, the rate for which is quoted on a bank discount basis, a yield (expressed as a percentage) calculated in accordance with the following formula:

$$\text{Money Market Yield} = \frac{D \times 360}{360 - (D \times M)} \times 100$$

where "D" refers to the per annum rate for the security, quoted on a bank discount basis and expressed as a decimal; and "M" refers to, if the Designated Maturity approximately corresponds to the length of the Calculation Period in respect of which the Money Market Yield is being calculated, the actual number of days in that Calculation Period and, otherwise, the actual number of days in the period from, and including, the applicable Reset Date to, but excluding, the day that numerically corresponds to that Reset Date (or, if there is not any such numerically corresponding day, the last day) in the calendar month that is the number of months corresponding to the Designated Maturity after the month in which that Reset Date occurred.

Section 7.4. Corrections to Published and Displayed Rates. For purposes of determining the Relevant Rate for any day

(a) in any case where the Relevant Rate for a day is based on information obtained from any published or displayed source (including, without limitation, H.15(519) or Composite 3:30 P.M. Quotations for U.S. Government Securities), that Relevant Rate will be subject to the corrections, if any, to that information subsequently published or displayed by that source within 30 days of that day;

(b) in any case where the Relevant Rate for a day is based on information obtained from any source used because H.15(519) is not yet available, that Relevant Rate will (except in the case of rates based on quotations from Reference Banks or Reference Dealers) be subject to correction based upon the applicable rate, if any, subsequently published in H.15(519) within 30 days of that day; and

(c) in the event that a Fixed Rate Payor or Floating Rate Payor for any Rate Swap Transaction notifies the other party to the Rate Swap Transaction of any correction referred to in subsection (a) or subsection (b) above no later than 10 New York Banking Days after the expiration of the 30-day period referred to in such subsection, an appropriate amount will be payable as a result of such correction (whether such correction is made or such notice is given before or after the Termination Date of the Rate Swap Transaction), together with interest on that amount at a rate computed on the basis of the "Federal Funds" Floating Rate Option with daily Reset Dates for the period from, and including, the day on which, based on such correction, a payment in the incorrect amount was first made to, but excluding, the day of payment of the refund or payment resulting from such correction.

ARTICLE 8
ROUNDING

All percentages resulting from any calculations referred to in this Code will be rounded upwards, if necessary, to the next higher one hundred-thousandth of a percentage point (*e.g.*, 9.876541% (or .09876541) being rounded to 9.87655% (or .0987655)), and all Dollar amounts used in or resulting from such calculations will be rounded to the nearest cent (with one half cent being rounded up).

ARTICLE 9
GROSS PAYMENTS AND NET PAYMENTS

Section 9.1. Gross Payments. "Gross Payments" means that, subject to Section 10.2 of this Code, each Fixed Amount and each Floating Amount is to be paid in full on the applicable Payment Date.

Section 9.2. Net Payments. "Net Payments" means that, subject to Section 10.2 of this Code, (a) on any Payment Date when amounts would otherwise be payable in respect of a Rate Swap Transaction by each of two parties to the other, neither party will be obligated to make a payment of any such amount to the other party, but if the amount that would have been payable by one party exceeds the amount that would have been payable by the other party, the party by which the larger amount would have been payable will be obligated to pay to the other party the excess of the larger amount over the smaller amount and (b) on any Payment Date when a Fixed Amount or Floating Amount would be payable in respect of a Rate Swap Transaction by only one party, such amount is to be paid in full by that party.

Section 9.3. Net Payments—Corresponding Payment Dates. "Net Payments—Corresponding Payment Dates" means that "Net Payments" will be applicable and that, subject to Section 10.2 of this Code, on any day when amounts would (after giving effect to Section 9.2 of this Code) otherwise be payable under a Rate Swap Agreement by each of two parties to the other, neither party will be obligated to make a payment of any such amount to the other party, but if the aggregate amount that would have been payable by one party exceeds the aggregate amount that would have been payable by the other party, the party by which the larger aggregate amount would have been payable will be obligated to pay to the other party the excess of the larger aggregate amount over the smaller aggregate amount.

Section 9.4. Payment Basis If Not Specified. If a payment basis is not specified for a Rate Swap Transaction, payments will be made as if "Net Payments" had been specified.

ARTICLE 10

PAYMENTS

Section 10.1. Payment Procedures. Payments in respect of a Rate Swap Transaction will be timely if made in same day funds not later than 2:00 p.m., local time at the designated place of payment, on the day on which they are due. Any amount due on a day on which banks are not open for business in the designated place of payment will be payable (without interest) on the first following day on which banks are open in that place.

Section 10.2. Conditions Precedent. Each obligation of each party to a Rate Swap Agreement to pay any amount due under the Rate Swap Agreement in respect of any Calculation Period is subject to (a) the condition precedent that no Event of Default (as defined in Section 11.2 of this Code), or event that with the giving of notice or lapse of time (or both) would become an Event of Default, in respect of the other party has occurred and is continuing and (b) each other applicable condition precedent specified in the Rate Swap Agreement.

Section 10.3. Default Rate. "Default Rate" means, in respect of a Rate Swap Transaction, the rate specified as such for the Rate Swap Transaction; if a Default Rate is specified, a party that defaults in the payment of any amount due will, to the extent permitted by law, be required to pay interest on such amount to the other party, on demand, for the period from, and including, the original due date for payment to, but excluding, the date of actual payment at the Default Rate (using the same Floating Rate Day Count Fraction that would apply under this Code if such Default Rate were a Floating Rate and such period were a Calculation Period).

ARTICLE 11

EARLY TERMINATION

Section 11.1. Early Termination Date. "Early Termination Date" means a Business Day on which the parties to a Rate Swap Agreement will settle out, on a "lump-sum" basis, their payment obligations for the Rate Swap Transactions governed by that Rate Swap Agreement (or, if the Early Termination Date occurs as the result of an Event of Default or Termination Event to which the parties have specified that "Limited Early Termination" applies, their payment obligations for the Rate Swap Transactions governed by that Rate Swap Agreement and affected by that Event of Default or Termination Event) in respect of each Calculation Period for any such Rate Swap Transaction that would, but for the occurrence of the Early Termination Date, end after the Early Termination Date. Subject to any conditions to designation of an Early Termination Date set forth in a Rate Swap Agreement, a party to a Rate Swap Agreement may designate an Early Termination Date (a) if an Event of Default in respect of the other party has occurred and is continuing at the time the Early Termination Date is designated or (b) if a Termination Event in respect of either party has occurred and is continuing at the time the Early Termination Date is designated and the party has the right to designate an Early Termination Date as provided in Section 11.6 of this Code or in the Rate Swap Agreement. If an Early Termination Date is designated in accordance with the preceding sentence, the Early Termination Date will occur on the date so designated, whether or not the Event of Default or Termination Event is continuing on the Early Termination Date; *provided, however,* if the Rate Swap Agreement specifies that upon the occurrence of a particular Event of Default or Termination Event "Immediate Early Termination" will occur, the Early Termination Date will occur immediately upon the occurrence of such Event of Default or Termination Event, without any Early Termination Date being designated and without any other action being taken by either party to the Rate Swap Agreement, and the amount payable pursuant to Article 12 of this Code will be determined as of such Early Termination Date or as soon thereafter as practicable, regardless of when either party learns of the occurrence of the Event of Default or Termination Event, and will be paid promptly after notice of the amount due and owing under Article 12 of this Code. A party entitled to designate an Early Termination Date in accordance with this Section 11.1 may do so by giving to the other party to the Rate Swap Agreement such notice as the Rate Swap Agreement requires (specifying in reasonable detail in such notice the basis upon which it is given).

Section 11.2. Event of Default. "Event of Default" means, in respect of a party and a Rate Swap Agreement (or, in the case of an Event of Default to which "Limited Early Termination" applies, a Rate Swap Transaction governed by that Rate

Swap Agreement and affected by that Event of Default), any event specified in that Rate Swap Agreement as an Event of Default in respect of that party.

Section 11.3. Termination Event. "Termination Event" means, in respect of a party and a Rate Swap Agreement (or, in the case of a Termination Event to which "Limited Early Termination" applies, a Rate Swap Transaction governed by that Rate Swap Agreement and affected by that Termination Event), any event specified in that Rate Swap Agreement as a Termination Event in respect of that party.

Section 11.4. Defaulting Party. "Defaulting Party" means the party in respect of which an Event of Default has occurred.

Section 11.5. Affected Party. "Affected Party" means each party in respect of which a Termination Event has occurred.

Section 11.6. Right To Terminate Following Termination Events. Upon the occurrence of a Termination Event in respect of a party and a Rate Swap Agreement (or, if "Limited Early Termination" applies, a Rate Swap Transaction), (a) if such Termination Event is a "Tax Event", a party that is an Affected Party will have the right to designate an Early Termination Date, (b) if such Termination Event is "Illegality", either party will have the right to designate an Early Termination Date and (c) otherwise, the party that is not the Affected Party will have the right to designate an Early Termination Date. If the Rate Swap Agreement specifies "Assignment To Avoid Illegality" or "Assignment To Avoid a Tax Event", an Early Termination Date may not be designated as a result of "Illegality" of the type described in Section 11.8(a) (i) of this Code or a "Tax Event" unless the applicable provisions of Section 18.3 of this Code have been complied with.

Section 11.7. Specifying Events of Default and Termination Events. The parties to a Rate Swap Agreement may specify as Events of Default or Termination Events such events as they may agree. Such events may, but need not, include any of the events described in this Section and need not be limited to the events described in this Section. If used for purposes of specifying Events of Default or Termination Events in a Rate Swap Agreement, the following terms will, subject to the passage of any applicable cure period or the giving of any applicable notice specified in that Rate Swap Agreement, have the indicated meanings in respect of a party:

(a) "Breach of Covenant" means failure by the party to comply with or perform any agreement or obligation (not including an obligation to make a payment or to give notice of an Event of Default or Termination Event and not including any Tax Covenant) to be complied with or performed by the party in accordance with the Rate Swap Agreement.

(b) "Credit Support Default" means (i) default by the party or any applicable Specified Entity with respect to any obligation which the party (or such Specified Entity) has under any Credit Support Document relating to the Rate Swap Agreement or to any Rate Swap Transaction governed by the Rate Swap Agreement or (ii) the expiration or termination of such Credit Support Document, or the ceasing of such Credit Support Document to be in full force and effect, prior to the Termination Date of each Rate Swap Transaction governed by the Rate Swap Agreement and to which the Credit Support Document applies without the written consent of the other party to the Rate

Swap Agreement or (iii) the party (or such Specified Entity) repudiates, or challenges the validity of, such Credit Support Document.

(c) "Default Under Specified Swaps" means the occurrence of an event of default in respect of the party or any applicable Specified Entity under any Specified Swap that, following the giving of any applicable notice and the lapse of any applicable grace period, has resulted in the designation or occurrence of an Early Termination Date in respect of that Specified Swap.

(d) "Failure To Give Notice of Events of Default or Termination Events" means failure by the party to notify the other party of the occurrence of an Event of Default or Termination Event in respect of the party within 10 days after the occurrence of such Event of Default or Termination Event.

(e) "Failure To Pay" means failure by the party to pay, when due, any amount required to be paid by it under the Rate Swap Agreement.

(f) "Failure To Pay Under Specified Swaps" means failure by the party or any applicable Specified Entity to pay, when due, following the giving of any applicable notice and the lapse of any applicable grace period, an amount to be paid by the party (or such Specified Entity) under any Specified Swap.

(g) "Misrepresentation" means a representation (other than a Payee Tax Representation or a representation that the party is "Exempt From Withholding") made or repeated or deemed to have been made or repeated by the party or any applicable Specified Entity in the Rate Swap Agreement or any Credit Support Document relating to the Rate Swap Agreement proves to have been incorrect or misleading in any material respect when made or repeated or deemed to have been made or repeated.

(h) "Tax Misrepresentation" means a Payee Tax Representation or a representation that the party is "Exempt From Withholding" made or repeated or deemed to have been made or repeated by the party proves to have been incorrect or misleading in any material respect on the Trade Date of any Rate Swap Transaction governed by the Rate Swap Agreement.

Section 11.8. Specifying Termination Events. If used for purposes of specifying Termination Events in a Rate Swap Agreement (in addition to or in lieu of any of the events described in Section 11.7 of this Code or in addition to such other events as the parties may agree), the following terms will, subject to the passage of any applicable cure period or the giving of any applicable notice specified in that Rate Swap Agreement, have the indicated meanings in respect of a party:

(a) "Illegality" means, due to the adoption of, or any change in, any applicable treaty, law, rule or regulation after the Trade Date of a Rate Swap Transaction governed by the Rate Swap Agreement or due to the promulgation of, or any change in, the interpretation by any court, tribunal or regulatory authority with competent jurisdiction of any applicable treaty, law, rule or regulation after the Trade Date of that Rate Swap Transaction, it becomes unlawful for the party (i) to perform any absolute or contingent obligation to make a payment or to receive a payment in respect of that Rate Swap Transaction or to comply with any other material provision of the Rate Swap Agreement relating to that Rate Swap Transaction or (ii) to perform, or for any applicable Specified Entity to perform, any absolute or contingent obligation which the party (or such Specified Entity) has under any Credit Support Document relating to that Rate Swap Transaction.

(b) "Tax Event" means the occurrence in respect of a party of any event specified in the Rate Swap Agreement as a Tax Event. If used for purposes of specifying Tax Events in the Rate Swap Agreement, the following terms will have the indicated meanings in respect of the party referred to below as an "Affected Party":

(i) "Tax Event upon Payment of Additional Amounts" means that an Affected Party determines that it is required to pay to the other party an additional amount in respect of an Indemnifiable Tax as provided in Section 19.1 (b) of this Code (except in respect of default interest).

(ii) "Tax Event upon Substantial Likelihood of Gross-up" means that, in the written opinion of independent legal counsel of recognized standing, there is a substantial likelihood that an Affected Party will be required on the next succeeding Payment Date to pay to the other party an additional amount in respect of an Indemnifiable Tax as provided in Section 19.1 (b) of this Code (except in respect of default interest) and such substantial likelihood results from either (A) a Change in Tax Law or (B) an action taken by a taxing authority, or brought in a court of competent jurisdiction, on or after the Trade Date of a Rate Swap Transaction governed by the Rate Swap Agreement (regardless of whether such action was taken or brought with respect to a party to the Rate Swap Agreement).

Section 11.9. Certain General Definitions Relating to Events of Default and Termination Events.

(a) "Credit Support Document" means any agreement or instrument which is specified as such in a Rate Swap Agreement.

(b) "Indemnifiable Tax" and "Change in Tax Law" have the meanings set forth in Section 19.5 of this Code.

(c) "Specified Entity" has the meaning set forth in Section 17.1 of this Code.

(d) "Specified Swap" means, for purposes of an Event of Default or Termination Event specified in a Rate Swap Agreement, any rate swap, rate cap, currency exchange transaction or similar transaction specified or described as such in that Rate Swap Agreement with respect to a party to that Rate Swap Agreement (or any applicable Specified Entity) and that Event of Default or Termination Event.

Section 11.10. Cure Period and Notice. For purposes of determining whether, and when, an Event of Default or Termination Event has occurred

(a) if a Rate Swap Agreement does not specify, in respect of a party and an Event of Default or Termination Event, a period of days to be the applicable "Cure Period" and does not specify "After Notice", such Event of Default or Termination Event in respect of that party will arise immediately upon the occurrence of the event or commencement of the condition giving rise to the Event of Default or Termination Event;

(b) if the Rate Swap Agreement specifies, in respect of a party and an Event of Default or Termination Event, a period of days to be the applicable "Cure

Period" and specifies "After Notice", such Event of Default or Termination Event in respect of that party will arise the specified period of days after notice of the event or condition giving rise to the Event of Default or Termination Event is given to the party by the other party to the Rate Swap Agreement if such event or condition is continuing after such period has elapsed;

(c) if the Rate Swap Agreement specifies, in respect of a party and an Event of Default or Termination Event, a period of days to be the applicable "Cure Period" but does not specify "After Notice", such Event of Default or Termination Event in respect of that party will arise the specified period of days after the occurrence of the event or commencement of the condition giving rise to the Event of Default or Termination Event if such event or condition is continuing after such period has elapsed; and

(d) if the Rate Swap Agreement specifies, in respect of a party and an Event of Default or Termination Event, "After Notice" but does not specify a period of days to be the applicable "Cure Period", such Event of Default or Termination Event in respect of that party will arise immediately upon notice of the event or condition giving rise to the Event of Default or Termination Event being given to the party by the other party to the Rate Swap Agreement if such event or condition is continuing at the time such notice is given.

ARTICLE 12

PAYMENTS ON EARLY TERMINATION

Section 12.1. Measures of Damages. For purposes of determining the amount payable on an Early Termination Date (or, if Immediate Early Termination applies, promptly after notice of the amount due and owing) in respect of a Rate Swap Transaction or a Rate Swap Agreement, as the case may be,

(a) "Agreement Value" means that on the Early Termination Date (or, if Immediate Early Termination applies, promptly after notice of the amount due and owing), if there is a Defaulting Party or only one Affected Party, that party will be obligated to make a payment to the other party in the amount, if any, by which the Market Quotation determined by the other party exceeds zero. If "Agreement Value" is the applicable measure of damages and notice of the Early Termination Date is given as a result of a Termination Event but there is more than one Affected Party, the payment to be made will be determined as if the parties had specified "Agreement Value—Two Way Payments" as the applicable measure of damages.

(b) "Agreement Value—Limited Two Way Payments" means that on the Early Termination Date (or, if Immediate Early Termination applies, promptly after notice of the amount due and owing), if there is a Defaulting Party, that party will be obligated to make a payment to the other party in the amount, if any, by which the Market Quotation determined by the other party exceeds zero. If notice of the Early Termination Date is given as the result of a Termination Event, the payment to be made will be determined as if the parties had specified "Agreement Value—Two Way Payments" as the applicable measure of damages.

(c) "Agreement Value—Two Way Payments" means that on the Early Termination Date (or, if Immediate Early Termination applies, promptly after notice of the amount due and owing), (i) if there is a Defaulting Party or only one Affected Party, that party will, if the Market Quotation determined by the other party exceeds zero, pay the amount of such excess to the other party, and the other party will, if the Market Quotation determined by it is less than zero, pay the amount of such deficiency to the Defaulting Party or the Affected Party, as the case may be, and (ii) if there is more than one Affected Party, each party will determine a Market Quotation, and the party with the lower Market Quotation will pay an amount equal to one-half of the difference between the two Market Quotations to the party with the higher Market Quotation.

(d) "Indemnification" means that on the Early Termination Date (or, if Immediate Early Termination applies, promptly after notice of the amount due and owing), if there is a Defaulting Party or only one Affected Party, that party will be obligated to make a payment to the other party in an amount equal to the positive amount, if any, of the other party's Loss. If "Indemnification" is the applicable measure of damages and notice of the Early Termination Date is given as the result of a Termination Event but there is more than one Affected Party, the payment to be made will be determined as if the parties had specified "Indemnification—Two Way Payments" as the applicable measure of damages.

(e) "Indemnification—Limited Two Way Payments" means that on the Early Termination Date (or, if Immediate Early Termination applies, promptly after notice of the amount due and owing), if there is a Defaulting Party, that party will be obligated to make a payment to the other party in an amount equal to the positive amount, if any, of the other party's Loss. If notice of the Early Termination Date is given as the result of a Termination Event, the payment to be made will be determined as if the parties had specified "Indemnification— Two Way Payments" as the applicable measure of damages.

(f) "Indemnification—Two Way Payments" means that each party will determine its Loss, and on the Early Termination Date (or, if Immediate Early Termination applies, promptly after notice of the amount due and owing), the party with the Loss that is less will be obligated to make a payment to the party with the Loss that is greater in an amount equal to one-half of the difference between their Losses.

(g) "Formula" means that on the Early Termination Date (or, if Immediate Early Termination applies, promptly after notice of the amount due and owing), if there is a Defaulting Party or only one Affected Party, that party will be obligated to make a payment to the other party in an amount equal to the excess, if any, of the Formula Settlement Amount of the Defaulting Party or Affected Party, as the case may be, over the Formula Settlement Amount of the other party. If "Formula" is the applicable measure of damages and notice of the Early Termination Date is given as the result of a Termination Event but there is more than one Affected Party, the payment to be made will be determined as if the parties had specified "Formula—Two Way Payments" as the applicable measure of damages.

(h) "Formula—Limited Two Way Payments" means that on the Early Termination Date (or, if Immediate Early Termination applies, promptly after notice of the amount due and owing), if there is a Defaulting Party, that party will be obligated to make a payment to the other party in an amount equal to the excess, if any, of the Formula Settlement Amount of the Defaulting Party over the Formula Settlement Amount of the other party. If notice of the Early Termination Date is given as the result of a Termination Event, the payment to be made will be determined as if the parties had specified "Formula—Two Way Payments" as the applicable measure of damages.

(i) "Formula—Two Way Payments" means that on the Early Termination Date (or, if Immediate Early Termination applies, promptly after notice of the amount due and owing) the Formula Settlement Amounts of the parties will be netted, and the party with the higher Formula Settlement Amount will be obligated to make a payment to the party with the lower Formula Settlement Amount in an amount equal to the difference between their Formula Settlement Amounts.

Section 12.2. Alternative Measures of Damages. If for any reason the amount payable in respect of an Early Termination Date cannot be determined, or is not determined, pursuant to the applicable measure of damages, (a) if "Agreement Value", "Agreement Value—Limited Two Way Payments" or "Agreement Value—Two Way Payments" is specified as the applicable measure of damages, the amount payable in respect of the Early Termination Date will be determined on the basis of the alternative measure of damages specified by the parties or (b) if "Formula", "Formula—Limited Two Way Payments" or "Formula—Two Way Payments" is specified as the applicable measure of damages, the amount payable in respect of the Early Termination Date will be determined on the basis of "Indemnification", "Indemnification—Limited Two Way Payments" or "Indemnification—Two Way Payments", respectively, as the alternative measure of damages.

Section 12.3. Aggregation. If "Aggregation" is specified in a Rate Swap Agreement in respect of a measure of damages or an alternative measure of damages, (a) all references to "Market Quotation" in Section 12.1 of this Code will be deemed references to "Aggregate Market Quotation", all references to "Formula Settlement Amount" in Section 12.1 will be deemed references to "Aggregate Formula Settlement Amount", and all references to "Loss" in Section 12.1 will be deemed references to "Aggregate Loss", and (b) if "Formula", "Formula—Limited Two Way Payments" or "Formula—Two Way Payments" is the applicable measure of damages, the amount of any damages determined on that basis will be increased or reduced, as appropriate, by an amount determined on the basis of "Indemnification", "Indemnification—Limited Two Way Payments" or "Indemnification—Two Way Payments", respectively, applying Aggregation, for all Rate Swap Transactions for which there is more than one Floating Rate Payor.

Section 12.4. Certain Definitions Relating to Agreement Value.

(a) "Market Quotation" means, with respect to a Rate Swap Transaction and a party to the Rate Swap Transaction making the determination, an amount (which may be negative) determined on the basis of quotations from Reference Market-makers for the Dollar amount that would be payable on the Early Termination Date, either by the party to the Rate Swap Transaction making the determination (to be expressed as a positive amount) or to such party (to be expressed as a negative amount), in consideration of an agreement between such party and the quoting Reference Market-maker and subject to such documentation as they may in good faith agree, with a Term commencing on the Early Termination Date (unless the Effective Date has not yet occurred, in which case the Term of such agreement will commence on the Effective Date), that would have the effect of preserving for such party the economic equivalent of the payment obligations of the parties in respect of each Calculation Period for that Rate Swap Transaction that would, but for the occurrence of the Early

Termination Date, end after the Early Termination Date (excluding any unpaid amounts in respect of any Calculation Period ended on or prior to the Early Termination Date but otherwise including, without limitation, any amounts that would, but for the occurrence of the Early Termination Date, have been payable (assuming each applicable condition precedent had been satisfied) on the next applicable Payment Date in respect of any Calculation Period in which the Early Termination Date occurs). The party making the determination (or its agent) will request each Reference Market-maker to provide its quotation as of 11:00 a.m., New York City time, on the Early Termination Date (or, if Immediate Early Termination applies, as of a time as soon thereafter as practicable). If more than three such quotations are provided, the Market Quotation will be the arithmetic mean of the quotations, without regard to the quotations having the highest and lowest values. If exactly three such quotations are provided, the Market Quotation will be the quotation remaining after disregarding the quotations having the highest and lowest values. If fewer than three quotations are provided, the Market Quotation in respect of the Rate Swap Transaction will not be determined for either party and the alternative measure of damages will apply.

(b) "Reference Market-makers" means four leading dealers in the relevant rate swap market selected by the party determining a Market Quotation in good faith from among dealers of the highest credit standing which satisfy all the criteria that such party applies generally at the time in deciding whether to offer or to make an extension of credit.

(c) "Aggregate Market Quotation" means, with respect to a Rate Swap Agreement and a party, the sum of the Market Quotations (both positive and negative) determined by such party for all Rate Swap Transactions governed by that Rate Swap Agreement with respect to which an Early Termination Date has occurred and for which a Market Quotation is determined, plus, for each Rate Swap Transaction governed by that Rate Swap Agreement with respect to which an Early Termination Date has occurred and for which a Market Quotation is not, or cannot be, determined, (i) if "Formula", "Formula—Limited Two Way Payments" or "Formula—Two Way Payments" is the alternative measure of damages specified by the parties, (A) in respect of each Rate Swap Transaction for which there is not a Floating Rate Payor or there is only one Floating Rate Payor, an amount (whether positive or negative) equal to the other party's Formula Settlement Amount less such party's Formula Settlement Amount and (B) in respect of each Rate Swap Transaction for which there is more than one Floating Rate Payor, an amount equal to such party's Loss, or (ii) if "Indemnification", "Indemnification—Limited Two Way Payments" or "Indemnification—Two Way Payments" is the alternative measure of damages specified by the parties, an amount equal to such party's Loss.

Section 12.5. Certain Definitions Relating to Loss.

(a) "Loss" means, with respect to a Rate Swap Transaction and a party, an amount equal to the total amount (expressed as a positive amount) required, as determined as of the Early Termination Date (or, if Immediate Early Termination applies, as of a time as soon thereafter as practicable) by the party in good faith, to compensate the party for any losses and costs (including loss of bargain and costs of funding but excluding attorneys' fees and other out-of-pocket expenses) that it may incur as a result of the early termination of the obligations of the parties in respect of the Rate Swap Transaction. If a party determines that it would gain or benefit from the early termination of the obligations of the parties in respect of the Rate Swap Transaction, such party's Loss will be an amount (expressed as a negative amount) equal to the amount of the gain or benefit as determined by that party.

(b) "Aggregate Loss" means, with respect to a Rate Swap Agreement and a party, the sum of such party's Losses (both positive and negative) for all Rate Swap Transactions governed by that Rate Swap Agreement with respect to which an Early Termination Date has occurred and for which a Loss is determined.

Section 12.6. Certain Definitions Relating to Formula.

(a) *General Definitions.*

(i) "Aggregate Formula Settlement Amount" means, with respect to a Rate Swap Agreement and a party, the sum of such party's Formula Settlement Amounts for all Rate Swap Transactions governed by that Rate Swap Agreement with respect to which an Early Termination Date has occurred and for which there is not a Floating Rate Payor or there is only one Floating Rate Payor and for which the Formula Settlement Amount can be determined for each party.

(ii) "Current Value" means, in respect of any amount, the value of that amount on the Early Termination Date after discounting that amount on a semiannual basis from the originally scheduled date for payment on the basis of the Treasury Rate.

(iii) "Treasury Rate" means a per annum rate (expressed as a semiannual equivalent and as a decimal and, in the case of United States Treasury bills, converted to a Bond Equivalent Yield) determined to be the per annum rate equal to the semiannual equivalent yield to maturity for United States Treasury securities maturing on the Termination Date, as determined by interpolation between the most recent weekly average yields to maturity for two series of United States Treasury securities, (A) one maturing as close as possible to, but earlier than, the Termination Date and (B) the other maturing as close as possible to, but later than, the Termination Date, in each case as published in the most recent H.15(519) (or, if a weekly average yield to maturity for United States Treasury securities maturing on the Termination Date is reported in the most recent H.15(519), as published in H.15(519)).

(b) *Definitions Relating to the Basic Formula.*

(i) "Formula Settlement Amount" means, with respect to a Rate Swap Transaction and a party, the sum of such party's (A) Current Calculation Period Adjustment (if the Early Termination Date is not an applicable Period End Date) and (B) Cost of Termination.

(ii) *Definitions Relating to the Current Calculation Period Adjustment.*

(A) "Current Calculation Period Adjustment" means, with respect to a Rate Swap Transaction and a party, the sum of (I) the Adjusted Fixed Amount, if such party is a Fixed Rate Payor, or the Adjusted Floating Amount, if such party is a Floating Rate Payor, and (II) the Redeployment Adjustment, if applicable.

(B) "Adjusted Fixed Amount" means, in respect of a Rate Swap Transaction and a Fixed Rate Payor, an amount equal to:

(I) if the Fixed Amount payable by the Fixed Rate Payor in respect of the Calculation Period in which the Early Termination Date occurs is a specified amount, such amount multiplied by a fraction the numerator of which is the actual number of days in the period from, and including, the most recent applicable Period End Date (or, if the Early Termination Date occurs before the first applicable Period End Date, from, and including, the Effective Date for the Rate Swap Transaction) to, but excluding, the Early Termination Date and the denominator of which is the actual number of days in the applicable Calculation Period in which the Early Termination Date occurs; or

(II) if the Fixed Amount payable by the Fixed Rate Payor is determined on a formula basis, an amount determined on that basis, as specified for the Rate Swap Transaction, for a hypothetical Calculation Period from, and including, the most recent applicable Period End Date (or, if the Early Termination Date occurs before the first applicable Period End Date, from, and including, the Effective Date for the Rate Swap Transaction) to, but excluding, the Early Termination Date.

(C) "Adjusted Floating Amount" means, in respect of a Rate Swap Transaction and a Floating Rate Payor, an amount determined to be the Floating Amount that would be payable by the Floating Rate Payor, computed on the basis of the applicable Floating Rate Option, the applicable Spread, if any, and the other variables specified for the Rate Swap Transaction, for a hypothetical Calculation Period from, and including, the most recent applicable Period End Date (or, if the Early Termination Date occurs before the first applicable Period End Date, from, and including, the Effective Date for the Rate Swap Transaction) to, but excluding, the Early Termination Date (except that if no Reset Date would otherwise occur during this hypothetical Calculation Period, the first day of this hypothetical Calculation Period will be deemed to be a Reset Date).

(D) A Redeployment Adjustment will be calculated only for a Rate Swap Transaction in which each Floating Rate is determined by reference to a single Reset Date for the Calculation Period to which the Floating Rate applies, and if positive the Redeployment Adjustment will be included in the Current Calculation Period Adjustment of the Fixed Rate Payor, and if negative the Redeployment Adjustment will be included (but as a positive amount) in the Current Calculation Period Adjustment of the Floating Rate Payor. "Redeployment Adjustment" means, with respect to a Rate Swap Transaction and a party for which it is applicable, an amount equal to the product of (I) the Notional Amount, (II) the Redeployment Rate and (III) a fraction, the numerator of which is the number of days remaining (from, and including, the Early Termination Date) in the Calculation Period in which the Early Termination Date occurs and in respect of which a Floating Amount would have been payable (assuming each applicable condition precedent had been satisfied) had the Early Termination Date not occurred and the denominator of which is the denominator of the Floating Rate Day Count Fraction that would otherwise have been applicable to that Calculation Period, after discounting that product, on a semiannual basis, from the Payment Date in respect of that Calculation Period to the Early Termination Date on the basis of the Treasury Rate.

(E) "Redeployment Rate" means a per annum rate (which may be positive or negative), expressed as a decimal, equal to (I) a hypothetical Relevant Rate for the Early Termination Date computed as if the Early Termination Date were a Reset Date and as if the Designated Maturity were approximately equal to the length of the period from the Early Termination Date to the next scheduled Payment Date but otherwise on the basis of the applicable Floating Rate Option and the other variables specified for the Rate Swap Transaction, less (II) the Floating Rate utilized to calculate the Adjusted Floating Amount.

(iii) *Definitions Relating to Cost of Termination for Future Calculation Periods.*

(A) "Cost of Termination" means (I) in respect of a Rate Swap Transaction and a Fixed Rate Payor, the Fixed Rate Payor's Discounted Remaining Fixed Amount Payments and (II) in respect of a Rate Swap Transaction and a Floating Rate Payor, the Alternative Financing Costs adjusted to give effect to the Floating Rate Spread Adjustment, if applicable.

(B) "Discounted Remaining Fixed Amount Payments" means, in respect of a Rate Swap Transaction and a Fixed Rate Payor, an amount equal to the sum of the Current Values of the Fixed Amounts (after subtracting, in the case of the next scheduled Fixed Amount, the Adjusted Fixed Amount if the Early Termination Date does not coincide with an applicable Period End Date) that would have been payable (assuming each applicable condition precedent had been satisfied) by the Fixed Rate Payor after an Early Termination Date if the Early Termination Date had not occurred.

(C) "Alternative Financing Costs" means, in respect of a Rate Swap Transaction, an amount which equals (I) if "Formula" is the applicable measure of damages and the Defaulting Party or Affected Party is a Fixed Rate Payor or "Formula—Limited Two Way Payments" is the applicable measure of damages and the Defaulting Party is a Fixed Rate Payor, the sum of the Current Values of each payment of interest the Floating Rate Payor would receive after the Early Termination Date (after subtracting from any such payment of interest any amount earned in respect of any period prior to the Early Termination Date) from an Alternative Fixed Rate Investment, (II) if "Formula" is the applicable measure of damages and the Defaulting Party or Affected Party is a Floating Rate Payor or if "Formula—Limited Two Way Payments" is the applicable measure of damages and the Defaulting Party is a Floating Rate Payor, the sum of the Current Values of each payment of interest the Fixed Rate Payor would pay for an Alternative Fixed Rate Borrowing and (III) if "Formula—Limited Two Way Payments" is the applicable measure of damages and the Early Termination Date occurs as the result of a Termination Event or if "Formula—Two Way Payments" is the applicable measure of damages, the arithmetic mean of the amounts described in clauses (I) and (II) above, unless a Treasury Rate Spread is expressly provided for the purpose of this clause (III), in which case Alternative Financing Costs will be the amount described in clause (I) above (adjusted to give effect to that Treasury Rate Spread).

(D) "Alternative Fixed Rate Borrowing" means, in respect of a Rate Swap Transaction, at the option of the Fixed Rate Payor, either

(I) a loan in a principal amount equal to the Notional Amount that is or could have been obtained by the Fixed Rate Payor on the Early Termination Date, maturing on (or as close as possible to) the Termination Date and bearing interest payable semiannually (with a short first period, if necessary) at a per annum rate equal to (x) if a Treasury Rate Spread is expressly provided for the purpose of this clause (I), the Treasury Rate adjusted to give effect to that Treasury Rate Spread, (y) if a Treasury Rate Spread is not expressly provided for the purpose of this clause (I) and the Fixed Rate Payor has actually obtained such a loan, the actual fixed rate of interest the Fixed Rate Payor is required to pay for it and (z) if a Treasury Rate Spread is not expressly provided for the purpose of this clause (I) and the Fixed Rate Payor has not actually obtained such a loan, the arithmetic mean of the rates that two banks of nationally recognized standing in the United States, selected by the Fixed Rate Payor in good faith, estimate to be the lowest fixed rate of interest at which the Fixed Rate Payor could have borrowed such a loan on the Early Termination Date from responsible lenders or, if the Fixed Rate Payor is a bank, funded such a loan on the Early Termination Date in the London interbank market; or

(II) if a Treasury Rate Spread is not expressly provided for such purpose and the Fixed Rate Payor is a bank subject to the reserve requirements and insurance assessments described below, certificates of deposit of the Fixed Rate Payor in an amount equal to the Notional Amount which are or could have been issued by the Fixed Rate Payor on the Early Termination Date, with repayment of principal due on (or as close as possible to) the Termination Date and bearing interest payable semiannually (with a short first period, if necessary) at a per annum rate equal to the sum of (x) the quotient of (1) the arithmetic mean of the respective bid rates quoted to the Fixed Rate Payor as of 11:00 a.m., New York City time, on the Early Termination Date by each of three certificate of deposit dealers in New York City of recognized standing selected by the Fixed Rate Payor in good faith for the purchase at face value of such certificates of deposit, divided by (2) one minus the maximum aggregate reserve requirements (expressed as a decimal) imposed under Regulation D of the Board of Governors of the Federal Reserve System on nonpersonal time deposits of $100,000 or more having a maturity similar to such certificates of deposit, as in effect on the Early Termination Date, plus (y) the net assessment rate per annum payable to the Federal Deposit Insurance Corporation (or any successor) for the insurance of domestic deposits of the Fixed Rate Payor during the calendar year in which the Early Termination Date occurs, as determined by the Fixed Rate Payor on the Early Termination Date.

(E) "Alternative Fixed Rate Investment" means, in respect of a Rate Swap Transaction, an investment in United States Treasury securities in a principal amount equal to the Notional Amount maturing on (or as close as possible to) the Termination Date which are or could have been purchased by the Floating Rate Payor on the Early Termination Date, yielding interest at a per annum rate equal to, at the option of the Floating Rate Payor, either (I) if the Floating Rate Payor has actually made such an investment, the per annum rate equal to the semiannual equivalent yield to maturity of such securities (expressed as a decimal and, in the case of United States Treasury bills, converted to a Bond Equivalent Yield), or (II) if the Floating Rate Payor has not actually made such an investment, the Treasury Rate, in either case plus or minus the Treasury Rate Spread, if applicable.

(c) *Definitions Relating to Certain Adjustments to the Basic Formula.*

(i) A Treasury Rate Spread will be used only if the parties to a Rate Swap Transaction specify a rate to be used for that purpose in determining Alternative Financing Costs under clause (III) of Section 12.6 (b) (iii) (C) of this Code, an Alternative Fixed Rate Borrowing under Section 12.6 (b) (iii) (D) of this Code or an Alternative Fixed Rate Investment under Section 12.6 (b) (iii) (E) of this Code. "Treasury Rate Spread" means, in respect of any calculation for which it is applicable, the per annum rate, if any, specified as such for the Rate Swap Transaction (expressed as a decimal). For purposes of applying a Treasury Rate Spread, if positive the Treasury Rate Spread will be added to the Treasury Rate or other rate to which it is applicable and if negative the Treasury Rate Spread will be subtracted from that rate.

(ii) *Definitions Relating to a Floating Rate Spread Adjustment.*

(A) A Floating Rate Spread Adjustment will be calculated only for a Rate Swap Transaction in which the Floating Amount reflects a Spread specified by the parties. "Floating Rate Spread Adjustment" means an amount equal to the Discounted Remaining Spread Amounts. In computing the Cost of Termination, the Floating Rate Spread Adjustment will be added to the Alternative Financing Costs if the Spread is positive and subtracted from the Alternative Financing Costs if the Spread is negative.

(B) "Discounted Remaining Spread Amounts" means, in respect of a Rate Swap Transaction, an amount equal to the sum of the Current Values of the Spread Amounts (after subtracting, if the Early Termination Date does not coincide with an applicable Period End Date, that portion, if any, of the Adjusted Floating Amount attributable to the Spread from the Spread Amount determined in respect of the Calculation Period in which the Early Termination Date occurs) computed for each Calculation Period ending after the Early Termination Date in respect of which a Floating Amount would have been payable (assuming each applicable condition precedent had been satisfied) if the Early Termination Date had not occurred.

(C) "Spread Amount" means, in respect of a Rate Swap Transaction and a Calculation Period, an amount equal to the product of (I) the Notional Amount, (II) the Spread (for such purpose deemed to be positive) and (III) the Floating Rate Day Count Fraction that would otherwise have been applicable to that Calculation Period.

Section 12.7. Limited Indemnification for Expenses. A Defaulting Party (unless the appropriate measure of damages contemplates "Two Way Payments") and, if there is only one Affected Party, the Affected Party (unless the appropriate measure of damages contemplates "Limited Two Way Payments" or "Two Way Payments") will, on demand, indemnify and hold harmless the other party for and against all reasonable out-of-pocket expenses, including attorneys' fees and all stamp, registration, documentation or similar taxes or duties, incurred by such other party by reason of the enforcement and protection of its rights under a Rate Swap Agreement or by reason of the early termination of the Rate Swap Agreement or any Rate Swap Transaction governed by that Rate Swap Agreement, including, but not limited to, costs of collection.

Section 12.8. Statement of Calculations. A party to a Rate Swap Agreement requesting payment of any amount under Article 12 of this Code will provide to the other party a statement in reasonable detail showing the calculation of such amount (including all relevant quotations). Absent written confirmation of a quotation obtained in determining a Market Quotation or Alternative Financing Costs from the source providing such quotation, the records of the party obtaining such quotation will be conclusive evidence of the existence and accuracy of such quotation.

ARTICLE 13

SUBMISSION TO JURISDICTION

Section 13.1. Submission to Jurisdiction. With respect to any claim arising out of a Rate Swap Agreement, (a) each party irrevocably submits to the nonexclusive jurisdiction of the courts of the State of New York and the United States District Court located in the Borough of Manhattan in New York City, and (b) each party irrevocably waives any objection which it may have at any time to the laying of venue of any suit, action or proceeding arising out of or relating to the Rate Swap Agreement brought in any such court, irrevocably waives any claim that any such suit, action or proceeding brought in any such court has been brought in an inconvenient forum and further irrevocably waives the right to object, with respect to such claim, suit, action or proceeding brought in any such court, that such court does not have jurisdiction over such party.

Section 13.2. Jurisdiction Not Exclusive. Nothing in this Code will be deemed to preclude either party to a Rate Swap Agreement from bringing an action or proceeding in respect of the Rate Swap Agreement in any other jurisdiction.

ARTICLE 14

NOTICES

Section 14.1. Notices. Any notice or communication in respect of a Rate Swap Agreement will be sufficiently given to a party if in writing and delivered in person, sent by certified or registered mail (airmail if overseas) or the equivalent (with return receipt requested) or by overnight courier or given by telex (with answerback received) addressed to the party at its address or telex number provided for that purpose.

Section 14.2. Effectiveness of Notice. A notice or communication will be effective, if delivered by hand or sent by overnight courier, on the day it is delivered (or if that day is not a day on which commercial banks are open for business in the city specified in the address for notice provided by the recipient (a "Local Banking Day"), or if delivered after the close of business on a Local Banking Day, on the first following day that is a Local Banking Day), if sent by telex, on the day the recipient's answerback is received (or if that day is not a Local Banking Day, or if after the close of business on a Local Banking Day, on the first following day that is a Local Banking Day) or, if sent by certified or registered mail (airmail if overseas) or the equivalent (return receipt requested), three Local Banking Days after dispatch if the recipient's address for notice is in the same country as the place of dispatch and otherwise seven Local Banking Days after dispatch (or, in either case, if delivered after the close of business on a Local Banking Day, on the first following day that is a Local Banking Day).

Section 14.3. Addresses. Either party by notice to the other may designate additional or different addresses or telex numbers for subsequent notices or communications.

ARTICLE 15

REPRESENTATIONS

Section 15.1. Representations of the Parties. On the date as of which it enters into a Rate Swap Agreement, on the Trade Date of each Rate Swap Transaction governed by the Rate Swap Agreement and at any additional times specified in the Rate Swap Agreement, each party makes to the other party and to any Specified Entity of the other party the applicable representations specified in that Rate Swap Agreement. If used for purposes of specifying representations in a Rate Swap Agreement, the following terms will have the indicated meanings in respect of a party to the Rate Swap Agreement:

(a) "Basic Representations" means that the party represents that: (i) it is duly organized, validly existing and in good standing under the laws of the jurisdiction of its organization or incorporation; (ii) it has the power to execute and deliver the Rate Swap Agreement and any other documentation relating to the Rate Swap Agreement that it is required by the Rate Swap Agreement to deliver and to perform its obligations under the Rate Swap Agreement and any obligations it has under any Credit Support Document and has taken all necessary action to authorize such execution and delivery and performance of such obligations; (iii) its execution and delivery of the Rate Swap Agreement and any other documentation relating to the Rate Swap Agreement that it is required by the Rate Swap Agreement to deliver and its performance of its obligations under the Rate Swap Agreement and any obligations it has under any Credit Support Document do not violate or conflict with any law, rule or regulation applicable to it, any provision of its charter or by-laws (or comparable constituent documents), any order or judgment of any court or other agency of government applicable to it or any of its assets or any contractual restriction binding on or affecting the party or any of its assets; (iv) all authorizations of and exemptions, actions or approvals by, and all notices to or filings with, any governmental or other authority that are required to have been obtained or made by the party at the time this representation is made with respect to the Rate Swap Agreement or any Credit Support Document to which it is a party have been obtained or made and are in full force and effect and all conditions of any such authorizations, exemptions, actions or approvals have been complied with; and (v) each of the Rate Swap Agreement and any Credit Support Document to which it is a party constitutes the party's legal, valid and binding obligation, enforceable against the party in accordance with its terms (subject to applicable bankruptcy, reorganization, insolvency, moratorium or similar laws affecting creditors' rights generally and subject, as to enforceability, to equitable principles of general application (regardless of whether enforcement is sought in a proceeding in equity or at law)).

(b) "Absence of Certain Events" means that the party represents that no event or condition has occurred that constitutes (or would with the giving of notice or passage of time or both constitute) an Event of Default or, to the party's knowledge, a Termination Event with respect to the party, and no such event would occur as a result of the party's entering into or performing its obligations under the Rate Swap Agreement or any Credit Support Document to which it is a party.

(c) "Absence of Litigation" means that the party represents that there is not pending or, to the party's knowledge, threatened against the party or any of its Affiliates any action, suit or proceeding at law or in equity or before any court, tribunal, governmental body, agency or official or any arbitrator that purports to draw into question, or is likely to affect, the legality, validity or enforceability against the party of the Rate Swap Agreement or any Credit Support Document to which it is a party or the party's ability to perform its obligations under the Rate Swap Agreement or such Credit Support Document.

(d) "Accuracy of Financial Information" means that the party represents that all financial information furnished to the other party to the Rate Swap Agreement pursuant to Section 16.1(a), 16.1(b) or 16.1(c) of this Code, or included in any report on Form 10-K, Form 10-Q or Form 8-K (or any successor form) filed by the party with the Securities and Exchange Commission which is furnished by the party to the other party to the Rate Swap Agreement, is, as of its date, true, accurate and complete in every material respect.

(e) "Accuracy of Specified Information" means that the party represents that all applicable information that is furnished in writing by or on behalf of the party to the other party to the Rate Swap Agreement and is identified in the Rate Swap Agreement is, as of the date of the information, true, accurate and complete in every material respect.

ARTICLE 16

AGREEMENTS

Section 16.1. Agreements of the Parties.   Each party to a Rate Swap Agreement agrees to perform any additional obligations specified in that Rate Swap Agreement as agreements in respect of that party for so long as the party has any obligations under the Rate Swap Agreement or under any Credit Support Document. If used for purposes of specifying agreements in a Rate Swap Agreement, the following terms will have the indicated meanings in respect of a party to the Rate Swap Agreement:

(a) "Furnish Annual Financial Statements" means that the party agrees to furnish to the other party, as soon as available and in any event within 120 days (or as soon as practicable after becoming publicly available) after the end of each of its fiscal years, a copy of the annual report of the party (or of such other entity as is specified in the Rate Swap Agreement) containing audited consolidated financial statements for such fiscal year certified by independent certified public accountants and prepared in accordance with accounting principles that are generally accepted in the country in which the party (or such entity) is organized.

(b) "Furnish Quarterly Financial Statements" means that the party agrees to furnish to the other party, as soon as available and in any event within 60 days (or as soon as practicable after becoming publicly available) after the end of each of its fiscal quarters, unaudited consolidated financial statements of the party (or of such other entity as is specified in the Rate Swap Agreement) for such quarter prepared in accordance with accounting principles that are generally accepted in the country in which the party (or such entity) is organized and on a basis consistent with that of the annual financial statements of the party (or such entity).

(c) "Furnish Investor Reports and Regular Public Reporting Documents" means that the party agrees to furnish to the other party, promptly after public availability, each regular financial or business reporting document that is (i) distributed or made generally available by the party (or by such other entity as is specified in the Rate Swap Agreement) to its shareholders or investors or (ii) filed by the party (or such entity) with such regulatory authorities as are specified in the Rate Swap Agreement and made available for public inspection.

(d) "Furnish Specified Information" means that the party agrees to furnish to the other party, upon request or as provided in the Rate Swap Agreement, such information as is specified in the Rate Swap Agreement as required to be so furnished.

(e) "Give Notice of Default and Certain Events" means that the party agrees, upon learning of the occurrence of any event or commencement of any condition that constitutes (or that with the giving of notice or passage of time or both would constitute) an Event of Default or Termination Event with respect to the party, promptly to give the other party notice of such event or condition (or, in lieu of giving notice of such event or condition in the case of an event or condition that with the giving of notice or passage of time or both would constitute an Event of Default or Termination Event with respect to the party, to cause such event or condition to cease to exist before becoming an Event of Default or Termination Event).

(f) "Maintain Authorizations and Comply with Laws" means that the party agrees (i) to maintain in full force and effect all authorizations of and exemptions, actions or approvals by, and all filings with or notices to, any governmental or other authority that are required to be obtained or made by the party with respect to the Rate Swap Agreement or any Credit Support Document to which it is a party and will use all reasonable efforts to obtain or make any that may become necessary in the future and (ii) to comply in all material respects with all applicable laws, rules, regulations and orders to which it may be subject if failure so to comply would materially impair its ability to perform its obligations under the Rate Swap Agreement or any Credit Support Document to which it is a party.

ARTICLE 17

SPECIFIED ENTITIES

Section 17.1. Definition of Specified Entity. "Specified Entity" means an entity specified as such in a Rate Swap Agreement with respect to a party to that Rate Swap Agreement and one or more Events of Default, Termination Events, representations, or agreements or other obligations.

Section 17.2. Definition of Affiliate. "Affiliate" of a party means any entity controlled, directly or indirectly, by the party, any entity that controls, directly or indirectly, the party or any entity under common control with the party. For purposes of this definition, "control" of an entity or of a party means ownership of a majority of the voting power of the entity or party.

Section 17.3. Representations and Agreements by Specified Entities. If a Rate Swap Agreement or an instrument or agreement relating to a Rate Swap Agreement indicates that any representation or agreement of a kind referred to in Section 15.1, 16.1, 19.2, 19.3 or 19.4 of this Code is made by any Specified Entity, for purposes of the Specified Entity's representation or agreement, all references to "the party" in Section 15.1, 16.1, 19.2, 19.3 or 19.4 will be deemed references to "the Specified Entity" and, if the Specified Entity is not a party to the Rate Swap Agreement, all references to "the Rate Swap Agreement" in Section 15.1, 16.1, 19.2, 19.3 or 19.4 will be deemed references to "the instrument or agreement executed by the Specified Entity in connection with the Rate Swap Agreement".

Section 17.4. Performance of Obligations by Specified Entities. If an obligation of a party under a Rate Swap Agreement is fully performed for the party by an applicable Specified Entity that is a party to a Credit Support Document or a party to the Rate Swap Agreement, such obligation will be deemed to have been fully performed by the party.

ARTICLE 18

CROSS BORDER PROVISIONS

Section 18.1. Payment in the Contractual Currency. To the extent permitted by applicable law, any obligation to make payments under a Rate Swap Agreement or Credit Support Document in any currency (the "Contractual Currency") will not be discharged or satisfied by any tender in any currency other than the Contractual Currency, except to the extent such tender results in the actual receipt by the party to which payment is owed, acting in a reasonable manner and in good faith in converting the currency so tendered into the Contractual Currency, of the full amount in the Contractual Currency of all amounts due in respect of the Rate Swap Agreement or Credit Support Document. If for any reason the amount in the Contractual Currency so received falls short of the amount in the Contractual Currency due in respect of the Rate Swap Agreement or Credit Support Document, the party or Specified Entity required to make the payment will, to the extent permitted by applicable law, immediately pay such additional amount in the Contractual Currency as may be necessary to compensate for the shortfall. If for any reason the amount in the Contractual Currency so received exceeds the amount in the Contractual Currency due in respect of the Rate Swap Agreement or Credit Support Document, the party receiving the payment will refund promptly the amount of such excess. To the extent permitted by applicable law, the obligation to pay an additional amount in accordance with the second preceding sentence will be enforceable as a separate and independent cause of action for the purpose of recovery in the Contractual Currency of such additional amount, will apply notwithstanding any indulgence granted by the party to which payment is owed and will not be affected by judgment being obtained for any other sums due in respect of the Rate Swap Agreement or Credit Support Document.

To the extent permitted by applicable law, if any judgment or order expressed in a currency other than the Contractual Currency is rendered (a) for the payment of any amount owing in respect of a Rate Swap Agreement or Credit Support Document, (b) for the payment of any amount relating to any early termination in respect of a Rate Swap Agreement or any breach of a Credit Support Document or (c) in respect of a judgment or order of another court for the payment of any amount described in clause (a) or clause (b) above, the party seeking recovery, after recovery in full of the aggregate amount to which such party is entitled pursuant to the judgment or order, will be entitled to receive immediately from the other party, or from the applicable Specified Entity required to make such payment, the amount of any shortfall of the Contractual Currency received by such party as a consequence of sums paid in such other currency and will refund promptly to the other party, or such Specified Entity, any excess of the Contractual Currency received by such party as a consequence of sums paid in such other currency, if such shortfall or such excess arises or results from any variation between the rate of exchange at which the Contractual Currency is converted into the currency of the judgment or order for the purposes of such judgment or order and the rate of exchange at which such party is able, acting in a reasonable manner and in good faith in converting the currency received into the Contractual Currency, to purchase the Contractual Currency with the amount of the currency of the judgment or order actually received by such party. The term "rate of exchange" includes, without limitation, any premiums and costs of exchange payable in connection with the purchase of or conversion into the Contractual Currency.

Section 18.2. Waiver of Immunities. Each party or Specified Entity entering into a Rate Swap Agreement or Credit Support Document irrevocably waives, to the fullest extent permitted by applicable law, with respect to itself and its revenues and assets, all immunity on the grounds of sovereignty or other similar grounds from (a) suit, (b) jurisdiction of any court, (c) attachment of its assets (whether before or after judgment) and (d) execution of judgment to which it might otherwise be entitled in any suit, action or proceeding relating to the Rate Swap Agreement or Credit Support Document in the courts of any jurisdiction and irrevocably agrees, to the extent permitted by applicable law, that it will not claim any such immunity in any such suit, action or proceeding.

Section 18.3. Assignment To Avoid Illegality or a Tax Event.

(a) If (i) Illegality occurs and a Rate Swap Agreement specifies "Assignment To Avoid Illegality" or (ii) a Tax Event occurs and the Rate Swap Agreement specifies "Assignment To Avoid a Tax Event", the Defaulting Party or, if there is only one Affected Party, the Affected Party will have the obligation to use all reasonable efforts (which shall not require the party to incur a loss) to make within 30 days, subject to the consent of the other party (which consent will not be withheld if the other party's policies in effect at the time would permit it to enter into a Rate Swap Agreement with the proposed assignee), an assignment of its rights and delegation (and transfer) of its obligations under the Rate Swap Agreement (or, if "Limited Early Termination" applies, its rights and obligations under the Rate Swap Agreement in respect of all Rate Swap Transactions governed by the Rate Swap Agreement and affected by the Illegality or Tax Event) to another of its offices, branches or Affiliates for the purpose of causing such Illegality or Tax Event to cease to exist, so long as such assignment and delegation will not create another Illegality or Tax Event. If the Defaulting Party or, if there is only one Affected Party, the Affected Party is not able to make such an assignment and delegation for such purpose after a reasonable effort to do so, and if the Rate Swap Agreement specifies that "Two Way Assignment" applies to Assignment To Avoid Illegality (in the case of Illegality) or Assignment To Avoid a Tax Event (in the case of a Tax Event), the Defaulting Party or the Affected Party may, for such purpose, request the other party to assign its rights and delegate its obligations under the Rate Swap Agreement (or, if "Limited Early Termination" applies, its rights and obligations under the Rate Swap Agreement in respect of all Rate Swap Transactions governed by the Rate Swap Agreement and affected by the Illegality or Tax Event) to another of its offices, branches or Affiliates for the purpose of causing such Illegality or Tax Event to cease to exist, so long as such assignment and delegation will not create another Illegality or Tax Event. Upon such request, such other party will have the obligation to use all reasonable efforts (which shall not require such other party to incur a loss) to make such an assignment and delegation within 30 days, subject to the consent of the Defaulting Party or the Affected Party (which consent will not be withheld if the Defaulting Party's or the Affected Party's policies in effect at the time would permit it to enter into a Rate Swap Agreement with the proposed assignee). Any such assignment and delegation will become effective upon (A) delivery to the nonassigning party of notice of the assignment and delegation and evidence reasonably satisfactory to such nonassigning party that the assignee and delegatee has, pursuant to such assignment and delegation, legally and effectively accepted all the rights, and assumed all the obligations, of the assigning and delegating party under the Rate Swap Agreement (or, if "Limited Early Termination" applies, its rights and obligations under the Rate Swap Agreement in respect of all Rate Swap Transactions governed by the Rate Swap Agreement and affected by the Illegality or Tax Event), (B) the nonassigning party's written consent to the assignment, (C) delivery to the nonassigning party of (I) a letter of credit, guarantee or other Credit Support Document satisfactory to the nonassigning party, if the nonassigning party's policies in effect at the time would require such a letter of credit, guarantee or other Credit Support Document in connection with a Rate Swap Agreement with the proposed assignee, and (II) such tax forms, certificates and opinions as the nonassigning party may reasonably request and (D) payment by the Defaulting Party or the Affected Party to the other party of all reasonable costs incurred by such other party in connection with the assignment and delegation (including but not limited to attorneys' fees and any costs of negotiating or executing Credit Support Documents). Upon the effectiveness of any such assignment and delegation as provided in this Section, the assigning and delegating party will be released from all its obligations under the Rate Swap Agreement (or, if "Limited Early Termination" applies, its obligations under the Rate Swap Agreement in respect of all Rate Swap Transactions governed by the Rate Swap Agreement and affected by the Illegality or Tax Event) except as otherwise expressly provided in connection with such assignment and delegation.

(b) In the event that clause (i) or clause (ii) of the first sentence of Section 18.3(a) of this Code is applicable and there is more than one Affected Party, each party will use all reasonable efforts to reach agreement within 30 days on action to be taken for the purpose of causing the Illegality or the Tax Event to cease to exist, which action may require one party or both parties to effect an assignment and delegation on the basis described in Section 18.3(a) of this Code, and the parties will share equally the costs incurred in connection with any such assignment and delegation.

Section 18.4. Definitions of "Illegality" and "Tax Event". For purposes of Section 18.3, the terms "Illegality" and "Tax Event" have the meanings set forth in Section 11.8(a)(i) and Section 11.8(b) of this Code, respectively.

ARTICLE 19
Certain Provisions Relating To Tax Matters

Section 19.1. Tax Gross-Up.

(a) All payments under a Rate Swap Agreement are to be made without any deduction or withholding for or on account of any Tax except as provided in this Section 19.1.

(b) Subject to Section 19.1(c) of this Code, if a party to a Rate Swap Agreement is required by any applicable law, rule or regulation to make any deduction or withholding for or on account of any Tax from any payment to be made by it under the Rate Swap Agreement, then that party (the "Withholding Party") will (i) promptly notify the other party (the "Taxed Party") of such requirement, (ii) pay to the relevant authorities the full amount required to be deducted or withheld (including the full amount required to be deducted or withheld from any additional amount paid by the Withholding Party to the Taxed Party pursuant to this Section 19.1(b)) promptly upon the earlier of determining that such deduction or withholding is required or receiving notice that such amount has been assessed against the Taxed Party, (iii) promptly forward to the Taxed Party an official receipt (or a certified copy), or other documentation acceptable to the Taxed Party, evidencing such payment to such authorities and (iv) if such Tax is an Indemnifiable Tax, pay to the Taxed Party, in addition to the payment to which the Taxed Party is otherwise entitled under the Rate Swap Agreement, such additional amount as is necessary to ensure that the net amount actually received by the Taxed Party (free and clear of Indemnifiable Taxes, whether assessed against the Withholding Party or the Taxed Party) will equal the full amount the Taxed Party would have received had no such deduction or withholding been required.

(c) A party to a Rate Swap Agreement will not be required to pay any additional amount to the other party pursuant to Section 19.1 (b) of this Code to the extent that such additional amount would not be required to be paid but for (i) the failure of a Payee Tax Representation made by the other party to be accurate and true or (ii) the failure by the other party to comply with or perform any Tax Covenant made by it in the Rate Swap Agreement. However, the preceding sentence will not apply to a failure with respect to a Payee Tax Representation or Tax Covenant that is specified in the Rate Swap Agreement to be subject to the occurrence of a "Change in Tax Law", if such failure would not have occurred but for a Change in Tax Law.

(d) If (i) a party to a Rate Swap Agreement (the "Withholding Party") is required by any applicable law, rule or regulation to make any deduction or withholding from a payment received by the other party (the "Taxed Party") for or on account of a Tax in respect of which the Withholding Party would not be required to pay an additional amount to the Taxed Party pursuant to Section 19.1 (b) of this Code, (ii) the Withholding Party does not so deduct or withhold and (iii) a liability resulting from such Tax is assessed directly against the Withholding Party, then, except to the extent the Taxed Party has satisfied or then satisfies the liability resulting from such Tax, the Taxed Party promptly will pay to the Withholding Party the amount of such liability (including any related liability for interest, but including any related liability for penalties only if the Taxed Party has agreed to "Give Notice of Breach of Payee Tax Representation or Tax Covenant" and has failed to comply with or perform such agreement).

Section 19.2. Payee Tax Representations. At all times during the Term of any Rate Swap Transaction governed by a Rate Swap Agreement, each party makes to the other party and to any Specified Entity of the other party the representations specified in that Rate Swap Agreement as "Payee Tax Representations" in respect of that party. If used for purposes of specifying Payee Tax Representations in the Rate Swap Agreement, the following terms will have the indicated meanings in respect of a party to the Rate Swap Agreement:

(a) "Effectively Connected" means that the party represents that, if it is acting through a branch, agency or office in the United States of America (including only the States and the District of Columbia) in respect of a Rate Swap Transaction governed by the Rate Swap Agreement, any payment received or to be received by it in connection with the Rate Swap Transaction is effectively connected with its conduct of a trade or business in the United States.

(b) "Eligible for Treaty Benefits" means that the party represents that it is fully eligible for the benefits (if any) of the "Business Profits" or "Industrial and Commercial Profits" provision, as the case may be, the "Interest" provision, and the "Other Income" provision (if any), of the Specified Treaty with respect to any payment described in such provisions and received or to be received by it in connection with a Rate Swap Transaction governed by the Rate Swap Agreement.

(c) "Ordinary Business Use" means that the party represents that each payment received or to be received by it in connection with a Rate Swap

Transaction governed by the Rate Swap Agreement relates to the regular business operations of the party (and not to an investment of the party).

(d) "Qualify as Business Profits" means that the party represents that each payment received or to be received by it in connection with a Rate Swap Transaction governed by the Rate Swap Agreement (other than default interest) qualifies as "business profits" or "industrial and commercial profits", as the case may be, under the Specified Treaty.

Section 19.3. Withholding Tax Representation. If a Rate Swap Agreement specifies "Exempt from Withholding" in respect of a party (the "first party"), then on the date as of which it enters into a Rate Swap Agreement, on the Trade Date of each Rate Swap Transaction governed by the Rate Swap Agreement, and at any additional times specified in the Rate Swap Agreement, the first party represents to the other party and to any Specified Entity of the other party that the first party is not required by any law, rule or regulation of the jurisdiction (a) of the first party's incorporation, organization, management and control, or seat, (b) where a branch or office through which the first party is acting for purposes of the Rate Swap Agreement is located or (c) in which the first party executes the Rate Swap Agreement, to make any deduction or withholding for or on account of any Tax from any payment (other than default interest) to be made by the first party to the other party under the Rate Swap Agreement. In making this representation the first party may rely on (i) the accuracy of any Payee Tax Representations and the satisfaction of any Tax Covenants made or deemed to be made by the other party under the Rate Swap Agreement and (ii) the accuracy and effectiveness of any document provided by the other party pursuant to any Tax Covenant.

Section 19.4. Tax Covenants. Each party to a Rate Swap Agreement agrees to perform any additional obligations specified in that Rate Swap Agreement as "Tax Covenants" in respect of that party for so long as the party has any obligations under the Rate Swap Agreement or under any Credit Support Document. If used for purposes of specifying Tax Covenants in the Rate Swap Agreement, the following terms will have the indicated meanings in respect of a party to the Rate Swap Agreement:

(a) "Give Notice of Breach of Payee Tax Representation or Tax Covenant" means that the party agrees to give notice of any failure described in the first sentence of Section 19.1(c) of this Code with respect to any Payee Tax Representation or Tax Covenant made or deemed to have been made by the party, promptly upon learning of such failure.

(b) "Provide Form 1001" or "Provide Form 4224" means that the party agrees to Provide Tax Forms and to complete, accurately and in a manner reasonably satisfactory to the other party, and to execute and deliver to the other party, a United States Internal Revenue Service Form 1001 or 4224 (as the case may be), or any successor form, (i) before the first Payment Date under the Rate Swap Agreement, (ii) promptly upon reasonable demand by the other party and (iii) promptly upon learning that any such form previously provided by the party has become obsolete or incorrect.

(c) "Provide Tax Forms" means that the party agrees to complete, accurately and in a manner reasonably satisfactory to the other party, and to execute, arrange for any required certification of, and deliver to the other party (or to such government or taxing authority as the other party reasonably directs), any form or document that may be required or reasonably requested in order to allow the other party to make a payment under the Rate Swap Agreement without any deduction or withholding for or on account of any Tax or with such deduction or withholding at a reduced rate, promptly upon the earlier of (i) reasonable demand by the other party and (ii) learning that the form or document is required.

Section 19.5. Certain Definitions Relating to Tax Matters.

(a) "Specified Treaty" means the treaty specified as such in a Rate Swap Agreement with respect to one or more Payee Tax Representations.

(b) "Change in Tax Law" means the enactment, promulgation, execution or ratification of, or any change in or amendment to, any treaty, law, regulation or ruling (or in the application or official interpretation of any treaty, law, regulation or ruling) that occurs on or after the Trade Date of any Rate Swap Transaction governed by a Rate Swap Agreement.

(c) "Tax" means any present or future tax, levy, impost, duty, charge, assessment or fee of any nature (including interest, penalties and additions thereto) that is imposed by any government or other taxing authority in respect of a payment under a Rate Swap Agreement, other than a stamp, registration, documentation or similar tax.

(d) "Indemnifiable Tax" means any Tax other than a Tax that would not be imposed in respect of a payment under a Rate Swap Agreement but for a present or former connection between the jurisdiction of the government or taxing authority imposing such Tax and the recipient of such payment (including, without limitation, a connection arising from such recipient being or having been a citizen or resident of such jurisdiction, or being or having been organized, present or engaged in a trade or business in such jurisdiction, or having or having had a permanent establishment or fixed place of business in such jurisdiction, but excluding a connection arising solely from such recipient having executed, delivered, performed its obligations or received a payment under, or enforced, the Rate Swap Agreement).

ARTICLE 20

Miscellaneous

Section 20.1. No Waiver of Rights. A failure or delay in exercising any right, power or privilege in respect of a Rate Swap Agreement will not be presumed to operate as a waiver, and a single or partial exercise of any right, power or privilege will not be presumed to preclude any subsequent or further exercise of that right, power or privilege or the exercise of any other right, power or privilege.

Section 20.2. Counterparts. A Rate Swap Agreement and each Credit Support Document or other written agreement relating to the Rate Swap Agreement may be executed in counterparts, each of which will be deemed an original.

Section 20.3. Governing Law. A Rate Swap Agreement and each Credit Support Document or other written instrument or agreement relating to the Rate Swap Agreement will, unless otherwise expressly provided, be governed by and construed in accordance with the laws of the State of New York, without reference to choice of law doctrine.

Section 20.4. Headings. The article and section headings used in this Code or in a Rate Swap Agreement are for convenience of reference only and are not to affect the construction of or be taken into consideration in interpreting this Code or any Rate Swap Agreement.

Glossary

Note: This glossary includes all terms boldfaced anywhere in the text except those boldfaced in Chapter 10. Chapter 10 deals with swap documentation and many of the terms used in that chapter have subtle legal meanings. The reader who does not find a desired term in this glossary should check the ISDA's 1986 Code that appears as an Appendix to Chapter 10.

Absolute advantage   The ability of one country to produce more of a given good with its endowed resources. In the context of swaps, the ability of one party to borrow at a lower rate of interest in a given currency than another party.

Add-on factor   Part of the bank capital guidelines adopted by the Federal Reserve in 1989. In the case of swaps and other off-balance sheet positions, it is a percentage of the notional principal.

Adjustable-rate mortgages (ARMs)   Any mortgage contract containing a provision to reset the mortgage coupon rate in response to a change in market rates. The coupon is usually tied to a specific rate or index such as the one-year constant Treasury maturity or the eleventh district cost of funds.

Affected party   A counterparty to a swap that has experienced a termination event.

Agreement value method   One of three allowable methods for determining damages upon the early termination of a swap. This method is now almost universally employed in swap documentation. The method assesses damages based upon "market quotations" for obtaining a replacement swap.

All-in cost   Also called *effective annual percentage cost* (the latter term is often applied to component costs individually). An important measure of the total cost of a financing that expresses the cost on an annual percentage basis. This measure is very useful for comparing alternative financing opportunities.

American option   An option that can be exercised at any time up to the time of its actual expiration.

Amortization schedule   A loan repayment schedule which describes the payment process by which the principal on a loan will be amortized. Such schedules usually also depict the interest payments and the total payments (principal and interest combined).

Amortizing   *See* **Amortizing debt.**

Amortizing debt   Any form of debt in which the principal balance is repaid gradually over the term of the loan.

Amortizing swap   Any swap in which the notional principal amortizes over the tenor of the swap. Thus, interest exchanges are made on a progressively smaller notional principal.

And interest   The normal way in which bond prices are quoted. Accrued interest is not included in the price quote and thus the bond buyer pays the bond seller the agreed price and any accrued interest. This contrasts with quotes on a "flat" basis which do include accrued interest.

Annuity   A series of equal-sized payments made at equal intervals in time.

A-Pack   A software package for use on IBM-type microcomputers published by MicroApplications (telephone # 516-821-9355). The package contains many useful analytical techniques with applications in finance, statistics, investment analysis, mathematical analysis, and management science. The full name of the software is *A-Pack: An Analytical Package for Business.*

Ascending yield curve   *See* **Upward sloping yield curve**.

Asset-based swaps   Any swap written to transform the cash flow characteristics of an asset in order to replicate the cash flow characteristics of another asset. The combination of the original asset together with the swap often constitutes a synthetic instrument.

Asset/liability management The management of assets and/or liabilities in such a way as to match cash flows, durations, or maturities of assets and liabilities.

Assignment The transfer of one's rights and obligations under a contract to another party.

At-the-money A situation in which an option's strike price and the current market price of the underlying asset are the same.

Average life A measure of interest-rate sensitivity based on principal repayments alone. Often used to determine the maturity-equivalent Treasury note for purposes of pricing long-dated swaps.

Back-to-back loans A loan arrangement involving two distinct loans between the same parties. In the first loan, Party 1 is the lender and Party 2 is the borrower. In the second loan, Party 2 is the lender and Party 1 is the borrower.

Bank discount yield Also known as *discount basis*. A yield measure used to express the yield on certain non-coupon bearing securities, such as T-bills, that always sell at a discount from face value.

Baseline instrument Also known as a *benchmark instrument*. An instrument selected to serve as the benchmark to which other instruments are compared. In hedging strategies, the benchmark instrument functions as a kind of common denominator.

Basis point An interest rate equal to 1 one-hundredth of 1 percentage point, that is, 0.01 percent. The term "basis points" is often abbreviated in the text as "bps."

Basis risk (1) The degree to which the difference between two prices fluctuates. (2) The residual risk that remains after a hedge has been placed.

Basis swap *See* **Floating-for-floating interest rate swap.**

Basle Accord An agreement in principle reached in December 1987 by the Basle Supervisors Committee that redefined bank capital requirements.

Basle Supervisors Committee A group of bank supervisors and regulators that met in Basle, Switzerland to redefine bank capital and to standardize capital requirements.

Bearer bonds   A negotiable bond whose title rests with the bearer. That is, it is presumed by law that the bearer of the bonds is the owner of the bonds.

Black/Scholes option pricing model   Often called the *OPM*. The first complete option pricing model. Published by Fischer Black and Myron Scholes in 1973.

Bid-ask spread   Also called *bid-asked spread*. The difference between the bid price and the asked price for any marketed instrument. In dealer markets, the bid-asked spread is the dominant source of the dealer's income.

Bond equivalent yield (BEY)   Also known as the *coupon equivalent yield*. A method of calculating and stating the yield on a coupon bearing instrument. Most often assumes semiannual compounding.

Book   (1) Market slang which means that a transaction giving rise to a position is recorded among the institution's assets and/or liabilities. (2) Market slang that refers to an institution's portfolio of some specific asset type such as a "swap book," a "foreign exchange book," and an "options book."

Book entry   Refers to ownership of a financial instrument in which ownership is evidenced by a notation on the record-keeping agent's books (or, in modern usage, computer data files). Ownership of such a financial instrument is transferred via a computer entry.

Bretton Woods Agreement   A multinational accord which established the post World War II international monetary system for participating nations. The accord served as the basis for the international monetary system until it broke down in the early 1970s.

British Bankers' Association (BBA)   A London-based trade association that deals with matters of common interest to member banks. In recent years, the BBA has dealt extensively with standardization of instrument documentation including swaps and forward rate agreements.

Bullet transaction   A banking term that describes a loan in which the principal is repaid in a single transaction upon maturity of the instrument. *See also* **nonamortizing debt.**

Butterfly spread   An option strategy involving four options with the same expiration date and all of the same class. Two of the options have the same strike price and this is between the other two. The two middle strikes are sold and the two end strikes are purchased.

Buy-down   The up-front sum that will be received by a swap bank for writing an off-market swap with itself as the receiver of fixed rate when the swap requires a coupon below current market.

Buy-up   The up-front sum that must be paid by a swap bank for writing an off-market swap with itself as the receiver of fixed rate when the swap requires a coupon above current market.

Calculation date   The date specified as such for the calculation of the cash settlement amount on a interest-rate or exchange-rate contract. If the calculation and settlement dates differ, the calculation date will precede the settlement date.

Call   (1) An option that grants the holder the right to buy the under-lying asset from the option writer. (2) The act of redeeming an instrument prior to its scheduled maturity.

Call date   The first date that a callable debt instrument or a callable derivative instrument can be called by the party holding the right to call the instrument.

Call price   The price that the issuer of a callable bond must pay the holder of the bond in the event the issuer chooses to call the bond. The call price is specified in the bond's indenture.

Call provision   A provision in a bond indenture or derivative contract which grants a party the right to call the instrument.

Call risk   The risk borne by the holder of a callable instrument that the party holding the right to call the instrument will choose to do so.

Callable bond   Any bond that can be called by the issuer on or after the call date.

Callable swap   A swap that may be terminated prior to its scheduled maturity at the discretion of the fixed-rate payer.

Capital   An important tool of bank regulation and safety. Consists of long-term debt and equity and protects depositors by acting as a cushion against losses.

Capital markets groups   Those groups within banks responsible for making markets in capital market instruments and related derivative products.

Capital market instruments   Equity and debt instruments having a maturity of one year or more.

Caps   Provisions in floating-rate loan agreements that place an upper limit on the contractual interest rate. *See also* **Interest-rate caps.**

Caption   An option on a cap. The term "Caption" is a registered servicemark of the Marine Midland Bank. The Caption purchaser has the right to enter a specific interest-rate cap at a set premium for a specified period of time.

Cash-flow stream   The series of cash flows associated with a debt instrument, swap, or other derivative instrument.

Cash flows   The payments made by one party to a contract to another party to the contract.

Cash position   A position in any asset, including a financial instrument, with the exception of a position in a derivative instrument unless the derivative instrument is itself the underlying asset for another derivative instrument. In the latter case, the position in the derivative instrument can itself be regarded as a cash position.

Cash settlement   (1) A transaction made for immediate settlement. (2) In futures trading, refers to contracts that do not provide for physical delivery of the underlying asset. Instead, contracts are settled in cash on a final settlement date using a mark-to-market procedure.

Cash settlement options   Option contracts that are cash settled on the basis of the value of the underlying asset on the expiration date.

Ceiling rate   The contract rate on an interest-rate cap that serves as the cap's strike price. Also sometimes called the *cap rate*, and the *contract rate*.

Certificate of deposit (CD)   A negotiable certificate issued by a bank or thrift that evidences a deposit. The certificate may be interest bearing or discounted. If interest bearing, the interest rate may be fixed or floating.

Cheapest-to-deliver   On an interest-rate future, the least costly to acquire an allowable delivery instrument. The term is most often used with respect to T-bond and T-note futures.

Chicago Board of Trade (CBOT)   The oldest futures exchange in the Unites States. Dates back to the 1860s when it was established to trade grain futures contracts. The CBOT has since expanded to trade a wide variety of futures including financial futures. Its subsidiaries include the Chicago Board Options Exchange (CBOE).

Chicago Board Options Exchange (CBOE)   The oldest and largest options exchange in the United States. Opened in 1973 as a subsidiary of the Chicago Board of Trade to provide an organized exchange for the trading of listed stock options.

Chicago Mercantile Exchange (CME)   Also known by its nickname *the Merc*. A leading futures exchange located in the city of Chicago. Originally an agricultural exchange, but now trades many non-agricultural commodities and financial futures as well. Its subsidiary, The International Monetary Market (IMM), trades currency futures, Eurodollar futures, and DIFFs.

Circus swap   A combination involving a fixed-for-floating interest-rate swap and a fixed-for-floating currency swap in which both floating rate sides are LIBOR based. Allows for the creation of a fixed-for-fixed or floating-for-floating currency swap.

Clearing association   *See* **Clearing house.**

Clearing house   (1) An organization that tracks, matches, and guarantees transactions in futures and options. Also known as a *clearing association* and, if so organized, as a *clearing corporation*. (2) An organization which acts as a custodian for bearer securities in international markets.

Closing trade   Also called an *offsetting trade*. A trade that closes an existing position by taking an offsetting position equal and opposite to that of the existing position.

Code, 1986   The International Swap Dealers Association's Code of Standard Wording, Assumptions and Provisions for Swaps, 1986 edition. A revision and expansion of the ISDA's 1985 code.

Coefficient of determination   An important statistical measure equal to the square of the correlation coefficient. Often used as a measure of hedge effectiveness in which case it measures the percentage of the variation in the price of a cash position "explained" by the variation in the price of the hedging instrument.

Collar   *See* **Interest-rate collars.**

Collar swap   *See* **Mini-max swap.** *See also* **Interest-rate collars.**

Collateral   Something of value pledged by a borrower to a lender as backing for a debt obligation in order to improve the creditworthiness of the borrower.

Collateral trust bond   A bond secured by personal property such as securities or inventory.

Collateralized mortgage obligation (CMO)   A bond backed by a pool of whole mortgages or by mortgage pass-throughs that is issued in distinct tranches. Ordinarily, interest flows to all tranches but principal only flows to the fastest-pay tranche.

Commercial paper   Short-term corporate IOUs often used as part of a rollover strategy to obtain long-term financing at a lower cost. Often called *paper* and sometimes denoted *CP*. This paper may be placed directly or through commercial paper dealers.

Commission   A fee paid by a principal to an agent for the sevices of the agent in executing a transaction on behalf of the principal.

Commodity Futures Trading Commission (CFTC)   The agency of the U.S. government responsible for oversight and regulation of the futures industry. The CFTC was created in 1974 by the Commodity Futures Trading Act and its authority was extended by the Futures Trading Act of 1978.

Commodity swaps   Swaps that are structured to convert floating prices paid (or received) for commodities to fixed prices, or vice versa. These swaps have a similar structure to interest-rate swaps.

Comparative advantage   A situation in which one country (or firm) can produce a good (or engage in a borrowing) at less cost than another country (or firm) in the special sense that it must sacrifice less of an alternative good to achieve production. The term is associated with the Theory of Comparative Advantage used to explain trading between nations.

Composite hedge   A hedge consisting of more than one hedging instrument.

Confidence interval   The range of values centered around the mean that captures a specified percentage of the outcomes form a stochastic process.

Confidence level   The number of times out of 100 that a stochastic process will generate an outcome in a prescribed range. Expressed as a percentage.

Confirmation   A statement in writing transmitted by mail, telex, or fax, detailing the relevant economic terms involved in a transaction. The transaction is usually initiated via phone conversations.

Contract rate   The rate of interest (or exchange) to serve as the basis of a cash settlement on a forward contract or an option contract. More precisely, the difference between the contract rate and the reference rate serves as the basis of the cash settlement.

Conventional mortgages   Also known as *level payment mortgages.* Mortgages having a fixed term and a fixed coupon rate with all payments of equal size.

Conversion arbitrage   Any strategy that seeks to combine (or to disassemble) instruments having one set of investment characteristics in order to obtain one or more instruments having a different set of investment characteristics. The resultant instruments are often described as ''synthetic.''

Convertible bond   Long-term collateralized debt instruments that are convertible into other assets of the issuer, usually common stock. *See also* **Convertible debt.**

Convertible debentures   Intermediate- to long-term debt instruments that are not secured by collateral and that are convertible into other assets of the issuer. *See also* **Convertible debt.**

Convertible debt   A debt instrument that is convertible into some other asset of the issuer—usually common stock.

Core business risks   Those risks faced by a business that are peculiar to the business concerned. Such risks include production risks, market share, useful outcomes from research and development, and so on.

Correlation coefficient   A widely used statistic that measures the degree of linear relationship between two variables. The correlation coefficient must lie in the range of -1 to +1. These extreme values represent perfect negative and perfect positive correlation, respectively.

Cost of a hedge   The difference between the expected terminal value of an unhedged cash position and the expected terminal value of the same cash position when hedged.

Cost of carry   The cost of carrying a position over a period of time. This includes all explicit costs but also includes implicit costs such as the opportunity cost of money (if not included among the explicit costs).

Counterparty   A principal to a swap or other derivative instrument, as opposed to an agent such as a broker.

Coupon   (1) The periodic interest payment on a debt instrument. (2) The periodic interest payment on the fixed-rate side of an interest rate or currency swap.

Coupon rate   (1) The fixed rate of interest on a debt instrument. (2) The fixed rate of interest on the fixed-rate side of a swap.

Coupon bonds   Bonds that pay periodic interest. The periodic payment is called the *coupon*.

Covered interest arbitrage   A strategy requiring the borrowing of funds in one currency for lending in another currency with two simultaneous foreign exchange transactions (one spot and one forward) in order to exploit interest-rate and exchange-rate differentials between the two markets.

Covered   (1) The offsetting of a position by an equal but opposite transaction. (2) The return of borrowed securities used for a short ·sale.

Credit risk   The risk that a counterparty to a contract (particularly a swap) will be unable to fulfill its obligations due to bankruptcy or other cause.

Credit risk equivalent   Part of the bank capital guidelines adopted by the Federal Reserve in 1989. Determined by marking off-balance sheet positions to their market values and then adding a prescribed add-on factor.

Creditor (lender)   One who is owed money by another. The creditor relationship usually arises as a consequence of lending money, but it may arise in other ways as well.

Creditworthiness A reference to the likelihood that a party to a contract will default on its obligations. The greater the likelihood of default, the less creditworthy the party.

Cross hedge A hedge employing contracts written on an underlying instrument that differs in a meaningful way from the instrument that is the subject of the hedge.

Cumulative A feature common with preferred stock that requires any unpaid preferred dividends to accrue such that they must be paid prior to any dividend payments to common shareholders.

Currency futures Future contracts written on currencies. In the U.S., currency futures prices are stated in American terms. For example, $0.4800 per deutschemark.

Currency markets Also known as *foreign exchange markets*, *FOREX markets*, and *FX markets*. These are the markets in which the world's currencies are exchanged. With the exception of futures markets in currencies, the currency markets are dealer markets made, for the most part, by commercial banks.

Currency matching An asset/liability management technique applied to multi-currency balance sheets. Involves the matching of the currency denominations of assets and liabilities.

Currency swap An agreement between two parties for the exchange of a future series of interest and principal payments in which one party pays in one currency and the other party pays in a different currency. The exchange rate is fixed over the life of the swap.

Date sensitive Refers to the risk associated with a swap portfolio from mismatches in payment dates on matched swaps. As a swap portfolio gets larger, it becomes progressively less sensitive to this form of risk.

Debentures In the United States, an unsecured debt of a corporation.

Debt-for-equity swap The use of an equity issue by a firm to buy back some or all of its outstanding debt (or vice versa).

Debt markets Also referred to as *credit markets*. The markets for the borrowing and lending of money. The debt markets include the markets for short-term as well as long-term debt and include both privately placed and publicly traded debt.

Debtor (borrower) One who owes money to another. The opposite of a creditor. The debtor relationship usually arises as a consequence of a borrowing but can arise in other ways as well.

Dedicated portfolio An asset/liability management technique that seeks to structure an asset portfolio in such a fashion as to generate cash flows that precisely match the cash flows on the underlying liabilities.

Default risk (1) The risk that a party to a contract will fail to make a payment when required to do so. Usually associated with an inability to make the payment due to insolvency or bankruptcy. When used in this way, the term is synonymous with credit risk. (2) In swap banking, the term is used more broadly to describe the risk of an "event of default." (3) In swap banking, the term is sometimes used to describe a swap bank's exposure from the combination of credit risk and market risk.

Defaulting party A counterparty to a swap that has experienced an event of default.

Deferred delivery A contract delivery schedule that involves a period of time longer than that customary for spot contracts. Both futures and forward contracts involve deferred delivery.

Deferred swap *See* **Forward swap.**

Delayed rate-setting swap Also called a *deferred rate-setting swap*. A fixed-for-floating interest-rate swap in which the swap commences immediately but the swap coupon is not set until later.

Delivery month The month when a futures or option contract is due to deliver or settle.

Delivery risk Also called *settlement risk*. The risk that is created by the differences between market settlement hours which may result in exchanges of interest and/or principal at different times or even on different days. The first paying party is exposed to the risk that the later paying party will default after the first paying party has made its required payment but before the later paying party has made its payment.

Derivative instruments An instrument that is defined on, and whose value is a function of, some other instrument or asset. Examples include futures, options and swaps.

Diagonal spread   A spread in options that is both vertical and horizontal simultaneously. *See* **Vertical spreads** and **Horizontal spreads.**

Discount bond   A bond selling below its par (face) value.

Discriminant analysis   A multivariate forecasting technique often used to determine which financial ratios or combination of financial ratios is most reliable for predicting business failure.

Dollar value of a basis point (DVBP)   The dollar value change that would result from a 1 basis point change in an instrument's yield. In order to make the definition usable, the DVBP must be stated per some amount of face value.

Domestic issue   A debt or equity instrument sold in the country in which the issuer is domiciled.

Downside risk   Focuses on only negative deviations from an expected outcome, as opposed to risk more generally which includes any deviation, either positive or negative, from an expected outcome.

Duration   A measure developed by Frederick Macaulay that allows for accurate measurement of a debt instrument's price sensitivity to yield changes. Duration is the instrument's weighted average time to maturity.

Duration-based hedging model   A hedging model based on the ratio of the duration of a cash position and the duration of the hedging instrument.

DVBP model   A hedging model that allows for the determination of the appropriate hedge ratio by employing an instrument's DVBP and comparing this DVBP to that of a benchmark instrument.

Earnings per share (EPS)   A firm's after tax earnings divided by the number of shares of common stock outstanding (fully diluted).

Economies of scale   Any production situation, including the provision of financial services, in which the cost per unit produced decreases as the number of units produced increases. Per unit cost should not be confused with total cost. The latter will rise directly with the quantity produced irrespective of the behavior of per unit costs.

Effective annual percentage cost (1) Any financial cost expressed on a percentage basis as an effective annual rate. Very useful for comparing alternative financing methods. (2) Often used to convert the one-time premium paid for multi-period options to re-express the cost of these options on a basis that is more easily understood.

Efficient markets hypothesis A theory that holds that all competitive markets price assets correctly in the sense that, at any given point in time, the market price accurately reflects all available information.

Efficiency of a hedge The degree to which a hedge achieves a given level of risk reduction at minimum cost.

Efficient hedge A hedge that achieves a given level of risk reduction at minimum cost.

End user In the context of swaps, the final counterparty—as opposed to intermediary counterparties such as swap dealers. Also called, for purposes of this text, *counterparty clients* and *corporate users*.

Environmental risk Risks to which a firm is exposed and over which it has no direct control. The forms of environmental risk with which this book deals are price risks. Examples of other environmental risks faced by a typical firm include such things as changes in tax law and changes in customer demographics.

Eurobond A debt instrument issued in the Euromarket (excluding money market instruments).

Eurobond market Any Euromarket for longer-term debt instruments (specifically excludes the money markets).

Eurodollar bonds Dollar-denominated bonds and bond-like instruments sold outside the United States.

Eurodollar convention The rules stipulated to quote rates on Eurodollar deposits (LIBOR).

European option An option that can only be exercised during a limited exercise period at the very end of the option's life.

Euro-rate differential futures (DIFFs) Futures contracts traded on the Chicago Mercantile Exchange that are structured to allow a U.S. based firm to hedge nondollar money market rates.

Events of default An event that is indicative of a credit problem. Occurrences that constitute events of default are specified in the swap documentation. The occurrence of such an event terminates all swaps governed by the same master agreement between the parties.

Exchange of borrowings The simplest form of a currency swap in which each counterparty to the swap obtains funds from third-party lenders and then exchanges the funds so obtained.

Exchange rate Also called *foreign exchange rate*. The price of a unit of one currency stated in terms of units of another currency.

Exchange-rate differentials The differences between spot and forward (or forward and forward) exchange rates for the same currencies.

Exchange-rate options Also known as *currency options*. Options on which the underlying asset's price takes the form of an exchange rate. Such options can be single period or multiperiod in nature.

Exchange-rate risk The risk that a future spot exchange rate will deviate from its expected value.

Exercise price *See* **Strike price.**

Extendable swap A fixed-for-floating interest-rate swap in which one counterparty has the right to extend the swap beyond its scheduled maturity date.

Fastest-pay tranche The tranche on a collateralized mortgage obligation that is presently scheduled to receive principal. *See also* **Collateralized mortgage obligation.**

Federal Home Loan Mortgage Corporation (FHLMC) One of several federally sponsored corporations that sell securities backed by pools of mortgages. The FHLMC guarantees the ultimate payment of principal and the timely payment of interest on its certificates (also known as participation certificates). Known by its nickname *Freddie Mac.*

Federal National Mortgage Association (FNMA) One of several federally sponsored corporations that sell securities backed by pools of mortgages. The FNMA guarantees the timely payment of interest and principal on its mortgage certificates. Presently owned entirely by private stockholders. Known by its nickname *Fannie Mae.*

Final settlement The date on which cash-settled futures are marked-to-market using the spot price as the final settlement price. On this date, the contracts cease to exist.

Financial engineering At the most general level, the work of those individuals responsible for the creation of new financial instruments, new financial processes, and new solutions to problems in finance. More narrowly, the term is often used synonymously with risk management.

Financial intermediary A financial institution which stands between two end users of the intermediary's products. In the traditional context, one user is represented on the asset side and the other is represented on the liabilities side of the intermediary's balance sheet. In the context of swaps and related instruments, however, the products are off-balance sheet.

Fisher Equation An equation that relates nominal rates of interest to required real rates of interest and expected rates of inflation. Named for Irving Fisher.

Fixed-for-floating interest-rate swap A swap in which one counterparty pays a floating rate of interest while the other counterparty pays a fixed rate of interest. This is the most common type of swap.

Fixing date The date on which the reference rate is observed for purposes of calculating the cash payment due on a multi-period interest-rate option such as a rate cap or rate floor.

Flat (1) Without premium or discount. (2) A bond quotation which includes accrued interest. *See also* **And interest.**

Floating-for-floating interest-rate swap Also called a *basis swap*. A swap in which both counterparties pay a floating rate of interest but these are tied to different reference rates.

Floating-rate CDs Certificates of deposit on which the interest rate is periodically reset to reflect changing market conditions.

Floating-rate debt Also known as *adjustable-rate debt* and *variable-rate debt*. Any form of debt on which the interest rate is periodically reset to reflect changing market conditions.

Floating-rate notes (FRNs) Also known as *floaters*. Any note paying interest on a floating-rate basis.

Flotation costs   The costs borne by the issuer that are associated with selling a new issue of securities.

Floor   *See* **Interest-rate floor.**

Floor broker   An exchange member who trades on the floor of the exchange on behalf of others in return for a commission.

Foreign exchange markets   *See* **Currency markets.**

Foreign issue   A debt issue sold outside the country in which the issuer is domiciled.

Foreign-pay   As used herein, refers to payments on debt or equity instruments in which the payments are denominated in a currency other than the native currency of the recipient.

Formula method   One of three methods for determining damages upon the early termination of a swap. No longer widely used.

Forward contract   Also called a *forward*. A contract for deferred delivery traded in over-the-counter dealer-type markets. Less standardized than a futures contract but more easily tailored to commercial users' idiosyncratic needs than futures.

Forward discount   The difference between a forward rate and a spot rate when the forward rate is below the spot rate.

Forward exchange agreement (FXA)   A type of cash settled forward agreement used to hedge changes in exchange rate differentials. These contracts are widely used in Europe but are not yet popular in the United States.

Forward exchange rate   A current rate of exchange for a foreign exchange transaction scheduled to take place at a later date. Also called a *forward rate*, but the latter term can also refer to a forward interest rate.

Forward premium   The difference between a forward rate and a spot rate when the forward rate is above the spot rate.

Forward rate agreement (FRA)   An interest-rate forward contract written on a notional principal and cash settled on the basis of the difference between the contract rate and the prevailing reference rate on the settlement date. The resultant settlement value is discounted to adjust for an up-front settlement.

Forward swap   Also called a *deferred swap*. A fixed-for-floating interest-rate swap in which the swap coupon is set at the outset but the start of the swap is delayed.

FRABBA terms   Standard terms for forward rate agreements established by the British Bankers' Association and generally used on all interbank FRAs.

Front-end fee   As used here, a fee paid up-front for the origination of a swap or other derivative instrument. Front-end fees have largely disappeared and are only imposed today when the swap, or similar instrument, involves some special financial engineering. Front-end fees are also imposed when the swap involves some option-like feature. In these cases the fee is best viewed as an option premium.

Fully registered   A security whose ownership is recorded by a registrar in the name of the holder or his nominee. Transfer of ownership requires the signature of the registered owner.

Futures contract   Also known as a *futures*. Standardized contracts for deferred delivery (or cash settlement) of commodities and financial instruments. Always traded on a designated futures exchange and regulated by the Commodity Futures Trading Commission.

Futures exchanges   In the United States, markets designated as such by the Commodity Futures Trading Commission. Highly standardized futures contracts are traded on these exchanges using a dual auction open outcry system.

Futures series   All futures contracts having identical terms (including the same delivery month) and trading on the same exchange constitute a series.

Futures strip   A series of futures contracts with successive delivery (settlement) months. Most often used to refer to a series of interest-rate futures such as Eurodollars.

Generally Accepted Accounting Principles (GAAP)   The accepted rules of accounting as defined by the Federal Accounting Standards Board (FASB).

Government National Mortgage Association (GNMA)   A wholly owned corporation of the U.S. government that guarantees mortgages which are insured by the Federal Housing Authority or guaranteed by the Veterans Administration. These mortgages, which are assumable, are pooled for subsequent issue of pass-through certificates. Commonly known by its nickname *Ginnie Mae*.

Grace period   A period of time built into an amortization schedule during which none of the principal amortizes.

Graduated payment mortgage (GPM)   Any fixed-rate mortgage schedule in which the mortgage payments get larger, usually resulting in a period of negative amortization. Most often, the payments on such mortgages periodically reset to a new level and then remain constant at that new level for some period of time before resetting again. After some period of time, usually five years, the payment is fixed for the remainder of the term of the mortgage.

Graduated equity mortgage (GEMs)   The purest form of a graduate payment mortgage in which each mortgage payment is larger than the last by some percentage amount or by some absolute amount.

Gross national product (GNP)   The total market value of all goods and services produced for final consumption in the course of a single year.

Guaranteed bonds   Bonds that are secured by a guarantee provided by another entity. Most often, such a bond is issued by a subsidiary corporation and guaranteed by a parent corporation

Guaranteed income contract (GIC)   A pension/insurance type contract that guarantees a fixed stream of income to the contract holder for some period of time.

Hedge   A position taken in order to offset the risk associated with some other position. Most often, the initial position is a cash position and the hedge position involves a risk-management instrument such as a swap or a futures contract.

Hedge effectiveness   The degree to which a hedge offsets the price risk associated with a cash position or an anticipated cash position. Hedge effectiveness is most often measured with the aid of the coefficient of determination.

Hedge efficiency   The degree to which a hedge provides risk reduction per unit of cost.

Hedge optimality   In the language of economics, hedging with the goal of utility maximization. In layman's terms, an effort to determine the best hedge given the trade-off between risk reduction and cost.

Hedge ratio   The number of units of a hedging instrument that must be held to minimize the overall portfolio variance (cash position and hedge combined).

Hedging   The act of calculating the size of the necessary position and the taking of that position in derivative cash instruments in order to create a risk equal but opposite that associated with a cash derivative position or an anticipated cash or derivative position.

Horizontal bear spread   A horizontal spread in options in which the spreader is long the near (front) month and short the back (far) month.

Horizontal bull spread   A horizontal spread in options in which the spreader is long the back (far) month and short the front (near) month.

Horizontal spread   Also known as a *calendar spread* and as a *time spread*. An option position involving simultaneous long and short positions in options of the same class. Both options have the same strike price but they have different expiration dates.

In-the-money   In the case of a call option, a situation in which the price of the underlying asset exceeds the strike price of the option. In the case of a put option, a situation in which the price of the underlying asset is below the strike price of the option.

Income bond   A bond which pays interest subject to the income of the issuer.

Indenture   Also known as a *trust deed*. An indenture is the contractual relationship between a bond issuer and the bondholders.

Indemnification method   One of three methods for assessing damages upon the early termination of a swap. No longer widely used.

Indicative swap pricing schedule   Industry term used to describe the pricing schedule for the swaps in which a bank makes a market. The term "indicative" is meant to imply that these rates are obtained at the start of the business day and apply to plain vanilla swaps written at market. Actual rates may vary depending on the timing and other conditions surrounding a specific swap. The term "indication" is sometimes used instead of "indicative."

Inefficient hedges   Any hedge such that there exists another hedge offering the same level of risk reduction at less cost or any hedge such that there exists another hedge having the same cost and that is more effective.

Informationally efficient   Prices that accurately reflect the value of all available information. Closely associated with the efficient markets hypothesis.

Insurable risk   Any risk such that the risk exposures of those who bear the risk are not highly correlated and that there are many who bear a similar risk.

Insurance   A policy that transfers a financial risk from one party to another in exchange for an up-front fee called a *premium*.

International Monetary Market (IMM)   A subsidiary of the Chicago Mercantile Exchange. The IMM is the major market maker in the United States for currency futures and Eurodollar contracts. It recently introduced Euro-rate Differential Futures (DIFFs).

IMM settlement dates   The settlement dates of IMM Eurodollar futures contracts. These dates are often used as settlement dates on forward rate agreements and swap contracts.

IMM swaps   Short-dated swaps that are priced off the IMM's Eurodollar futures strip.

Interest-rate cap   Also called a *rate cap* and, sometimes, just a *cap*. Multi-period cash settled options on interest rates. The cap purchaser receives a cash payment whenever the reference rate exceeds the ceiling rate (also called the *cap* and sometimes called the *contract rate*) on a fixing date.

Interest-rate collar   Also called a *collar*. A combination of an interest-rate cap and an interest-rate floor such that a cap is purchased and a floor is sold or vice versa. The effect is to place upper and lower bounds on the cost of funds.

Interest-rate floor   A multi-period interest-rate option that provides a cash payment to the holder of the option whenever the reference rate is below the floor rate (also called the *floor* and sometimes the *contract rate*) on a fixing date.

Interest-rate futures   Futures on debt instruments or debt indexes. The value of interest-rate futures contracts moves inversely with changes in the level of interest rates.

Interest differential   (1) The difference between the amount of interest Party 1 must pay Party 2 and the amount Party 2 must pay Party

1. (2) The rate differential between the rates on two different instruments having the same maturity. In this context, the preferred term is "interest-rate differential." (3) The rate differential between instruments of the same maturity but denominated in different currencies.

Interest Rate and Currency Exchange Agreement A multi-currency standard form agreement published by the ISDA in 1987. It does not reference the 1986 Code but employs virtually identical provisions. Designed to serve as a master swap agreement.

Interest-rate option An option in which the underlying asset is a debt security such that the instrument's price changes with changes in its yield or an option in which the underlying asset's price is stated as an interest rate or yield. Such options can be single period or multi-period in nature. The latter include caps and floors.

Interest-rate parity A relationship between the nominal interest rates and the spot and forward exchange rates for two countries currencies. Interest-rate parity is the consequence of arbitrage. In brief, parity implies that the real rate of interest on equivalent risk instruments in two countries should be the same.

Interest-rate risk (1) The risk that a future spot interest rate will deviate from its expected value. (2) The price risk associated with holding a fixed-rate debt instrument as a result of fluctuations in the instrument's yield.

Interest-rate swap An agreement between two parties to engage in a series of exchange of interest payments on the same notional principal denominated in the same currency.

Interest Rate Swap Agreement A standard form swap agreement published by the ISDA in 1987 that is based on the 1986 Code and incorporates the Code by reference. It is meant exclusively for U.S. dollar interest-rate swaps. Intended to serve as a master swap agreement.

Internal rate of return (IRR) The discount rate that equates the sum of the present values of the cash flows associated with an investment with the initial cost of the investment.

International Swap Dealers' Association (ISDA) A New York-based trade association that deals with matters of common interest to member swap dealers. In recent years, this organization has concentrated on standardizing documentation.

Intrinsic value   A major component of an option's value. It is the greater of the amount by which an option is in-the-money or zero.

Investment grade bond   Any bond that has been rated as such by a rating agency. In the case of Moody's and Standard & Poor's, these would be ratings of Baa or better BBB or better, respectively.

Investor   A person (or an institution) that holds an asset in order to enhance his financial position. Also sometimes called a *holder*.

Issue   Also called an *issuance*. The full set of securities issued as part of the same offering.

Issuer   The party that offers its securities for sale.

Law of one price   An equilibrium relationship that is enforced by arbitrage. The "law" states that the difference between the prices of the same commodity offered in two different markets should never differ by more than the cost of transporting the commodity between the two markets.

Leverage   (1) In investment finance, the use of any instrument or mechanism to magnify potential returns with concomitant magnification of financial risk. The use of futures, options, and securities purchased on margin all provide leverage. (2) In corporate finance, the use of debt in the capital structure.

Liquidity premium theory   A theory of interest-rate-term structure which holds that the shape of the yield curve is explained by a risk premium demanded by investors. The longer the maturity of the instrument the larger the risk premium demanded.

Listed option   Any option traded on an organized exchange and having standardized terms. This is in contrast to options that trade over the counter.

LIBOR   An acronym for *London Interbank Offered Rate*. This interest rate is the standard rate for quoting interbank lendings of Eurodollar deposits.

LIBOR flat   LIBOR quoted without any premium or discount.

Long   A party is said to be *long* an instrument when he or she owns the instrument.

Long-dated swaps   Any swap with a tenor of two years or more.

Long the option   Describes the position of the owner of an option.

Long volatility   Also called *long vols*. An option position that is structured to produce a profit should the price of the underlying asset change significantly (irrespective of direction).

Macro-hedge   A hedge taken to offset the residual risk between a firm's assets and liabilities. Unlike a micro-hedge, macro-hedges are not identified with a specific asset or liability.

Margin   (1) In securities trading (stocks and bonds), refers to the portion of the purchase price paid in cash by the purchasing principal (with the remainder of the purchase price borrowed—usually from the principal's agent). (2) In futures trading, refers to a required performance bond tendered by a party to a futures contract. Also sometimes called *earnest money*.

Market maker   Also known as a *dealer*. A party that makes a market in an instrument by offering to both buy and sell the instrument. The market maker profits from the difference between its bid and ask prices.

Market risk   (1) Often used interchangeably with price risk including interest-rate risk and exchange-rate risk. (2) The risk that it will be difficult for a swap bank to offset a swap with a matched swap with a second counterparty.

Marking-to-market   The practice of periodically adjusting a margin account by adding or subtracting funds based on changes in market value. The practice has long been employed in futures trading and for writers of options. Many swap dealers are now employing the practice to limit risk on swaps portfolios.

Master swap agreement   A document written in such a fashion that its terms govern all swap activity between the counterparties. Each new swap is viewed as a supplement.

Matched needs   When two end users have identical, but mirror image, needs and so can satisfy each other's requirements by entering into a mutually beneficial relationship.

Matched swaps   A pair of swaps that have identical but mirror image provisions.

Max function   A mathematical function that selects the highest value from a set of values. It contrasts with the Min function which selects the smallest value from a set of values.

Mean   A statistical measure of "central tendency." The value to which a simple average tends upon repeated sampling from the same distribution.

Micro-hedge   A hedge clearly identified with a specific cash position.

Mini-max swap   Also called a *collar swap*. A fixed-for-floating interest-rate swap in which the floating-rate side is bounded between an upper and a lower limit.

Mismatch risk   The risk to a swap bank from failing to precisely match the provisions of the various swaps in its swap book. The term can also be applied, in a similar context, to other types of portfolios held by a bank.

Modified duration   A modified form of duration obtained by dividing the duration measure developed by Macaulay by 1 plus the yield divided by the frequency of the coupon payments.

Money market instruments   Debt instruments having a maturity of less than one year.

Money market yield   Also known as *money market basis* and *yield basis*. A method of calculating the yield on certain money market instruments. The method uses actual days over 360 in the yield calculation.

Moody's   One of two dominant firms in the bond rating business.

Mortgage   A debt instrument secured by real property.

Mortgage bonds   Bonds secured by real property.

Mortgagee   The lender in a mortgage contract.

Mortgagor   The borrower in a mortgage contract.

Natural hedge   The tendency of certain risks to be coincidentally offsetting.

Negative amortization   Any amortization schedule in which the principal or, in the case of swaps and related instruments, the notional principal increases from the initial level.

Net asset value (NAV)   The pro rata share of the asset value (less liabilities) of any pooled investment vehicle such as a mutual fund.

Netting   (1) The standard practice in swap documentation requiring that only the interest differential on interest-rate swaps be exchanged with the higher paying party making payment of this difference to the lower paying party. (2) The reduction of risk exposures by netting payments under a master swap agreement.

Nonamortizing *See* **Nonamortizing debt.**

Nonamortizing debt A debt obligation in which the full principal is repaid in a single transaction upon maturity of the debt with no repayments of principal prior to maturity. *See also* **Bullet transaction.**

Noncumulative In reference to dividends on preferred stock and coupons on bonds, if payments are missed they are not carried forward.

Notional principal The amount of principal on which the interest is calculated on a swap or related instrument including FRAs and interest rate options. In the case of interest-rate swaps, FRAs, and interest-rate options, the principal is purely ''notional'' in that no exchange of principal ever takes place.

Off-balance sheet A position with potential financial consequences that does not appear on either the asset side or the liabilities side of a balance sheet.

Off market Whenever a swap or other instrument must be priced with a coupon or floating rate that deviates from currently prevailing market conditions.

Off the run Those U.S. Treasury securities that are not the most recent issues for their respective maturities.

Offering price The price at which a public offering of securities is scheduled to be offered for sale by the underwriters.

On the runs Those U.S. Treasury securities that are the most recent issues for their respective maturities.

Over-the-counter Known more commonly by the acronym *OTC*. A dealer market in which transactions take place via telephone, telex, and other electronic forms of communication as opposed to trading on the floor of an exchange. Such markets allow for great flexibility in product design.

Optimal hedge The hedge that maximizes the hedger's utility.

Option Any contract or provision of a contract that grants a right without an obligation to do something.

Option Clearing Corporation (OCC)   The clearing house for all listed stock options and most commodity options traded in the United States.

Option holder   Also called the *option purchaser*. The owner of an option. The holder is said to be "long the option."

Option writer   Also known as the *option grantor*. The party who grants an option by selling the option instrument. The option writer is said to be short the option.

Options on futures   Options written on futures contracts. If the option is exercised, the futures contract is the delivered instrument.

OECD   Organization of Economic Cooperation and Development. An organization of European states for mutual economic gain.

Out-of-the-money   In the case of a call option, a situation in which the price of the underlying asset is below the strike price of the option. In the case of a put option, a situation in which the price of the underlying asset is above the strike price of the option.

Overnight repo   A repurchase agreement that provides for a secured lending for a period of one business day.

Parallel loans   An arrangement in which two parent companies agree to make loans to each other's subsidiaries. The parallel loan is a precursor of the modern swap and serves a similar purpose as a currency swap. The structure of parallel loans, however, is generally considered inferior to that of swaps.

Participating cap   An interest-rate cap in which the purchaser reduces the up-front premium by agreeing to pay the writer a portion of the difference between the reference rate and the ceiling rate whenever the reference rate is below the ceiling rate on the fixing date.

Pass-through certificates   Also known as *participation certificates*. Mortgage-backed securities that represent a pro rata claim on a pool of whole mortgages.

Pass-through rate   The rate of interest paid on pass-through certificates. This rate is equal to the mortgage rate less the servicing agent's fee and the guarantor's fee (if any).

Payoff profile   A visual depiction, by way of a graph, of the profits (and losses) associated with a position in a financial instrument.

Per unit pricing   The accepted practice of quoting the prices of financial instruments on a per unit basis irrespective of the number of units of the asset actually covered by the contract.

Perfect negative correlation   A perfect linear, but inverse, relationship between two variables. *See also* **Correlation coefficient.**

Perfect positive correlation   A perfect linear, and direct, relationship between two variables. *See also* **Correlation coefficient.**

Perfectly correlated   A perfect linear relationship (either positive or negative) between two variables. *See also* **Correlation coefficient**.

Plain vanilla   The simplest form of a financial instrument. Often associated with the first manifestation of an instrument (e.g., a plain vanilla swap).

Pledged account mortgage (PAM)   A mortage contract requiring a separate time deposit account dedicated to making a portion of each mortgage payment.

Points   Each point is one percent of the principal amount. Often used to describe the front-end or origination fee associated with a mortgage.

Portfolio immunization   An asset/liability management strategy that seeks to select assets in such a fashion as to minimize the difference in interest-rate sensitivities between assets and liabilities.

Positioning a swap   Also called *booking a swap*. The taking of a position in a swap by a swap dealer. This contrasts with a broker in which the swap facilitator acts as an agent in a swap and does not take the swap on its own books.

Premium   The name given to the price paid for an option or an option-like feature. The premium is determined by two types of values called *intrinsic value* and *time value*.

Prepayments   Repayments of borrowed principal in advance of those prescribed by the amortization schedule.

Prepayment risk   A form of risk borne by investors in certain types of debt instruments. The risk that the lender will repay sooner than desired.

Present value   The current value of a sum of money to be received at some later date.

Present value annuity factor   The present value of one dollar to be received at a later point in time.

Price risk   Any financial exposure faced by a firm as a consequence of a change in the prices of physical or financial assets and/or liabilities.

Primary government securities dealer   One of 40+ dealers in U.S. Treasury securities designated by the Federal Reserve to participate in making both the primary and the secondary markets in government securities.

Primary market   The market in which new issues of securities are initially distributed for sale.

Prime cap   An interest-rate cap in which the reference rate is tied to the prime rate of interest. The prime rate is the rate charged by commercial banks to their best business customers for short-term loans.

Principle of comparative advantage   A well-established theory first developed by David Ricardo in the nineteenth century to explain trade between nations. The concept is equally applicable in explaining trade more generally and for explaining the benefits that accrue to the counterparties to a swap. In brief, the theory holds that, assuming an appropriate exchange rate, both parties will benefit from trade if each concentrates production in that good in which it holds a comparative advantage and then trades its surplus production for the surplus production of the other. Refinements of the theory allow for transaction costs.

Principle of offsetting risks   This is an extension of portfolio theory which states that risk can be reduced if two simultaneous positions are held such that manifestations of the individual risks, which take the form of deviation from expected values, are in opposite directions.

Productizing   The process of taking a customized solution to a specific client's needs and converting it to an off-the-shelf financial tool.

Profit diagram   A graphic portrayal of the profit from an investment as of a certain point in time under a range of values for the underlying asset. Often drawn to depict the profit potential of option strategies but can be drawn for any derivative instrument.

Promissory note   Any of a variety of debt instruments evidenced by a note promising to repay borrowed money together with interest according to a specified repayment schedule.

Protective covenants   Provisions written into an indenture to protect the interests of the lender.

Purchasing power parity   A relationship that explains the exchange rate between two countries' currencies on the basis of the average price of the average good in each of the two countries. Not widely accepted in a pure form by traders.

Purchasing power risk   The risk that, upon liquidation, the proceeds from an investment will have less purchasing power than expected.

Pure arbitrage   Also known as *academic arbitrage*. Any arbitrage situation which is affected without any risk and without any investment. As a practical matter, most real world arbitrage involves at least some modest risk.

Pure expectations theory   A theory of interest-rate term structure that explains the shape of the yield curve on the basis of unbiased expectations of future short-term rates of interest and complete risk neutrality.

Put   An option that grants its holder the right to sell the underlying asset to the option writer at the option's strike price.

Putable swap   A fixed-for-floating interest-rate swap in which the floating-rate payer has the right to terminate the swap prior to its scheduled maturity date.

Rate-capped swap   A fixed-for-floating interest-rate swap in which the floating-rate side is capped. Can be created as a unit or by combining an interest-rate swap with a separate interest-rate cap.

Reference rate   A rate (such as six-month LIBOR or three-month T-bill) designated as such on any cash settled interest-rate contract including swaps, forward rate agreements, and interest-rate options. The reference rate is the rate that is observed on the calculation or settlement date for purposes of determining the amount of any cash settlement.

Refunding   The process of retiring an existing issue of debt with funds obtained from the sale of a new issue of debt.

Refunding restrictions Also known as *refunding provisions*. These are special covenants often included in the indenture of a callable bond which specifically prohibit the retirement of a bond by call if the funds that are used for the call are obtained by issuing a new bond.

Registered bonds Bonds for which ownership is recorded by a registrar and transfers of ownership require the signature of the registered owner.

Registered with respect to principal only A registered bond in which interest is paid to the party submitting interest coupons but in which the principal can only be paid to the registered owner. *See* **Registered bonds.**

Regression analysis Statistical procedures used to fit lines to data. The most used form is linear regression which fits a straight line to data. This line is the "best" fit in the sense that it minimizes the sum of squared errors.

Reinvestment risk The risk that the general level of interest rates will have changed from some initial level by the time the cash flows from an investment are due to be reinvested.

Replacement swap A swap that is entered to replace a swap that is terminated prematurely. This most often becomes necessary when a one of a pair of matched swaps is terminated early.

Repurchase agreement Also known as a *repo* and an *RP*. A method of borrowing that involves the sale of a security with the simultaneous agreement to buy it back at a specific later date and at a specific price. These agreements are widely used in the securities industry as a means of obtaining relatively inexpensive short-term financing.

Reset An adjustment in a floating rate of interest that marks the rate to that prevailing in the market.

Reset dates The scheduled dates for the resets of the floating rate of interest on rate swaps.

Retail market Any market specifically designed to handle securities transactions of a relatively small size and, hence, geared to the individual investor. Contrasts with the wholesale market designed for large trades among institutions.

Return on assets (ROA)   A widely used measure of corporate profitability. ROA is defind as the firm's earnings after taxes divided by
its total assets.

Return on risk-adjusted assets (RORA)   A new financial ratio introduced to measure a bank's profitability as a function of its risk-
weighted assets. It is defined as the ratio of the firm's earnings after
taxes to its total risk-weighted assets.

Reverse-annuity mortgage   A mortgage in which homeowners with
substantial equity in their homes receive periodic payments from a
mortgage lending institution. Each such payment represents a reduction in the homeowner's equity and an increase in the mortgage
principal. The mortgage is repaid in whole at a single point in time.

Reverse butterfly   Also known as a *sandwich spread*. This is the
opposite of a butterfly spread. The two middle strikes are purchased
and the two end options are sold. *See* **Butterfly spread.**

Reverse repurchase agreement   Also known as a *reverse* and a
reverse repo. The opposite of a repurchase agreement. The purchase
of a security with the simultaneous agreement to sell it back at a
specific later date and at a specific price.

Right of assignment   The right to transfer one's interest in a contractual relationship without seeking permission of the other party to the
contract.

Right of set off   The right to terminate payments on an obligation
upon the failure of another party to make its required payments on a
contractually separate obligation.

Risk averse   A dislike of risk. The risk averse individual suffers a
loss of utility (called *disutility*) from the presence of risk. The
greater the risk the greater the loss of utility. Risk aversion as a
component of rational behavior is a tenet of almost all financial
theory.

Risk profile   A visual depiction, by way of a graph, of the financial
consequences of a change in a price.

Risk weighted asset   Part of the bank capital guidelines adopted by
the Federal Reserve in January of 1989. Obtained by multiplying the
credit risk equivalent by a risk weighting factor.

Roller coaster swap   Any swap in which the notional principal increases for a period and then amortizes to zero over the remainder of its tenor.

Rollover   The re-issue of short-term money market securities on the date of their maturity in order to fund the retirement of the existing issue.

Samurai bonds   Any foreign bonds issued in Japan.

Sandwich spread   *See* **Reverse butterfly.**

Search costs   The cost, both direct and indirect, of finding a party having matched needs.

Seasoned   A security that is not exempt from registration with the SEC but which has been outstanding for a period of not less than 90 days following the completion of its distribution.

Secondary market   The market in which a security or other instrument trades after its initial issue. The initial issue takes place in the primary market.

Securities   Marketable claims on, or interest in, the assets of a legal entity. These instruments may be in either book entry or bearer form and may or may not be evidenced by certificates.

Segmented markets theory   Also known as the *segmentation theory*. A theory of the term structure of interest rates which explains the shape of the yield curve by the existence of distinct markets for debt of different maturities.

Semiannual rate   An annual rate of interest that is paid in two semiannual installments. Not to be confused with a "half-year rate" which is a rate of interest stated on a six-month basis.

Separate Trading of Registered Interest and Principal of Securities   Known by the acronym *STRIPS*. A Treasury program which allows for the separation of coupons and principal on conventional notes and bonds having original issue maturities of not less than ten years. The program allows for the efficient creation of zero coupon Treasuries from conventional Treasuries.

Serial bond   An issue of securities consisting of two or more blocks with each block having a different maturity. Individual blocks may carry the same or different coupons but are all governed by the same prospectus.

Series   (1) With respect to bonds, a subset of mortgage bond issue sharing common features. (2) With respect to options, all options of the same type, written on the same underlying asset, having the same expiration date and the same exercise price. (3) With respect to futures, all futures listed on the same exchange and having the same terms, including the same delivery month.

Settlement date (1) In securities trading, the date a transaction is cleared. (2) In futures trading, the date a cash settled contract is marked to the spot price or index. (3) The date that the cash settlement is due on an interest-rate contract. This may or may not coincide with the calculation date.

Settlement price The price established by the clearing house to be used as the basis of the daily marking-to-market of margin accounts.

Settlement risk *See* **Delivery risk**

Shared appreciation mortgage (SAM) A mortgage made at a below market interest rate but in which capital appreciation is shared between the homeowner and the mortgage lender.

Short A party is said to be short securities if he or she has borrowed the securities (usually for purposes of a short sale). A party is said to be short futures and options if he or she has sold the contracts.

Short-dated swaps Swaps with tenors of less than two years.

Short sales (1) With respect to securities, sales of borrowed securities. (2) With respect to options and futures, the creation of position by way of the sale of the instrument.

Short the option The position of an option writer.

Short volatility Any position in which the position taker will benefit from a decline in volatility of an underlying asset's price. Most often associated with a short straddle (short both a call and a put).

Straddle An option position consisting of a long (or short) position in both a call option and a put option.

Strip A series of successive contracts of a particular type and the accompanying price structure. The most important is the IMM strip. This is the set of Eurodollar futures traded on the IMM and often used to price swaps and forward rate agreements.

Simple rate of interest Also known as the *effective annual rate of return*. The clearest and simplest statement of yield. It is obtained by dividing the value of a position at the end of a one-year period by the value of the position at the beginning of the one-year period and then deducting one.

Sinker   Any bond or note having a sinking fund provision.

Sinking fund   (1) A provision written into a debt instrument's indenture requiring the gradual amortization of the instrument either by periodic repurchases of portions of the outstanding issue or by deposits to a trust account. (2) Often used to describe an amortization schedule in which a fixed percentage of the principal is amortized each period.

Sovereign risk   The risk that an issuer may be barred by its government from making interest and principal payments on its debt. In the context of swaps, the risk that a counterparty will be barred by its government from fulfilling its swap obligations.

Speculative grade bonds   Also known as *high yield* or *junk bonds*. These are bonds having a less than investment grade but still not in default.

Spot exchange rate   Also known as a *spot rate*. The exchange rate quoted for immediate delivery of a currency. As a practical matter, immediate delivery is understood to be two business days. *See also* **Exchange rate.**

Spot rate   *See* **Spot exchange rate.**

Spread   (1) The difference between the bid price and the ask price (*see also* **Bid-ask spread**). (2) Simultaneous long and short positions in options of the same class but having different expiration months. (3) Simultaneous long and short positions in futures written on the same underlying asset (but different delivery months) or different underlying assets (with the same delivery month). (4) The difference between the offering price and the proceeds to the issuer for a public offering which accrues to an underwriter as a compensation for its services. (5) The number of basis points added to the Treasury yield curve to determine the absolute yield on swaps.

Standard deviation   A statistical measure of dispersion around some central (mean) value. Obtained by taking the square root of the variance.

Standard form agreements   Standardized swap contract documentation published in 1987 by the International Swap Dealers Association. Published in two forms including the *Interest Rate Swap*

Agreement (U.S. dollar contracts only) and the *Interest Rate and Currency Exchange Agreement* (multi-currency).

Stock-index futures   Futures contracts written on stock indexes. All such contracts are cash settled.

Stop out bid   The highest accepted competitive bid on an auction of securities.

Stop out price   The lowest accepted price on a competitive offering of a securities issue.

Strike price   Also known as the *exercise price*. The amount that must be paid (or the price that will be received) by an option holder to buy (or sell) the underlying asset from the option writer.

Subordinated debentures   A security in which the holders' claims on the assets of the issuer rank behind the claims of other debt holders for purposes of repayment in the event of liquidation.

Supervening illegality   A change in applicable law, the imposition of foreign exchange controls, or similar condition that makes it impossible for a counterparty to a swap to fulfill its obligations.

Swap   A contractual agreement providing for a series of exchanges of principals and/or interest in the same or different currencies. At a more general level, the term includes the exchange of fixed-for-floating payments on a given quantity of commodity (i.e., a commodity swap). *See also* **Interest-rate swaps** and **Currency swaps.**

Swap broker   An agent acting on behalf of one or more principals that finds parties with matching swap needs in exchange for a commission.

Swap coupon   The fixed rate of interest on the fixed-rate side of a swap.

Swap dealer   Also known as a *market maker*. A financial intermediary that makes a market in swaps and that profits from its bid-ask spread. Unlike a swap broker, the swap dealer becomes a counterparty to each swap.

Swap driven   A term loosely used to describe pricing behaviors in non-swap instruments that are brought about through a linkage to the swap market. Examples include price movements in the Eurobond futures and forward markets.

Swaption An option on a swap. The swaption purchaser has the right to enter a specific swap for a defined period of time.

Synthetic instruments A basket of instruments that behaves, in terms of its cash flow stream, like some real instrument not included in the original basket. The basket constitutes the synthetic instrument.

Systematic risk The degree to which the fluctuations in the value of a financial instrument are associated with fluctuations in the value of the market more generally for instruments of that particular type.

Tail The difference between the average price and the stop-out price in a competitive securities offering.

Tax driven swaps Asset-based swaps that are used to alter the tax character of a cash flow stream.

Teaser rate An artificially low (and temporary) initial interest rate on an adjustable-rate mortgage. Used to induce borrowers to opt for an adjustable-rate mortgage as opposed to a conventional mortgage.

TED spread The difference between the interest rate on Treasury bills and the interest rate on Eurodollar deposits of similar maturities. The definition applies to both cash instruments and futures contracts.

Tenor The length of the life (term-to-maturity) of a multi-period derivative instrument such as a rate cap, a rate floor, or a swap.

Term repo A repurchase agreement having a maturity of 30 days or more.

Term structure of interest rates The relationship between the maturity of debt instruments and yield-to-maturity when all other yield influencing factors are held constant.

Term-to-maturity Also referred to as *term*. The length of time from the present until the maturity of an instrument.

Termination clauses Provisions in a swap agreement that provide for the assessment of damages in the event of early termination due to the occurrence of an event of default or a terminating event.

Termination events Any event other than those indicative of credit problems that results in automatic termination of a swap contract. Unlike an event of default, a termination event only results in termination of the affected swaps.

Time to expiration Also called *time to expiry*. The period of time from the present until an option contract expires.

Time value That portion of the fair option premium in excess of the option's intrinsic value. Time value is a function of time to expiration, price volatility of the underlying asset, the amount by which the option is in-the-money, and the level of interest rates.

Trademarks In a securities industry context, the names given to the proprietary products of investment banks and commercial banks.

Tranche One of two or more instruments governed by the same documentation even though they may have different terms. The term is most often associated with collateralized mortgage obligations.

Transaction costs The costs associated with engaging in a financial transaction. These include such explicit costs as commissions and front-end fees and indirect costs such as a bid-ask spread.

Transfer pricing rate (TPR) The cost to a department within a bank of intrabank borrowings of funds or securities. Also sometimes called the *cost of carry* although the latter term has other uses as well.

Treasury bills Also known as *T-bills*. Short-term securities sold at a discount from face value by the U.S. Treasury as part of its ongoing funding operation. Offered in maturities of 13 weeks, 26 weeks, and 52 weeks.

Treasury notes Also known as *T-notes*. Intermediate-term coupon-bearing securities sold at periodic auctions by the U.S. Treasury to fund its ongoing operations. Offered in two, three, four, five, seven and ten year maturities.

Treasury bonds Also known as *T-bonds*. Long-term coupon-bearing securities sold at periodic auctions by the U.S. Treasury to fund its ongoing operations. Offered in 30 year maturities.

Treasury receipts A Treasury-based, generic zero coupon product which has been superseded by the STRIPS program.

Trustee An institution appointed by an issuer to look after the interest of the holders.

Underlying asset The asset on which an option or futures contract is written.

Underwriter   One who commits to purchase securities from an issuer for a guaranteed price for the purpose of distributing the securities in resale. Generally, an investment banking activity but also practiced, on a limited scale, by commercial banks.

Underwriter's discount   Also called the *gross spread*. The difference between the offering price for securities and the sum promised to the issuer by the underwriter. This sum does not necessarily accrue to the underwriter, who may be forced to sell the securities below the offering price.

U.S.-pay   Dividends, coupons, and principal payments made in U.S. dollars.

Unsystematic risk   The extent to which the fluctuations in an instruments value are not associated with fluctuations in the value of the market more generally for instruments of that particular type.

Upward sloping yield curve · Also called an *ascending yield curve*. The normal shape of the yield curve when short-maturity instruments have lower yields than long-maturity instruments.

U.S. Treasury securities   Also called *Treasuries*, sometimes called *governments*, and, in market slang, sometimes called *govies*. The latter two terms are often used to include government securities in addition to those issued by the Treasury. Debt issues of the U.S. Treasury consist primarily of Treasury bills (T-bills), Treasury notes (T-notes), and Treasury bonds (T-bonds).

Value diagram   A graphic device used to depict the value of a derivative instrument as of some specific date over a range of values for the underlying asset.

Value weighting   Any weighting scheme that employs value-based weights to determine an index value. Duration is an example of such a value-weighted index.

Variance   A widely used statistic that measure deviations from a central or mean value. Often converted to a standard deviation by taking the square root of the variance.

Variation margin   (1) Money added to or subtracted from a futures account to reflect changes in the value of the position as a consequence of daily marking-to-market. (2) The amount of margin necessary to bring a futures margin back to its initial level.

Vertical bear spread   A vertical spread in options in which the spreader is long the *higher* strike price option and short the *lower* strike price option.

Vertical bull spread   A vertical spread in options in which the spreader is long the *lower* strike price option and short the *higher* strike price option.

Vertical spread   Also called a *price spread* and a *money spread*. An option position involving simultaneous long and short positions in options of the same class. Both options have the same expiration date but they have different strike prices.

Volatility   The degree to which the price of an asset fluctuates around some mean value. Usually measured as the variance or the standard deviation of the price.

Volatility unit (vol)   Industry terminology for one standard deviation. *See* **Standard deviation.**

Warehouse receipts   Documentation representing ownership of goods (including commodities) held in a public warehouse. Often used as the mechanism for transferring ownership of stored commodities.

Warehousing   Also called *running a book*. Refers to the act of managing a portfolio of some specific type of instrument. Warehousing swaps, for example, means holding a portfolio of swaps.

Wholesale market   Any financial market specifically geared to handling large transactions in order to service the institutional investor.

Yankee bonds   A foreign bond issued in the United States.

Yield   (1) Used in a general sense to refer to the annual return (expressed as a percentage) on a debt instrument. In this usage, the rate can refer to any yield measure that is customary for quoting the instrument in question. (2) More narrowly, used to mean the *yield-to-maturity*.

Yield beta   The historic change in the yield of one instrument divided by the historic change in the yield of another instrument (usually a benchmark instrument). Obtained by a regression of the former on the latter.

Yield curve   A graphic portrayal of the relationship between the yields-to-maturity of instruments of a given class and the terms-to-maturity of those instruments. *See also* **Term structure of interest rates.**

Yield-to-maturity Also called *yield*. The discount rate that equates the present value of the cash flow stream associated with an instrument and the current price of that instrument. This calculation assumes that cash flows can be reinvested to earn the same rate.

Zero coupon bond Also called a *zero*. A bond that does not pay periodic coupons. In lieu of periodic coupons such bonds are sold at a steep discount from par and redeemed at par.

Zero coupon-for-floating swap A variant of the fixed-for-floating interest-rate swap in which the fixed-rate paying party pays all interest upon the termination of the swap.

Zero coupon yield curve A graphic portrayal of the relationship between yield and maturity when the instruments involved are zero coupon bonds. Usually drawn for Treasury-based zeros.

Zero-sum game An economic term used to describe any type of financial transaction in which the profits to the winners exactly equal the losses of the losers. Futures and options trading are examples of zero sum games if one ignores transaction costs.

Index

S